Teaching
in Physical
Education

Teaching in Physical Education

Editors:

Thomas J. Templin, Ph.D.
Janice K. Olson, Ph.D.

Purdue University

**Big Ten Body of Knowledge
Symposium Series, Volume 14**

Human Kinetics Publishers, Inc.
Champaign, Illinois 61820

Production Directors
Margery Brandfon
Kathryn Gollin Marshak

Editorial Staff
Peg Goyette
John Sauget

Typesetters
Sandra Meier
Carol McCarty

Text Layout
Lezli Harris

Cover Design
Jack Davis

Library of Congress Catalog Number 83-81455

ISBN 0-931250-48-X

Printed in the United States of America

Human Kinetics Publishers, Inc.
Box 5076, Champaign, IL 61820

CIC
Big Ten Symposium
Research on Teaching
in Physical Education

November 12-13, 1982
Purdue University
West Lafayette, Indiana

Sponsors:
Big Ten Directors of Physical Education
Indiana State Board of Health
Indiana Inter-agency Council
Purdue University:
School of Humanities, Social Science, and Education
Department of Physical Education, Health, and Recreation Studies

CIC

The Committee on Institutional Cooperation is made up of members from several of the Big Ten universities and The University of Chicago. Its objective is to foster cooperation among the member institutions through the sharing of human and material resources for educational and research purposes.

CIC CONFERENCE GROUP ON BODY OF KNOWLEDGE IN PHYSICAL EDUCATION

Margaret J. Safrit, University of Wisconsin-Madison, Chairperson
D.W. Edington, University of Michigan
Dale L. Hanson, Purdue University
Charles Mand, Ohio State University
Wynn F. Updyke, Indiana University

CONTENTS

Preface

Not long ago, Lawrence Locke (1977) stated:

> The new science of research on teaching physical education is only a fledgling, but if its significance is recognized it can be nurtured and made to grow. The research and knowledge we have tomorrow need not be like what we have today. We can escape the grim prologue of our past. (p. 13)

Locke's words were quite prophetic, considering that in the brief time since then research on teaching in physical education, and to a lesser degree research on teachers, has blossomed. As Siedentop suggests in his keynote address, the "bastard child" called research on teaching in physical education has suddenly been recognized as legitimate.

This growth in research on teaching and teachers in physical education over the last decade served as the impetus for proposing and conducting the 1982 Committee for Institutional Cooperation Big Ten Physical Education Body of Knowledge Symposium. We were quite pleased to have organized the Symposium with the assistance of our colleagues, Anthony Annarino and Dale Hanson, for it marked two firsts in the long history of the annual meeting: research on teaching in physical education as the focus, and Purdue University as the host.

We made every attempt to encourage presentation of a wide variety of topics by outstanding professionals in the area of pedagogy. As this text reflects, the information presented is currently at the forefront of pedagogical research in physical education. The order in which the various papers are presented herein is quite arbitrary and, for the most part, represents the order in which the papers were presented at the conference. With the exception of the opening and closing papers, we have separated the presentations by topic and prefaced each section with a brief introduction of the papers within it.

We are very grateful to have been involved in the organization of the 1982 Symposium, and our thanks go out to everyone who contributed to its success. Although the 2-day session was quite intense, both presenters and conferees made the Symposium a special event. Certainly, pedagogical research must continue to grow and we look forward to the next C.I.C. Symposium on Research on Teaching and Teachers in Physical Education.

Thomas J. Templin, Ph.D.
Janice K. Olson, Ph.D.
Purdue University
West Lafayette, IN
May 23, 1983

References

LOCKE, L. Research on teaching physical education: New hope for a dismal science. *Quest*, 1977, **25**, 2-16.

Teaching
in Physical
Education

Welcoming address

Dale L. Hanson
Purdue University

As an official member of the CIC Body of Knowledge Symposium Committee, it is my privilege to welcome you to this symposium. This is the 14th in a series initiated in 1968 by the Big Ten physical education directors to encourage the development and dissemination of knowledge considered basic to a discipline of physical education. It is their desire to provide such a forum for the exploration of new ideas and concepts within physical education as we continue our quest for excellence.

This symposium has as its focus research on teaching in physical education. This is the first time that research on teaching in physical education has served as a theme for a Big Ten CIC Symposium. And it's about time! The great interest shown by your collective presence and the high quality of the papers will affirm the timeliness.

This is also a first for Purdue University—the first time that Purdue University has hosted a CIC Big Ten Symposium. This occasion will be especially meaningful because it is probable that this symposium on research on teaching in physical education will be noted as a significant historical event within the study of physical education pedagogy.

Let me provide a brief review of the previous 13 symposia. The first symposium focused on the sociology of sport and was held at the University of Wisconsin in 1968. The last symposium, held at the University of Michigan in 1981, focused on exercise physiology. Following is a historical record of the symposium series.

1968, Sociology of Sport, University of Wisconsin;
1969, Motor Learning, University of Iowa;
1970, Biomechanics, Indiana University;
1971, History of Sport, Ohio State;
1972, Physiology of Fitness and Exercise, University of Minnesota;
1973, Administrative Theory, University of Michigan;
1974, Physical Education for the Handicapped, University of Iowa;
1975, Measurement and Evaluation, Indiana University;
1976, Motor Control and Learning, University of Wisconsin;
1978, Sport Sociology, University of Minnesota;
1979, Motor Skill Development, University of Iowa;
1980, Biomechanics, Indiana University;
1981, Exercise Physiology, University of Michigan.

Some "thank you" acknowledgments are in order: To each one who will present a paper at this symposium, we appreciate your willingness to share your important work with us. We are grateful for the financial support in underwriting the costs of this symposium, to each of the physical education departments at the Big Ten universities, to the Indiana State Board of Health, and to the Department of PEHRS at Purdue University. Gratitude is expressed to professors Tom Templin, Janice Olson, and Anthony Annarino of Purdue University for their work in planning this symposium. Finally, to you who have taken the time from your busy schedules to attend this symposium, your being here gives the symposium a special meaning. Thank you.

Having predicted earlier that this symposium will become an historically significant event in the recognition of research on teaching in physical education, I am confident given the program and this gathering of scholars that such will be the case. Let us celebrate it! May the spirit of celebration be experienced throughout all of our time together. After all, this is a most festive occasion. And let us engage each other playfully as we share our insights and experiences about teaching physical education.

So, welcome to Purdue University and to the Big Ten Physical Education Body of Knowledge Symposium on "Research on Teaching in Physical Education." May we experience the playful celebration of this historically significant event.

Research on teaching in physical education

Daryl Siedentop
The Ohio State University

As a teaching researcher in a Big Ten university, symbolically at least, I feel like a bastard child who, just as he is beginning to make it on his own, is suddenly recognized by his parents as legitimate. We have finally been accepted into the family. With this symposium, we have been asked to sit at the main table and discuss our concerns with the full approval and recognition of the parents.

In 1964, the Western Conference Physical Education Directors created the Body of Knowledge project and formed a steering committee to develop it substantively and give it expression with a series of scholarly symposia. The steering committee subsequently decided that the Body of Knowledge of physical education would be defined through six subareas: exercise physiology, biomechanics, motor learning and sport psychology, sociology of sport, history and philosophy of sport, and administrative theory. Pedagogy, of course, was not among the areas defined. These areas provided the focus for the yearly symposia and also, it seems (McKristal, 1970, p. ix), for the format of the agendas at annual meetings of the Big Ten directors.

The first symposium, held in Madison in 1968, was chaired by Gerald Kenyon and focused on the sociology of sport. The second symposium was held in Iowa City, chaired by Leon Smith and devoted to motor learning. The stated purpose of these symposia was to bring physical education scholars into substantive contact with scholars from related disciplines. The lineups at those early symposia read like a who's who of our recent past. In Madison, physical educators such as Kenyon, Loy, Lüschen, and Kleinman were brought together with the likes of Greg Stone, Brian Sutton-Smith, and Harry Webb. In Iowa City, Franklin Henry, Dick Schmidt, and Walt Kroll interacted with Ina Bilodeau, Dennis Holding, Karl Smith, and the Ammons'. After each major presentation, there was a reaction paper followed by extended discussion among the conferees. Those papers, reactions, and discussions provide some of the very best literature ever produced in physical education.

As I reflect on those years, I cannot but wonder how much more quickly teaching research would have developed in physical education had pedagogy been included within the definition of what constituted the proper body of knowledge in physical education. What good outcomes might have derived had John Nixon, Larry Locke, Tony Annarino, and Bill Anderson been brought together with Nate Gage, Don Medley, and Ned Flanders? But, it did not happen. Indeed, we were largely left out of that entire scene. The teaching act, which constitutes one of if not the most central act in sport education, was simply left out. We were certainly part of the family, still obviously a part of every department of physical education in the Big Ten. But we were bastardized—branded as illegitimate, if not directly, then certainly by implication.

I sincerely hope that this symposium marks the end of that era. The days of lusting after a discipline of physical education defined by its relationship to parent disciplines seems to be near its end. Lis Bressan (1982) recently described quite clearly how the parent child metaphor was a mistake and how debilitating that original mistake has been to the development of a cohesive sport science. Jan Broekhoff (1982) has also fairly well debunked the cross-disciplinary model ascribed to the discipline of physical education. At last there are clear signs that scholars and researchers in our field are increasingly defining their interests by reference to our subject matter—sport—rather than by pirating questions from their supposed parent disciplines. If questions continue to develop from the subject matter itself, then clearly our concerns with teaching research will gradually move into the central role that they always should have occupied. Thus, rather than spend time marking the end of the discipline era, it behooves us to celebrate the beginning of a new era, one that holds much promise for us and for the enterprises with which we are associated.

The degree to which teaching research in physical education has blossomed during the past decade is remarkable. Teaching research sessions are evident at every national and international conference. Indeed, there are enough people, ideas, and data for specialized conferences.

At the recent Commonwealth Games conference in Brisbane, Larry Locke (Note 1) keynoted the subsection on research on teaching by reviewing the accomplishments of the past 15 years. Many colleagues played important roles in those developments. There *is* a great deal to celebrate. Fundamental contentions such as "Can teaching be studied systematically?" and "Do teachers really make a difference?" have been put to rest with rather clear, affirmative answers.

We have learned a great deal about data collection. We have many different tools for collecting data and a new book describing those many tools (Darst, Mancini, & Zakrajsek, 1983). There is a healthy attention to and discussion of what constitutes good data, precisely the kind of interest that is characteristic of one of the most important self-correcting mechanisms of science, the continual asking, in one way or another, of the fundamental scientific question "How do you know?" which translates most often into "What methods did you use to collect your data?"

Greatly enhancing this attention to methodological improvement are the dissemination mechanisms we have developed. Anytime one goes public, one becomes fair game for the critical mechanisms through which knowledge needs to be filtered. We now have an audience that sustains and supports these crucial, critical systems. We get time on conference agendas. We present papers. We have panels. We now have journals in which one can be fairly sure of a review by peers who are knowledgeable in our own field. We have seen in the past 5 years, the development of a critical structure that will require us to improve our work continuously, and those are exactly the contingencies necessary for a science to grow and prosper.

Methodologically, teaching research is often on more solid ground than any area of research in educational or social psychology. As I argued in Houston (Siedentop, Note 2), teaching research moved away from its thoroughly undistinguished history of no significant differences when it began to adopt some of the methodological commitments of the natural sciences, particularly those of absolute unit based measurement and systematic replication. In so doing, it put aside many of the debilitating measurement tactics of the psychometric sciences. To the extent that teaching research continues on that course, it will continue to prosper.

First-generation researchers have trained a group of graduate students who have continued to do research. In turn, this second generation has trained yet another large cadre of teaching researchers whose mark is currently being left on our collective enterprise. Most importantly, research programs have developed in a number of institutions, and these programs have devoted themselves to the exploration of a certain set of questions using a certain set of methods.

To date at least, researchers within the field have shown an admirable willingness to prosecute their positions without rancor and to respond to criticism without defensiveness. Researchers whose basic assumptions differ markedly, and whose methodological commitments reflect those differences, still find ways not only to talk to and provide mutual support for one another, but also to learn in ways that sharpen and improve their own positions. I hope that we can protect and nurture this collegiality. To be able to criticize and debate without personalizing the dialogue, and without developing turf battles, is not only a sign of the maturity of the individuals involved, but it clearly is the best way to improve our science.

While it might seem that the immediate area for application of teaching research is teaching, it is more likely true that the most immediate application is in teacher education. It does appear that teaching research has begun to make inroads into teacher education. It is not uncommon for undergraduates today to know and utilize some of the technical language of teaching research, even though they may not have been directly exposed to the research itself. That is, the language and concepts developed in teaching research are often alive and well in the verbal repertoire of the newly certified teacher. Methods textbooks increasingly pay attention to the results of teaching research. Supervision practices appear to be changing, reflecting a basic commitment to systematic observation as an important way to know about teaching. This gradual adoption of a common technical language by researchers and practitioners should help immensely in future research.

This is not to suggest that teaching in schools will automatically improve, or that it is any better now than it was 15 years ago. There is no good evidence to answer that question one way or the other. I do believe that many newly certified teachers are in a better position to teach well than were their counterparts 15 years ago. To the degree that they understand the crucial importance of classroom management, have some managerial skills, have an expanded repertoire of discipline skills, and understand the importance of student engaged time, they likely would be in a better position to teach well.

The possibility that they may not be teaching better should serve as a rather clear cue that the induction period—the time from student teaching to the time of permanent appointment—is sufficiently powerful that it deserves to be studied very carefully. It should also tell us something about the manner in which we conceptualize and implement our training programs, an item which I will address later.

I am convinced that during the next 10 years our research will progress rapidly toward issues and problems that are even more central to effective teaching. If the same filtering and dissemination mechanisms continue to operate, then our undergraduates will probably know even more about the issues and skills directly related to the contingencies that do indeed affect day-to-day performance in teaching. At that point, if teaching still does not improve, then the induction and training questions will become the most crucial ones to answer.

My optimism about our research progress is based on recent efforts that I believe have begun to move us very close to the variables most central to effective teaching. We have begun to move through the era when teaching research was characterized primarily by the "add and divide" strategy—where category systems consisting primarily of phenomenal units (Dunkin & Biddle, 1974) were applied through continuous or time sampled measurement systems, category totals calculated, and some measure of rate or percentage achieved through dividing by time or totals. Do not mistake my intent here. This era of category systems was a necessary and useful step in our progress if for no other reason than it allowed us to develop and improve our methodological skills. For certain purposes, these category systems will continue to remain eminently useful. But, for a more thorough understanding of the dynamics of teaching, they were clearly inadequate.

The development of more complex, ecologically valid analytic units began to move us toward that more thorough understanding. From Robert Soar's (1979) explanation of the importance of established structures in classroom processes, Walter Doyle (1979) began to develop the notion of task structures as a basic unit of analysis. That work has been pioneered in physical education by Marielle Tousignant (1982), who described the difference between rule-governed task systems and contingency-developed task systems, and the extraordinary degree to which teacher accountability mechanisms, mediated by the degree of active supervision, affects the behavior of students as they respond to stated task demands.

If systematic, replicative efforts verify these relationships, and if we then can produce predictable changes in student behavior experimentally through the manipulation of formal and informal accountability systems, then we can reasonably expect this information to disseminate so that undergraduates might not only understand the key roles of active supervision and accountability, but also have at their disposal a greatly expanded repertoire of techniques through which accountability systems can be brought to bear on student behavior.

If all this were to occur, it just might help to improve the practice of physical education. I take it almost as an assumption that most of us are not only concerned with the improvement of practice, but have it as a central commitment. Indeed, I have been continually impressed with the extent to which my colleagues in this enterprise over the past decade have been willing to adopt an activist role concerning the improvement of practice. It is only recently that sport psychologists have adopted a more activist stance; sport sociologists still appear reluctant to do so. We seem to have avoided both the basic/applied wars and the value-free/activist debates. There seems to be widespread agreement among teaching researchers that our efforts must be directed eventually toward improving practice; indeed, our efforts have little meaning without such a mission.

Perhaps it is this shared commitment that has helped us over the years to develop our research questions from studies of the practice of teaching, rather than to borrow questions deduced from theories in related disciplines. We have managed to keep our research enterprise securely grounded in our subject matter, a characteristic the absence of which has tended to bedevil several other areas in the sport sciences. The first important question we asked was "What is going on in the gym?" and from those answers have developed many of our research directions. Needless to say, I am convinced that our best hope for continuing research productivity is to keep our research firmly rooted in the realities of teaching and coaching.

I also believe that recent developments in teaching research that may lead us beyond the add/divide strategy and toward more complex, ecologically valid analytic units will help put to rest the important concern as to whether results from classroom teaching research generalize to the gymnasium. I have argued (Siedentop, 1982) that our early efforts in teaching research in physical education have produced data that looks more similar to than different from classroom studies data. Still, there have been some differences, and when viewed from the add/divide strategy of category systems, no doubt there will continue to be some important variations in the two data sets. But, as we move toward more complex analytical units, it is my guess that even these differences will disappear. For example, in the task structure model developed by Doyle and applied to our field by Tousignant, it appears that accountability is the centrally important variable in both the classroom and the gymnasium. Doyle (Note 3) concluded, "If there is no accountability, then there is no task and whatever effects are obtained will depend upon the personal interests and motivations of students." Tousignant (1982) concluded, "When there was no formal accountability on the students' performances, the instructional task system was suspended, and the informal contingencies controlled the accomplishment of those tasks" (p. 145). Accountability as a generic phenomenon tends to eradicate differences in context.

Let me forecast about the degree to which generic variables operate in similar ways across subject matters and contexts. When a study is designed to decipher the dynamics of student teaching as an experience through which to improve teaching performance, the major conclusion will be as follows. The teaching performance of interns is determined primarily by the degree of accountability from the preparation program mediated through the supervisor. To the extent that this accountability system is lacking, the teaching performance of the intern will then be determined primarily by the informal accountability provided by the cooperating teacher; this accountability system will have a more direct impact on the managerial task performance of the intern than on the instructional task performance. In the absence of even that level of accountability, teaching performance is determined by the students taught by the intern; and gaining and maintaining their cooperation will be the main "task structure" of the experience. Beyond that, the student teacher will do as little or as much as is determined by his/her own interests and predispositions.

That prediction can be made simply by generalizing the results of current classroom teaching research to student teaching. If it proves to be an accurate prediction, then concepts such as rule-governed versus contingency-developed task systems, the role of active supervision, and the central importance of accountability will be further established as generic functions.

To the extent that we verify the existence of generic teaching skills and a paradigm that is valid across subject matters and contexts, it will become more important that teacher education change so that the generic skills and paradigms become central program commitments, visible in terms of credit hours, course titles, field experiences, and even certification rules. But there is less reason to be optimistic here for although teacher education has changed somewhat as the result of recent teacher effectiveness research, it is clear that the changes have not been nearly as pervasive as one might argue they should have been.

At our teaching research workshop in Columbus in the spring of 1982, Dean Pease, in one of the evening open forums, asked whether anybody knew how to do teacher education so that teachers would graduate with the relevant skills and the predispositions to use them. Nobody there was willing or able to answer. I think there is at least a partial answer.

The answer, or rather the problems that the question addresses, has two levels. One was identified by Don Medley (1979) in his milestone review of teacher effectiveness research. After reviewing those studies, Medley concluded:

Teacher education, both at the preservice and the inservice level, should adopt as primary goals the development of the competencies needed to create and maintain the learning environment, to engage pupils in learning-related activities, and to implement the kind of instruction that research indicates is provided by effective teachers. There is an abundance of practical

knowledge available about how to do these things; what has been missing in
the past is the clear conviction on the part of teacher educators that these
things are what teachers ought to be doing. (pp. 25-26)

It seems apparent to me that there is no widespread "clear conviction" to
do so on the part of teacher educators. Many still lack knowledge about
teacher effectiveness research, although one hopes that the relative
numbers of this group will continue to diminish. Others know about
teacher effectiveness strategies but do not believe that they are the skills
to emphasize in the program. Within this latter group are a large number
of teacher educators who continue to insist that preservice teachers acquire a romantic vision of education and learning, one that is at considerable odds with the view derived from research. A third group knows
about teaching skills, believes them to be important, but tends to treat
them only as information, alluding to them in methods lectures but failing to treat them as acquirable skills, let alone as central program commitments.

It is within this third group that one can find the remaining part of the
answer to Dean's question. I believe that during the next decade many
teacher educators will become convinced that the teaching skills about
which we are talking are the skills that teachers ought to be doing. What
will then be lacking is the companion conviction that the undergraduate
program should be designed and implemented so that they do indeed acquire them, and that if they do not, they do not graduate from the program. In other words, we may feel secure about what teachers ought to
be doing, but we will still feel insecure that our programs should ensure
that undergraduates can indeed do these things.

I must say in all candor that there is no lack of knowledge about how
to help undergraduates acquire and perfect those skills. That knowledge
is available right now. What is lacking is the conviction that teacher
education should be a behavior change system. What we seem to be unwilling to do is engage directly in the control of the behavior of our
undergraduates — there is nothing to gain from using a softer description.
Surely we try to influence our students, but if we continue to be content
just to exert influence, we probably will continue to be mostly ineffective. Webster defines influence as the attempt to affect or alter the conduct, thought, or character of a person by indirect or intangible means.
The indirect, intangible means derive from the original meaning of the
word — "an ethereal fluid thought to flow from the stars and to affect the
actions of men." (Webster's Third International Dictionary, 1971, p.
1160) To exert influence is certainly to control behavior, but it is a weak
form of control. Perhaps most importantly, it is a form of control that
allows us to continue believing that we are not engaging in control.

This dilemma has existed in counselor education for some time, where it is known as the Krathwohl-Carkhuff Paradox, the notion that there are certain skills and predispositions which, while necessary for successful practice, are inappropriate to state explicitly and to deliberately teach in training programs. There is no question that it *can* be done. But, there is considerable thought that it should *not* be done.

Thus, in the very near future, I believe that someone will be able to answer Dean's question about how to do it. And I believe that no matter what rhetoric embellishes the answer, the message will be: "We know what skills are important and we know how to ensure that undergraduates acquire those skills. We are just not sure that we *ought* to be doing it." When we are unwilling to hold undergraduates directly accountable for their teaching performance, we should at least proceed cautiously in our criticism of their inability or unwillingness to hold students accountable in school physical education classes.

We are unwilling to design and implement our undergraduate programs in that manner because to do so would run counter to most of the views of education that have prevailed in this century and the models of human development that underly them. It is often difficult to talk about, let alone criticize, basic philosophical commitments about education and human development. But we greatly need to generate these kinds of discussions. Teaching research and teacher education too often move blindly ahead without questioning the assumptions on which their decisions are made. Have you ever talked to a teacher educator about time on task research without realizing that the person to whom you are talking believes that children are born virtuous and that society tends to corrupt them (the traditional school being the main agent of corruption), or to one who is most at home with the "gardener" metaphor of education and believes that self-esteem is the major goal of education. Teacher educators with those assumptions believe that time on task research is the enemy—the weapon of those who would ruin children. The fact that the data are clear and convincing is irrelevant to that kind of discussion. The data speak to issues about effective teaching. The assumptions speak to issues about the purposes of schools, which in turn are always based on assumptions about human development.

I believe this notion of assumptions is so important that I would favor the addition of a brief preliminary section in research studies that might be called "anthropological commitments" or "the view of man from which these methodologies derive." Such a section would not only alert the reader to the basic point of view of the researcher but, more importantly would require the researcher to consider seriously the implications of the questions asked and the assumptions underlying the methodologies used to answer those questions.

My guess is that presently very few of us would know enough about our assumptions to write that section in any coherent fashion. There is a very lively and serious literature attending to such issues but, unfortunately, too few teaching researchers keep in touch with it.

For example, most would agree on the importance of investigating popular notions such as student attitudes, student self-concept, physical self-awareness, or locus of control. Most would choose a psychometric instrument to measure the phenomenon in question. The instrument would be a "test," administered once, probably to a large number of subjects. In an experimental paradigm it would be administered twice, pre- and post-intervention, and subsequent changes would become the dependent variable subjected to analysis. What assumptions underly such a research question and the choice of a psychometric instrument for measurement?

Certainly one set of assumptions is that there are phenomena such as basic abilities and that behavior is a manifestation of these central, stable properties. These internal states can be measured, indirectly and/or projectively, only by measuring observed variability in human behavior, the most typical of which is responding to written questions on a paper and pencil test. These abilities are thought to be stable and measurable in a one-shot effort, given that the test instrument has sufficient reliability.

Another set of assumptions is that central abilities are rather fixed, often at birth, and will realize their full potential if nurtured in such a way that the developing person can explore the potential of those abilities in ways characterized mostly by the absence of direct control by adults, such control thought to interfere with development. The abilities are often thought to be sequential and hierarchically arranged such as in the current developmental models of Piaget and Kohlberg.

The intellectual traditions from which these assumptions derive are to be found in the Enlightenment, particularly with the shift during that time toward the notion of the person as an autonomous moral agent (McIntyre, 1981). The notion of a "self," distinct from the obligations and definitions provided by social roles, is an outgrowth of that dramatic shift in intellectual thought.

In the 18th and 19th centuries, this tradition gave rise to romantic educational philosophies based on the notion of an autonomous self, equipped with a set of assumptions about children's inner resources and how they might best be realized. The most influential ideas in that movement derived from the romantic, natural philosophy and educational program of Jean Jacques Rousseau.

In the 19th century, educational psychology developed as a way of measuring the central phenomena that gave definition to the autonomous person. Using manifest variability in projective human responses as a basis for defining internal characteristics and dispositions, this new approach in the social sciences was greatly enhanced by the emergence during the same period of a calculus of probability. The social and educational psychology movement introduced into science an entirely new definitional and measurement strategy. Observed variability was described; from these descriptions not only were internal, hypothetical phenomena defined, but units for scaling them and subsequently measuring them were created. It was in this tradition that educational psychology emerged in the late 19th century, for example, in the mental measurement movement pioneered by Francis Galton. He worked under the assumption that mental abilities were normally distributed, and arranged the theoretical distribution of those supposed abilities onto a 14-step, equal interval scale. With one fell swoop, Galton invented not only the concept of intelligence but a means for measuring it as well.

This approach to the measurement of internal states — psychometrics — was carried to its logical conclusions in the works of Binet in intelligence and Cattell in personality. This supposed measurement of essentially dimensionless inner states gave credibility and a trapping of scientific objectivity to the romantic philosophies that began to dominate views of human development and schooling. For, although the early pioneers were careful not to attribute to these internal states any causal significance, educationists, and later educational psychologists, were not so careful. Maslow (1970), for example, proclaimed that persons live by their inner laws rather than in response to outer pressures. In a companion field to ours, Rainer Martens (1979) has recently suggested that the determinants of behavior are to be found in the mind. In fact, what has happened over time has been the reintroduction into science, albeit by different names, of a whole class of explanatory variables whose origins are philosophical and religious rather than empirical.

These philosophical assumptions and the measurement tactics that proceed from them can, and should, profoundly affect the manner in which many of us pursue some of the practical research questions that most interest us and that most urgently need to be investigated. For example, under what conditions will inservice teachers most optimally improve their managerial and instructional performance? The manner in which a simple but important question like that is defined and subsequently attacked would differ dramatically, depending on what set of assumptions one holds about how persons develop, whether or not they can change, or under what conditions they might change most quickly and with least resistance. Any different approaches to those underlying assumptions would require entirely different kinds of measurement tactics. To mix assumptions, approaches, and measurement tactics is to render research unintelligible.

Therefore, let me suggest that part of our efforts in the next few years be directed toward a lively debate concerning basic assumptions and research strategies compatible with each set of assumptions. It seems to me that such a debate would be the best way we could avoid becoming efficient technocrats who cannot see beyond their data nor integrate those data so that they eventually might have an impact on some of the larger questions facing our profession. Without that kind of debate, we might risk becoming a group that knows more and more about less and less, and in so becoming, loses any chance to exert control over the future directions of sport education in our society. We have made a very good beginning at teaching research. There is much about which we can be rightfully proud. But it is not time to put ourselves on a pedestal. Rather, it is time for us to put ourselves on the spot — to ask more of ourselves so that 10 years from now we can again look back with satisfaction and ahead with optimism.

Reference Notes

1. Locke, L. *Research on teaching physical education: A modest celebration.* Paper presented at the VII International & Commonwealth Conference on Sport, Physical Education, Recreation & Dance. Brisbane, Australia, September 1982.
2. Siedentop, D. *Recent advances in pedagogical research.* Paper presented at annual meeting of American Academy of Physical Education, Houston, April 1982.
3. Doyle, W. *Student mediating responses in teaching effectiveness.* Unpublished manuscript, North Texas State University, 1980.

References

BRESSAN, E. An academic discipline for physical education: What a fine mess! *NAPEHE Annual Conference Proceedings*, 1982, **III**.

BROEKHOFF, J. A discipline — Who needs it? *NAPEHE Annual Conference Proceedings*, 1982, **III**.

DARST, P., Mancini, V., & Zakrajsek, D. *Systematic Observation Instrumentation for physical education.* West Point: Leisure Press, 1983.

DUNCAN, M., & Biddle, B. *The study of teaching.* New York: Holt, Rinehart & Winston, 1974.

DOYLE, W. Classroom tasks and students' abilities. In P. Peterson & H. Walberg (Eds.), *Research on teaching: Concepts, findings, and applications.* Berkeley, CA: McCutchan, 1979.

MARTENS, R. About smocks and jocks. *Journal of Sport Psychology*, 1979, **1**, 94-99.

MASLOW, A. *The farther reaches of human nature.* New York: Viking, 1970.

MCINTYRE, A. *After virtue.* Notre Dame: University of Notre Dame Press, 1981.

MCKRISTAL, K. The symposium series: An historical perspective. In L. Smith (Ed.), *Psychology of Motor Learning.* Chicago: Athletic Institute, 1970.

MEDLEY, D. The effectiveness of teachers. In P. Peterson & H. Walberg (Eds.), *Research on teaching: Concepts, findings, and applications*. Berkeley, CA: McCutchan, 1979.

SIEDENTOP, D. *Developing teaching skills in physical education* (2nd ed.). Palo Alto, CA: Mayfield, 1982.

SOAR, R., & Soar, R. Emotional climate and management. In P. Peterson & H. Walberg (Eds.), *Research on teaching: Concepts, findings, and applications*. Berkeley, CA: McCutchan, 1979.

TOUSIGNANT, M. *Analysis of the task structures in secondary physical education classes*. Unpublished doctoral dissertation. The Ohio State University, 1982.

Section one
Teacher
decision making

Research on teacher thinking, planning, and decision-making has received increased attention by classroom researchers (Shavelson & Stern, 1981), but only recently has this focus been extended to the physical education setting (Sherman, Note 1). The papers by Michael Sherman, Shirl Hoffman, and Judith Placek reflect this new direction in research on teaching and teachers in physical education.

Michael Sherman presents a paper illustrating how the teacher initiates a planned routine (i.e., Mosston's pre-impact decision set), evaluates learner progress and, most importantly, decides to continue the routine or make in-class adjustments. Based on this model, Sherman describes the decision pathways that novice versus expert teachers take in maintaining or altering a routine. He reports on three studies that reflect major differences between novices and experts in terms of diagnostic competence and pedagogical memory.

Shirl Hoffman's paper supports Sherman's work, as it focuses on teacher decision-making concerning the learner's performance of a motor skill. Hoffman presents a hypothetico-deductive model of diagnosis, in which the teacher initially hypothesizes about a learner's performance and then decides which pathways to present to the student in correcting motor skill deficiencies. The author shares the results of experimental studies that compare the diagnostic skills of inservice physical education teachers and classroom teachers and those of preservice physical education majors. Based on the seemingly "abysmal" diagnostic skills of inservice physical educators (versus the superior skills of undergraduate students), Hoffman suggests how the professional preparation process may be changed to enhance the diagnostic competence of physical educators.

Finally, Judith Placek presents two qualitative studies examining how physical education teachers and undergraduate majors perceive success in teaching. Through interview data, both studies reveal that inservice and preservice teachers alike associate success in teaching to student enjoyment, participation, and good behavior. Placek describes how these three factors direct teacher planning, and how this in turn affects student learning.

Sherman, Hoffman, and Placek offer some thought-provoking insights into teacher thinking, planning, and decision-making. Although each paper has its own emphasis, together they shed light on the relationship between teacher thought and action in the gymnasium. Undoubtedly, the consequences of teacher thinking, teacher beliefs, and teacher planning are critical to the teaching/learning process.

Reference Note

1. Sherman, M. *Teacher thinking in physical education: A cognitive view of clinical expertise.* Symposium presented at the annual meeting of the Pennsylvania State Association for Health, Physical Education, Recreation, and Dance. Pittsburgh, December 1981.

References

MOSSTON, M. *Teaching Physical Education.* Columbus, OH: Merrill, 1981.

SHAVELSON, R.S., & Stern, P. Research on teachers pedagogical thoughts, judgments, decisions, and behavior. *Review of Educational Research*, 1981, **51**, 455-498.

Pedagogical cognitions in physical education: Differences between expert and novice teachers

Michael A. Sherman
University of Pittsburgh

Standing at the water's edge, the potential swimmer notices the magnificent and powerful waves rushing inward toward the beach. The undulating white caps are audible, visible, and easy to count. Upon entering the surf, the swimmer soon feels the more mysterious undertow that washes the once wild waves back into the sea. This tow is quite powerful but remains invisible and silent.

These bidirectional currents are intrinsic to the perpetual motion of the sea. To focus attention exclusively on one creates a blurred image of hydrodynamics. The same is true at the beachfront of research on teaching physical education, where most scholars ride the waves of behavior rather than fight the undertow of cognition.

What are the implications of this choice? How might our conceptions of teaching be affected by looking at it exclusively from a behavioral perspective?

Behaviorists are concerned with the analysis of overt teaching acts. They are often motivated to write prescriptions for teaching effectiveness based on correlational results from process-product research (Graham & Heimerer, 1981). These correlations suggest that more or less of a given teaching act is statistically associated with more or less of a particular learning outcome, but they fail to specify when, with whom, or for what purpose to use or not use the designated act. Although process-product research is relevant for determining how variations in observable teaching behavior are related to variations in student achievement, it disregards the causes and reasons for behavioral differences among teachers. Recently, the "mainstream" behavioral paradigm has come under sharp attack. For example, Shavelson and Stern (1981) argue that, by itself, a behavioral model of teaching is conceptually incomplete because it does not account for predictable variations in teachers' behavior that result from differences in their pedagogical cognitions. These sentiments have been echoed by Huber and Mandl (Note 1), who pressed for research on critical links between teachers' classroom behavior and their action-directing cognitions before, during, and after the clinical encounter with learners.

Research on teacher thinking is being coaxed along by cognitive psychological studies about the nature of problem-solving expertise within knowledge-rich domains such as chess, physics, and medical diagnosis (Chi, Glaser, & Rees, 1982). These studies attempt to comprehend the underlying mechanisms that differentiate more and less intelligent individuals, and the results already indicate that conceptual knowledge and cognitive skills are responsible for observable performance differences.

This paper will not debate whether behavioral or cognitive paradigms should guide research on teaching physical education. Both are essential for understanding pedagogical dynamics. However, if one is predisposed to plunge beneath the surface and look at the mental lives of teachers, then some unique methods must be employed. One approach for capturing teachers' thoughts, judgments, and decisions is *stimulated recall*, a technique whereby an investigator elicits introspective verbal reports from a teacher about action-relevant cognitions during a recently completed instructional episode (Ericsson & Simon, 1980; Peterson & Clark, 1978; Peterson, Marx, & Clark, 1978). The basic assumptions of introspective inquiry are: (a) teachers can accurately recall, reconstruct, and report their most intimate thoughts; (b) reported cognitions are action-directing; and (c) reported cognitions can be faithfully interpreted by another person.

Introspective methods are still in the formative stage and require cautious application in research on teachers' cognitive processes (Shulman & Elstein, 1975; Huber & Mandl, Note 1). Consequently, the work described in this paper is quite exploratory but should suffice to generate several hypotheses about the antecedents of teaching behavior.

The reported work described decision-making during interactive teaching and compared the decision tendencies of expert and novice teachers. The theoretical framework for analyzing decisions made by teachers with varying levels of expertise is synthesized below.

Interactive teaching decisions

Decisions involve making choices among known alternatives. Given the classical teaching problem in physical education, that of transforming an unskilled learner into a skilled performer, the teacher must decide upon strategies to facilitate the conversion. These strategies are called teaching routines. They include details about content, activities, materials, teaching styles, and other elements of what Doyle (Note 2) refers to as the "task environment."

Theoretically, decisions about teaching routines are made "preimpact" or before class (Mosston, 1981). Routines can either be retrieved from memory or created from scratch. Once developed, they seem to function as mental scripts, images, or plans that get carried out during interactive teaching; they maintain the activity flow of the lesson and keep learner responses within tolerable limits (Joyce, 1978-79).

Interactive decision-making assumes that classroom teaching involves the implementation of planned teaching routines. Morgenegg (1980) suggests that a common routine in physical education begins when the teacher uses structuring and soliciting moves to elicit learner responses. The teacher then monitors the response cues and determines whether they match the performance criteria. Periodically, the teacher emits reacting moves that offer feedback to the learner. According to Joyce (1978-79), Peterson and Clark (1978), Shavelson (1976), and Snow (Note 3), interactive decision-making starts when the teacher initiates the planned routine, monitors and evaluates the learner, and decides whether to continue the routine unchanged or make an "in-flight" adjustment.

Figure 1 illustrates the interactive decision model being used at the Teacher Behavior Laboratory, University of Pittsburgh. The model consists of rectangles, diamonds, and pointers. The rectangles depict planned or adjusted teaching behavior. The diamonds represent four binary decision points:

1. Are the cues (learner's response) within the limits of tolerance?
2. Is an alternative routine necessary?
3. Is an alternative routine available?
4. Is an alternative routine initiated?

By asking stimulated recall questions of the teacher, each reported decision can be coded as a "yes" or "no" response. The combined responses fall into the five different interactive decision pathways marked on the

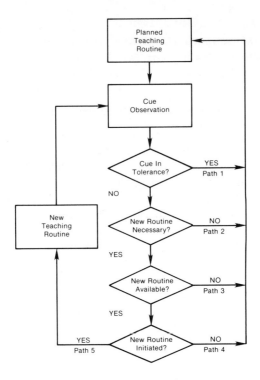

Figure 1 — A model of interactive teaching decisions.

pointers. The path options are also shown in Table 1 in relation to the responses at each decision point.

Paths 1 through 4 reflect decisions to continue the planned teaching routine unchanged. Path 1 ("full speed ahead") is generally taken when cues are judged within tolerable limits. Path 2 means that cues are perceived outside tolerable limits, but an immediate adjustment is un- necessary ("darn the torpedos, full speed ahead"). Shavelson and Stern (1981) speculated that Path 2 might imply that the teacher has opted to store the information and delay corrective action rather than disrupt ongoing events. The condition of helplessness seems synonymous with Path 3, where the teacher is essentially forced to continue the lesson un- changed because he or she doesn't know what else to do. Path 4 suggests that the teacher considers an alternative action both necessary and available, but chooses to stick with the original plan after all, rather than "change horses in midstream." Path 5 infers the decision to deviate from the planned routine. The model assumes that every in-flight adjustment requires the teacher to perceive learner response cues outside tolerable limits, consider it necessary to adjust the routine, have one or more alter- native routines in memory, and decide to implement the alternative ac-

Table 1

Responses Associated with Five Decision Paths during Interactive Teaching

	Decision pathways				
Interactive decisions	1	2	3	4	5
Cue in tolerance?	Yes	No	No	No	No
New routine necessary?	—	No	Yes	Yes	Yes
New routine available?	—	—	No	Yes	Yes
New routine initiated?	—	—	No	No	Yes

tion. This entire sequence requires no-yes-yes-yes responses across the respective decision points.

A recent review of research on pedagogical cognitions (Shavelson & Stern, 1981) cited only 13 studies on interactive teaching decisions. With two exceptions, these studies employed stimulated recall. The accumulated evidence suggests that interactive decision-making is not pervasive because most teachers are reluctant to risk management problems that could result from abruptly shifting teaching routines. MacKay (1977) reported that teachers make about 10 interactive decisions per hour. Morine-Dershimer and Vallance (1975) set the per lesson rate between 9.6 and 13.9 decisions. Concerning the number of alternatives considered at critical moments, MacKay reported that the teacher seldom ponders more than two options, while Morine-Dershimer and Vallance found mean values ranging from 2.2 to 3.2 per lesson for four different teacher groups.

Even when adjustments are made, they tend to be fine tuning rather than major revisions (Joyce, 1978-79). Shavelson and Stern offered three possible reasons why teachers are inclined to follow original plans during interactive teaching. One possibility is that the original plan was considered the best available for teaching a given task. Second, the plan might be the only one known by the teacher. Third, altering the routine might overload the information processing system and compel the teacher to devote more attention to the routine instead of the learner's responses.

The analysis of expertise

Are interactive decision tendencies dependent upon one's level of expertise in teaching physical education? Expertise has been defined as "the possession of a large body of knowledge and procedural skill" (Chi, Glaser, & Rees, 1982, p. 8). This definition suggests that an expert physical educator has advanced competence in the knowledge and skills of an academic discipline *and* in the knowledge and skills of teaching that discipline to others. The expert physical education teacher should be highly proficient at solving pedagogical problems in sport, dance, and exercise. Such proficiency might be associated with the tendencies to sustain planned routines during interactive teaching, probably because such routines are keeping learner responses on target, or to make quick but relatively small in-flight revisions when learner responses become intolerable.

Chi and Glaser (1980) proposed that, based on psychological models of memory, experts know more than novices. Knowing more means that one's semantic network contains more central concepts, more defining features for each concept, and more robust relationships among concepts. The semantic network of an expert is dense, with many related clusters of information, whereas the novice's network is sparse, with relatively few closely connected clusters.

Expert/novice differences also occur in the planning, execution, and evaluation of problem-solving strategies. Anderson (1980) described experts as routine planners and called novices creative planners. Routine planning involves the retrieval of prestored solution strategies from memory, while creative planning requires the production of new strategies. The expert's planning strategy involves a rapid initial analysis of a problematic situation so that it can be "transformed" into a problem for which the expert already has a solution routine in memory (Resnick & Glaser, 1976).

The expert/novice literature is quite clear about the quantitative aspects of problem-solving activity. Experts solve problems more accurately and much faster than novices, are more confident that the chosen path will lead to a solution, and are less dependent upon executive control functions (i.e., "metacognition") such as searching for possible errors (Chi & Glaser, 1980; Chi, Glaser, & Rees, 1982). Simon and Simon (1978) reported that experts make fewer metacomments about their solution routines than do novices, who are uncertain and constantly use self-interrogations to check their solution procedures and results.

The decision pathways taken during interactive teaching might be related to expertise in pedagogical problem solving. Such differences should first unfold at point 1 of the interactive decision model when the teacher judges whether observed cues are within limits of tolerance. This decision demands that the teacher knows the performance criteria and can recognize mismatches between cues and criteria. A study of more and less experienced tennis teachers has shown that novices report more false alarms than do experts (Armstrong & Hoffman, 1979). That is, inexperienced teachers perceive more errors than actually occur, especially when some uncertainty exists. Experienced teachers are more conservative and, when unsure, refrain from reporting errors until they gather more evidence. It is also possible that novices have ambiguous or different schema for evaluating learner responses. Thus, at the outset of the interactive decision cycle, novices might be prone to report intolerable cues and, therefore, take Path 1 less often than experts.

Differences in Path 1 might also be attributed to pedagogic as well as diagnostic expertise. Because of more experience with various teaching routines, experts should enter the classroom with strategies that have kept learner responses within tolerable limits on previous occasions. Learners taught by experts should respond appropriately more often than those taught by novices; thus, experts should have opportunities to follow Path 1 relatively more often than novices.

When inappropriate cues are perceived, the teacher's next decision is whether an immediate adjustment is necessary. Expert/novice differences are probable here at decision point 2. First of all, experts may have a different threshold for determining the necessity of adjustments. A minor cue deviation to an expert may be considered major by a novice. In the second place, experts might have greater confidence in their planned routines and, hence, be reluctant to change unless the lesson becomes totally disrupted. Taheri's (1982) study of fitness teachers revealed that experts were more confident and less anxious than novices before conducting a lesson. Experts may respond with patience when cues are perceived intolerable, whereas novices may panic because of greater uncertainty about their routines to begin with. The result should be seen in Path 2, which experts might take relatively more often than novices because of greater willingness to follow their plans and delay corrective actions.

The influence of expertise on Path 3 tendencies seems obvious. This path is taken when adjustments are considered necessary but the teacher lacks an alternative. The novice is expected to use Path 3 more than the expert. According to the definition of expertise, novices know fewer routines and might have included their *only* routine in the original plan. Even when novices know an alternative, they may be reluctant or unable to initiate the routine. Due to insufficient experience, they might not know the outcomes of the new routine. Furthermore, comparing alternative and original routines in-flight places heavy demands on their information processing system. The tendency to reject available alternatives and continue teaching unchanged is associated with Path 4. Novices will likely follow this path more frequently than experts. Experts might take Path 4 on some occasions. However, they often know before the lesson that critical moments are possible, and come to class with contingency plans that they fully intend to use if necessary (Sherman, Note 4).

Both experts and novices change their teaching routines (Path 5) when alternatives are necessary and available. However, this tendency should be more prevalent among novices because they have, or think they have, more problems. The actual and perceived magnitude of these changes might also differ for teachers with varying levels of expertise. The fitness experts studied by Taheri (1982) reported making mostly fine-tuning adjustments, while the novices usually reported major revisions.

Overall, we suspect that experts have fewer real and perceived problems during interactive teaching than do novices. When problems are noticed, the experts will be more likely to reject the necessity of immediate adjustments and continue their teaching routines unchanged. When immediate adjustments are considered necessary, experts will make them directly. Novices should react quite differently, sometimes by making adjustments and on other occasions by continuing planned routines because they lack or are reluctant to initiate alternatives.

Expert/novice comparisons

Three studies were conducted to check hypothesized relationships between pedagogical expertise and interactive decision-making. Stimulated recall was employed in all cases to trace pathway tendencies during actual lessons.

The inverted balance study (IBS)

This work was done by DiCicco, Housner, and Sherman (Note 5) to describe teachers' cognitions during a 30-minute lesson on inverted balance. The lesson was conducted in a laboratory setting and involved five children, ages 9 to 11 years, selected from a university campus school and randomly assigned to teachers.

Six physical education teachers served as paid volunteer subjects. Three were specialists in elementary physical education (mean age = 28.7 years), with full-time experience ranging from 2 to 12 years. The others were undergraduate college students of health and physical education (mean age = 21.0 years), with no full-time experience. Both groups included one male and two females. The a priori classification of teachers was confirmed by self-ratings of experience and expertise, and observed measures of learner engagement and improvement. The mean scores of experts were superior on all measures.

Teachers were allocated 60 minutes for lesson planning. Following the lesson, they viewed five 2-minute video segments of their teaching and responded to a series of structured interview questions to stimulate recall of decision path tendencies during interactive teaching. The questions were basically the same as those shown in Figures 1 and 2. Verbal responses were first audiotaped and then transcribed verbatim. One trained coder analyzed the transcripts and tapes by coding "yes" or "no" at each decision point. The procedure was rather straightforward, except when more than one decision path was reported per segment. Such cases typically occurred when a teacher simultaneously reported going full speed ahead for one learner while making an adjustment for another. Though these events introduced some complexity into the coding procedure, they were easily accommodated by carefully reviewing tapes and transcripts. A study (Peterson & Clark, 1978) using a similar pathway coding system reported interobserver agreement coefficients as high as 91%.

The body composition study (BCS)

The second study (Taheri, 1982) focused on the interactive decision-making of teachers from a university department of health, physical, and recreation education. Subjects were five expert and five novice teachers in the area of health-related physical fitness. The experts included full-time faculty ($n = 2$) and doctoral students ($n = 3$) with special competence in exercise physiology. The novices were freshman ($n = 2$) and sophomore ($n = 3$) undergraduate majors in health and physical education. The learners were 60 children, ages 11 to 13 years, selected from the university's campus school, randomly divided into small groups ($n = 6$ per group), and randomly assigned to teachers.

There were several obvious differences between the experts and novices. On the average, experts were older (34.6 vs. 21.0 years), better educated (five graduate degrees vs. no undergraduate degrees), and more experienced in teaching health-related physical fitness (5.6 vs. 0.0 years). Experts were also more involved in fitness oriented professional activities and averaged 5.0 as opposed to 1.6 for novices on self-ratings of expertise in teaching health-related physical fitness (1-to-6 scale). On self-ratings of knowledge about body composition, the means were 6.0 and 3.2 for experts and novices, respectively.

Each teacher planned, conducted, and reviewed a lesson on body composition and its relationship to health-related physical fitness. Lessons were taught in the same laboratory used for the IBS. The post-lesson recall questions were asked on five preselected occasions after a 2-minute videotape replay. Recall sessions lasted about 90 minutes. Audiotaped responses were coded by one investigator.

The geometric figure study (GFS)

The GFS was conducted by Sherman (Note 6) as part of a professional presentation for teachers and teacher educators. Subjects were nine adults who attended a state AAHPERD convention, specifically, a session entitled "Teacher Thinking in Physical Education." Following an overview of the interactive decision model and coding procedures, the attendees selected a partner for an informal experimental activity. Each dyad was asked to designate a teacher and a learner. The dyads were randomly split into two groups.

Expertise levels were induced by providing both groups with different color coded instructions for teaching a geometric pattern consisting of five interconnected rectangles. The exact pattern varied between and within groups but always included five rectangles. The rectangle chain is often used in workshops about 1- and 2-way communication. The guidelines for experts ($n = 5$) included initial and alternative routines that encouraged teachers to give demonstrations, maximize practice, observe learner responses, offer feedback, and answer questions. Novices ($n = 4$) were given fewer and obviously (we assumed) poorer initial routines but no backups. They were asked to talk steadily, refrain from repeating or rephrasing directions, and not demonstrate or show the original figure. They were not given any of the same routines as experts, but were simply told to teach like a public address system. At five randomly selected points in the 15-minute lesson, a stop signal sounded and teachers conducted self-analysis of decision pathways using a coding form and replica of Figure 2.

Statistical findings

The coding procedure provided absolute and relative frequency counts for each of the five decision paths. Individual scores were combined for the various expert and novice groups and treated by analysis of variance for repeated measures to determine whether the proportional use of pathways depended upon expertise. Figure 2 illustrates the decision patterns for all expert and novice teachers across the three studies. The expertise X pathway interaction was statistically significant in the BCS, $F(4,32) = 5.72$, $p < .001$, but not in the IBS or GFS.

Tables 2 and 3 provide more detail about the results of each study. The experts in BCS and GFS perceived cues in tolerance relatively more often than did novices. This trend was reversed in IBS, possibly due to expert C.K. who was experienced in elementary physical education but quite naive about inverted balance. This subject never reported tolerable cues and, from an interactive decision viewpoint, was very different from all other experts.

When cues were judged outside tolerable limits, both experts and novices in all studies considered immediate adjustments necessary more often than not. However, novices were more prone to respond affirmatively to the necessity question, 100% of the time in BCS and GFS and 92.1% in IBS. The Path 2 data seem to support the notion of an expert's greater tendency to delay corrective action when cues deviate from tolerable limits.

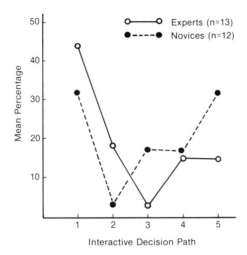

Figure 2 — Expertise X pathway interaction across three studies of physical education teachers.

When cues were reported outside the limits and adjustments were deemed necessary, both groups usually had alternative routines but the experts were 2.7% (GFS), 16.6% (IBS), and 19.5% (BCS) higher in "yes" responses to the availability question and, overall, followed Path 3 less often than did novices.

Path 4 results were mixed. Experts were higher in the IBS and GFS but lower in the BCS. Generally, when alternative routines were thought necessary and available, the dominant tendency of both groups was not to initiate the alternative. When adjustments were reported, novices were more likely to make them in all three studies, especially the GFS where their in-flight changes (Path 5) were 28.2% more frequent than those of experts. Path 5 differences were 3.6% in IBS and 15.9% in BCS, with novices higher in both cases.

The combined results indicate that both experts and novices tend to continue rather than change routines during interactive teaching. This tendency, however, appears stronger among experts. The results also suggest differential reactions at critical moments depending upon the subject matter for the lesson. In the IBS and GFS, the novices were twice as likely to make adjustments when cues were outside tolerable limits. The mean values for changes at critical moments were 21.0% for experts and 42.9% for novices in IBS, and 36.8% for experts and 76.9% for novices in GFS. Finally, when cues were perceived outside tolerable limits, experts showed two major reactions. They either delayed action or made immediate adjustments. On the contrary, novices almost always reacted to problems more diffusely, distributing their decisions among Paths 3, 4, and 5.

Table 2

Percentage of Binary Responses at Four Interactive Decision Points

	Cues within tolerance?		Alternative teaching routines					
			Necessary?		Available?		Initiated?	
Teachers	Yes	No	Yes	No	Yes	No	Yes	No
Inverted balance								
Experts (n = 3)	22.7	77.3	66.0	34.0	100.0	0.0	31.4	68.6
Novices (n = 3)	29.2	70.8	92.1	7.9	83.4	16.6	38.2	61.8
Body composition								
Experts (n = 5)	55.1	44.9	56.1	43.9	92.9	7.1	16.6	83.4
Novices (n = 5)	25.9	74.1	100.0	0.0	73.4	26.6	25.9	74.1
Geometric figure								
Experts (n = 5)	58.7	41.3	66.1	33.9	94.6	5.4	18.1	81.9
Novices (n = 4)	42.3	57.7	100.0	0.0	91.9	8.1	49.4	50.6

Note. Percentage figures are only for teachers who reached each decision point. Not all teachers answered each question on every occasion because of variations in path tendencies.

Table 3

Interactive Decision Tendencies of Expert and Novice Physical Education Teachers

	Percentage of decisions				
Teachers	Path 1	Path 2	Path 3	Path 4	Path 5
Inverted balance					
Experts (n = 3)	22.7	26.3	0.0	35.0	16.0
Novices (n = 3)	29.2	5.6	15.3	18.0	31.9
Body composition					
Experts (n = 5)	55.1	19.7	4.0	5.7	15.4
Novices (n = 5)	25.9	0.0	26.6	28.5	19.0
Geometric figure					
Experts (n = 5)	58.7	14.0	3.6	6.5	17.2
Novices (n = 4)	42.3	0.0	8.1	4.2	45.4

Concluding remarks

The three studies summarized in this paper investigated relationships between pedagogical expertise and interactive decision-making. These studies were based on a conceptual model that assumes that teachers are periodically faced with the decision to continue or change their planned routines. The model further assumes that this decision requires knowledge of the task, performance criteria, and pedagogical alternatives, plus the skills to solicit, monitor, and evaluate learner responses. The critical factors for interactive decision-making seem to be (a) diagnostic competence, the ability to recognize correct and incorrect responses, and (b) pedagogical memory, the availability of alternative routines for making in-flight adjustments when responses are judged outside tolerable limits and changes are considered necessary. The possible effects of insufficient routines were most striking in the GFS where novices made in-flight changes 2.7 times more often than experts.

Although the results of these exploratory efforts are quite suggestive of expert/novice differences with respect to the five path options, the cognitive mechanisms responsible for these differential tendencies have not been isolated. To some degree, interactive decisions might reflect varying strategies of instructional planning. In the body composition study (Taheri, 1982), a significant correlation ($r = .78$) was reported between Path 1 and the number of information cues requested during planning. Also significant were correlations for Path 2 versus cue requests ($r = .68$) and preimpact decisions ($r = .79$), and for Path 3 versus total planning decisions ($r = -.72$). Overall, Taheri's experts requested more information and made more preimpact decisions than did novices, but the mean planning times for experts and novices, respectively, were 33.6 and 63.6 minutes. Peterson, Clark, and Marx (1978) reported slight positive relationships among experience, Path 1, and students' academic achievement. Hopefully, such correlational evidence will stimulate future research on the determinants and consequences of the tendency to follow through with planned routines during interactive teaching.

Mosston's (1981) theory of teaching begins with the axiom: "Teaching behavior is a chain of decision making." This fundamental assumption suggests that overt teaching acts result from decisions made before, during, and after every teaching/learning transaction. It implies that "teachers are rational professionals who, like other professionals such as physicians, make judgments and carry out decisions in an uncertain, complex environment" (Shavelson & Stern, 1981, p. 456). It also suggests that teaching behavior is somehow influenced by pedagogical thoughts, judgments, and decisions and that such cognitions might explain predictable variations in teaching behavior or account for why some teachers are better pedagogical problem solvers than others.

Psychological studies of expertise in problem solving indicate that competent performance is dependent upon the semantic structure of long-term memory and the cognitive skills of planning, evaluating, and revising solutions. The expert's semantic memory is not only saturated with conceptual knowledge, but contains elaborate production systems as well (Anderson, 1980). Production systems are "if . . . then" rules that enable individuals to match problems and solutions. The key distinction between expert and novice is not whether more or less of a given action is taken, but whether it is appropriate for the problem at hand. Experts are adept at matching and, once the optimal match is planned, can work out their problems with relatively few mistakes. However, when experts commit errors, the errors are quickly detected and corrected.

Compared with experts, the problem solving of novices is crude, inconsistent, and less automatic (Chi & Glaser, 1980). The inability of novices to accept or reject solutions accounts for their frequent mistakes and tendencies toward checking and switching routines. These tendencies can be traced to the absence or incompleteness of their production systems.

Although the knowledge and production systems of physical education teachers have not been studied, the interactive decision tendencies of our experts and novices seem empirically and theoretically consistent with the problem-solving literature. Future research on the action-directing cognitions of physical educators seems advisable, particularly by scholars who view teaching as a problematic activity or "open skill" (Jensen, 1980). As long as scholars acknowledge the bounded rationality of teaching, there is room to study pedagogical cognitions. However, such research ought not remain submerged too long. Eventually, it must come up for air to observe behavioral phenomena and discover meaningful links between teachers' thoughts and actions. While the immediate goal of research on pedagogical cognitions is conceptual clarity, its ultimate challenge is to discover ways of educating more intelligent teachers.

Reference Notes

1. Huber, G.L., & Mandl, H. *Methodological questions in describing teacher cognitions.* Paper presented at annual meeting of the American Educational Research Association, New York, March 1982.
2. Doyle, W. *Student mediating responses in teaching effectiveness: Final Report* (Project No. 0-0645). Department of Education, North Texas State University, March 1980.
3. Snow, R.E. A model of teacher training system: An overview. *Research and Development Memorandum No. 92.* Stanford, CA: Stanford Center for Research & Development in Teaching, 1972.
4. Sherman, M.A. *A study of expert and novice gymnastics teachers.* Paper presented at the annual meeting of the Pennsylvania State Association for Health, Physical Education, Recreation, and Dance, Philadelphia, December 1979.
5. DiCicco, G., Housner, L.D., & Sherman, M.A. *Expert-novice differences in planning and teaching physical education.* Abstract of a presentation at the annual meeting of the Pennsylvania State Association for Health, Physical Education, Recreation, and Dance, Pittsburgh, December 1981.

6. Sherman, M.A. *Teacher thinking in physical education: A cognitive view of clinical expertise.* Symposium presented at the annual meeting of the Pennsylvania State Association for Health, Physical Education, Recreation, and Dance, Pittsburgh, December 1981.

References

ANDERSON, R. *Cognitive psychology and implications.* W.H. Freeman, San Francisco, 1980.

ARMSTRONG, C.W., & Hoffman, S.J. Effects of teaching experience, knowledge of performance competence, and knowledge of performance outcomes on performance error identification. *Research Quarterly*, 1979, **50**, 318-327.

CHI, M.T.H., & Glaser, R. The measurement of expertise: Analysis of the development of knowledge and skill as a basis for assessing achievement. In E.L. Baker & E.S. Quellmalz (Eds.), *Educational testing and evaluation: Design, analysis and policy.* Beverly Hills, CA: Sage, 1980.

CHI, M.T.H., Glaser, R., & Rees, E. Expertise in problem solving. In R. Sternberg (Ed.), *Advances in the psychology of human intelligence* (Vol. 1). Hillsdale, NJ: Erlbaum Associates, 1982.

ERICSSON, K.A., & Simon, H.A. Verbal reports as data. *Psychological Review*, 1980, **87**, 215-251.

GRAHAM, G., & Heimerer, E. Research on teacher effectiveness: A summary with implications for teaching. *Quest*, 1981, **33**(1), 14-25.

JENSEN, M. Teaching: An open skill, implications for teacher training. *Quest*, 1980, **32**(1), 60-70.

JOYCE, B. Toward a theory of information processing in teaching. *Educational Research Quarterly*, 1978-1979, **3**, 66-67.

MacKAY, A. The Alberta studies of teaching: A quinquereme in search of some sailors. *CSSE News*, 1977, **3**, 14-17.

MORGENEGG, B.L. Pedagogical moves. In W.G. Anderson & G.T. Barrette (Eds.), *What's going on in gym: Descriptive studies of physical education classes* (A special monograph of Motor Skills: Theory into Practice. Newtown, CT), 1980.

MORINE-DERSHIMER, G., & Vallance, E. *A study of teacher and pupil perceptions of classroom interaction* (Tech. Rep. 75-11-6).San Francisco: Beginning Teacher Evaluation Study, Far West Laboratory, November 1975.

MOSSTON, M. *Teaching physical education.* Columbus, OH: Charles E. Merrill, 1981.

PETERSON, P.L., & Clark, C.M. Teachers' reports of their cognitive processes during teaching. *American Educational Research Journal*, 1978, **15**(4), 555-565.

PETERSON, P.L., Marx, R.W., & Clark, C.M. Teacher planning, teacher behavior, and student achievement. *American Educational Research Journal*, 1978, **15**, 417-432.

RESNICK, L.B., & Glaser, R. Problem-solving and intelligence. In L.B. Resnick (Ed.), *The nature of intelligence*. Hillsdale, NJ: Erlbaum Associates, 1976.

SHAVELSON, R.J. Teachers' decision-making. In N.L. Gage (Ed.), *The psychology of teaching methods* (Yearbook of the National Society for the Study of Education). Chicago: University of Chicago Press, 1976.

SHAVELSON, R.J., & Stern, P. Research on teachers' pedagogical thoughts, judgments, decisions, and behavior. *Review of Educational Research*, 1981, **51**(4), 455-498.

SHULMAN, L.S., & Elstein, A.S. Studies of problem-solving, judgment, and decision-making. In F.N. Kerlinger (Ed.), *Review of Research in Education* (Vol. 3). Itasca, IL: Peacock, 1975.

SIMON, D.P., & Simon, H.A. Individual differences in solving physics problems. In R. Siegler (Ed.), *Children's thinking: What develops*. Hillsdale, NJ: Erlbaum Associates, 1978.

TAHERI, M.A. *Analysis of expertise in planning and interactive decision-making among health fitness teachers*. Unpublished doctoral dissertation, University of Pittsburgh, 1982.

Clinical diagnosis as a pedagogical skill

Shirl J. Hoffman
University of Pittsburgh

The behaviors of teachers are manifestations of a continual stream of decisions made before and during the course of instruction. These decisions are the antecedents of behavior and, according to instructional theorist Richard Shavelson (1973), the ability to make correct decisions on the basis of all available pertinent information constitutes "the basic teaching skill." Of the various decisions teachers make during the course of instruction, many (perhaps the majority) are based on information gleaned from an analysis of the learner's performance. This most certainly is the case in sport skill instruction where teachers and coaches traditionally have emphasized the importance of observing students' motor skill performances. Whether considered as discrete units or members of a behavioral class, the motor responses of students comprise the basic data upon which physical education and sport skill teachers make major pedagogical decisions.

Making decisions and judgments on the basis of cues or symptoms informally collected during a systematic observation of a sample case constitutes what medical science labels clinical diagnosis. Within the context of this paper, clinical diagnosis refers specifically to decisions made by skill instructors regarding the nature of the learner's performance problems and the factors that give rise to them. Over the past several years, I and some of my students have been studying some cognitive and behavior components of clinical diagnosis, an operation that appears to be critically important in motor skill instruction. This paper briefly outlines the framework in which our research has been conducted and summarizes some of the data collected to date.

Clinical diagnosis in motor skill instruction

The importance of diagnosis in teaching was highlighted several years ago by a "law of teaching behavior" proposed by instructional theorists Norman Wallen and R.M.W. Travers (1963). According to Wallen and Travers, teaching can be expressed as an equation: $T = f(\text{Rg}, \text{Ri})$. Quite simply, teaching is a function of the goal to be attained (Rg) and the present behavior of the learner (Ri). The law underscores the fact that pedagogy is driven by teacher judgments regarding the discrepancy between the learner's present behavior and the behavior required to attain the skill goal. Teaching is not, as Mary Jensen has told us, something to be performed like a closed skill (Jensen, 1980). It is an adaptive-interactive process and the principal controlling stimulus in this reactive system is the learner's behavior, particularly as it relates to the goal that the teacher had in mind.

Compared to the elegant systems and microscopic analyses of teaching performance presented in this symposium, the diagnostic-prescriptive model depicted in Figure 1 is rather primitive, yet it redirects attention to this oft-neglected aspect of teaching. The model suggests that the discrepancy between actual and desired behavior is the focal point of instruction. The discrepancy represents the principal cues disclosed in the instructor's analysis of the learner's performance. The nature of this discrepancy and what the teacher determines to be its cause influence the course of instructional events which follow. This, of course, presumes that specific performance deficits require specific pedagogical interventions for their remediation. The model also suggests that the accuracy of the teacher's prescription will be determined, to a large extent, by the accuracy of the diagnosis. In this respect, the analogy between teaching and medicine is nearly direct. As the physician's decisions regarding medical treatment are contingent upon his diagnosis of the patient's ailments, so are decisions regarding feedback, verbal prompts, or the nature of practice experiences contingent upon the instructor's diagnosis of the learner's performance deficiencies. Obviously, then, the teacher's ability to correctly ascertain the learners' problems, and allow that assessment to inform subsequent decisions about the prescriptive part of teaching,

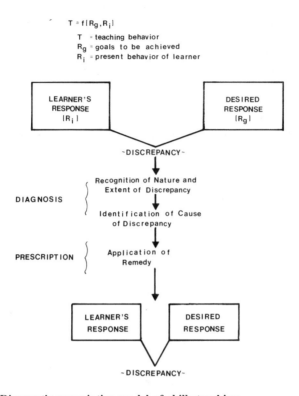

$T = f[R_g, R_i]$

T = teaching behavior
R_g = goals to be achieved
R_i = present behavior of learner

Figure 1 — Diagnostic prescriptive model of skills teaching.

would appear to be a major determinant of his/her effectiveness in helping learners attain the skill goal.

Skills teachers are confronted with three major clinical-diagnostic decisions:

1. The first is whether or not the learner has performed the skill correctly. In skills where outcomes are of the discrete yes/no variety (i.e., shooting a basketball, catching a ball) this may be a rather easy task. However, in skills where outcomes are graded on a continuous scale (i.e., discus throwing, passing a soccer ball to a moving teammate), substantial knowledge about the skill, standards of performance, and the competitive context is required for an accurate decision. Knowledge about standards of performance is especially important in evaluating responses of "form-specific skills" such as diving and gymnastics.

2. If the teacher decides that the learner has not performed the skill correctly, he/she must decide which features of the performance are in error. Often, it is not all that difficult to recognize that a perfor-

mance is of relatively poor quality, but even the most enthusiastic teachers can be stymied when asked to describe how the performance differed from an ideal performance.

Errors can be primary or secondary. Secondary errors are those that reflect errors committed at some earlier point in the response sequence. Secondary errors are important because they furnish clues about the learner's "real problem," the causative or primary error. Thus, primary errors are the principal concern of the clinician. For example, the secondary errors which mar the diver's performance in flight are signals to the experienced instructor that primary errors were committed while the performer was still in contact with the board. Any attempt to eliminate a secondary error without taking into account its complementary primary error is doomed to fail.

3. Finally, the instructor is confronted with clinical decisions regarding prescriptions for remediating the primary errors. Experienced teachers seem to have stored in memory a selection of instructional strategies (prompts, cues, drills, etc.), time-proven methods for treating particular performance deficits. Effective skills teaching seems largely a matter of fitting the correct instructional strategy to the primary error judged to be hindering the learner's attempt to attain the skill goal.

A hypothetico-deductive model

These decisions are incorporated into the hypothetico-deductive model of clinical inquiry presented in Figure 2. It should be noted that the model is intended for illustrative purposes only. The binary decision tree may vary dramatically depending upon the instructor's knowledge and experience, the type of motor skill being analyzed, the learner's competence in the skill, the nature of the performance problems, and the relative cost to the instructor of making a particular diagnostic error. It also should be noted that no data yet available permit us to say with any degree of assurance that skill instructors actually approach diagnosis in such a logical and systematic fashion, nor do we know if they make reasonable judgments based on the data at hand.

The initial question ("Was the goal attained?") must always be considered within the framework of a host of contingencies. The learner's age and experience, and the level of competition for which the performer is preparing, invariably are factored into the clinician's decision about goal attainment. What may be an acceptable golf swing for a 13-year-old novice may be woefully inadequate for a member of the high school golf team. The dotted line in the flow chart represents the highest possible standard attainable.

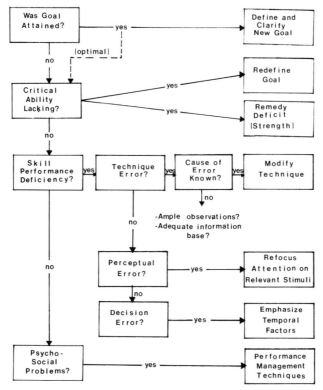

Figure 2 — Diagnostic problem-solving in skill instruction.

If the instructor decides the goal was not attained, a series of follow-up questions guides the troubleshooting process designed to uncover the reasons. Operating on the basis of information supplied by secondary errors and his/her long-term store of clinical knowledge, the instructor attempts to pinpoint the primary errors preventing the learner from attaining the skill goal.

Hypothetico-deductive reasoning is a process of collecting data or cues and generating alternative hypotheses about the nature of the problem under investigation. As the clinical workup proceeds, some early hypotheses may be discarded and newer ones added as additional information is collected and weighed in light of alternative hypotheses. The hypotheses entertained by the skill instructor fall into three major categories: abilities, skill deficiencies, and psychosocial factors. One hypothesis may be that the learner lacks a requisite ability or abilities to successfully perform the skill. If that hypothesis is confirmed, the appropriate prescription depends upon the nature of the ability judged to be lacking. If the learner is deficient in an enduring trait that cannot be remediated to any appreciable degree (i.e., visual acuity, movement speed, etc.), the teacher has no choice but to redefine the skill goal within the limitations of the learner's abilities. If, however, the ability is one that can be modified (i.e., strength, endurance, etc.), the instructor must prescribe activities to remediate the deficiency before progress will be evident.

If a critical ability is not judged to be lacking, a second major hypothesis may be that the learner suffers from a skill deficiency. Skill deficiencies are variations of one of three major types: technique or output errors, perceptual errors, and decision errors (Marteniuk, 1976). Technique errors are movement errors, and in most cases, the most obvious type of error. Because the relationships between movement sequences are governed by fundamental laws of mechanics, primary technique errors often can be deduced on the basis of secondary technique errors. That a knowledge of mechanics is essential for accurate diagnosis of motor skills is, of course, a firmly held tenet by contemporary biomechanists, but I am not so sure. Experienced clinicians teaching skills with which they are familiar may not resort to trouble shooting. Through repeated analyses of the skill, they have learned to focus directly on the source of difficulty. Some may not even appreciate or understand the mechanical laws that govern the relationship between secondary and primary errors. Granted, this does not mean that a knowledge of mechanics would not improve their diagnostic capabilities, but that remains a question yet to be examined.

If, in the clinician's judgment, the technique is acceptable but the learner continues to fail the skill goal, the breakdown may be due to perceptual or decision errors. Perceptual errors are mistakes in interpreting sensory input. Decision errors occur when inappropriate responses are made to what may or may not be correctly interpreted input. For example, if a batter's swing appears to be mechanically correct but the batter continues to miss the ball, the clinician is cued to a possible error in the learner's visual analysis of the ball's flight path (perceptual error), or an error in judgment about when to initiate his swing in order to make contact with the ball (decision error). Perceptual errors depend for their remediation upon a redirection of the learner's attention to critical environmental events (i.e., the motion path of the ball). Decision errors are eliminated only when the performer learns to pay closer attention to the temporal relationship between their movements and relevant signals in the environment.

If the learner possesses the requisite abilities and technical skills but still fails to perform in the expected manner, the instructor may entertain a third hypothesis: The problem may be related to psychosocial factors. The most frequently encountered problems in this domain are motivational, particularly among highly skilled athletes who suffer from what industrial psychologists have called the "you really oughta wanna syndrome" (Mager & Pipe, 1970). Other psychosocial obstacles include fear, guilt, and anxiety. When such problems are severe and beyond the professional scope of the instructor, referral is in order. Less complex problems such as lack of motivation, may be solved by using a variety of different approaches. One such approach is an application of behavioral management techniques.

The model raises several important questions about the nature of the diagnostic process. Do skill instructors actually employ a hypothetico-deductive model of diagnosis and, if so, how do the diagnostic strategies employed by experienced instructors differ from the strategies used by novices? Can specific diagnostic strategies be associated with rapid learning gains for particular classes of skill, age groups, and levels of competence and, if so, how can those strategies be taught to preservice and inservice teachers?

The model also raises questions about the knowledge base required for making clinical decisions. The importance of clinical memory in diagnosis was underscored by Arthur Elstein (Note 1), who, along with his colleagues at Michigan State, has given considerable attention to the role of diagnosis in both medicine and the teaching of reading:

> The set of solutions entertained by the clinician is limited by the contents of long-term memory, for clearly one cannot consider, even hypothetically, a condition one has never heard of or knows nothing about. (p. 6)

The same can be said of clinical memory subserving motor skill instruction. Presumably, the teacher's memory store contains technical ("how-to") information about the skill being analyzed as well as an integrated body of theoretical knowledge about human performance as it relates to that skill. If the decisions presented in Figure 2 in any way resemble those demanded of a skills teacher, it is obvious that he/she must draw *simultaneously* from what are normally considered widely disparate bodies of knowledge such as exercise physiology, motor learning, motor development, sport psychology, and biomechanics.

The implication of this is painfully obvious for conventional teacher training programs that typically downplay the importance of technical information about sport skills, and that compartmentalize theoretical knowledge about human performance into isolated course offerings. Skill teachers and coaches can no more spontaneously evolve effective diagnostic strategies for gymnastics or volleyball instruction out of the melange of theoretical coursework offered up by academics, (most of whom are neither interested nor knowledgeable in the kind of clinical decision-making required in pedagogy) than medical students could spontaneously evolve an effective method of diagnosing encephalitis from a basic course in anatomy and physiology. If diagnostic com-

petence is to be acquired, it must be taught as a clinical skill and supported by a thoroughly integrated knowledge base that is directly relevant to the decisions confronting the instructor.

Perception as a critical component of clinical diagnosis

Unfortunately, this model of clinical inquiry, focusing as it does on the
search for primary errors, neglects the distinguishing feature of
diagnoses conducted in motor skill settings, the single characteristic that
sets them apart from diagnoses conducted by internists, radiologists,
electronic maintenance technicians, and reading teachers. I refer to the
transitory nature of the data base upon which sport skill instructors must
make their clinical decisions. Except in rare instances where performances are preserved on film or videotape, the principal diagnostic cues
are available for inspection only for an instant. Unlike radiologists who
can leisurely examine shadows on roentgenograms, motor skill instructors are allowed only a brief glimpse of their diagnostic data, thus com-
pounding the uncertainty surrounding their clinical decisions.

Because clinical inquiry is a series of chain-linked decisions, uncertainty at the front end of the diagnostic workup introduces uncertainty into
all decisions that follow. Consequently, the instructor's ability to visually
capture and retain, if only for a brief interval, details of a learner's motor
response strongly influences the accuracy of the final clinical determina-
tion. This is not to say that perceptual facility guarantees that faulty decisions will not be made at some later step in the diagnostic workup, but it
is obvious that any clinical judgment can never be better than the
evidence upon which that judgment is made. Quite simply, the upper
limits of accuracy in clinical inquiry are set by the accuracy of the instructor's initial observation.

Data from three modest studies have suggested that physical education
teachers—generalists who teach a variety of sport skills—experience extraordinary difficulty in this initial stage of data collection. In order to
assess performance in this front end operation of diagnosis, care must be
taken not to confound subjects' proficiency when collecting the data with
their skill when evaluating or interpreting the data (Hoffman, 1977). One
method of isolating data collection from these subsequent operations is
to require subjects to recognize a previously viewed motor response
without making judgments regarding the quality of the performance.
Such a paradigm was followed in these three studies.

In two studies, subjects were shown a discrete response (prototype) of
a sports skill performance several times, after which they attempted to
recognize that performance when it appeared in a series of 10 performances of the same skill by the same subject. If the test item was judged
to differ from the prototype, subjects selected from among three short
phrases the one which accurately described the discrepancy. In a control

condition, subjects were also tested on recognition accuracy for a novel movement task with which they had no prior experience.

In the first study (Biscan & Hoffman, 1976), physical education teachers with a mean of 3 years' service, undergraduate preservice physical education teachers, and classroom teachers observed and attempted to recognize a single cartwheel performed by a junior high school student. The physical education teachers were accurate in 65% of the cases, the undergraduate students in 77% of the cases, and the classroom teachers in only 44% of the cases. Although the physical education teachers were more accurate in their recognitions than the classroom teachers, they were significantly poorer in recognition performance than were the undergraduate trainees.

A second study (Hoffman & Sembiante, 1975) employed the same paradigm to test recognition accuracy of a baseball swing. Subjects were a group of town recreation baseball and softball coaches with no formal training in physical education theory or kinesiology, a group of physical education teachers with no intensive experience in softball or baseball but with at least a baccalaureate degree in physical education and at least one course in kinesiology, and a control group with no formal training in physical education theory and no intensive experience in softball or baseball. Results revealed significantly higher accuracy scores for the coaches (74% accuracy) than either of the other two groups, but scores for physical education teachers (66% accuracy) were not significantly higher than scores for the controls (64% accuracy). In both the Biscan and Hoffman and Hoffman and Sembiante studies no differences were observed in recognition performance between the groups when subjects viewed a novel movement sequence, a finding that underscores the importance of experience in this kind of diagnostic ability.

A third study, which used a different method for comparing recognition accuracy of a gymnastic skill (a front handspring), involved gymnastic coaches (specialists), veteran physical education teachers with an average of 5 years' teaching experience who taught at least one unit of gymnastics each year (generalists), and a group of undergraduate preservice physical education students with no special interest or experience in gymnastics (Imwold & Hoffman, 1983). The test required subjects to view a film depicting a discrete response of the skill and then try to remember the position of the performer's body at two, three, or four critical phases in the performance. The phases were *hurdle, hand placement, midflight,* and *landing*. Recognition performance was assessed by having subjects recognize a contour drawing (created from the film) which depicted the position of the body at a phase from among four alternative contour drawings. On some trials, subjects were required to recognize body positions at two or three phases, and on others at all four phases of the skill on a single trial.

We had anticipated that the specialists, by virtue of their greater experience with the skill, would score higher on the recognition task than either the generalists or novices and, for the same reason, that generalists would score higher than novices. In addition, we anticipated that as the task became increasingly complex by requiring subjects to monitor and remember a greater number of components of the performance, differences between the groups would increase because of the specialists' more efficient perceptual strategy for processing large amounts of information.

Results tended to follow the pattern observed in the two previous studies. The gymnastic specialists were significantly more accurate in their recognitions (54% accuracy) than were either the generalists (47%) or the novices (46%). Once again, veteran physical education teachers were found to be no more reliable in recognizing previously presented motor performances than were inexperienced undergraduate students. Although no significant interaction was observed to suggest that specialists improved relative to the other two groups as the task increased in complexity, the predicted trend was observed for specialists relative to generalists. Surprisingly, as the task increased in complexity, the novices improved relative to the veteran teachers.

The data collected in these modest investigations are far from conclusive but they do underscore the critical importance of intensive visual and possibly kinesthetic experience with the skill, if skill teachers are to develop this important perceptual ability. On one hand, teacher educators will be encouraged to learn that perceptual ability is not fixed but appears to be modifiable through intensive experience. On the other hand, they will not be encouraged when they learn that the amount of skill-specific experience required seems far in excess of that provided in traditional programs of professional preparation, and probably beyond what physical education teachers acquire during years of duty in the schools.

Clearly, one of the most disturbing findings has been the abysmal performance of veteran physical education teachers relative to undergraduate novices. It is hardly novel to suggest that survival in the real world of teaching depends upon skills that have little, if anything, to do with diagnosing performance errors and probably little to do with pedagogy. Consequently, one shouldn't be surprised to discover that diagnostic proficiency appears to decline during the years following graduation from the teacher training institution. Nevertheless, the findings are striking, particularly in the case of the teachers sampled in the Imwold and Hoffman study. If recognition performance on the experimental task truly reflected the ability of subjects to hold information about the learner's response in short-term memory, and if, as has been suggested, this data is essential for accurate diagnosis, it follows that the physical education teachers sampled in this study will correctly diagnose a learner's response in the handspring in no more than 47% of the cases they confront. Given ample opportunity for committing further mistakes in the subsequent steps of the workup, the accuracy rate probably will be considerably less.

Reference Note

1. Elstein, A. *Human factors in clinical judgment: Discussion of Scrivan's "The Logic of Clinical Inference."* Paper presented at the Fifth Transdisciplinary Symposium on Philosophy and Medicine, UCLA, April 1977.

References

BISCAN, D., & Hoffman, S.J. Movement analysis as a generic ability of physical education teachers and students. *Research Quarterly*, 1976, **47**, 161-163.

HOFFMAN, S.J. Competency-based training in skill analysis. In R.E. Stadulis (Ed.), *Research and practice in physical education.* Champaign, IL: Human Kinetics, 1977.

HOFFMAN, S.J., & Sembiante, J. Experience and imagery in movement analysis. *British Proceedings of Sports Psychology* (British Society of Sport Psychology), 1975, pp. 288-295.

IMWOLD, C., & Hoffman, S.J. Visual recognition of a gymnastics skill by experienced and inexperienced instructors. *Research Quarterly for Exercise and Sport*, 1983, **54**(2), 149-155.

JENSEN, M. Teaching: An open skill, implications for teacher training. *Quest*, 1980, **32**, 60-70.

MAGER, R., & Pipe, P. *Analyzing performance problems.* Belmont, CA: Lear Siegler Inc./Fearon, 1970.

MARTENIUK, R. *Information processing in motor skills.* Holt, Rinehart, & Winston, 1976.

SHAVELSON, R. What is the basic teaching skill? *The Journal of Teacher Education*, 1973, **14**, 144-151.

WALLEN, N., & Travers, R.M.W. Analysis and investigation of teaching methods. In N.L. Gage (Ed.), *Handbook of research on teaching.* Rand McNally, 1963.

Conceptions of success in teaching: Busy, happy and good?

Judith H. Placek
San Diego State University

In the past, most of the research on teaching has focused upon interactive teaching, that is, the events that occur when the students are present in the classroom. In addition to providing a description of classroom processes, examination of student/teacher interaction has focused on the question "what teaching strategy works best?" Recently, researchers have narrowed the focus of their attention to systematically observing the classroom with an eye toward relating particular observed variables to student learning and thus, indirectly, producing estimates of teacher effectiveness. The ultimate target of such product/process research has been the construction of reliable and comprehensive theories that would serve to improve teaching and teacher preparation.

In contrast to examining interactive teaching, recent interest in the hidden or inner world of the teacher has led some educational researchers to focus on an area called cognitive information processing, or research on teachers' thinking. For example, Michigan State University's Institute for Research on Teaching (IRT), founded in 1976, is examining teachers' mental lives and decision making (Shulman & Lanier, 1977). The IRT's cognitive information processing approach is based on the belief that how teachers behave and what they do is directed to a large extent by what they think. Thus, the relationship between thought and action becomes the critical issue in research on teaching. This paper will present the results of two studies that examined how physical education teachers and undergraduate majors think about success in teaching. The findings of the first study, which examined teachers' planning, provided the inspirational spark for the second study, which directly investigated conceptions of success in teaching.

Teachers' planning study

One facet of the research on teachers' thinking involves investigating an area Jackson (1968) calls preactive teaching, which defines the time when teachers are planning lessons, grading papers, or preparing materials rather than interacting with students.

Planning, one component of preactive teaching, is a process in which teachers should engage in careful and thoughtful deliberation in preparation for teaching. Under ideal conditions, preactive decisions call upon a teacher's ability to blend theoretical knowledge and practical experience in order to produce an effective learning environment for students. During this time teachers have the opportunity to collect materials, consider student characteristics, wrestle with their subject matter, and then make judgments about teaching that should produce a well constructed plan for action. In short, thoughtful planning should result in more effective teaching and improved student learning.

In order to investigate planning in a public school context, a recent study examined the planning of physical education teachers (Placek, 1982). The study was conducted in a natural setting—the gymnasia, fields, and offices where teachers work. Four physical education teachers were observed for 2 weeks each, and the observers' field notes were combined with teachers' written plans and interviews to provide data for this study.

One question asked in this study was, "What are the influences on the teachers' planning?" All the teachers (alias Jerry, Ted, Paula, and Sue) perceived that many factors influenced their planning. For example, all four said their past teaching experiences, students, safety considerations, weather, and equipment and facilities affected their planning for classes. Two influences, however, student behavior and environmental unpredictability, had the greatest impact on their planning. This paper will discuss only the influence of student behavior. The majority of teachers' statements during the observation dealt with the students, and the teachers' comments in the final, formal interview abounded with references to the students.

The teachers most frequently mentioned student feedback in three specific areas as influencing their planning: student enjoyment, participation, and incidents of misbehavior. All the teachers were concerned that students would not like physical education classes; their statements expressed concern about

- (classes) not being fun or exciting;
- playing something they (students) want to play;
- student enthusiasm;
- if kids really like it (class or activity);
- (if students were) having a good time, talking about class, cheering, excited, happy.

The second area of student feedback that influenced the teachers' planning, student participation, was reflected in teachers' statements about

- kids being active and busy;
- total participation;
- don't want long lines;
- include as many people as possible in the activity;
- not a lot of wasted time.

The third student-related area that influenced the teachers' planning was student misbehavior. When a student misbehaved, the teachers usually reprimanded the student or made her or him take a "time out" and leave the activity. However, if many students were unruly, the teachers tended to deal with the misbehavior during the next class period. For example, Jerry said, "The plan was we've always met on the circle . . . but I'm not that pleased with that. Behavioral problems were developing on the circle . . . so I've tried to have them go right into an activity" (Placek, 1982). Paula was concerned with one class's inability to focus on the lesson at the beginning of each class. So she had them get in lines and do calisthenics at the beginning of each period. She said, "They are a hyper group and I thought . . . making them line up . . . would get them thinking a little bit, hopefully, in the right direction" (Placek, 1982). Thus, student behavior, and specifically enjoyment, participation, and misbehavior, seemed to influence the teachers' planning decisions to a greater degree than any other factor.

How, then, did the major influence of student response affect the physical education teachers' planning? Student influences affected the explicit decisions teachers made about what to teach in their classes. The teachers focused upon which activities to teach rather than which objectives to choose. The choice of activities seemed to be influenced by three student-related questions.

1. What activities will the students enjoy?
2. What activities will provide the most participation for the students?
3. What activities will give me the fewest discipline problems?

The physical education teachers seemed to define the teaching situation in terms of keeping students busy, happy, and good.

As a result of this view, student learning was not of much concern to the teachers. In fact, if student skill level improved, the teacher might even ask why. For example, as Paula left a volleyball class one day, she mused, "I wonder why they played so much better today than during the last class?" On another occasion she wondered aloud why students didn't move to the ball (playing volleyball), but she didn't ask herself what she could do in class that would help students learn to move to the ball. She was concerned that students were not accomplishing the tasks she wanted them to; but she did not move to the next step of asking, "What can I do to help the students learn?" She did not say, "I have some responsibility for student learning."

In summary, the teachers in this study were more concerned about student behavior than about transmitting a body of knowledge. All of them cared about their students and went out of their way to talk to them outside of class, trading jokes or asking about their families. This personal level of caring, however, did not transfer to a direct feeling of responsibility for their learning. The teachers did not even say, for example, "Each student will be able to bump, set, and serve correctly at the completion of this volleyball unit." They provided activities for the students to participate in, and did their best to ensure that the students had a good time and kept active. Thus, it seems the teachers viewed learning as relatively unimportant to their perceptions of success in teaching.

This study's discovery that the teachers were concerned mainly with the students and their behavior corresponds with Jackson's (1968) findings that, although teaching is usually conceived of as being concerned with learning, teachers are not concerned with this "unseen harvest." The elementary teachers in Jackson's study measured their progress by students' daily behavior rather than by student achievement or learning. This finding led Jackson to distinguish between primary and ultimate concerns of teachers. He observed that teachers seem to be primarily activity-oriented rather than learning-oriented. The teachers in Jackson's sample were interested in achieving and maintaining student involvement in activities.

Other recent studies by Zahorik (1980) and Earls (1981) support this view of how teachers perceive their tasks as teachers. Zahorik selected six teacher verbal behaviors (directions, lecturing, questioning, answering, praise, reproofs and clarifications), and asked 31 elementary teachers to describe and identify recommended and nonrecommended ways of using each behavior, and to give reasons for their recommendations. As might be expected, the teachers recommended many ways to use each verbal behavior. The reasons the teachers gave for their recommendations, however, provided the most interesting findings in the study. Zahorik classified the positive and negative reasons into four groups: a) motivation, b) involvement, c) thinking, and d) self-concept. He states, "The most striking aspect of this study was the nearly total absence of the use of the terms 'achievement' or 'learning' by the teachers" (p. 48).

Earls (1981) interviewed distinctive physical education teachers and found that they believed the "satisfaction of teaching relates primarily to interactions with the students" (p. 64). However, he also noted that signs of student enjoyment and success, as well as long term effects, were important to the teachers.

Conceptions of success study

Zahorik (1980), Earls (1981), and Placek (1982) did not ask teachers directly to identify their basis for judging success in teaching. The findings about teaching and learning were obtained indirectly as parts of larger studies. A logical next question seemed to be, "What would the response be if teachers or preservice students were asked directly how they thought about success in teaching?" The literature revealed only one study that asked teachers how they view success in teaching. Harootunian and Yarger (1981) asked 237 teachers to list any events in their teaching that they regarded as successes. Several results are noteworthy. First, elementary teachers were able to report significantly more successes than senior high teachers (4.96 vs. 3.75). Second, teachers defined their successes in terms of student behavior rather than themselves or other criteria. Third, teachers reported more successes of an affective nature than a cognitive nature (e.g., positive student attitude rather than good grades on quizzes and tests).

How do physical educators and future physical educators view success in teaching? In order to specifically answer this question, a critical incident technique (Flanagan, 1954) was used to examine conceptions of success and nonsuccess in teaching physical education. The subjects for the study were junior and senior college physical education majors enrolled in specific subject methods classes. All of the majors (N = 47) volunteered to complete the questionnaire during the class. However, only data on those majors who had been involved in actually teaching K-12 students in physical education classes are included in this study (N = 29, 15 females, 14 males).

The critical incident technique asks subjects to recall specific behavioral details of a particular situation. Thus, the subjects were asked to identify a specific instance of success in teaching and a specific instance of nonsuccess in their teaching experience. They were asked to describe the instance in some detail, providing information on the setting in which it occurred and what actually happened.

The instances of success reported in the questionnaire were examined and all were listed. Fifteen of the 29 subjects had written more than one example of success in their description (e.g., students learned to work together and the students were all active). Categories were then developed as similar instances of success were grouped together. The descriptions of nonsuccess in teaching were also listed. Again, multiple listings occurred as 10 subjects identified more than one nonsuccess in their example (e.g., students standing around, and students not liking the activity, both in the same example). Each response detailing the nonsuccess was then separated into two or three parts. In all responses, the subjects had identified the cause of the problem. In some responses, the subjects then listed both the problem itself (behavior) and its consequences. In some cases, however, the subjects did not distinguish between the behavior and the consequences; and only two categories were used for those responses. Categories were then developed for the cause of the problem, and the behavior and/or consequence.

The subjects' responses concerning successful instances in their teaching experience fell into three categories. First and most frequently, the subjects were concerned that students in physical education classes enjoyed themselves. Forty-eight percent of the subjects reported feeling successful if students displayed some indication of liking physical education. For example,

- they all enjoyed themselves;
- the students thoroughly enjoyed the soccer unit;
- make physical education a fun experience;
- students had a great time and really got into it.

Second, 44% of the preservice subjects stated that success was indicated by student learning. Three specific subareas of learning were identified under this broader category of student learning (see Table 1). Thirty-one percent of the subjects indicated that they felt successful when students had learned or improved a physical skill. Three subjects (10%) reported feeling successful when social skills were improved, and one subject (3%) stated a cognitive success. Below are some examples of statements made about learning:

- most of the class got 100% correct on the test (cognitive);
- using progression to move a student into the act of performing an activity they could not previously do (physical skill);
- less talented students would make nice plays and be complimented by their teammates (social skill).

High participation levels by students in the class was the third indicator of success, with 31% of the subjects commenting about keeping students busy. For example,

- everyone was able to participate during total class time;
- everybody was busy;
- a well-organized, busy class.

Table 1

Undergraduate Physical Education Majors
Indicators of Success in Teaching

Indicators of success	Percent of total responses*
Student enjoyment	48%
Student learning	44%
a. Physical skill (31%)	
b. Cognitive skill (3%)	
c. Social skill (10%)	
High participation levels of students	31%
Lack of student misbehavior	7%
Other	17%

*The percentages total more than 100% due to multiple successes listed by the subjects.

When the answers were categorized by the source of the success, the overwhelming focus of success, not surprisingly, was the students. Students were the measuring stick of success for 83% of the subjects. The remainder of the subjects directly linked success to their own action (e.g., I had a concise, well-organized lesson plan; I could help students pick out the faults).

Responses to the question asking subjects to give an example of non-success in teaching were placed into two or three categories. First, what did the subjects perceive to be the cause of the problem? In 65% of the statements, the subjects indicated that the problem was due to circumstances over which they felt they had no control. Such statements as, "the previous teacher had exercised little control," "there wasn't enough equipment," and "it was the day before Halloween," gave the impression that the subjects felt the source of the problem was external to them or outside their control.

Thus, only 35% of the subjects blamed themselves for the unsuccessful drill or lesson. These subjects blamed such things as a poor choice of activity, lesson not well prepared, or their own lack of confidence as the major reason for their unsuccessful experience.

The second categorization of the unsuccessful teaching experiences provides insight into the subjects' view of the actual problem or its consequences. The most frequently perceived problem or consequence was control or discipline; that is, the K-12 students didn't do what the teacher had anticipated or asked them to do. Forty-nine percent of the subjects indicated that discipline problems were the major factor in their unsuccessful teaching, and Table 2 shows some of their reasoning on this. Only

Table 2

Samples of Subjects' Unsuccessful Teaching Experiences

Cause of problem	Problem	Consequences
Students couldn't do drill properly	Balls flying all over	Students running all over out of control
Lack of organization by teacher	Students waiting	Kids running around playing tag and yelling
Differences in students' skill level	Only skilled got to contact ball	Unskilled students became disruptive
Poor choice of activity	Students hated game	Students wouldn't follow directions
Teachers turned back on students	Students stopped exercising	
Windy weather	Students couldn't do parachute activity properly	

four subjects (14%) equated nonsuccess with lack of learning by the students. Therefore, the following statement was rare: "I didn't know all the skill levels of the students and thus I taught moves that were too advanced in my wrestling class, and many of the students couldn't learn the skills." Also, only six subjects reported nonsuccess related to students' lack of participation or not enjoying the class.

Thus, it appears that the absence of "successful" events does not necessarily make an experience unsuccessful. That is, success was considered to be student enjoyment, student participation, and student learning, but nonsuccessful events were not entirely defined as a lack of these three categories. The main factor in the subjects' unsuccessful experiences was discipline problems. Only two subjects had reported the lack of discipline problems as a success. Only one-third of the subjects reported the lack of learning, enjoyment, or participation as nonsuccesses. It seems the subjects had different definitions of what constitutes success and nonsuccess in teaching.

Discussion

These answers to direct questions about success and nonsuccess in physical education teaching provide support for the answers obtained through observation in the physical education planning study (Placek, 1982). The fact that similar results were obtained with two different samples (inservice teachers and preservice students) indicates that the focus upon busy, happy, and good students is not the sole province of experienced teachers in the field. Junior and senior physical education majors with limited teaching experience seem to view success in much the same way as do experienced teachers. Less than half of the college students listed success as related to student learning. Success, in many cases, is not Sharon or Bob learning to shoot a jump shot correctly. Success is related to the immediate, observable happenings in the gym. Are the students participating (busy), enjoying themselves (happy), and doing as the teacher directs (good)?

What implications do these findings have for researchers and teacher educators? The results of these studies underscore the fact that teachers and students apparently view success very differently than do researchers who design studies to tease out variables of effective teaching. The process/product paradigm, with student achievement as the dependent variable, certainly dovetails with current calls for accountability for student learning in the schools. If researchers, utilizing the results of process/product studies, begin to tell teachers how to teach in order to produce more student learning—when teachers themselves do not see this as related to success in teaching—it seems inevitable that problems will arise. In fact, the ensuing collision may register a 10 on the Richter scale if teachers' perceptions of the process and product of teaching differ fundamentally from those of researchers.

Fenstermacher (1979), in support of the view that teachers' thought processes are important and worthy of attention, argues that educational research should examine what he calls the subjectively reasonable beliefs of teachers. He believes that even if researchers should find which teacher performances result in student learning, and are therefore able to tell teachers how to produce learning, a crucial question still has not been addressed. That is, why do teachers engage in performances that are not found to be effective for student learning? He says, "the researcher should possess a conception of schooling that accounts for the fact that the school situation is made up of persons who act intentionally within a complex social system" (p. 159). He feels that understanding the subjectively held views of teachers should become the initiating focus for teacher effectiveness research.

The small sample size of the two studies presented here precludes generalization, but it does provide food for thought for teacher educators. Many teacher educators who supervise student teachers may know intuitively that these findings ring true. A few days of observing happy games of beach ball or bombardment provide much informal data to support these studies. It is depressing, to say the least, if teachers feel that student learning is not really of great concern to them. It is even more discouraging, however, that physical education majors may already equate much success with keeping students busy, happy, and good. It tells us that our goals as teacher educators to produce teachers who are concerned not only with student enjoyment, but also student learning, may be fantasy. Even while students are within our grasp at the university, they may be slipping into an unconscious acceptance of the status quo in many school programs.

Of course, we do not know if our physical education majors come to the university with a preconceived notion about what success in teaching is all about. Also, it is not known exactly why experienced teachers equate success in teaching with busy, happy, and good students. What is it in the schools, the teaching situation, college education, or background of the teachers that causes them to view learning as relatively unimportant? Or perhaps they really do view learning as an ultimate goal, but believe that busy, happy, and good are necessary prerequisites for learning to take place. After all, it is difficult for learning to occur if gymnasiums are truly chaotic. And, although the evidence in physical education is limited to one study (Silverman, 1982), studies of elementary classrooms have shown a positive relationship between time on task (busy) and student learning (e.g., Fisher, Filby, Marliave, Cahen, Dishaw, Moore, & Berliner, 1972). Busy, happy, and good could be regarded as the means to an end. Let's hope the pursuit of these characteristics does not become the ultimate end.

References

EARLS, N.F. Distinctive teachers' personal qualities, perceptions of teacher education and the realities of teaching. *Journal of Teaching in Physical Education*, 1981, 1(1), 59-70.

FENSTERMACHER, G.D. A philosophical consideration of recent research on teacher effectiveness. In L.S. Shulman (Ed.), *Review of research in education, No. 6.* Itasca, IL: F.E. Peacock, 1979.

FISHER, C., Filby, N., Marliave, R., Cahen, L., Dishaw, M., Moore, J., & Berliner, D. *Teaching behaviors, academic learning time, and student achievement: Final report of Phase III-B, Beginning Teacher Evaluation Study.* San Francisco: Far West Laboratory for Educational Research and Development, 1972.

FLANAGAN, J.C. The critical incident technique. *Psychological Bulletin*, 1954, 51(4), 327-358.

HAROOTUNIAN, B., & Yarger, G.P. *Teachers' conceptions of their own success.* Washington, DC: ERIC Clearinghouse on Teacher Education, 1981. (ERIC Document Reproduction Service No. ED 200 518)

JACKSON, P. *Life in classrooms.* New York: Holt, Rinehart & Winston, 1968.

PLACEK, J.H. An observational study of teacher planning in physical education. (Doctoral dissertation, University of Massachusetts, 1982). *Dissertation*

Abstracts International, 1982, **43/04**, 1081-A. (University Microfilms No. DA8219838)

SHULMAN, L.S., & Lanier, J.E. The institute for research on teaching: An overview. *Journal of Teacher Education*, 1977, **23**(4), 44-49.

SILVERMAN, S.J. The relationships among student achievement, student engagement, and selected student characteristics in physical education. (Doctoral dissertation, University of Massachusetts, 1982). *Dissertation Abstracts International*, 1982, **43/04**, 1082-A. (University Microfilms No. DA8219849)

ZAHORIK, J.A. Teachers' experiential knowledge about teacher verbal behavior. *Journal of Teacher Education*, 1980, **31**(1), 44-49.

Section two
Social psychological perspectives of teaching physical education

This section contains five papers that reflect to varying degrees the social psychological dynamics of teaching physical education. They have been grouped here because each represents two features that define social psychology: "1) the individual within a social situation and 2) the underlying processes associated with the impact the social situation has upon individual behavior" (Carron, 1980, p. 2).

Thomas Martinek's paper reflects his continued focus on Pgymalion theory, which points to a self-fulfilling prophecy in the gym—the phenomenon whereby students perform according to their teachers' expectations. Martinek reviews research conducted in classrooms and gymnasia. He shows how different sources of teacher expectations (i.e., student's sex, attractiveness, and psychomotor abilities, as well as teacher characteristics) influence teacher-student interaction and, as a consequence, create positive or negative effects in relation to student behavior or performance.

Patricia Griffin's paper mirrors her emphasis on investigating sex equity in physical education classes. Operating from a qualitative research paradigm, Griffin offers ethnographic data that reveal how boys and girls differ in their participation and interaction in a gymnastics class. Analyses of between-gender and across-gender interaction reveals how an "us versus them" and "our events and their events" atmosphere may prevail in the gym and contribute to sex-differentiated participation and interaction.

Teacher/coach role conflict is the focus of Linda Bain's essay, which reviews recent research about that topic. Bain presents the results of research examining preservice teachers' perceptions of, and preferences for, the roles of the teacher and coach. Factor analysis reveals that prospective physical educators perceive the roles of teacher and coach as requiring rather similar abilities concerning interpersonal relations, instructional skills, and subject matter competence. Such findings, in contrast to previous research, suggest that inter-role conflict is not perceived by preservice teachers to be as great of a problem as previously suggested. Bain also discusses role preference, and here again her findings contrast with previous research.

Patsy Kollen presents some interesting results of a phenomenological study based on her interviews with high school students concerning their perceptions of physical education. Kollen paints a bleak picture of physical education as the students see it, and suggests that the typical physical education setting promotes inactivity, conformity, and alienation. Furthermore, Kollen contrasts the natural highs that some students experience during physical activity with the near impossibility of "being into movement" in the physical education class.

In the final paper in this section, Don Hellison explains his "experiment of one." He tells of his experiences in working with alienated adolescents, and how he developed and implemented goals, teaching strategies, and evaluation procedures with these students. Hellison shows how his experiment evolved, and cites evidence about the effectiveness of his work with high risk youths.

The social/psychological dynamics of the physical education setting becomes apparent in these five papers. The papers reflect different foci, yet they indicate that the degree to which physical education is a positive force in our schools depends upon our ability to structure equitable and exciting settings, which are led by individuals who are equally committed to teaching and coaching and are not deterred by the demands of multiple role conflicts.

References

CARRON, A. *Social psychology of sport*. Ithaca, NY: Mouvement Publication, 1980.

Creating Golem and Galatea effects during physical education instruction: A social psychological perspective

Thomas J. Martinek
University of North Carolina at Greensboro

Teachers' attitudes toward students have a profound effect on their relationships with those students and on actual student performance. The Pygmalion theory to which this paper is addressed focuses on specific social psychological forces that have considerable effect on the interactions of the teacher and student. Pygmalion theory basically explains the phenomenon of the self-fulfilling prophecy in which students perform in accordance with expectations of their teachers. Often this produces what social psychologists call "Galatea" or "Golem" effects in physical education instruction. Galatea effects occur when there is a positive effect from the teacher's expectations. In other words, if the teacher expects a particular student to perform well and begins acting toward that student accordingly, these biased interactions may well result in superior student performance. Likewise, Golem effects occur when a teacher expects a particular student to be a low achiever and behaves accordingly toward that student. The student may react adversely, fulfilling the prophecy that he/she is a low achiever.

Although these relationships appear reasonably straightforward, there are important exceptions to consider. For example, research has shown that poor performance does not always come from low expectations. Similarly, high expectations have been found to not always guarantee good performance (Brophy & Good, 1974; Good & Brophy, 1978; Martinek, Crowe, & Rejeski, 1982; West & Anderson, 1976). Therefore, there are significant differences in the opinions about the degree to which teachers' expectations about their students are likely to function as self-fulfilling prophecies.

A 1948 paper by Robert Merton established an initial foothold in explaining the occurrences of certain social phenomena, but it was not until approximately 20 years later that Merton's concept of the self-fulfilling prophecy came to the attention of educational researchers (Clark, 1963; Goldberg, 1963; Rosenthal & Jacobson, 1968). Since Rosenthal and Jacobson's infamous Oak School experiment, educational researchers have conducted well over 100 studies relating to teacher expectations; other writers have provided scholarly critiques that have both supported and debated the degree to which teacher expectations affect student performance. Historically, physical education researchers have not conducted investigation in this potentially important area. Not until recently have physical education researchers and sport psychologists begun to build a significant body of knowledge to support the notion that the self-fulfilling prophecy prevails in the gymnasium as well as in the classroom (Brown, 1979; Crowe, 1977; Martinek, 1981a; Martinek & Johnson, 1979; Oien, 1979; Rejeski, Darracott, & Hutslar, 1979; Martinek & Karper, Note 1; Martinek & Karper, Note 2).

In order to approach this topic with reasonable clarity, it is important that the reader first obtain a realistic picture of what is presently known about self-fulfilling prophecy effects and to what extent Golem and Galatea effects result from variable teacher expectations.

Realities of Pygmalion effects

There have been numerous reviews of published research related to teacher expectations (i.e., Braun, 1976; Brophy & Good, 1974; Cooper, 1979; Good, 1980). These authors have demonstrated that there is a remarkable degree of agreement regarding the theoretical implications from these studies as well as their empirical findings. Although most agree that teacher expectations do act as self-fulfilling prophecies, many disagree about the strength of expectancy effects. West and Anderson (1976) argue that the self-fulfilling prophecy effects related to teacher expectations are relatively small, producing only a 5% to 10% difference in student achievement. This is largely due to the fact that teacher expectations are generally accurate. That is, a teacher's perception of a student's ability is usually in line with what the student can actually achieve (Brophy, Note 3).

However, even this conclusion needs to be interpreted with a great deal of caution and consideration. First, while teachers' expectancies appear to account for only a small variability in student performance, a significant amount of error variance due to inadequate achievement measures, sampling error, and motivational status of the student not accounted for in many studies may be significantly suppressing the 5% to 10% figure. Second, who is to say that a 5% difference in performance outcomes is unimportant? This question becomes even more salient when we consider that expectation effects become compounded across school years (Brophy, Note 3). In addition, much of the expectancy research reported thus far represents average performance scores across a large number of teachers. Therefore, it is quite probable that teacher expectancy effects for some teachers may have much greater influence on student performance than the 5%-10% range reported. This is especially true for those teachers who are highly susceptible to Pygmalion effects in their teaching. Third, many studies on self-fulfilling prophecy effects have looked at induced expectancy effects where teachers were given phony information about their students without having prior exposure to them.

Other studies have assessed naturally formed expectations where teachers were asked to rate their students after having worked with them during the school year. Teachers in these natural setting studies, therefore, had previous exposure to their students and were more in tune with what their students could do and could not do. Consequently, the expectancy effects found by using the latter methodology may be discounted since teacher-student interactions and performance outcomes may be due to the student's behavior rather than the teacher's expectations (Martinek, Crowe, & Rejeski, 1982; West & Anderson, 1976).

Finally, it is important to note that most of the research concerning expectancy effects has focused exclusively on performance measures. Few, if any, studies reported have attempted to look at expectancy outcome measures such as self-concept, student attitudes, peer relations, motivational levels, etc., all of which can significantly interact with various types of performance scores. This becomes even more critical when we consider that teachers have other expectations, such as those for the students' social relationships with peers and cooperative behavior in class (Martinek, 1980). In any case, most researchers agree that when teachers' expectations are inaccurate and consistently communicated, student performance becomes self-prophetic.

Teacher personal characteristics

Among the factors already mentioned are the roles that teacher characteristics play in the self-fulfilling prophecy. Examples of teacher characteristics would include such variables as intelligence, self-concept, reactive versus nonreactive personality, rigid versus flexible character, etc. (Brophy, Note 3). Although few studies have looked at this dimension, some have shown interesting findings regarding "high bias" and "no bias" teachers. Babad, Inbac, and Rosenthal (in press) reported conflicting results when comparing high bias and low bias teachers on data collected using quantitative and qualitative measures. The objective measures showed no significant differences between high bias teachers and no bias teachers in terms of educational ideology, dogmatism, political views, defensiveness, locus of control, extroversion, and impulsiveness. However, qualitative analysis showed that high bias teachers were regarded as more autocratic, rigid, distant, impulsive, and preferential in their teaching behavior. It appears, therefore, that high bias teachers produce most of the self-fulfilling prophecy effects and that most of these are described as Golem effects rather than Galatea effects.

Other combinations of characteristics can also produce considerable variability among teachers in the way that they interact with their highs and lows. For example, while some teachers may think that low-expectancy students require more structured learning experiences than high-expectancy students, they may in fact be unable to provide the necessary structure because of their own personal style of teaching (Hamachek, 1972). This is especially true where a teacher is impulsive by nature and mediates a large degree of student decision-making during the teaching process. This becomes an apparent problem when the personality style is so inflexible that it gets in the way of the teacher's ability to plan and organize appropriate teaching strategies for low-expectancy students. Brophy (Note 3) believes that we are a long way from being able to predict with any accuracy why teachers differ in respect to the way they are affected by their own expectations. He has found, for example, that some teachers feel less responsible to do something about their low achievers. On the other hand, some teachers will make extraordinary efforts to monitor and interact with them (Rejeski et al., 1979). In either case, it appears that future research must take into account individual teacher characteristics when developing clearer interpretations of effective and ineffective teaching strategies.

Pygmalion effects in physical education

During the last decade, teacher expectancy research in physical education has begun to provide some rather consistent findings regarding the operational characteristics of the Pygmalion phenomenon in the gymnasium. Researchers have generally looked at three processes that have been operational during the expectation cycle. Specifically, these processes indicate: (a) that teachers' perceptions of students are formed by a number of impression cues such as students' somatotype, sex, disabling conditions, etc.; (b) that these expectations in turn influence the interactions between the teacher and student in such a way that is consistent with the teacher's expectations; and (c) that the student often interprets these expectations through the social interaction with the teacher and responds in accordance with the teacher's expectations.

Although there will be no attempt to review all of the studies that have investigated these processes, some of the more recent findings regarding this subject will be discussed.

Impression cues and expectancy formation

While many classroom researchers have examined the differential effects that specific cues or student characteristics have on expectancy formation, only recently has similar research emerged from the instructional setting of physical education. One salient cue in impression formation of physical educators is physical attractiveness. In a study by Martinek (1981a), teachers found that highly attractive students were expected to do better in physical performance and be more socially adept with their peers than less attractive students. They also appeared to affect the teacher-student interactions as well. It was shown that highly attractive students in the sixth grade received more acceptance for their ideas from their teachers than did the students in the lower grades.

Another impression cue that has been found to influence teacher expectations is the amount of perceived effort that a student exhibits during physical education instruction. Rejeski and Lowe (1980) have suggested that perceived nonverbal expression of effort has a profound impact on the teacher's expectation for the child's future performance. Recent studies by Martinek and Karper (1982; Note 4) have demonstrated that both effort and attractiveness in upper elementary grades were directly related to overall teacher expectations, especially for social prowess and thinking ability. This finding becomes more relevant when we look at the numerous ways teachers reward and punish in order to elicit higher levels of motivation and participation rather than better performance.

The dynamics of expectancy formation has also been studied within mainstreamed physical education classes where handicapped and nonhandicapped children were taught together in the same setting. Data from this research have attempted to answer questions about the success or continuation of mainstreamed physical education programs. One such study by Martinek and Karper (1981) demonstrated that elementary physical educators have significantly lower expectations for their handicapped students' social relations with classmates than they do for nonhandicapped children. However, nonsignificant differences were found between the two groups for expectations for physical performance, cooperative behavior, and ability to reason. Given that the intended outcomes of mainstreaming are to develop and improve the social integration of handicapped and nonhandicapped children, these findings have implications regarding those problems encountered by handicapped children who are mainstreamed into programs with social goals.

Communication of teacher expectations

Other investigations have focused on the ways that expectations are communicated. Much of this research has attempted to describe the differential dyadic interactions between teacher and student. Rosenthal (1974) devised a four-factor theory that emerged from a meta-analysis of over 30 studies that looked at specific behaviors related to only positive expectancy effects. From this theory, it was hypothesized that maximum learning could be enhanced if teachers would:

1. Create a warm socioemotional climate with their students (climate);
2. Give them more feedback about their performance (feedback);
3. Teach more material as well as more difficult material (input);
4. Give a greater number of response opportunities (output).

While Rosenthal's four factors provided a rather substantial beginning in the development of social psychological theory, teachers of physical education today might benefit if additional specific behaviors were identified and implemented for education and inservice purposes. In addition, since teachers appear to be affected more by low expectations than high expectations, there is a special need to find how these low expectations are being communicated. Martinek and Karper (Note 1) have identified several recent studies describing specific teaching behaviors related to low teacher expectations in the physical education setting:

1. Teachers gave less praise (verbal and nonverbal) to low-expectancy students (Crowe, 1977; Martinek & Johnson, 1979; Rejeski, Darracott, & Hutslar, 1979; Martinek & Karper, Note 2);
2. They asked less analytic questions and provided fewer response opportunities to lows (Crowe, 1977; Martinek & Johnson, 1979);
3. Teachers gave lows less evaluative comments to their responses Crowe (1977);
4. Unanswered questions were rephrased or repeated less for lows Crowe (1977);
5. Fewer dyadic contacts were directed toward lows (Brown, 1979; Martinek & Johnson, 1979; Oien, 1979);
6. Less information on content-related behaviors was directed toward lows (Brown, 1979; Rejeski et al., 1980; Martinek & Karper, Note 2);
7. More criticism was directed toward lows (Templin, 1981; Martinek & Karper, Note 2);

8. Acceptance and use of a student's ideas and actions were less for lows (Martinek & Johnson, 1979; Martinek & Karper, 1982).

Interaction effects of student behavior with teacher behavior

At this point, it is important to mention that the effect of the student's own behavior on teacher expectations may be a variable interacting with the operation of the self-fulfilling prophecy phenomenon. Students differ in intelligence, ability, achievement motivation, learning styles, and class conduct. Therefore, these differences exert pressures on teachers and condition their behavior in part (Brophy, Note 3). Consequently, whether teachers interact in certain ways with their students because of feedback regarding positive learning behaviors (i.e., student continually staying on task) or whether it is because of their preconceived high expectations remains empirically unanswered.

One such study by Templin (1981) indirectly investigated this concept by looking at the physical education student's role as a socializing agent in the formation of student teachers' pupil control ideology. To determine to what degree students' behavior affected the student teacher's concept of behavior control, Templin investigated 28 preservice student teachers before, during, and after teaching. By using both quantitative and qualitative methodologies, he examined the degree to which high- and low-achieving students' behavior affected their teachers' ideas about dealing with their own behavior. Results of the study revealed that all 28 teachers shifted from a humanistic approach to pupil control and, further, to one that was more custodial in nature. Concerning high and low achievers, the results also indicated that the student teachers did, in fact, formulate positive and negative attitudes in accordance with certain student attributes. That is, the teachers appeared to have a more positive bias toward students who were conforming, cooperative, orderly, and high-achieving. This in turn affected the teachers by causing them to use more controlling behaviors (i.e., making them run laps, giving the evil eye, etc.) with low-achieving students.

An important implication of this study was that the low-achieving students' off-task behavior preoccupied most of the teachers' attention, causing them to become more custodial during the student teaching term. Similar results were also reported by Martinek and Karper (Note 2), who found that low teacher expectations for the social behavior of early elementary students caused teachers to distribute more convergent direction-giving behaviors to these students. It was also found that these expectations were positively related to the amount of off-task behavior that low-expectancy students displayed during physical activity instruction.

Although it is difficult to determine the extent that student behavior covaries with teacher expectations and teacher-student interactions, this area of inquiry nevertheless remains a most important consideration for furture research.

The effects of the social climate on expectancy effects

At this point, the reader can appreciate the problems of sorting out clear explanations of Pygmalion effects. The picture becomes even more complex as one tries to consider contextual variables that interact with the operational characteristics of the self-fulfilling prophecy cycle. Taguiri (1958) has suggested that along with teacher characteristics and student attributes, the various social conditions in which interaction takes place can have a significant impact on how expectancy effects operate. For example, a teacher may direct very different behaviors toward his or her low-expectancy players during skill practice that typically emphasizes individual skill development, team camaraderie, and problem-solving skills — as compared to a game or to more competitive situations. In other words, the social consequences (winning/losing) inherent in a competitive social environment may cause low-expectancy performers to receive more reprimand and less tolerance from the coaches, who may perceive the game's outcome as a direct reflection on their coaching ability (as compared to the different perceptions about practice). To prove this hypothesis in a physical education setting with small children, Martinek and Karper (Note 4) conducted a study in which students were exposed to two experimental phases: one that stressed individualized instructional methodology and one that was a highly competitive setting. Each experimental condition was taught twice by the same teacher, using an A-B-A-B experimental design.

Their study was to describe the effects of competitive and noncompetitive instructional climates on the communication of teacher expectations. In addition, the researchers looked at the effect of the treatment conditions on the social preferences among the high- and low-expectancy students. The purpose for looking at social preference was to determine, in an indirect way, whether students were fulfilling teacher expectations about their classmates during competitive and noncompetitive involvement. In order to obtain social preference information, the researchers asked each student to list in rank order the three students they most preferred playing with and the three they least preferred playing with. This procedure was followed after each experimental phase. The results of the study indicated that low-expectancy students received significantly more dyadic contacts and more encouragement than did high expectancy students during noncompetitive participation. In addition, low-expectancy students appeared to receive more direct instruction during competitive involvement. An important finding from this study was that low-expectancy students appeared to receive more teacher attention than did the high-expectancy students during the noncompetitive phases. This appears to indicate that noncompetitive instructional climates may help to facilitate more interaction between teachers and low achievers as well as to increase the amount of teacher encouragement directed toward lows.

Analysis of the social preference data showed that for some of the teachers' classes, high-expectancy students were least preferred by their classmates during the two noncompetitive phases. On the other hand, there were no significant differences between the two groups in most preferred and least preferred dimensions for both competitive phases, indicating that perhaps the communication of expectations may work to the disadvantage of high-expectancy students. At first, this may lead one to believe that low-expectancy students readily reject those classmates they perceive as receiving preferential treatment due to the teacher's high expectations for them in noncompetitive social climates. However, since lows received more dyadic contacts and encouragement from their teachers, this conclusion may be somewhat questionable. Perhaps lows were perceiving other teacher behaviors that were directed toward highs and that were not addressed in this study.

Considerations for causal connections in Pygmalion effects

One of the thorny issues facing researchers is determining the existence of a causal linkage between teacher expectations and student outcomes. Recall that earlier in this paper, we referred to the interaction effects that student behaviors have on teacher expectations and dyadic interactions. For example, when the amount of teacher encouragement directed toward high achievers has been found related to student motivation, it has not been known whether the teacher's encouragement motivated students or whether poorly motivated students received less encouragement simply because they gave the teacher little reason for commending them. This example represents some of the uncertainty found in much of the research on the self-fulfilling prophecy.

In order to gain a clear perspective on causality, let us consider two conceptual models that attempt to illustrate cause and effect relationships. One way of viewing a causal linkage is to view once again Rosenthal's four-factor theory that was proposed to explain the Pygmalion phenomenon. He felt that the teacher expectations (the cause) resulted in biased teacher behaviors (mediating variables) and that these behaviors influenced student behavior and performance. Within this framework, the relationship between expectancy and student performance is characterized as *unidirectional causation*. Another way of describing this relationship is to view Pygmalion effects in terms of *reciprocal causa-*

tion. That is, the teacher's perception and student behavior is characterized as a dynamic interactive process. The student's behavior continually reinforces the teacher's original expectations (Martinek et al., 1982).

While it is not quite clear how the concept of *reciprocal causation* operates during physical education instruction, studies have shown that there is a high degree of stability of teacher expectations over time. For example, Parker (1980) and Martinek (1980, 1981b) found that coaches' and teachers' expectations for performance, social relations, and cooperative behavior were relatively constant over several months of instruction. This might indicate, therefore, that student behavior continually interacts with teacher expectations over time, thus playing a major role in self-fulfillment. These findings further indicate that once students are labeled as high or low achievers, they will no doubt remain in their respective categories (Martinek et al., 1982).

In summary, it is clear that researchers need more definitive approaches to delineate the causal network responsible for Pygmalion effects. By developing more tightly controlled research procedures and by utilizing applied experimental methodologies, researchers may begin to take a foothold in the discovery of those factors affecting instructional decisions and methodologies.

Reference Notes

1. Martinek, T., & Karper, W. *A causal model for determining expectation effects in physical education instruction.* Unpublished manuscript, Motor and Social Behavior Laboratory, University of North Carolina at Greensboro, 1982.
2. Martinek, T., & Karper, W. *Multivariate relationships of specific impression cues with teacher expectations and dyadic interactions in elementary physical education classes.* Unpublished manuscript, Motor and Social Behavior Laboratory, University of North Carolina at Greensboro, 1982.
3. Brophy, J. *Research on the self-fulfilling prophecy and teacher expectations.* Paper presented at the annual meeting of the American Educational Research Association, 1982.
4. Martinek, T., & Karper, W. *An analysis of competitive and non-competitive social climates on teacher expectancy effects.* Unpublished research report, Motor and Social Behavior Laboratory, University of North Carolina at Greensboro, 1982.

References

BABAD, E., Inbac, J., & Rosenthal, R. Pygmalion, Galatea, and the Golem: Investigations of biased and unbiased teachers. *Journal of Educational Psychology* (in press).

BRAUN, C. Teacher expectation: Social psychological dynamics. *Review of Educational Research*, 1976, **46**, 185-213.

BROPHY, J., & Good, T. *Teacher-student relationships: Causes and consequences*. New York: Holt, Rinehart & Winston, 1974.

BROWN, J.P. *Description of dyadic student-teacher interaction in the physical education activity class*. Unpublished doctoral dissertation, University of North Carolina at Greensboro, 1979.

CLARK, K.B. Educational stimulation of racially disadvantaged children. In A.H. Passow (Ed.), *Education in depressed areas*. New York: Columbia Press, 1963.

COOPER, H. Pygmalion grows up: A model for teacher expectation communication and performance influence. *Review of Educational Research*, 1979, **49**, 389-410.

CROWE, P. *An observational study of expectancy effects and their mediation mechanisms on students of physical education activity classes*. Unpublished doctoral dissertation, University of North Carolina at Greensboro, 1977.

GOLDBERG, M. Factors affecting educational attainment in depressed urban areas. In A.H. Passow (Ed.), *Education in depressed areas*. New York: Columbia Press, 1963.

GOOD, T. Classroom expectations: Teacher-student interactions. In J. McMillan (Ed.), *The social psychology of school learning*. New York: Academic Press, 1980.

GOOD, T., & Brophy, J. *Looking in classrooms*. New York: Harper & Row, 1978.

HAMACHEK, D. Personality styles and teacher behavior. *Education Forum*, 1972, **36**, 313-322.

MARTINEK, T. Stability of a teacher expectations for elementary school aged children. *Perceptual and Motor Skills*, 1980, **51**, 1269-1270.

MARTINEK, T. Physical attractiveness: Effects on teacher expectations and dyadic interactions in elementary age children. *Journal of Sport Psychology*, 1981, **3**, 196-205. (a)

MARTINEK, T. Pygmalion in the gym: A model for the communication of teacher expectations in physical education. *Research Quarterly for Exercise and Sport*, 1981, **52**, 58-67. (b)

MARTINEK, T., Crowe, P., & Rejeski, W. *Pygmalion in the gym: Causes and effects of expectations in teaching and coaching*. West Point, NY: Leisure Press, 1982.

MARTINEK, T., & Johnson, S. Teacher expectations: Effects on dyadic interactions and self-concept in elementary age children. *Research Quarterly*, 1979, **50**, 60-70.

MARTINEK, T., & Karper, W.B. Teacher expectations for handicapped and non-handicapped children in mainstreamed physical education classes. *Perceptual and Motor Skills*, 1981, **53**, 327-330.

MARTINEK, T., & Karper, W. Canonical relationships among motor ability, expression of effort, teacher expectations and dyadic interactions in elementary age children. *Journal of Teaching in Physical Education*, 1982, **1**, 26-39.

MERTON, R. The self-fulfilling prophecy. *Antioch Review*, 1948, **8**, 193-210.

OIEN, F. Teacher directed behavior toward individual students. In Cox (Ed.), *Symposium papers II: Teaching behavior and women in sport*. Washington, DC: AAHPERD Publications, 1979.

PARKER, L. *The perception of effort and interpersonal expectations*. Unpublished master's thesis, Wake Forest University, 1980.

REJESKI, W., Darracott, C., & Hutslar, S. Pygmalion in youth sport: A field study. *Journal of Sport Psychology*, 1979, **1**, 311-319.

REJESKI, W., & Lowe, C. The role of ability and effort in sport achievement. *Journal of Personality*, 1980, **48**, 233-244.

ROSENTHAL, R. *On the social psychology of the self-fulfilling prophecy: Further evidence for Pygmalion effects and their mediating mechanisms*. New York: MSS Modular Publications, 1974.

ROSENTHAL, R., & Jacobson, L. *Pygmalion in the classroom: Teacher expectations and pupil intellectual growth*. New York: Holt, Rinehart & Winston, 1968.

TAGUIRI, R. Person perception. In G. Lindzay & E. Aronson (Eds.), *Handbook of social psychology*. Cambridge, MA: Addison-Wesley, 1969.

TEMPLIN, T. Student as socializing agent. *Journal of Teaching in Physical Education*, 1981, pp. 71-79 (introductory issue).

WEST, C., & Anderson, T. The question of preponderant causation in teacher expectancy research. *Review of Educational Research*, 1976, **46**, 613-630.

"Gymnastics is a girl's thing": Student participation and interaction patterns in a middle school gymnastics unit

Patricia S. Griffin
University of Massachusetts

Title IX of the Educational Amendments Act of 1972 prohibits assigning students to classes by sex. The purpose of this requirement is to eliminate sex discrimination by providing girls and boys with the same opportunity for instruction in a school physical education program. The assumption behind Title IX is that sex-integrated classes will be more equitable than sex-segregated classes.

However, there is reason to doubt the success of the sex integration of classes as an effective tool, in and of itself, in eliminating sex stereotyping and discrimination in physical education. Studies of teacher-student interaction in sex-integrated physical education classes show that teachers interact differently with girls and boys (Allard, 1979; Griffin, 1981a). In some programs, activities perceived as difficult to teach in sex-integrated classes have been eliminated. As a result, activities like wrestling, dance, or gymnastics have been dropped so that student choices have actually become more limited. In other programs, though classes are sex integrated, teachers continue to group students within classes by sex.

In addition, casual conversations with teachers reveal a yearning on the part of some, both male and female, for the "good old days" of sex segregation in physical education. Men often complain of "watered down" programs in which boys must "hold back" because of the girls. Women complain about the extra "discipline problems" posed by boys and lament that they are teaching less because boys only want to "play the game." Many teachers of both sexes agree that students would prefer single-sex classes if given the choice. Other teachers openly acknowledge that worrying about whether boys and girls are working together in a drill, or passing the ball to each other in a game, is not a priority for them. Thus, if students resist sex-integrated groups, then class groups are sex segregated.

Studies by Solomons (1977), Wang (1978), and Griffin (1981a) support the assertion that sex is a salient category of differentiation among students in physical education classes. Solomons found that boys often left girls out of game interactions. Even when girls were included in game play, they tended to give away scoring opportunities to boys. Moreover, girls and boys perceived boys to be more highly skilled, even when objective skill tests identified girls to be more talented than boys. In Griffin's study, the boys had more contacts with the ball and girls had less contacts with the ball than was expected based on the number of boys and girls actively participating in class games. The students in Wang's study not only separated themselves by sex within the physical education class, but also stratified themselves as evidenced by who sat where in squad lines (boys sat in the front and girls sat in the rear).

These student preferences and behaviors become more powerful when examined in the context of research showing that what students say and do has a strong influence on what actually occurs in a physical education class (Templin, 1981). The primary concerns of teachers in Placek's (1982) study of teacher planning were to keep students "busy, happy, and good." Wang found that even when the teacher's explicit purpose was to promote integrated and nondiscriminatory participation, students subverted this intention with their hidden curriculum of segregation and stratification along lines of sex, race, and skill. If sex-segregated and stratified groups keep students busy, happy, and good, and if a teacher's stated goals of sex integration and nondiscrimination can be subverted by the students' preference for sex segregation and stratification, then it is necessary to understand the nature of student interaction and participation more fully in assessing the "lived" status of sex equity in physical education.

Methodology

The purpose of this study was to describe female and male student interaction and participation in a sex-integrated middle school gymnastics unit. The participation and interaction patterns identified are part of the data collected during a 3-month qualitative study of sex equity in a middle school physical education program. Specifically, these participation and interaction patterns were identified during observations of 20 sixth- and seventh-grade gymnastics classes and informal discussions with the three physical education teachers.

Field notes taken during each observation session were guided by two initial focusing questions.

1. How do girls and boys participate in the gymnastics unit?
2. How do girls and boys interact in the gymnastics unit?

Researcher observations were checked with teacher perceptions in informal discussion between classes. After each observation day, field notes were analyzed to identify patterns of participation and interactions among students. The patterns identified formed the observation focus for the next visitation. As patterns were identified and confirmed, a search for negative cases or atypical interactions and participation among students became an observation focus. The patterns of participation and interaction reported are a synthesis of the observation and teacher interview data.

Profile of North Ridge Middle School

North Ridge Middle School is located in a small town in southern New England. The community of North Ridge is almost exclusively white and middle class. Students in the sixth, seventh, and eighth grades attend North Ridge Middle School and are all required to take physical education twice a week. All classes are sex integrated (50% boys and 50% girls) unless students are given a choice of activities; then the percentage of females and males in each class depends on student activity preference. There are three physical education teachers at North Ridge this semester: two full-time teachers, Mr. Warren and Miss Graham, and Mr. Freeman, a student teacher from the state university 12 miles away.

It is the end of October. Students have just finished their first unit in physical education and are beginning a new unit today. Seventh-and eighth-graders will have a choice between gymnastics and flag football. The sixth-graders are required to take gymnastics. It is first period. There are 45 seventh-graders sitting on the three rows of pull-out bleachers along the side wall of the gym. The students have segregated themselves by sex as they do every class period. Boys sit on one side of the bleachers and girls sit on the other. Most students wear the required gym uniform of black shorts and red and white tee shirts. Running shoes and tube socks complete the uniform. Three girls wear leotards with sweaters over them instead of the regular uniform. Mr. Freeman and Miss Graham stand to one side, while Mr. Warren stands directly in front of the bleachers. He explains the activity choices to the students and hands a clipboard to a boy. The sign-up process takes about 5 minutes as students pass the clipboard around the bleachers. Mr. Warren takes the clipboard from the last girl to sign up and announces, "Ok, everyone signed up for flag football go out to the field with Miss Graham." This process is repeated with minor variations for each of the other two seventh-grade classes meeting that day. The sign-up process results in class composi-tions heavily weighted for each activity according to sex. The boys in each class number 26, 21, and 22, respectively, with 4, 1, and 11 (same order) of them choosing gymnastics. Girls in each class number 19, 18, and 17, respectively, with only 3, 0, and 4 of them choosing flag football. Since the sixth-graders are required to take gymnastics, there are 20 boys and 20 girls in each of the two sixth-grade classes.

Nearly half of the gym is covered by the floor exercise mat. The balance beam is set up along one side of the gym with a thick crash pad abutting the end of the beam for dismounts. The approach for vaulting runs beside the beam, with the vaulting box on the other end of the gym. The unevens and parallel bars are side by side. The rings hang in the far corner. The pommel horse is between the parallel bars and the floor exer-cise mat. For the seventh-grade classes, Mr. Warren and Mr. Freeman teach gymnastics while Miss Graham teaches flag football. For the sixth-grade classes, all three teachers team teach gymnastics. For each class, students are divided among the three or two gymnastics teachers. Students rotate to different events, staying in the same group. There are three stations in most classes: a) balance beam and vaulting, b) unevens, parallel bars, and rings, and c) horse and floor exercise. Within this con-text, then, how do students participate and interact with each other?

Student participation in gymnastics

Three aspects of student participation were observed: choice of activities, choice of events within gymnastics, and participation patterns in each event.

Two statements made by boys on the first day of the unit during the sign-up process seemed to capture the prevailing opinion among many boys.

"Gymnastics is a girl's thing."
"Only wimps and fairies take gymnastics."

Of the 69 seventh-grade boys, only 16 elected to take gymnastics. Of the 54 seventh-grade girls, only 7 elected flag football. These numbers do not necessarily represent a positive activity choice for everyone. Some students chose gymnastics to avoid going outside in the cold weather. For other students, the choice was between the lesser of two evils.

> Girl: (muttering under her breath after an unsuccessful try at a backward roll) "I hate gymnastics."
> Boy: "What did you take it for?"
> Girl: "I hate football more."

Even with these exceptions, though, the choices that students made conformed closely to sex-stereotyped perceptions of each activity: Gymnastics is for girls and flag football is for boys.

Once activity choices were made, observations focusing on students in gymnastics revealed clear and consistent patterns of participation among girls and boys. When students had options to choose partners or events, virtually all student groups were sex segregated. Squad lines and informal seating patterns for attendance were always sex segregated. Even within alphabetically assigned squads in the sixth-grade classes, boys sat at the front of the line and girls at the rear. This pattern of sex segregation was reinforced by teacher groupings within the class. Students were listed in the roll books by sex. Both Mr. Warren and Miss Graham divided students into sex-segregated groups for work on the gymnastic events. Only Mr. Freeman instructed students in sex-integrated groups. However, as soon as students in his group were given the option, they segregated themselves by their choice of partners or events.

In addition to a preference for segregated class groups, each sex showed distinct participation styles. Furthermore, these participation styles were related to specific gymnastic events. Thus, participation within the gymnastic classes was differentiated by what events students participated in and how they participated in each of the events.

Boys

Three styles of participation for boys emerged from the observation data.

1. Serious participation — Voluntary participation characterized by on-task behavior, repeated attempts at skill performance, and asking for help from a teacher or another student;
2. Frivolous participation — Voluntary or required participation characterized by clowning, half-hearted attempts at skill performance, teasing or laughing at others' mistakes, and approaching the event as a non-serious novelty;

3. Reluctant participation — Required participation only or in rare instances, voluntary participation characterized by one trial attempts at skills.

The following excerpts from field notes illustrate each style of participation:

Serious. Mr. Warren is working with a boy on the rings. Five other boys are lined up one behind the other waiting for their turn. Each boy intently watches the boy on the rings. Mr. Warren helps him swing up and into a skin-the-cat position. He hangs there and then drops to the mat. Immediately, the other boys crowd forward. Mr. Warren says, "Wait a minute. Let him try again." The boy looks up at the rings swinging crazily overhead, steps on the stool Mr. Warren has placed under the rings and, with a look of concentration on his face, reaches for the rings.

Frivolous. The boys in Mr. Warren's group are on the balance beam. Mr. Warren is working with the girls on vaulting. The boy on the beam announces to the rest of the boys, "I'm gonna do the dip." He walks across the beam doing exaggerated dip steps. Several other boys in line laugh at him. When he reaches the end of the beam, he grabs his chest as if he has been shot, and leaps off, still clutching his chest. He twists in the air to land on his back with a thud on the crash pad. The next boy does the dip step too. A boy in line calls out to him, "Cut the fancy stuff." Thereafter, each boy hurries across the beam in whatever way is quickest, pauses at the end to make sure everyone in line is watching, and then executes a dramatic fall, dive, or jump onto the crash pad complete with sound effects, "Superman!" "Awwagh!" "Look at this."

Reluctant. Three boys wander over to the unevens. They have been working on the parallel bars. Two of them swing tentatively on the low bar. Mr. Freeman asks if they'd like to try something. They say no and move back to the parallel bars.

These participation styles were related to specific gymnastic events. Boys tended to be more serious about their participation on the rings, horse, and parallel bars than they were in other events. On balance beam, vaulting, and floor exercise, boys were frivolous. The attraction of the balance beam and vaulting seemed to be the thrill of flying through the air, crashing on the mat, and laughing at each other. However, boys liked these events, as evidenced by their voluntary participation when given the option to choose. In contrast, though boys participated frivolously in floor exercise, they rarely chose this event voluntarily.

Practically all boys were reluctant in their participation on the unevens. Teachers never assigned boys to the unevens, though Mr. Freeman instructed boys and girls in his group when describing basic skills on the unevens.

Girls

For girls, gymnastics was a much more serious endeavor. Three to five girls wore leotards instead of shorts and tee shirts during each class period. The girls' general skill level was higher in gymnastics than the boys' skill, and they showed more serious interest in practicing skills in a wider variety of events. Analysis of the observation data for girls' participation yielded three styles of participation.

1. Serious participation — Voluntary participation characterized by ontask behavior, repeated attempts at skill performance, and asking for help from a teacher or another student;
2. Exploratory participation — Tentative or curious voluntary attempts at skill performance characterized by single-try experiments, giving up easily, and rarely asking for help;
3. Reluctant participation — Required participation only or in rare instances, voluntary participation characterized by one trial attempts.

The following excerpts from field notes illustrate each style of participation for girls:

Serious. Mr. Warren is working with a girl on the balance beam. She is standing on the beam with her eyes focused intently on the end of the beam. She takes slow steps forward, pointing her toes as she steps. She stops and squats. Mr. Warren steadies her. She places her hands for a forward roll. He guides her through the forward roll and back to a standing position. She pauses near the end of the beam with both arms extended over her head. She reaches down, places both hands on the beam and does a cartwheel onto the crash pad. Two girls waiting in line for the beam clap their hands.

Exploratory. Several girls have been doing cartwheels and round offs on the floor exercise mat. They are now watching three boys on the pommel horse. The boys move over to the parallel bars. The girls approach the horse. One of them grabs the pommels and jumps up, supporting her weight on her arms. She drops back to the mat and says, "That's hard." She walks back to the floor exercise mat. The other girls each try the same thing once and go back to the floor exercise mat. The first girl returns once later and tries the same thing again. After dropping back to the mat, she goes over to watch a girl on the balance beam.

Reluctant. Mr. Freeman has asked several girls in the back of the vaulting line to come to the front of the line and take a turn. Several boys in line yell at them to "come on, go." Each girl takes one turn and moves to the balance beam.

As was observed for the boys, girls' participation styles were related to specific gymnastic events. Girls were serious about participating on the unevens, balance beam, and floor exercise. On the rings, horse, and parallel bars, girls tended to be exploratory. Interestingly, though vaulting is a women's event in Olympic gymnastics, girls were reluctant about their participation in this event.

After these participation styles for girls and boys were identified, the investigator searched for negative cases — students who did not conform to the participation styles identified. However, participation patterns were so clearly established and accepted by the students that few exceptions were observed.

In summary, girls and boys participated differently. These participation styles were so universal that they served as unspoken rules that allowed a fairly accurate prediction of *how* girls and boys would participate in the seven gymnastic events taught. The patterns of *what* events girls and boys chose to do, though clear, appeared to be more flexible. Some boys chose the balance beam or tumbling, and some girls chose the rings or the horse. Boundaries for what events were perceived as appropriate seemed to be less rigid for girls. Girls were more exploratory or serious in their participation on the rings, horse, and parallel bars than boys were on the balance beam, floor exercise, vaulting, or unevens.

Student interaction in gymnastics

The investigator observed four aspects of student interaction: (a) boy to girl, (b) girl to boy, (c) boy to boy, and (d) girl to girl.

Boy-to-girl interactions

Boy-to-girl interactions in the gymnastics classes included hassling, ignoring, and separating.

Hassling. Hassling, the most frequently observed boy-to-girl interaction, was verbal and physical. In addition, individual boys hassled girls and groups of boys hassled girls (see Table 1). The following field note excerpts exemplify boy-to-girl hassles:

Two girls are waiting in line for the rings. There is a boy on the rings. Another boy walks over to the rings from the parallel bars. He cuts in front of the girl who is next in line to get a turn on the rings. The second girl in line says, "She was here first." The boy looks

Table 1

Kinds of Hassles Observed in Boy-to-Girl Interactions

	Group	Individual
Physical	Getting in the way	Butting in line
	Butting in line	Poking
		Getting in the way
Verbal	Giving orders	Giving orders
	Teasing	Teasing
	Mimicking	Mimicking
	Yelling at	Yelling at
	Laughing at	Laughing at
	Criticizing	Criticizing

straight ahead and shrugs his shoulders. No one does or says anything else.

Two girls and three boys are assigned to a mat to practice back rolls. One of the girls is very skilled in gymnastics. She does back rolls in excellent form. One of the boys is having trouble. He asks Mr. Warren, "How come she can do it?" Mr. Warren says, "Watch her and you'll learn something." The boy says, "Kathy thinks she's so good." He repeats this. Kathy ignores him and continues to practice. He says to her, "Kathy, we're not all gymnasts, you know." She is now doing a head stand. The boy stands up and does several karate kicks, his foot stopping several inches from her head. She continues to ignore him. He says, "She's a show off." The other girl on the mat says, "No she isn't."

In line for vaulting, all the boys are in the front of the line. The girls are huddled in the back. Mr. Freeman sees that the girls are not taking their turns. He calls for them to go ahead of the boys. The boys turn and start yelling at the girls, "C'mon, go, go, move it." The girls, one by one, run down the approach past the boys to do a vault. As each girl goes past, the boys yell at her and laugh if she makes a mistake on her vault. One boy says to the rest of the boys, "She goes . . ." He mimics her running approach. The other boys laugh.

There is a girl on the balance beam. A boy waiting in line for vaulting jumps on the beam in front of her. She tells him to get off. He walks to the end of the beam and dives onto the crash pad. Another boy jumps onto the crash pad just as the girl is getting ready to dismount. She yells at him to "get off."

Ignoring. Most interactions in this category were boys' reactions to girls' requests or demands to stop hassling. Two of the examples from field notes used to describe hassling also illustrate ignoring. When the boy butted in line on the rings, he ignored the girl's objection. The two boys hassling the girl on the balance beam ignored her demands that they stop.

Separating. Boys separated themselves from girls for attendance and for voluntary participation on the gymnastics equipment. The only time boys chose to be in groups with girls was when they were hassling them.

Girl-to-boy interactions

Girls rarely initiated interactions with boys. Girl-to-boy interactions in gymnastics were almost exclusively in response to hassles and included separating, acquiescing, ignoring, and requesting/demanding that boys stop.

1. Separating: Physically moving away from boys who are hassling them;
2. Acquiescing: Letting boys butt in line, leaving an event because of being hassled;
3. Ignoring: Continuing participation without acknowledging the boy's hassle;
4. Requesting/demanding that boys stop: Asking boys to stop, yelling at boys to stop, or physically pushing boys away.

Some of the field note excerpts used to describe boy-to-girl interactions also include examples of girls' responses to being hassled. Here is one more.

> Three girls are trying out the horse. A boy walks over to the horse, butts in front of the girls, and grasps the pommels with both hands. The girl whose turn it was reaches across, grabs his hands, and pushes them off of the pommels. She then grasps the pommels herself.

As with student participation patterns, exceptions to these interaction patterns were rare. They did occur, however.

> A boy and girl are working on the floor exercise mat. He says, "Mary, are my feet straight?" He does a cartwheel. She nods. He says, "Do that one again where you go like this." He does a cartwheel-like movement. She does a round off. He says, "Yeah, that."

These students were breaking interaction and participation patterns by working together. The boy was seriously participating in floor exercise and interacting with a girl without hassling her.

Table 2

Characteristics of Boy-to-Boy Interactions

Characteristic	Examples
Physical	Poking, punching, chasing, mock fights pushing, jumping on
Combative	Dares, challenges, jeers, name-calling
Public	Loud voices, big movements, calling for attention
Clown-like	Laughing, exaggerated movements in skill performance, intentional mistakes
Hassling	Appreciating other boys' hassles, participating in group hassles

Boy-to-boy interactions

Interactions among boys tended to be physical, combative, public, clown-like, and hassling. Though there were instances of boys interacting with each other in different ways, notably when working on the rings, horse, or parallel bars with a teacher present, the interactions described in Table 2 for boys were the norm in the gymnastics unit. Here are some examples of boy-to-boy interactions observed.

It is the last day of the gymnastics unit. Students have been asked to help put away the gymnastics equipment. The girls sit in tight little groups on the bleachers. The boys are all over the gym. They move equipment, swing on the unevens, help dismantle the parallel bars, bounce off crash pads, chase each other, balance on mat rollers, and yell to each other. They gym is a swarm of boys in action.

A girl has been asked to demonstrate a "bunny lift" for the rest of the class. She does one in excellent form. Several boys sitting together clap and say, "Oooh! Oooh!" very sarcastically.

Students are practicing tumbling skills. Four boys are working together on a mat. One boy does a backward roll, flops over sideways halfway through the roll, and sprawls on his back. His practice mates laugh.

Girl-to-girl-interactions

In contrast, girl-to-girl interactions were primarily verbal, cooperative, private, serious, and responding to hassles as described in Table 3. The following are examples of typical girl-to-girl interactions.

The class is practicing forward rolls. The teacher moves from mat to mat to help individual students. Some of the girls have done two or

Table 3

Characteristics of Girl-to-Girl Interactions

Characteristic	Examples
Verbal	Quiet talking, excited talking
Cooperative	Working on skills together, helping each other with skills, appreciating each other's skill performance
Private	Quiet, small groups, individual work, not asking for help
Serious	On task, talk about gymnastics, trying different events, wearing leotards, practicing skills before class
Responding to hassles	Standing up for friends, group ignoring, group separating

three forward rolls easily and begin doing back rolls, headstands, or handstands. They work quietly together, watching, spotting, and talking to each other about the skills they are practicing.

Mr. Warren has to leave the gym for a moment. His group was working on the unevens and the parallel bars. He tells them all to sit down and stay off the equipment until he returns. The boys sit on the mats around the parallel bars while the girls sit beside the unevens. They sit quietly talking. After about 15 seconds, one boy gets up and does a karate kick at another boy's head. Another boy reaches up and swings from the bar. Other boys start punching each other. In the span of one minute, the boys' group is transformed into a mock free-for-all. Each boy vies for the most dramatic fall, most realistic punch or kick, best sound effects, while the girls are still sitting just as they were when Mr. Warren left.

In summary, the interaction patterns observed among the students were sex differentiated and allowed a fairly accurate prediction of girl-boy, boy-boy, and girl-girl interactions within the gymnastics classes observed. Generally, boys only interacted with girls to hassle them. Girls, generally, only interacted with boys when responding to being hassled. Among boys, interactions tended to be physical, combative, public, clown-like, hassling girls. In contrast to those of boys, girls' interactions were verbal, cooperative, private, serious, and responding to being hassled by boys.

Conclusions

The observed student interaction and participation patterns limited the opportunities to learn gymnastics skills in several ways.

1. Serious participation in different gymnastic events was governed by the perceived sex appropriateness of the event. Boys and girls participated seriously only in events traditionally accepted as appropriate for their sex: girls on the unevens, balance beam, and floor exercise and boys on the rings, horse, and parallel bars.
2. Boys participated in "girl appropriate" events either frivolously or reluctantly, thus limiting their own opportunity to learn by approaching many events in a nonserious way.
3. Girls' participation in "boy appropriate" events was exploratory or reluctant. Girls were much more curious about the rings, horse, and parallel bars than boys were about the unevens or floor exercise. However, girls limited their opportunity to learn on the rings, horse, and parallel bars by giving up easily on skill attempts and by not asking for help. They also allowed themselves to be hassled off equipment.
4. Boys limited their own participation more strictly than girls. While girls were either serious or exploratory in six of the seven events taught, boys were serious in only three of the seven events.
5. Perceived sex appropriateness of gymnastics events seemed more important to boys than to girls. Boys tended to see "girls' events" not only as activities they should avoid or not take seriously, but also as lower status events. For example, they were more likely to make fun of each other on "girls' events," and were more protective of "boys' events," as evidenced by their butting in front of girls waiting for the rings, horse, or vaulting. Girls did not show the same concern about participating in "boys' events" or about boys participating in "girls' events."
6. Boys limited the girls' opportunity to learn by hassling them, thus interfering with girls' serious and exploratory participation in all events except the unevens. When girls were participating in "girls' events," the boys would hassle them by getting in the way; when girls explored "boys' events," boys hassled them by butting in line.
7. Girls did not limit the boys' opportunity to learn. They spent most of their time trying to ignore boys or separate themselves from them. Girls rarely hassled boys.
8. Boys limited each other's opportunity to learn by clowning. These boy-to-boy interactions set a norm that clowning for each other was the only accepted way to participate in most of the events being taught.
9. Girls limited their own opportunity to learn by accepting boys'

hassles. Rather than asking or demanding that boys stop, they usually tried to ignore boys or moved to another event.

10. Student self-segregation by sex within the class accentuated, exaggerated, and reinforced sex differentiated participation and interaction. It seemed to support "us vs. them" and "our events and their events" attitudes among the students. Sex-segregated groups also made it more difficult for any student to choose to interact or participate out of pattern.

Implications for teachers and teacher educators

It is important for readers to understand that the middle school physical education classes observed in this study were part of a high quality program. A casual visitor to the gym would see teachers conducting instructional rather than recreational classes. Teachers worked with small groups of students to provide maximum activity time in a safe environment. There was a sense of order and purpose in the way teachers had organized the instruction. The point is that the student participation and interaction patterns observed occurred within this context and operated as a hidden curriculum thriving within the teachers' explicit and well-organized gymnastics curriculum.

Teachers must recognize that students bring to the gym all of their sex-stereotyped beliefs about themselves, each other, teachers, and the activity being taught. To the extent that teachers and students accept the resulting interaction and participation patterns as a normal part of the day-to-day experience in sex-integrated classes, the opportunity to learn activity skills will be limited to student perceptions of sex-appropriate behavior.

Teachers need to take a fresh look at these stereotyped student participation and interaction patterns, reject the inevitability of such patterns, and address them clearly and specifically in their class planning and interactions with students. Teacher educators can assist teachers by providing workshops or classes designed to help teachers not only recognize sex-stereotyped student interaction and participation patterns in their classes, but also identify alternative class organization and individual interaction strategies to change these patterns.

As we move into the 80s, physical educators teaching sex-integrated classes have a unique opportunity to help girls and boys learn to enjoy sport, physical activity, and dance activities together. Teachers can help students overcome the artificial expectations and limitations that sex stereotyping imposes on their interests and abilities, and can help them learn to appreciate themselves and each other in physical education activities. Merely putting boys and girls together in one class is not enough. By taking action to address stereotyped interaction and participation patterns, teachers can help students move a little closer to the day when gymnastics is no longer perceived as a "girls' thing."

References

ALLARD, R. Teacher behavior directed toward individual students in physical education classes: The influence of student gender and class participation. (Doctoral dissertation, University of Massachusetts, 1979.) *DAI*, 1979, **40**, 2538-A.

GRIFFIN, P.S. Developing a systematic observation instrument to identify sex role dependent and sex role independent behavior among physical education teachers. (Doctoral dissertation, University of Massachusetts, 1980.) *DAI*, 1981, **41**, 2995-A. (a)

GRIFFIN, P.S. One small step for personkind: Observations and suggestions for sex equity in co-educational physical education classes. *Journal of Teaching in Physical Education*, Spring 1981, pp. 12-17. (b)

PATTON, M.Q. *Qualitative evaluation methods.* Beverly Hills, CA: Sage Publications, 1980.

PLACEK, J. *An observational study of teacher planning physical education.* Unpublished doctoral dissertation, University of Massachusetts, 1982.

SOLOMONS, H. Sex role mediated achievement behaviors and interpersonal dynamics of fifth grade co-educational physical education classes. (Doctoral dissertation, Bryn Mawr College, 1976.) *DAI*, 1977, **37**, 5445-A.

SPRADLEY, J. *Participant observation.* New York: Holt, Rinehart, & Winston, 1980.

TEMPLIN, T. Student as socializing agent. *Journal of Teaching in Physical Education.* Spring 1981, pp. 71-79.

WANG, B.W. An ethnography of a physical education class: An experiment in integrated living. (Doctoral dissertation, University of North Carolina, 1977.) *DAI*, 1978, **38**, 1980-A.

Fragmentation and integration in human movement

Patsy Phillips Kollen
Springfield, Illinois

Fragmented and integrated human movement, my main research interest, was sparked when I interviewed 20 high school seniors about their K-12 physical education experiences for my dissertation (Kollen, 1981). This study was a qualitative investigation using a phenomenological methodology. Phenomenologists are noted for being unable to say what they are about. I am no exception.

I want to present enough nuts and bolts from my dissertation to give you a sense of my starting point for wanting to understand fragmentation and integration in human movement. I interviewed students of varying ethnic origins and physical education/athletic experiences. These characteristics as well as others are delineated in Table 1. For a detailed description of each student, the reader is referred to Kollen (1981).

The four questions presented below represented the major foci of the study. In addition, 30 probes were helpful in teasing out answers to the main questions when necessary.

1. Tell me some things you remember about your physical education classes.

Table 1

Characteristics of Students Interviewed

10 Females, 10 Males

1 Chinese-American, 7 Blacks, 12 Whites
4 Athletes, 2 cheerleaders, 1 dancer
3 Students with learning disabilities
2 Overweight students
3 Handicapped students
4 Repeated physical education failures
7 Students who repeatedly elected physical education
5 Students who simply satisfied the requirement
8 A/B P.E. grade-receivers; 5 C-average; 6 C/D/E
1 Medically discharged from P.E.

2. How would you describe yourself as a student in these classes?
3. Would you describe a natural high you have had connected with sports or recreation. Have you had a similar experience in a physical education class?
4. What do you remember about moving/movement in your physical education classes?

Results

From these questions, student responses were reduced to the following themes:

1. Being "into" movement integrates self, requires risk/challenge and the freedom to interact and react spontaneously, results in feelings of joy, control/power, and is valued by all.
2. Increasing emphasis through the grades on norms, curriculum, grades, requirements, teaching methods, and standards has a negative effect on the enjoyment of movement.
3. The physical education environment is sterile and stresses conformity to teacher or institutional standards which result in physical education payoffs (grades, recognition, encouragement, freedom from punishment) *and* in "going through the motions" of movement to please the teachers.
4. The physical education environment is unsafe and is characterized by embarrassing situations, public humiliation, not being believed, unrealistic expectations, rigid irrelevant movement activities, angry teacher put-downs, discomfort, forced display of performance when the student feels incompetent, and feelings of vulnerability.
5. Students respond to the unsafe environment by withholding some-

thing of themselves through minimal compliance, lack of involvement, manipulation of the teacher, false enthusiasm, rebellion, leaving, failing class, isolation, or giving up.

6. Teachers assume that students who are independent and responsible make it on their own regardless of sports background or personal problems. They assume that students are innately lazy and must be *made* to do, that athletic status is the goal for all students, and that athletic status is achievable through concerted effort and self-discipline.

7. The movement standard in physical education is masculine-athletic-competitive. There are positive or negative repercussions when one does or does not measure up.

8. A safe, fruitful environment would include acceptance of differences, noncomparative feedback, and progress toward one's own movement and fitness goals, as well as concern, help, and support.

These themes were considered further in an attempt to identify underlying meanings:

1. Personal unity/completeness is threatened by the expectation of a dependent relationship in an unsafe/sterile environment.

2. Negation and denial of being is expected.

3. Withholding of oneself from the situation is the student's attempt to affirm his or her existence.

4. There is awareness of the spiritual poverty of the environment as manifested by absence of care, concern, acknowledgement of emotions, personalization, or positive feelings.

5. Absence of movement integrity surfaces as a "Catch-22" feeling.

6. Being out of place is the norm for the nonathlete.

7. The awareness of one's movement being visible to others—on display—permeates the physical education environment.

8. Being "into" movement includes losing oneself in the movement, thus creating the need for a safe environment that is free of damage to allow for this vulnerability. Physical education is not a safe place to be "into" movement.

After writing my dissertation, I felt I had made some useful suggestions for teachers to address the themes that emerged from the study. However, I felt I had not adequately dealt with the meanings underlying the themes in terms of practical suggestions. Since these findings were of most interest to me, and because I felt they were the more fundamental in terms of understanding what is really going on in teaching, I have focused some postdoctoral work on these findings.

This study led to a better understanding of existentialism and phenomenology, and to studies of embodied consciousness, particularly the work of Marcel, Sartre, and Merleau-Ponty. It led to renewed interest in

Table 2

Differences Between Fragmented and Integrated Movement

Fragmented movement	Integrated movement
Presence of self	Absence of self
Here/now time dimension	Timeless dimension
Comparison/judgment	No comparison/judgment
Comparing the moment with past/future	Living the moment
Becoming	Being
High from externals (beating self/others, praise, reward)	High from movement/seems like a completely new happening
Psychological pleasure if up/ psychological pain if down	Joyful
Image/standards in operation	No images or standards used
Presence of thoughts	Absence of thoughts
Conflict, struggle, striving	No conflict, struggle, striving
Learning through imitation, conformity, acquisition of skills/knowledge	Learning through doing, acting, creating

Heidegger, and a new interest in Eastern thinkers and/or interpreters, particularly Suzucki, Watts, and Krishnamurti. Based on this study, fragmented and integrated human movement can be categorized, though incompletely, as I have done in Table 2.

Discussion

As a result of this research, aren't we left with the inescapable fact that physical education has a significant, though negative, impact on students from the perspective of fostering integrated movement?

Is this fact inescapable for us? Can we look it squarely in the face? Haven't we all, at times at least, deeply known this to be true? How have we escaped facing it?

The easiest escape for teachers seems to be a belief that students are incapable of integrated movement. Before coming to us they have been ruined by bad teachers, bad parents, bad society, or they have psychological problems that we can't be expected to understand. If only they came to us first, uncontaminated, we say, things would be different. A paradox surfaced in my research that makes any such escape impossible for me. Students were unable to recall any examples of integrated movement within physical education but they were *all* able to report such experiences outside of physical education.

Another avoidance technique is simply saying that institutional settings by their very nature cannot foster this kind of movement experience. If we settle for this, we stop all possibility for inquiry into the truth or falseness of such a claim. Besides, students do vaguely recall in early elementary physical education an atmosphere of excitement, newness, and mystery.

As researchers, we seem to have avoided facing this fact by trying to point the finger at teacher ignorance of scientific findings, teacher inhumanity, poor methodology, or competition. Can we face the fact that students find little joy, learning, or meaning through movement activities in our classes? Do we want to feel good that students instead find self-importance, self-denigration, or anesthetization through movement activities in our classes?

Perhaps too much of our research energy has gone into making projections about what our teaching should be like. Maybe it is time to focus this energy on observing what is actually happening in our teaching. Were we to do this, I think we would quickly see very clearly that we are getting fragmented movement whereas what we want is integrated movement. As we continue to observe, I think we will find that fragmented movement stems from our deeply embedded ideology, which in practice uses a masculine-athletic-competitive image as our standard. The effects of this ideology in practice desperately need to be understood through inquiry and research.

Let me quickly say I don't think the problem is masculinity, athletics, or competition per se. While these are fragments in themselves and cannot lead to integration, the problem is that there is an image at all. What happens when we do movement activities according to an image? Imagine yourself doing your favorite sport or physical activity. Can you recall a time when it was perfect or near perfect? Can you remember a time that reflects the following description?

Being-into-movement is crossing a line into a different world, a world of pure excitement, exhilaration, and action. A tuning-in to the movement is balanced by a turning-off of the outside. Time disappears. You lose yourself as you become the movement. The atmosphere is one of newness, crispness, and mystery. Things stand out in bold relief and take on new meaning. The challenges or risks invite you to join and embrace them in a demonstration of power, control, and effectiveness. You feel good, accomplished, and complete, and these feelings weave throughout like quiet applause. Being-into-movement is a kind of freedom, a treasure.

Why do we consider these natural highs? Why aren't these the norm rather than the exception? Let's not say it is impossible. We don't know.

Say, for example, that you are out jogging and, for a second, things are perfect. All of a sudden something intrudes. Here are some examples from my own thoughts while jogging:

1. The thought comes in, "I should be running faster if I want to improve."
2. I wonder how far I've gone and begin to estimate and calculate.
3. I see some people up ahead. I don't want them to think I'm slow. I speed up and quickly become exhausted, and run around a corner so I can stop.
4. I think, "Wow! I'm running well today. Why can't I do this all the time?"

Now, the moment one of these intrusions comes in, the joy of movement is gone and the whole thing becomes fragmented. I am no longer there in the movement but am now condemning myself, or judging myself, or comparing myself, or feeling good about myself. And why? The image—the masculine-athletic-competitive image. It says to me that I should be able to work harder, go farther effortlessly and in good form, better than yesterday—and if I don't, somehow I have failed, and if I do, I can feel good about myself.

I can't have it both ways. If I'm going to be concerned with the image, the way I think I should be, then the jogging, the "what is," goes out the window. If I spend all of my movement time trying to be that *image*, I'll never be into the movement. I will be living in the past or in the future. My activities won't be alive and vital and dynamic and enjoyable. They won't lead to ease, learning, or health.

If I clearly see this, the image may drop away and leave me being-into-movement so that it is not a high, an exception, but instead is the rule for my movement activities. Impossible? I don't think we know. Let's look at another situation:

I remember the first time I ran a 5:55 mile and my reaction was, "Wow, me?" Afterwards, "I did that!" Almost anytime you increase your weight, bench press by a place, you think "Wow, that's pretty neat." Your pride. Knowing that you're one step better than what you were. In wrestling, winning by a lot or pinning a guy. My best record in pinning a guy was 10 seconds and I felt pretty *bad* after that.

How many of us can remember incidents when we felt like this in some activity or other? Of course, being masculine-athletic-competitive types more or less, it is not surprising that we recall more of these incidents than we do the movement-high kind. What happens, though, when we don't increase our weight or decrease our time, and improvement slows or stops? Don't we feel bad? Don't we move on to another activity? Why? The enjoyment wasn't from the physical movement but rather from the psychological status we gained. This is the norm in physical education.

The masculine-athletic-competitive "jocks" feel pretty good about themselves in our classes; the others feel pretty bad. And none of them enjoy the movement, the functioning with competence and enjoyment in the physical activity. We need to ask ourselves very seriously, being primarily jocks ourselves, if it is the physical activity we love or the psychological rewards we have gained over time.

Let me make one thing clear. It is not physical comparison or physical measurement that is the problem. Rather, it is the psychological comparison and measurement that leads to false pride or condemnation.

As physical educators, I think we are terribly confused about competition. If fully understood, I believe that competition and cooperation go hand in hand. The root words of compete mean to come together, to strive, and to belong. Interestingly, compete is also derived from a root word meaning feather. Feathers either fly or fall depending on the presence or absence of wind, a natural phenomenon. I doubt that a feather that flies feels it is "better" than the feather that falls. Perhaps feathers while flying learn that a certain angle or fanning pattern can influence the height or direction of flight. It seems ludicrous to say that because of this ability, that feather is better or more valuable.

Being-into-movement or integrated movement could happen in a competitive setting when the competition is based strictly on physical capabilities. Fragmentation occurs when the competition is used to make psychological distinctions and status is placed on these distinctions.

Our field has cornered the institutional market on conditioning young people's thoughts and feelings about their bodies and physical movement. Nothing is more fundamental to well-being than a healthy, harmonious relationship between mind, body, and spirit. We are dealing with very fragile and vulnerable perceptions. What an opportunity! What responsibility!

I am afraid that we have conditioned our students to think about themselves as moving beings by comparing themselves against this masculine-athletic-competitive image. I would like to see us go about unconditioning the profession, the professionals, and the students. I think we have two very important things going for us. First, I'm confident that each of us has experienced the movement high, not often, perhaps, but enough to have engendered in us a love of movement. Second, students love movement and want to fly like a feather.

To paraphrase Krishnamurti (1964), it is the function of physical education to help each student move freely and without fear. What an extraordinary thing it would be to create such an atmosphere in our classes, an atmosphere free of the fear of moving so that students would be constantly high on learning to move through moving together.

References

KOLLEN, P. The experience of movement in physical education: A phenomenology (Doctoral dissertation, The University of Michigan, 1981). *Dissertation Abstracts International*, 1981, **42**(2), 428A-893A. (University Microfilms No. 81-16, 272)

KRISHNAMURTI, J. *Think on these things*. New York: Harper & Row, 1964.

Teacher/coach role conflict:
Factors influencing role performance

Linda L. Bain
University of Houston

Teacher/coach role conflict has received considerable attention in recent physical education literature. Research by Locke and Massengale (1978), Templin (1980), Chu (1981), and Earls (1981) has indicated that employment of physical educators as both teacher and coach is a source of conflict and stress for those individuals.

There are two potential causes for the stress experienced by individuals occupying multiple roles simultaneously. Role conflict refers to being exposed to contradictory expectations at the same time (Getzels & Guba, 1954). Role strain or overload involves being exposed to demands which require more time, energy, and commitment than one has (Goode, 1960). There is reason to believe that teachers/coaches experience both role conflict and role strain. Locke and Massengale (1978) found that teachers/coaches perceive and experience both role overload and role conflict, although scores for *perceived* overload and conflict were higher than those for *experienced* overload and conflict. Templin (1980) obtained similar results with a sample of teachers/coaches and their principals.

Both role conflict and role strain have important practical implications for professional preparation and for employment practices in public schools. If role conflict exists, the expectations for each role differ. Many people are more capable of performing one than the other, and different preparation and abilities are required for each. Solutions to role conflict problems require that different individuals be employed for each of the roles or that individuals be specifically prepared to acquire the skills needed for each of the roles. Preparation for teaching would not be assumed to serve as preparation for coaching or vice versa. Solutions to role strain, the other potential source of stress for teachers/coaches, require that organizations attempt to reduce time demands on the individual (lighter teaching loads, more support services, etc.) and that individuals learn short-cuts to save time and energy. If teacher educators and school administrators are to respond appropriately to teacher/coach role conflict, they need more information about the characteristics of the two roles and the factors which influence role performance.

Figure 1 delineates a model of those factors hypothesized to influence role performance. In describing the model and examining the research related to its components, this discussion will focus on its application to teacher/coach role conflict in public schools—although it might be interesting to make a similar analysis of teacher/researcher role conflict among university faculty.

Much of the role conflict literature suggests that teaching and coaching require different characteristics and abilities. A physical educator's compatability with each of the roles depends upon the match between the individual's talents and the job expectations. This compatability has both a direct and indirect influence on role performance because of the impact upon the person's commitment to the role.

The critical factor in examining this component of the model is clarification of the expectations or performance capabilities associated with each role. Such clarification must precede estimates of compatability. Several attempts have been made to describe the roles of physical educators but this research has not always differentiated between the role expectations and qualifications of teachers and coaches. Weber (1977) developed a physical education teacher-role identification instrument which requires respondents to rate the importance of each of 89 competencies for a female high school physical education teacher. Weber (1974) used the instrument to conduct a study of the role definitions of prospective and public school physical eduation teachers, administrators, nonphysical education public school teachers, and physical education professional preparation faculty. Her study indicated that the role of the female physical education teacher was multidimensional, with 14 subroles being identified. The six groups of subjects had somewhat different definitions of the role, the greatest congruence being between the senior students and the university faculty. Pace (Note 1) also used the Weber instrument to compare the views of senior students and university

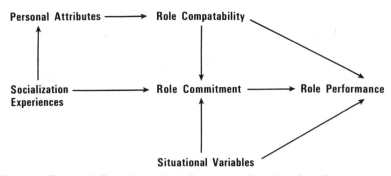

Figure 1—Factors influencing role performance of teachers/coaches.

faculty. In the Pace study, five subroles emerged: teacher, interpersonal interactant, planner, professional member of a school staff, and program manager. Kane (1975) conducted a study in England where 852 male and female physical education teachers from 568 schools rated the relative importance of each of 24 attributes and abilities for a physical education teacher. Factor analysis revealed seven dimensions measured by the instrument: personal education, social concern, rapport, knowledge of children, professional organization, assurance, and application. Results indicated that subjects considered rapport and application (knowledge of subject matter, capacity for hard work) most important. No differences were found between male and female subjects.

Hendry (1972, 1975a, 1975b) also has examined the role of physical educators in England, using a questionnaire which addressed seven aspects of the role: status within the school, relations with other staff, relations with the head teacher, relations with pupils, extracurricular duties, personal characteristics, and conscious motives for career selection (Hendry, 1975a). The sample included male physical education teachers, classroom teachers, pupils, and preservice physical educators. Subjects were asked to indicate both actual and ideal role conceptions. Preservice and inservice physical educators had similar perceptions indicating strong feelings of low status, subject marginality, and a social orientation in their teaching. Other subgroups seemed to have differing expectations of the physical educator, and physical educators seemed to agree with all of these views. Pupils wanted a counselor, head teachers wanted a disciplinary influence in the school, and colleagues valued success in athletic competition which brought prestige to the school. Hendry (1975b) describes the physical educator's role as marginal in the school because the social and disciplinary functions are perceived as less valuable than academic functions. He proposes that some physical educators attempt to survive in that marginal role by emphasizing competition and elitism in the athletic program in order to gain the esteem of colleagues. It should be noted that while Hendry's work describes role expectations, the emphasis is upon the situational variables which affect role performance. That is, the reward and prestige system of the school is hypothesized to influence both role commitment and role performance.

Only a few studies have examined teaching and coaching as separate roles. Research by Chu (1981) indicated that 28 of 30 secondary school physical education teachers/coaches perceived teaching and coaching as separate and distinct roles. The respondents were asked to indicate the skills they perceived as most important for teaching and coaching. Rankings for the two roles differed: Communication skills ranked first for teaching and subject matter knowledge ranked first for coaching. The teachers/coaches interviewed perceived their professional preparation as much less relevant in learning to coach than in learning to teach.

Earls (1981) interviewed 24 junior high school physical educators who had been identified as distinctive because of the quality of their teaching. The subjects indicated that different behaviors were required for success in teaching than in coaching. Coaching focused upon developing skilled performance, but teaching required an awareness of and responsiveness to a wider range of student needs.

An observational study conducted by Bain (1978) found differences in the manner in which teachers and coaches performed. Athletic team practices focused intensely upon attaining skilled performance. In contrast, physical education classes seemed to be more neutral, more diffuse, less individualized, and less achievement-oriented. This study, however, described actual performance of each of the roles, and these observed behaviors did not necessarily represent quality role performance.

A recent study conducted by the author and a colleague (Bain & Wendt, in press) examined prospective physical educators' perceptions of the two roles. A questionnaire developed for this study asked subjects to rate the importance of each of 12 characteristics or abilities for a teacher and then for a coach. Subjects were 70 undergraduate physical education majors in a large urban university in the Southwest. Table 1 reports the mean, standard deviation, and rank of each item rated for each of the two sets of ratings. In contrast to Chu's (1981) findings, communication skills were ranked as most important for both teachers and coaches. In general, the two sets of ranks were very similar ($\bar{r}_s = .93$).

Factor analysis yielded three factors for each set of ratings. Factor 1 for both roles appeared to focus upon interpersonal relationships with students (understanding, communication, motivation) and explained most of the common variance. However, some differences appeared in the constellation of variables for teaching Factor 1 and coaching Factor 1. For teaching, a high level of personal fitness was viewed as related to the interpersonal skills factor. One might speculate that "practicing what you preach" is perceived as important in motivating physical education

Table 1

Ratings of Importance of Selected Attributes for Roles of Teacher and Coach

	Teacher			Coach		
	M	SD	Rank	M	SD	Rank
Communication skills—teaching techniques	4.44	.70	1	4.49	.70	1
Understanding—concern for students	4.31	.81	2	4.41	.69	4
Ability to maintain discipline	4.27	.90	3	4.31	.94	5
Knowledge—activity being taught-coached	4.20	.96	4	4.46	.79	3
Ability to motivate to achieve	4.16	.83	5	4.47	.70	2
Ability to cope with stress	4.11	.94	6	4.16	.99	6
Efficiency in organization	3.94	1.19	7	3.99	1.00	8
Ability to judge performance	3.89	1.04	8	4.06	.80	7
Personal fitness	3.64	1.02	9	3.81	.98	10
Knowledge—general scientific information	3.61	1.25	10	3.84	1.16	9
Personal skill in activity taught/coached	3.31	1.17	11	3.23	1.28	11
Public relations ability	3.14	1.09	12	3.19	1.12	12
Average rating	3.92			4.04		

students. Credibility may also be related to interpersonal skills for coaches but may be dependent upon different characteristics. Knowledge of the specific activity being taught or coached and the ability to judge student performance loaded significantly on this factor for coaches. Ability to maintain discipline and to cope with stress also related to Factor 1 for both roles.

Factors 2 and 3 differed somewhat for the two roles. For teachers, Factor 2 seemed to identify a cluster of instructional skills and Factor 3 seemed to be a subject matter competence factor primarily based on personal skill in the activity taught. For coaches, Factor 2 seemed to be subject matter competence based on both personal skill and fitness while Factor 3 seemed to be a managerial factor comprised of public relations and organizational skills.

Based on the similarity of the ranks and the factor structures, this sample of prospective physical educators seemed to perceive the roles of teacher and coach as requiring rather similar characteristics or abilities. Several explanations might account for this inconsistency with previous role conflict research. A social desirability response may have caused subjects to rate all characteristics as important and thus may have masked differences in the two roles. A second explanation might be that awareness of role conflict develops only after employment in both roles. The professional preparation phase is a time of anticipatory socialization during which the individual acquires the beliefs, norms, and values of a role not yet occupied. If role conflict exists among inservice teachers/ coaches but is not perceived by prospective physical educators, questions might be raised about the effectiveness of current professional preparation procedures which fail to communicate realistic expectations for each of the roles. It is also possible that role strain, not role conflict, is the primary source of stress for teachers/coaches and that previous research has not adequately distinguished the two.

Role strain emphasizes the situational component of the model. Teaching and coaching assignments are so heavy that they create unreasonable time demands and affect role performance. The degree to which such strain or overload affects each role appears to be based upon an interaction with role commitment and role compatability or competence. That is, individuals experiencing role strain are likely to neglect the role for which they have least commitment and compatability. As indicated previously, physical educators who experience overload tend to report that the negative impact is primarily upon their teaching (Earls, 1981; Locke & Massengale, 1978).

One of the most important components of this model may be role commitment. A frequent response to role conflict or role strain is that one of the roles is adopted as the major role (Getzels & Guba, 1954). Marks (1977) has also argued that equally positive commitment to multiple roles minimizes role strain by increasing energy levels and flexible use of time. Segrave (1980) reported that among prospective physical education teachers, 76% of the males and 48% of the females identify coaching as the preferred role. Those subjects who were athletes also expressed greater interest in coaching than did non-athletes.

Other researchers have examined the factors related to selection of a physical education major but have not differentiated between preference for teaching and coaching. Pooley (1975) examined variables associated with anticipatory socialization of physical educators in the United States and England. Physical education recruits in the USA seemed to select the field because of their love of activity and their belief that the profession is useful to society. United States recruits, especially males, tended to have more athletic experience than their English counterparts. Anderson (Note 2) used Pooley's model of socialization to develop a questionnaire administered to 472 physical education majors in six Texas universities. His results indicated that the most frequent reason given for selecting physical education as a major was experience in competitive sports (72%). Although neither of these studies differentiated choice of teaching or coaching as a career goal, the importance of athletic experience may indicate higher commitment to coaching.

In the study conducted by Bain and Wendt (in press), undergraduate students were asked to indicate a preference for teaching only, coaching only, or teaching and coaching. Discriminant analysis was employed to identify which personal and background variables best differentiated among the role preference groups. Gender and athletic experience were significant predictors of job preference. A substantial number, 58% of the females and 45% of the males, indicated equal commitment to teaching and coaching. Males expressed greater preference for coaching only and females for teaching only. The teaching-only group reported less experience in athletics (3.3 years) than either of the other groups (6.2 years). The teaching and coaching group had more positive role models than the teaching-only and coaching-only groups. Skill variables were relatively unimportant in predicting job preference.

When the discriminant function was employed to predict job preference categories, 52.94% of the cases were correctly classified. Interestingly, 69% of the teaching-only and 81% of the coaching-only subjects were correctly classified, but only 29% of the teaching-coaching group were. This set of variables seems to distinguish those who prefer teaching only or coaching only, but the factors which influence a person to have equal commitment to teaching and coaching do not seem to have been identified.

Summary

Occupying the dual roles of teacher and coach appears to be a source of stress. Future research need not focus upon verification of the existence of this phenomenon, but rather upon understanding those factors which influence the severity of the problem and the responses of teachers/ coaches in coping with role conflict or overload. A model has been proposed to describe factors influencing role performance of teachers/ coaches. Existing research seems to support the explanatory potential of the three major influences on role performance: role compatability, role commitment, and situational variables. However, further research is needed to describe each of the links in the model.

Reference Notes

1. Pace, J. *Role definitions of college faculty and prospective physical educators.* Paper presented at the Annual Convention of the American Alliance for Health, Physical Education, Recreation and Dance, Detroit, April 1980.
2. Anderson, E.W. *A study of selected reasons for majoring in physical education.* Paper presented at Annual Convention of Texas Association for Health, Physical Education and Recreation, December 1981.

References

BAIN, L. Differences in values implicit in teaching and coaching behaviors. *Research Quarterly*, 1978, **49**, 5-11.

BAIN, L.L., & Wendt, J.C. Undergraduate physical education majors' perceptions of the roles of teacher and coach. *Research Quarterly for Sport and Exercise*, in press.

CHU, D. Functional myths of education organizations: College as career training and the relationship of formal title to actual duties upon secondary school employment. *NAPEHE Annual Conference Proceedings*, 1981, **II**, 36-46.

EARLS, N.F. Distinctive teachers' personal qualities, perceptions of teacher education and the realities of teaching. *Journal of Teaching in Physical Education*, 1981, **1**(1), 59-70.

GETZELS, J.W., & Guba, E.C. Role, role conflict, and effectiveness. *American Sociological Review*, 1954, **19**, 164-175.

GOODE, W.J. A theory of role strain. *American Sociological Review*, 1960, **25**, 483-496.

HENDRY, L.B. The coaching stereotype. In H.T.A. Whiting (Ed.), *Readings in sport psychology*. London: Kimpton, 1972.

HENDRY, L.B. The role of the physical education teacher. *Education Research*, 1975, **17**, 115-121. (a)

HENDRY, L.B. Survival in a marginal role: The professional identity of the physical education teacher. *British Journal of Sociology*, 1975, **26**, 465-476. (b)

KANE, J.E. Perceptions of personal characteristics by physical education teachers and coaches. In H.T.A. Whiting (Ed.), *Readings in sport psychology*, **2**. London: Lepus Books, 1975.

LOCKE, L.F., & Massengale, J.D. Role conflict in teacher/coaches. *Research Quarterly*, 1978, **49**, 162-174.

MARKS, S.R. Multiple roles and role strain: Some notes on human energy time and commitment. *American Sociological Review*, 1977, **42**, 921-936.

POOLEY, J.C. The professional socialization of physical education students in the United States and England. *International Review of Sport Sociology*, 1975, **10**, 97-105.

SEGRAVE, J.O. Role preferences among prospective physical education teacher/coaches. *NAPEHE Annual Conference Proceedings*, 1981, **II**, 53-61.

TEMPLIN, T.J. Teacher/coach role conflict and the high school principal. *NAPEHE Annual Conference Proceedings*, 1981, **II**, 70-81.

WEBER, M. *The role of the woman high school physical education teacher as viewed by selected university and public school personnel in Wisconsin*. Unpublished doctoral dissertation, University of Wisconsin, 1974.

WEBER, M. Physical education teacher role identification instrument. *Research Quarterly*, 1977, **48**, 445-451.

It only takes one case to prove a possibility . . . and beyond

Don Hellison
Portland State University

Since 1969, I have been shuttling back and forth between homemade theory and "real world" teaching or, more formally, practice. The real world teaching has taken place in a variety of settings — from inner city schools to diversion and detention programs — and in a variety of arrangements (e.g., half a day all year, 1 hour every day for 6 weeks, half a day on Fridays for 3 months). But in all cases I either taught or team taught. Also, in all cases the students were teenagers, usually categorized one way or another as high risk, alienated, or in trouble. My ego has been severely bruised in the process, my drawing board worn down by revisions, my shuttle craft nearly scuttled more than once.

This work doesn't really fit the criteria for qualitative research, nor does it resemble any of the alternative research strategies recently described by Silva and Parkhouse (1982). Taylor's description of the "resident professor" (1980), which includes field-based research, comes closer, but perhaps one could draw even more parallels between George Sheehan's research on running and my research methodology. Sheehan (1975) has said that he is an experiment of one. So am I. I have tried to fully participate in the process as it unfolds. Through the years, I have simply reported my biases, intentions, and experiences as I perceived them, including setting, students, goals, strategies, whatever data were gathered, and my impressions without trying to generalize beyond these specific experiences.

For this paper, I have tried to look back on the past 13 years from a research perspective. Three distinct phases have emerged from this analysis. The major premise underlying the first two phases was that it only takes one case to prove a possibility. I planned, experienced, and reported. In the third phase, my reports began to include the experiences and data collected by other teachers who attempted to replicate, with modifications, my model.

Phase 1 focused on the question: What's worth teaching? This question is partly a matter of sorting out values — that is, what kind of commitment is worth my time and energy and what sense of purpose will provide the most meaning? But there are psychological implications as well — that is, what should I identify with in order to feel "right," significant, or worthy? How does one go about researching such questions? My way has been to try out various goal models and then to reflect on how well they fit my sense of purpose and identity. Sport for the sake of sport or for leisure time pursuits is one such goal model; fitness for health is another. I've tried both. Neither holds much personal meaning for me in terms of the above criteria. Character development/social development, on the other hand, first appealed to me when I read about Hetherington's work at a reform school (Gerber, 1971, pp. 389-390) and held its appeal for me when I began teaching. I liked the idea of sport and exercise as an intervention medium in spite of my rather dismal failure at effectively teaching from this goal model. Teaching fitness for health and teaching skills seemed easier to do, but they didn't and still don't matter very much to me. I wanted to help "problem kids" become less of a problem to themselves and society; that seemed really worth doing.

Phase 1's finding led to another question which took about 10 years to answer and is still under investigation. The Phase 2 question was: To what extent could sport and exercise act as an intervention medium for high-risk youth in an educational setting? Each year, I first identified some goals in line with my answer to what's worth teaching and some strategies that seemed likely to bring about the changes I sought. Then I tried them out, evaluated the whole process, modified, added, deleted, and tried again — and again. There were three parts to this process: goal clarification, the search for appropriate strategies, and evaluation of results.

My first experience involved an attempt to develop the self-esteem of 50 11th- and 12th-grade males who had flunked physical education. Strategies were a) heavy curricular emphasis on combative activities and weight training, and b) my charisma. Without calibrating my charisma as John Cheffers has suggested we will eventually be able to do, it was easy to tell that the whole experience was a disaster from beginning to end. Students were out of control and off task much of the time, my feelings of frustration ran high almost all the time, and so on. I had one very vague goal, strategies that didn't work, and no formal evaluation procedures, although it didn't take much to size up the effectiveness of my program. That was in 1969-1970.

By 1974-1975, I had developed three goals, a program framework (the awareness levels), a wide range of strategies, and 11 evaluation procedures. All of this was reported in *Beyond Balls and Bats* (Hellison, 1978). Evaluation suggested *some* degree of success in moving the majority of students *toward* the goals. Recent changes have involved modifying and integrating goals and framework into four progressive levels/ goals, identifying principles for developing one's own strategies based on personal style and setting, and adding a variety of behavior checks to the evaluation procedures.

In the struggle to find out to what extent sport and exercise can act as an intervention medium for problem kids, goals, strategies, and evaluation procedures underwent a considerable evolution. The four goals of Hetherington and others of the education-through-the-physical perspective were obviously unmanageable from the start. The what's-worth-teaching perspective of Phase 1 helped to clarify the most personally satisfying kinds of intervention — for example, teaching kids to respect the rights of others. In addition, some goals such as involvement for its own sake were added to more fully integrate activity into the goal model. Attempts to locate and evaluate relevant strategies also helped to clarify goals. For example, self-esteem was too vague to give much direction, whereas self-direction provided a clearer notion of which strategies and evaluation procedures to employ.

I began without any teaching strategies other than command style instruction and play. I needed more structure and more student involvement in goal-related tasks, so teaching strategies such as reciprocal teaching, contracts, and behavior management were added each year. I also kept a daily record of goals for the day and goal-related strategies, and when I failed to keep track, my rhetoric remained quite oriented toward character development while my teaching reverted to its traditional roots. The daily records also helped to show the extent to which strategies matched goals. Did the strategies have face validity? Did each goal have at least one strategy? This search for a good fit often led to the development of new strategies to provide missing links.

Evaluation procedures had to be designed to determine which strategies were working and the extent of progress toward the goals. Subjective evaluations indicated the feelings of the students, other teachers, and me concerning progress as well as preferences. Objective data gave indications of behavior changes and attitude changes. Each year some procedures were added, some were deleted. However, the primary method utilized throughout Phase 2 (and Phase 1 for that matter) was self-reflection, sometimes by keeping a daily journal, sometimes by discussing the day's experiences with students and colleagues, but always by trying to judge what made emotional and intellectual sense and what seemed to work. For a "reliability check" on my self-reflection, others' opinions helped, as did the data (e.g., attendance records, number of students working independently or cooperatively, and so on). Crises also helped. For example, it was difficult to avoid analyzing my behavior when I pushed a student into the wall in response to his behavior of setting fire to an emotionally handicapped student's shirt.

During Phase 2, structure (i.e., specific guidelines and strategies) gradually replaced the time that had been allowed for my teacher artistry to blossom. It just wasn't blossoming! For example, carefully structured counseling days were created so that I could talk to students individually. However, by 1978-1979 I had finally internalized the goals and some of the teaching skills necessary to survive, so a trend toward structure reduction began. By Phase 3, options in structure had been developed for teachers.

Phase 3 really began early in this whole process. I just didn't pay much attention to it. Some teachers in schools in which I worked, and to a lesser extent in classes at Portland State University and workshops elsewhere, began to try for themselves this kind of intervention. They became their own "experiments of one" so that several cases could be reported to prove our possibility. Cases could also be reported to refute the possibility; as one teacher told me, "I tried your stuff—it doesn't work!" Other teachers began to visit the apparently successful programs and follow *their* lead. I didn't hear about some of these efforts until much later, and still don't know the extent of "adoption." In 1980-1981, the Oregon Governor's Council on Health, Fitness, and Sports asked me to develop a training program for physical education teachers and youth workers that would help to reduce delinquency. Six experienced teachers completed the training to include an internship teaching high-risk youth; their evaluation of this experience provided more data and more experiments of one. They are now conducting workshops and acting as consultants. Hopefully, more experiments of one will result from this work. From time to time, I hear of some adaptation that absolutely astounds me. Several Portland elementary physical educators have developed their own versions of the model for use with little children without any help from my trainers or me. A private high school in Calgary has developed a program far beyond the initial workshop. So has at least one Portland teacher. Last spring, thanks to Linda Bain, I met a Houston alternative school teacher who had implemented his own version by reading *Beyond Balls and Bats*. He wanted more help; I could only give him kudos. Some teachers in the California Youth Authority system made changes based on a 1-hour workshop, as I discovered later, 2 years after the workshop.

These cases provide variations in implementation based on teaching style, setting, and students, thereby offering options for others who would like to implement the program. They also provide evidence that this stuff works — sometimes. Daryl Siedentop and George Graham have encouraged me to take more advantage of their subjective impressions and their data such as attendance records in my reports to the profession.

Have I been researchy enough? Probably not. Graham and Siedentop are right, of course. However, both of them have also said that I need to do what I need to do. Choosing George Sheehan's work on running as my "hindsight" research model leaves me vulnerable to a number of criticisms, but it has one big advantage. It best reflects what I want to do and how I would like to contribute. I offer my work as an alternative or, more accurately, as another piece to the puzzle rather than as a replacement for other research methodologies.

My final thought is that Siedentop has suggested that we specify our assumptions. What are mine? Using the Wolfgang-Glickman (1980) continuum, I have clearly moved away from the non-interventionist end represented by Carl Rogers, and I have even dipped into the interventionists' (behaviorists') bag of tricks at the other end. Mostly, however, my efforts to get students to interact with my goals fall in the middle or interactionist orientation represented by Dreikurs and Glasser. Tune in next month for changes!

References

GERBER, E.W. *Innovators and institutions.* Philadelphia: Lea & Febiger, 1971.

HELLISON, D. *Beyond balls and bats: Alienated (and other) youth in the gym.* Washington, DC: AAHPERD, 1978.

SHEEHAN, G.A. *Dr. Sheehan on running.* Mountain View, CA: World Publications, 1975.

SILVA, J.M., & Parkhouse, B.L. On answering questions worth asking: Alternative designs for sport and exercise research. *Quest*, 1982, **34**, 43-52.

TAYLOR, J.L. The resident professor: A leadership role for connecting theory and practice. *Motor Skills: Theory Into Practice*, 1980, **4** 51-58.

WOLFGANG, C.H., & Glickman, C.D. *Solving discipline problems: Strategies for classroom teachers.* Boston: Allyn & Bacon, 1980.

Section three
Student teaching

This section's two papers focus on the student teaching experience as an agent of socialization. Specifically, student teaching may influence the attitudes and behavior of an individual in further developing his or her teaching identity. In contrast to most studies that depict the student teacher as passively and unconsciously socialized into traditional roles, the papers by Paul Schempp, and by Linda Marrs and Tom Templin, show how the student teacher plays an active role in shaping his or her own teaching identity.

Utilizing a critical incident technique, Schempp reveals that when student teachers have autonomy in planning and leading physical education classes, for students who view the classes as legitimate and valuable, student teachers feel satisfied and competent. Therefore, student teachers serve as their own socializing agents. They themselves identify those incidences (student social and emotional engagement in and conformity to student teacher-planned activities) critical to their development in the teaching role.

Marrs and Templin describe three strategies that student teachers use in directing their experience. Using the social strategy concept developed by Lacy (1977), the authors demonstrate how student teachers consciously defer to impression management and internalized adjustment in perpetuating the traditional model of physical education. Also illustrated is strategic redefinition, a strategy employed to redefine the instructional norms of a setting. The authors indicate that student teachers are not just passive recipients of the influences of various socializing agents, but in fact are actively engaged in developing their own teaching identities.

Hence, both papers in this section demonstrate that student teachers play a larger role in the socialization process than is normally attributed to them. Beyond the influence of cooperating teachers, students, university supervisors, and the school setting itself, student teachers are active agents of self-socialization.

Reference

LACY, C. *The socialization of teachers*. London: Metheun, 1977.

Learning the role:
The transformation
from student to teacher

Paul G. Schempp
Kent State University

Student teaching is an exercise many have experienced. Student teaching is also an institution with which many of us hold affiliation. Most importantly, student teaching has proven to be a fertile medium for research on teaching in physical education. The research in student teaching to date can be classified into two general camps. The first views student teaching as experiences contributing to the development of better teachers. Thus, research attempts to legitimate techniques and methods for effective teaching (Boehm, 1974; Dodds, 1975; Getty, 1977). The second approach regards student teaching as coercive by passively and unconsciously socializing teachers into traditional roles (Burlingame, 1972; Hoy, 1967; Templin, 1979; Templin, 1981). The common limitation in both these perspectives is the failure to illuminate interactions of student teaching with the environmental factors in the gymnasium. Furthermore, studies have viewed the student teacher as a source of manipulation, an object to be manipulated by the researcher or by a selected socializing variable.

Unfortunately, such research fails to consider the student teacher as part of the environment. Thus, we do not see the student teaching experience from the perspective of the student teacher. We do not come to know and understand how the prospective teacher mediates the environment to give meaning to his/her experiences. In short, we have little insight as to what the student teacher learns. As Zeichner (1980) stated:

> If we want field-based experiences to contribute to the development of thoughtful and reflective teachers, then we must focus our concerns on the quality of these experiences as they are actually implemented in the field. In this regard, we need more research that seeks to illuminate what is learned during these experiences as they are now constituted. (p. 52)

Therefore, this study attempts to understand how physical education students learn the role of physical education teacher. How do they transform from student to teacher through the student teaching experience? What experiences and incidents do the student teachers encounter and how do they give them meaning? Specifically, two research questions will frame the focus of this study on role transformation through student teaching. First, what modes of student interaction lead to role satisfaction for the prospective teacher? Secondly, what modes of student interaction lead to role competence for the novice teacher?

No single research method can provide all the answers regarding teaching in physical education. One method that seemed useful for answering the concerns of this study was the critical incident technique. This method was clearly explained by Flanagan (1954), who saw the value of this technique as:

> rather than collecting opinions, hunches and estimates, [the critical incident technique] obtains a record of specific behaviors from those in the best position to make the necessary observations and evaluations. (p. 355)

Thus, in physical education we may analyze the specific gymnasium events identified by student teachers as having significant impact on their role as physical education teachers.

The available population for this investigation consisted of 20 Kent State University physical education student teachers. All student teaching was conducted during the spring 1982 semester. The student teachers ranged in age from 20 to 25 and none had teaching experience prior to those associated with undergraduate preparation.

Data were collected during the second, sixth, and ninth week of the 10-week experience, the data collection instrument being a critical incident report form. Using this form, students were asked to report two specific incidents that occurred during their student teaching, one dealing with role satisfaction and the other with role competence. A total of 301 incidents were reported.

Data analysis in the critical incident technique served to summarize and describe the data as efficiently and accurately as possible. Analysis required the recognition and identification of recurring and consistent trends or patterns in the data. In reviewing the data, four patterns appeared consistent. These patterns, once identified and labeled, formed the data classification scheme for this study. The first identified pattern was the language coding system employed by student teachers to describe the incidents; this classification was labeled Incident Descriptors. A second pattern was the number and structure of individuals involved in the reported incidents; this classification system was titled Incident Involvement. Thirdly, the incidents appeared to clearly refer to specific domains of student behavior and activity, and this pattern formed the classification Incident Domain. The final pattern appeared after analysis of the second and third patterns. It was a combination of the two previous patterns and thus was called the Incident Involvement X Domain classification.

After the classification systems were established, data were again reviewed for trends within the classifications. These trends formed the categories for each classification system. For the Incident Descriptor classification, 88 words or phrases were identified as potential categories. After two passes through the data, those categories with a frequency of 10 or greater were used for analysis. The descriptor categories are reported in Table 1. The incidents reported involved either the entire class, a group of students, an individual student, or only the teacher. Thus, the four categories comprising the Incident Involvement were: class, group, individual, and teacher. The categories comprising the Incident Domain classification included cognitive, social, emotional, and psychomotor. The final classification system was a combination of two previous systems. Therefore, the categories for the Incident Involvement X Domain classification consisted of 16 possible category combinations of the previous two systems.

Once the four classification systems and their respective categories were derived, the next procedure was validation. Twenty incidents were randomly selected from the available 301. These incidents were then analyzed by this investigator and two judges not affiliated with this study. All 20 incidents were classified and categorized identically by the three individuals.

The classification and categories were then used to analyze the data in light of the research questions. Each of the subject-reported incidents related to one of the two research questions. Therefore, data analysis re-

Table 1

Incident Descriptor Categories

Rank	Descriptor	Frequency
1	Activity	69
2	Feel	51
3	Work	33
4	Time	31
5	Teacher	29
6	Tell	28
7	Lesson	22
8	Ask/question	20
9	Help	18
10	Listen	17
10	Detention	17
10	Teach	17
13	Know/understand	15
13	Learn	15
13	Enjoy	15
13	Teacher try	15
17	Sit	14
17	Talk	14
17	"I have (had) to. . ."	17
17	Progress/improve	14
21	Discipline	13
22	Plan	12
22	Involve/participate	12
22	Respect	12
25	Play	11
26	Frustrate	10
26	Directions	10

quired that the two discrete incidents be analyzed separately using the established systems.

The first research question asked: What modes of student interactions led to role satisfaction for the prospective teacher? Describing role satisfaction most often involved a description of a teacher-approved activity such as a game, sport, or skill performance. The exact nature of the activity was not necessarily described. Apparently, the importance was not in the activity itself, but rather in the student engagement of that activity. Lortie (1975) found similar results as teachers in his study overwhelmingly cited task-related outcomes in describing teaching satisfaction.

Student enjoyment and asking questions were tied for second rank in student teachers' role satisfaction descriptions. Ranking fourth and fifth were student work and teacher feelings. In summarizing the descriptors,

Table 2

Role Satisfaction

Rank	Classification category	Frequency
Incident Descriptors		
1	Teacher approved activity	35
2	Student ask/question	10
2	Student enjoy	10
4	Student work	9
5	Teacher feel	7
Incident Involvement		
1	Class	47
2	Individual	30
3	Group	10
4	Teacher	1
Incident Domain		
1	Emotional	39
2	Social	27
3	Cognitive	12
4	Psychomotor	9
Incident Involvement X Domain		
1	Individual-emotional	19
2	Class-social	17
3	Class-emotional	15
4	Class-cognitive	8
5	Class-psychomotor	7

student teachers appeared to derive satisfaction from their teaching role when students were working, enjoying and asking questions about an activity the teacher felt was appropriate.

Role satisfaction most often occurred for the student teachers when they were interacting with the entire class. Events occurring with individual students appeared next most satisfying. Events occurring with groups of students or without students seemed to provide little satisfaction for the prospective teacher.

The emotional domain of student actions was most often the focus of incidents leading to student teacher role satisfaction. Student emotional behaviors were defined as attitudes or feelings expressed or perceived relative to self, others, or events. The social domain was also a significant medium for role satisfaction. Student social domain was defined as a student's compliance or noncompliance with teacher-approved codes and rules of interactions with others. The two areas often said to be major purposes for physical education, the cognitive and psychomotor domains, seemed to hold little potential for student teacher role satisfaction. Cognitive domain was defined as student thought process, comprehension, or understanding. The psychomotor domain referred to student physical movements approved by the teacher.

The final classification system focused on both incident involvement and domain. The three top ranking categories were separated by less than five incident frequencies, and thus seemed to hold near equal satisfaction for the prospective teachers. Interacting with an individual student on an emotional level led to the greatest amount of role satisfaction. Interacting with an entire class in social and emotional domains, respectively, were also incidents leading to role satisfaction. Class cognitive and class psychomotor behavior provided little satisfaction for these teachers.

Based on the evidence available through this study, it was concluded that the teaching role was most satisfying for student teachers when the students, both individually and as a class, socially and emotionally engaged in a teacher-approved activity. This finding is consistent with and supports conclusions reached by Iannaccone (1963) and Lortie (1975).

The second research question asked: What modes of student interaction led to role competence for a student teacher? Describing role competence incidents most often involved a description of teacher-approved activity. This finding was similar to descriptions of role satisfaction. Incidents involving the teacher-planned lesson were ranked second. In this vein, the student teachers often described "successful" adjustments in lesson plans, having lessons "improve" with practice, or having planned lessons go "smoothly." This implied that role competence is achieved when the technical aspects of the lesson plan were mastered. The lesson plan was seen as a tool to be mastered so the class can operate with efficiency, control and prediction. Teachers' feelings ranked a close third, followed by an equally close student work category. Both these categories were also found in the top five rankings for role satisfaction, implying a relationship between role competence and satisfaction.

The fifth incident descriptor was teacher-tell. This category usually referred to teaching methodology. Telling students exactly what to do, when to do it and for how long, and having students do as they are told, seem to be hallmarks of role competence according to these student teachers. This belief appears compatible with the desire for classroom efficiency, control, and prediction. Further, it supports Hoffman's (1971) contention that "selection of a teaching style is probably determined more by expediency, practicality and conditions which are essentially unrelated to the teaching act than by the potential of the method for helping the students to learn" (p. 54).

In summarizing the descriptors, student teachers saw role competence as telling students to work on activities teachers felt were appropriate within the teacher-planned lesson, and then having students do as they

Table 3

Role Competence

Rank	Classification category	Frequency
Incident Descriptors		
1	Teacher approved activity	24
2	Teacher planned lessons	13
3	Teacher feel	12
4	Student work	11
5	Teacher tell	7
Incident Involvement		
1	Class	46
2	Individual	17
3	Teacher	8
4	Group	7
Incident Domain		
1	Social	27
2	Emotional	26
3	Cognitive	9
4	Psychomotor	8
Incident Involvement X Domain		
1	Class-social	20
2	Class-emotional	13
3	Individual-emotional	9
4	Class-cognitive	8
5	Class-psychomotor	5

are told. It was curious to note that role competency was described in terms of active teacher behaviors and relatively passive student behaviors. The role competence of a teacher appeared then to be the almost exclusive responsibility of the student teacher, with little regard for any outside factors. Burlingame (1972) reached a similar conclusion when he reported:

> If the new teacher learns anything from the world of work, it is that he operates alone and is rewarded alone. His experiences in the classroom are what count, for in that world he receives little or no support from fellow teachers, administrators or trainers. (p. 54)

Incidents indicative of role competence most often involved the whole class. Ranking a distant second were incidents involving a single student. Ranking still further behind were teacher and group categories. It therefore seemed that role competence was established through interaction with the entire class.

In analyzing Incident Domain, the social and emotional categories ranked a very close first and second, respectively. Once again, the cognitive and psychomotor category frequencies did not equal the frequencies of either of the first two categories. As with role satisfaction, the psychomotor category ranked last. It therefore seemed that competence as a physical education teacher had little to do with the ability to teach motor skills. The social and emotional behaviors of students in physical education appeared to be the primary concern of a competent teacher. In this regard, social behavior most often referred to in the reported incidents dealt with student compliance with school- or teacher-established codes of behavior. The emotional behavior most often referred to student attitudes toward the teacher selected activities. It seemed a competent teacher was one who could select activities or plan lessons in which all the students would participate and enjoy.

In analyzing the incidents by involvement and domain, class-social was predominant. This category held a slight advantage over the second ranked, class-emotional. In addition to selecting activities that prompted involvement and enjoyment, competent teaching incidents also incorporated mass conformity. Illustrative of this were incidents reported whereby the students would "follow directions," "pay attention and listen," and "show respect for me as a teacher." Incidents occurring with an individual student in the emotional domain, which ranked first in role satisfaction, ranked third in role competence. Class cognitive and class psychomotor categories ranked fourth and fifth, respectively. This was consistent with role satisfaction and offered further evidence of a relationship between teaching role satisfaction and competence. This consistent finding lent support to Lortie's (1975) conclusion that teachers "fused the idea of work gratification and the idea of work goals; they made little distinction between deriving satisfaction from their work and reaching classroom objectives" (p. 103).

Based on data analysis, it was concluded that student teachers believed themselves competent when they told students to work on a teacher-planned activity and the entire class responded with social and emotional behavior the teacher felt was appropriate. This finding remained consistent with other research on student teaching, particularly those completed by Burlingame (1972) and Templin (1979, 1981).

The results and conclusions of this investigation appeared consistent with the available literature on student teaching. As with most research, the completion of this investigation raised many more questions for the investigator than it answered. One such question was, what kind of environment exists in the gymnasium? Secondly, why do student teachers feel compelled to control and dominate the people in that environment? Is it any wonder that student attitudes toward physical education remain so poor? How many of us would prosper, learn, and grow in a situation that existed to dominate and suppress our thoughts, feelings, and social interactions? Are these the gymnasiums one finds in a democratic society? Perhaps if we can achieve a greater consciousness on the ways teachers develop perspectives on teaching through field experiences, we can design opportunities that encourage teachers to empathize with children, to create lively and varied learning experiences, and to be analytic about the teaching decisions they make.

References

BOEHM, J.M. *The effects of a competency-based teaching program on junior high school physical education student teachers and their pupils.* Unpublished doctoral dissertation, Ohio State University, 1974.

BRUNELLE, J., Tousignant, M., & Pieron, M. Student teachers' perceptions of cooperating teachers' effectiveness. *Journal of Teaching in Physical Education*, 1981, pp. 80-87. (Introductory issue)

BURLINGAME, M. Socialization constructs and the teaching of teachers. *Quest*, 1972, **18**, 40-56.

DODDS, P. *A behavioral, competency-based peer assessment model for student teacher supervision in elementary physical education.* Unpublished doctoral dissertation, Ohio State University, 1975.

FLANAGAN, J.C. The critical incident technique, *Psychological Bulletin*, 1954, **4**, 327-358.

GETTY, H.L. *Effects of instruction and supervision in interaction analysis on the teaching behavior of student teachers.* Unpublished master's thesis, Ithaca College, 1977.

HOFFMAN, S.J. Traditional methodology: Prospects for change, *Quest*, 1971, **15**, 51-57.

HOY, W. Organizational socialization: The student teacher and pupil control ideology. *Journal of Education Research*, 1967, **61**, 152-155.

IANNACCONE, L. Student teaching: A transitional stage in the making of a teacher, *Theory Into Practice*, 1963, **2**, 73-80.

LORTIE, D. *Schoolteacher: A sociological study.* Chicago: University of Chicago Press, 1975.

TEMPLIN, T. Occupational socialization and the physical education student teacher, *Research Quarterly*, 1979, **50**, 482-493.

TEMPLIN, T. Student as socializing agent, *Journal of Teaching in Physical Education*, 1981, pp. 71-79. (Introductory issue)

ZEICHNER, K.M. Myths and realities: Field-based experiences in preservice teacher education. *Journal of Teacher Education*, 1980, pp. 45-54.

Student teacher as social strategist

Linda K. Marrs
University of Texas

Thomas J. Templin
Purdue University

Student teaching has been described as the "one indisputably essential element in professional education" (Conant, 1963, p. 142). However short and parochial student teaching may seem in its role as a socializing agent, it certainly has been characterized by preservice and in-service teachers alike as one of the most valuable, useful, and earthy experiences during one's professional training.

Associated with this practicum is an area of research that examines the influence of student teaching on the attitudes, knowledge, values, and behavior of the neophyte (Burlingame, 1972; Zeichne, Note 1, Note 2). Specifically, research on teacher socialization has ta':en an important role within research on teaching in general and more recently, as an area of inquiry within physical education (Lawson, in press, Locke, 1979; Templin, 1979, 1981). Such research is aimed at understanding the various processes that influence one's development in the role of physical educator, that is, the influence of pre-training, training, and occupational factors that are "intended to change the neophyte into a mature practitioner" (Burlingame, 1972, p. 40).

This paper reports the results of an exploratory study (Marrs, 1982) that addressed the issue of the occupational socialization of the physical education student teacher. Unlike the majority of socialization studies, this study operated from the theoretical premise that although student teachers are necessarily constrained by the social-structural limitations of the schools and programs in which they teach, it should be recognized that student teachers may "at the same time play an active role in shaping their identities, often in ways which contradict the dominant norms and values which pervade the school setting" (Zeichner, Note 2, p. 3). In contrast to many functionalist studies of teacher socialization which suggest that student teachers are social puppets, easily manipulated to adhere to the basic value orientations and routines of various programs in which they teach, this study set to explore the dialectical nature of student teaching. Again, such a position not only recognizes the power of institutional constraints and biography (Templin, 1979; Zeichner, 1981), but more importantly, it recognizes the potential of self-determinism by the student teacher, who develops his or her own teaching identity through individual autonomy and situational adjustment. Unlike the submissive caricatures of student teachers that many studies portray, this study set out to describe if and how student teachers were involved in a process of self-socialization.

Lacey's social strategies paradigm

To investigate this process, the research turned to a useful model developed by Lacey (1977) that recognizes the dialectical nature of teacher socialization. Lacey forwards a social strategy concept which accounts for a "purposive, guiding, autonomous element within individual behavior" (1977, p. 67), as one interacts within the constraints of a specific situation and develops "action-idea" systems wherein individual purpose is accounted for. Lacey delineates three basic strategies student teachers use that reflect autonomous behavior.

One strategy proposed by Lacey and revealed in his research is that of *strategic compliance*, in which the individual complies with the authority figure's definition and constraints of a situation but retains reservations about them. This strategy is synonymous with strategies such as fronting (Zeichner, Note 2), and impression management (Goffman, 1959; Snyder, 1981) in which an individual consciously conforms to expectations and norms in order to control the image and impressions they project to others. These strategies, again, typically contradict one's behavioral preferences, yet are used in order to avoid conflict and to assure favorable sanctions from significant others. It is this distinction that is critical. The very fact that the neophyte presents an image to superordinates that is contrary to the image he or she would prefer to present is evidence that the socialization process is not complete.

A second strategy identified by Lacey, *internalized adjustment*, implies individual compliance, but compliance to constraints that the individual believes to be for the best. Although the behavioral product of internalized adjustment may be no different than that of strategic compliance, the underlying difference is that within internalized adjustment the individual develops an accompanying value commitment to the norms of the situation. Not only is one seen to be "good," but one really is good in relation to a value commitment to situational norms. It is here that the socialization influence of the setting and its agents may be thought of as most potent.

Finally, *strategic redefinition* implies that the student teacher is actively trying to change the range of acceptable behaviors within the school or physical education setting. Change is achieved, as Lacey suggests, "by causing or enabling those with formal power to change their interpretations of what is [or should or could be] happening in a situation" (1977, p. 73). Although student teachers have no formal power, strategic redefinition is typically manifested through their introduction of new ideas or methods to significant others such as the cooperating teacher. Hence, strategic redefinition not only allows the student teacher to behave autonomously, but may bring about change in the behavior of significant others and their definition of the instructional setting.

Hence, Lacey's social strategies model served as the basis for understanding the dialectical versus functionalist nature of teacher socialization. It should be clear that the intent of this study was to examine how student teachers might manipulate the social setting while being confronted with the constraints of various situations. Consequently, this research had a two-fold purpose: first, to identify and describe those social strategies as proposed by Lacey to which student teachers defer when confronted by the demands of the socialization setting and its agents, and secondly, to identify and describe other strategies beyond those proposed by Lacey (1977).

Results

The data, obtained through a series of three interviews with five randomly selected student teachers and their cooperating teachers and analyzed using a taxonomic method (Spradley, 1979), revealed that the student teachers did, in fact, engage in social strategizing in various situations at different times. The following presentation of representative interview data illustrates the use of these strategies.

Strategies compliance
In relation to strategic compliance, it is important initially to note that, in all cases, student teachers were presented the option and were en-

couraged to act autonomously. That is, cooperating teachers said that student teachers were free to explore the role of physical educator and to apply those instructional strategies that they deemed appropriate. In essence, beyond curricular and some managerial constraints, student teachers had the option to set their own instructional destiny—they were free to establish their own teaching identity.

> I'm going to give her as much freedom as I can—she's free to try new things and I would hope she tries to incorporate new ideas and handle discipline problems herself. (CT-D)

> I expect her to experience as much as possible and to be her own individual —never to rely on me. (CT-M)

Based on this data, strategic compliance was not expected to be a strategy to which student teachers would necessarily defer. They would not be forced to develop chameleon-like images as a utilitarian response to situational dictates.

With few exceptions, this seemed to be the case. Although student teachers maintained the same class routines (i.e., management and instructional processes) common to the programs in which they instructed, such adherence did not appear linked to strategic compliance. Rather, continuity in terms of a traditional model of physical education (Hoffman, 1971) seemed to represent self-direction or autonomy by the student teacher. One should be reminded that strategic compliance implies that an individual has qualms about compliance; in this study, interview data revealed few instances where student teachers had qualms about their instructional roles or role expectations.

> I can't control what is going on. I have to go along with them to keep the peace. I often caught myself falling into their shoes. They all are kind of laid back and don't really get into the class when they are teaching. I caught myself acting like _____ and _____. I don't want to be like that. I found myself slipping into the command style of teaching. I wish I could have used different styles. (ST-Ju)

Equally, little evidence was documented wherein student teachers offered alternatives to how they would behave or how they would structure the physical education setting.

> I would be more strict than I am—be more tough. Maybe getting them out of class or something 'cause you get to the point where you're always controlling the guys screwing up and don't have time to praise the kids doing it right. (ST-R)

> I'm easier than her—I slack up when she's not around. (ST-At)

> I wouldn't have a dress code. Shorts, shirts, and shoes are good enough for me. (ST-Ja)

It appeared that in these select cases, with one possible exception, student teachers agreed with the normal way of life in the gymnasium. Certainly the authors are well aware of the claim that the student teacher has no option other than conformity when faced with the possibility of retribution from significant others. That is, if one doesn't behave like a good student teacher, one will be punished. Such a claim is unfounded here; none of the student teachers expressed fear of negative sanctions for failing to comply, nor did cooperating teachers indicate that student teachers would be reprimanded or punished for nonconformity.

> I feel in charge and tell her what I'm doing. I feel comfortable telling her what I think. (ST-At)

> I'm not really worrying about a grade. I'm concentrating on my teaching and being me. (ST-Ja)

> I definitely wasn't going through student teaching just to get a grade. I wanted to try some things I had learned in school. (ST-R)

As pointed out earlier, cooperating teachers said they expected student teachers to do their own thing and it just so happened that, in most instances, doing one's own thing was compatible with the dominant patterns of gymnasium life. As one student teacher stated, "We do about the same thing. Seems like our styles are the same. It seems we are alike — not that I try to or have to copy things, I don't."

Although student teachers were not forced toward strategic compliance, this is not to conclude that strategic compliance wouldn't be a behavioral option in situations demanding strict conformity. As some data suggest, student teachers were quite prepared to comply strategically.

> I would have been real upset and it would have bothered me, but I would have done whatever she said. It was for a grade. (ST-Ju)

> I would have said "Okay." I probably wouldn't have fought her. I wanted to pass. (ST-An)

Internalized adjustment

Most functionalist studies on teacher socialization indicate significant shifts in the attitudes and values of beginning and student teachers toward various aspects of instruction or the schooling process in general. Through the use of various psychometric inventories, attitudinal shifts from one extreme toward another are typically reported and linked to the influence of the various socializing agents with whom the individual interacts or observes. For example, this has certainly been the case in the study of pupil control ideology as individuals shift from humanism toward custodialism (Templin, 1979; Willower, 1975). Such shifts may be representative of internalized adjustment in which student teachers not only follow the suggestions or mandates of their cooperating teachers, but develop beliefs that such behavior should be valued.

> [CT] made a big impression on me. After so many years he is still trying to get something positive out of everyone. This is how I want to handle my students — get something positive out of them — even if they're losers — don't write people off. (ST-R)

> She suggested to be more open with the students, to talk to them more. When I talk to them, it seems more that they like me and do things I want to do and I don't have many discipline problems. (ST-An)

> I learned how to socialize with the kids. [CT] has a great relationship with the students. This has rubbed off on me and how I want to treat kids — caring for them and having an interest in each kid. (ST-Ja)

Although documented in only a few instances, an interpersonal relations theme emerged as a few student teachers internalized the value of establishing more caring, warmer, and less distant interpersonal ties with their students. In essence, as student teachers complied with cooperating teacher suggestions to get to know and care for their students and to establish greater rapport with them, these student teachers developed and internalized more positive values toward the interpersonal dimensions of teaching.[1]

It must be remembered, as supported earlier, that internalized adjustment in these cases did not seem to reflect the presentation of a facade. In other words, having the freedom to behave independently without the fear of negative sanctions, student teachers appeared to critically evaluate compliance in terms of their own volition rather than as an act of strategic compliance. Finally, internalized adjustment reflects the strategy of studentship in which student teachers are not only able to assess how to behave, but to judge whether those values attached to behavior should be internalized. As one student teacher indicated, "I found myself starting to teach like . . . . She has a negative attitude . . . . I found myself with that attitude . . . . I caught myself." Thus, as suggested by this quote, conformity to values and behavior may vary quite independently.

Strategic redefinition

The third strategy within Lacey's model, strategic redefinition, also emerged from the interview data. Not surprisingly, this strategy was rare-

---

[1]Even though internalized adjustment may result in a change in one's attitudes and behavior, the change may not necessarily persist during or throughout one's "in-service" experience. The same may be true in the strategic redefinition of a school or class setting.

ly employed by student teachers. Redefinition was defined subtly in relation to a cooperating teacher's favorable recognition of new ideas, drills,
or methods of teaching brought to the gym by the student teacher, that
is, the acknowledgement of something that might be valuable to the
cooperating teacher in his or her own teaching.

> [CT] was timing students on sprints. I suggested that we use more stop-
> watches and have the students time each other. At first, Maria didn't like the
> idea; but before she could react, I reorganized it so they were timing each
> other. It worked. (ST-A)

> She taught me to try my hardest and to be more enthusiastic when I'm
> around the kids. (CT-M)

> Sometimes he underestimates kids. I've shown him new ways that enable the
> kids to do things (gymnastics) he thought they weren't able to do. I also
> showed him some new drills for volleyball. (ST-R)

One might think that persistence in redefining a situation from a position of weakness, like that of a student teacher, could lead to serious
problems for the neophyte; but again, because of the autonomy afforded
student teachers, those few instances of redefinition did not seem to be a
problem. In fact, it seemed to validate one major expectation held by
cooperating teachers — that of behavioral exploration or self-direction by
the student teacher.

Selective modeling, studentship, and self-legitimation

Beyond those strategies just presented, the data revealed the presence of
other strategies that illuminate the dialectical nature of the socialization
process. For example, throughout student teaching situations arose
wherein student teachers were actively involved in selective modeling
(Bucher & Stelling, 1977; Copeland, 1978). Through observation of or
discussion with significant others, student teachers made conscious decisions about those cooperating teacher traits and behaviors that they
chose to emulate, as well as those that they chose to ignore or reject.

> I found myself starting to teach like Jenny. She has a negative attitude and I
> found myself with that attitude. I caught myself and stopped. (ST-Ju)

> I had to incorporate a lot of things he did at first (class routines), and then I
> added my influence at different stages. I wanted to learn as much as possible
> from him, especially the part about getting something positive out of
> everyone. He really has a way with kids because he makes them feel like
> somebody. I take what he says and do what I want. (ST-B)

> She has her own style. She doesn't like the way I do some things and she
> doesn't do them. (CT-P)

This strategy is closely linked to the strategies of studentship (Olesen & Whittaker, 1968) and self-legitimation (Bucher & Stelling, 1977; Friebus, 1977) in which student teachers, again, evaluate not only their own performance but also the performance and suggestions of cooperating teachers as a means of formulating or validating their own behavior. Hence, student teachers actively control the level and direction of their efforts according to their own criteria of experience.

> I listened to what she has to say and if I like it, I'll try it. If I don't, I won't. I have my own way. She never smiles—she believes in that saying, "Don't smile until Christmas." I like how she levels with students. I agree with that and try. You should tell them why you do something. (ST-At)

> During the gymnastics unit, she was real hard on me. She told me I did a lot of things wrong—said that my lessons won't always be a total flop. I didn't think it was a total flop. That made me nervous, but I didn't change my plans or way to teach. (ST-Ju)

As Bucher and Stelling (1977) state, "Although signals from others are important to trainees, there are no cues more important than those trainees derive from looking at themselves" (p. 166).

Summary

This paper has presented some descriptive data that moves beyond the functionalist approach of many studies on teacher socialization. Any theory of socialization must be able to account for the rejection of norms, and this research seems to lead evidence away from an over-socialized concept of man (Wrong, 1961).

Although this research was purposely remiss in examining the influence of anticipatory or professional socialization factors, which probably accounted for student teacher behavior to some degree within the occupational setting, the study was able to document how student teachers defer to a combination of strategies promoting individual autonomy. In the cases studied, self-directed behavior was both congruent and contrary to the norms and role expectations of the socialization setting and its agents. Obviously, self-direction is the essence of this study and it supports, to some degree, of course, the theoretical bases of Lacey's dialectical model. Certainly the freedom granted to student teachers from the onset of their experience, as well as each student teacher's ability to positively execute the role of physical educator, added to this self-direction, but this does not negate the presence of social strategizing as one follows internal cues of behavior.

Reference Notes

1. Zeichner, K.M. *The student teaching experience: A methodological critique of the research.* Unpublished manuscript, 1978.
2. Zeichner, K.M. *The dialetics of teacher socialization.* Paper presented at the meeting of the Association of Teacher Educators, Orlando, FL, February 1979.

References

BUCHER, R., & Stelling, J. *Becoming professional.* Beverly Hills: Sage, 1977.

BURLINGAME, M. Socialization constructs and the teaching of teachers. *Quest*, 1972, **18**, 40-56.

CONANT, J. *The education of American teachers.* New York: McGraw Hill, 1963.

COPELAND, W. Processes mediating the relationship between cooperating teacher behavior and student teacher classroom performance. *Journal of Educational Psychology*, 1978, **70**, 95-100.

FRIEBUS, R. Agents of Socialization in student teaching. *Journal of Educational Research*, 1977, **7**, 263-268.

GOFFMAN, E. *The presentation of self in everyday life.* Garden City, NY: Double-Anchor, 1959.

HOFFMAN, S. Traditional methodology: Prospects for change. *Quest*, 1971, **15**, 51-57.

LACEY, C. *The socialization of teachers.* London: Metheun, 1977.

LAWSON, H. Toward a model of teacher socialization in physical education. *Journal of Teaching in Physical Education*, in press.

LOCKE, L. Supervision, schools, and student teaching: Why things stay the same. *The Academy Papers*, 1979, pp. 65-74.

MARRS, L. Student teacher as social strategist. Unpublished master's thesis, Purdue University, 1982.

OLESEN, V., & Whittaker, E. *The silent dialogue: A study in the social psychology.* San Francisco: Jossey-Bass, 1968.

SNYDER, M. Impression management: The self in social interaction. In Wrightsman & C. Deaux (Eds.), *Social Psychology in the 80's.* Monterey, CA: Brooks/Cole, 1981.

SPRADLEY, J. *The ethnographic interview.* New York: Holt, Rinehart, & Winston, 1979.

TEMPLIN, T. Occupational socialization and the physical education student teacher. *Research Quarterly*, 1979, **50**, 482-493.

TEMPLIN, T. Student as socializing agent. *Journal of Teaching in Physical Education*, 1981, pp. 71-79. (Introductory issue)

WILLOWER, D. Some comments on inquiries on schools and pupil control. *Teacher College Record*, 1975, **77**, 219-230.

WRONG, D. The oversocialized conception of man in modern sociology. *American Sociological Review*, 1961, **26**, 183-193.

ZEICHNER, K. Myths and realities: Field-based experiences in pre-service teacher education. *Journal of Teacher Education*, 1980, **31**, 45-54.

ZEICHNER, K., & Grant, C. Biography and social structure in the socialization of students: A re-examination of the pupil control ideologies of student teachers. *Journal of Education for Teaching*, 1981, **7**, 298-314.

Section four
Preservice and inservice professional preparation

The professional preparation process, particularly at the preservice level, has often been questioned in relation to its ability to promote teacher effectiveness. Two basic questions seem to persist: How can we train prospective teachers so that preparation has a strong positive influence on the trainees and, as a result, on their students? And, after these individuals become teachers, how can we meet their needs and concerns for professional growth? The four papers in this section address these questions to varying degrees, and offer guidance in structuring and evaluating preservice and inservice professional preparation processes.

The first paper—by Andrew Hawkins, Robert Wiegand, and Carl Bahneman—provides an evaluation design for examining the influence of the professional preparation process. Conceptually based in a diagnostic-prescriptive model of professional preparation and supported through faculty concensus, the authors set forth the components and significant principles from which to examine the training process. For example, they describe a sequential process in which data (i.e., ALT data, student and teacher behavior data, and pupil performance outcomes) are collected in various instructional settings throughout an individual's preparation. Finally, they point out how the evaluation data can be used for purposes other than program evaluation. Through the process, data provide an impetus for program and student behavior change, and a means for better understanding and refining the research on teaching.

In his paper, Herbert Haag describes a project in the Federal Republic of Germany whereby the aims and objectives of teacher training were identified, and from which a competency-based model of teacher training evolved. Through a content analysis of literature related to curriculum, instruction, teacher training, and sport pedagogy, Haag discusses four competency areas that are critical in the development of a physical education teacher: sportive competency, scientific competency, political competency, and teaching competency. Haag discusses the implications of a curriculum design that integrates the four areas.

The paper by Frank Rife shifts the attention to inservice education or staff development. Rife describes various characteristics of effective staff development, and then discusses a three-phase model developed for physical educators in the state of Massachusetts. He identifies the major concerns of physical educators, that is, the image of physical education and alternative careers. And he identifies the strengths of practitioners as resources in the staff development process. In Phase 2, Rife discusses the workshop or seminar, which addresses practitioner concerns both formally and informally. Here teachers are asked to assess any new concerns or to affirm their original responses. Rife summarizes by discussing plans to work with individual staffs and departments (phase three) and by citing the major contributions of staff development.

This section's final paper is by Susan Schwager and William Anderson, and illustrates their work in changing physical education programs in several New York school districts. They describe the Physical Education Program Development Center, which encourages teachers to evaluate their programs, identify needs for improvement, and to implement those improvements. Schwager and Anderson show how one program development activity, the Competency-Based Physical Education Project, served to upgrade elementary physical education in five school districts. The authors survey the project phases, the research methods used to assess each phase, program changes and student performance, and an assessment of project activities. The reader, then, is provided with an excellent example of the components and the benefits of inservice education.

The authors in this section offer principles and methods for examining both processes and, concerning inservice education, they illustrate how to enhance the professional growth of teachers.

Data-based evaluation of a physical education professional preparation program

Andrew Hawkins,
Robert Wiegand and Carl Bahneman
West Virginia University

This paper describes the data-based portion of the program evaluation design utilized by the Department of Professional Physical Education at West Virginia University. Our department has undergone significant change during the last 2 years with respect to the way our curriculum has been conceptualized, implemented, and evaluated. These changes climaxed with the writing of a training proposal in which we committed ourselves to utilizing data-based procedures to evaluate the effectiveness of the project.[1]

The design itself is not specifically a child of the training grant. It has developed into its present form during the last 2 years within the context of departmental programmatic revision. Moreover, the design was not

[1]Program to prepare regular physical educators to instruct West Virginia handicapped children. US Department of Education, Office of Special Education, Division of Personnel Preparation, Project No. 029CH20032A.

developed based on any established principles of program evaluation. However, several principles have emerged during the process on a more inductive basis. To a significant degree, these principles are what this paper is about, since we believe our design gains meaning when described in their light.

Conceptual foundation

During the fall of 1980, we found ourselves in what is perhaps an unusual situation. Four members of our professional physical education faculty had similar ideas on the conceptual basis for physical education and for professional preparation. Briefly stated, we all believed that the primary mission of physical education was to enhance the motor development of individuals across the life span.

In addition, we also agreed that for the instructional objectives related to the acquisition of individual skills, an individualized approach based on a diagnostic-prescriptive model was the most appropriate instructional strategy. Each of us had our own reasons for adopting individually prescribed instruction (IPI), but the common denominator involved our concern for mainstreaming exceptional children. We believed then, and do now, that the only way the direct integration of exceptional children could be accomplished — while at the same time providing appropriate skill-activity matches for both normal and disabled children — was to use some form of IPI.

This description of our assumptions was not intended to influence the conceptual foundation of any other program, nor even to defend our own. The point is that we largely agreed on *one* conceptual foundation, and this agreement was the first essential step in developing an evaluation design. It had been our collective experience that, regardless of how any training program appeared "on paper," what was actually taught was usually a function of the individual interests of faculty rather than a carefully reasoned and coherent statement of the fundamental mission of our profession. Sometimes faculty interests mesh quite nicely, but most often a coherent conceptual basis cannot readily be discerned from what is actually taught.

Hence, our first principle of evaluation design emerged: Establish a strong, coherent, conceptual basis for the training program. It is imperative that we know what kind of entity we are attempting to diagnose. The validity of any measure is arguable unless there is basic agreement about the nature of our profession and our program. Do all of our faculty understand and support the conceptual basis we have selected? Not entirely. However, no disagreements serious enough to create factions have arisen to date among our faculty. Concensus is nearly as important as principle (Smith, 1980).

Establishment of training competencies

We began to investigate ways in which our conceptual foundation could find its way into our teacher preparation curriculum. Our starting point was this simple question: What do our students have to do in order to enhance the motor development of all children? We established that, in general, students had to do three things: a) know the motor development needs of normal and exceptional children through the life span; b) select activities which can potentially meet those needs; and c) individualize instruction such that all children could engage in appropriate activities while in an integrated setting. Some courses in our curriculum were already addressing some of our concerns, whereas others needed only minor modification. However, significant content changes were implemented in the methods portion of our curriculum dealing primarily with the area of individualized instruction.

At this point we began to generate precise student outcomes for our instructional goals. In-depth program evaluations are often not undertaken due to the lack of clear student outcomes. In fact, what kind of teacher a program should produce is sometimes not apparent to the student. Even more often, however, students receive multiple contradictory messages about how they should behave as teachers (Smith, 1980), leaving them dangerously susceptible to adverse socializing influences. Those most likely to be swayed are those who don't have strong feelings about anything.

This, of course, marked another essential step in the development of our evaluation design, and the second principle emerged: Establish clear statements of performance outcomes. One of the primary reasons why many program evaluations center on job placement records and supervisor satisfaction ratings is that clear statements of how students should behave when they graduate are simply nonexistent. If there are no statements of performance outcomes, there is little to evaluate.

All of the performance outcomes we wrote essentially fell into the following categories: a) cognitive objectives relevant to knowing the motor needs of normal and exceptional individuals; b) cognitive objectives relevant to matching activities with needs; c) performance objectives relevant to the planning and implementation of individually prescribed instructional systems; and d) performance objectives relevant to the demonstration of generic teaching skills.

After viewing the multitude of performance objectives, we divided them among appropriate courses. Cognitive objectives relevant to motor needs of normal individuals throughout the life span were currently the focus of the motor learning/development course. The former adapted physical education course became primarily informational and currently deals with the motor development characteristics (needs) of special populations. The cognitive objectives regarding the needs-activity match were incorporated into the existing majors' activity sequence for secondary emphasis, and into two new elementary curriculum courses entitled Early Childhood Activities, and Middle Childhood Activities. The performance objectives were divided among the methods courses with IPI systems being the focus of the Elementary Methods course, while generic teaching skills became the core of the Secondary Methods course.

It was at this point that we came to a startling realization. Faculty with the interest and professional expertise to train these competencies lacked the time required to implement the training program with all of our majors. We were forced to swallow our pride, recognize that we couldn't do it alone, and seek extramural funding. It became obvious when analyzing the criteria by which federal funding agencies evaluate proposals that a significant portion of our project would be devoted to evaluating whether or not we had done what we said we would do. Since some of us had research interests in the area of behavior analysis, we were comfortable with a data-based approach to evaluation. We also believed that such an approach would make the proposal stronger, since we would be able to state what our students could do after leaving our program.

Planning the implementation of the evaluation design

If we really were going to devise a meaningful evaluation design, the question arose as to when and under what conditions would we collect data on our students. We decided to use a three-phase approach in our methods courses to assess the performance objectives.

The first phase of data collection was to take place in methods laboratories. Objectives were organized into units, and small group teaching simulations were planned in which students would demonstrate the competencies associated with each unit. After practicing the competencies in the simulations, students were to move to a check-out station. Students passing the check-out were deemed competent in a particular unit's objectives. Class peers were the simulation subjects for the Secondary Methods course. Elementary children were simulation subjects for the Elementary Methods course.

The next phase involved microteaching, which consumed approximately 50% of a semester's class time in each methods course. Microteaching involved individual students teaching both large and small groups. Secondary methods students taught their peers while elementary methods students taught elementary-age children.

The third phase involved field experiences. Students from both methods classes taught in the public schools. In addition to these field experiences, we arranged four on-campus clinics for exceptional youngsters to be staffed by graduate students and undergraduate methods students.

We established a mainstreamed motor development clinic for normal and mentally handicapped elementary children, a bowling program for physically disabled children, a swim program for emotionally handicapped children, and a sports camp for adolescent retarded youths.

Data were to be generated during each phase. Mastery of the specific competencies demonstrated during laboratory check-outs were to take the form of competency checklists. Category systems for both teacher and student behaviors were to be employed for microteaching, field experiences, and clinics.

In addition to all this evaluation, we proposed to follow some of our students 2 years into their teaching positions and compare their teaching methods with those of our graduates who had not been through the revised training sequence. Then we could say that perhaps our graduates who trained under the new curriculum behaved differently than those who graduated prior to its institution. At any rate, it is of little value to train competencies if those competencies are not retained and demonstrated when students become teachers. All of this brings us to our third principle: Give students numerous opportunities to be evaluated. We planned to have each student evaluated during every phase of his or her education, even during the phase after graduation.

Development of category systems

When we began to develop our category systems, we employed the only principle that came to us deductively. It made good sense that we should collect information on all behaviors relevant to the instructional process. The fourth principle states: Design evaluations to be as comprehensive as possible. Essentially, we desired to have a mutually exclusive category system encompassing every student and teacher behavior that could possibly be emitted, avoiding at all costs the category labeled "other." This task was relatively straightforward as far as student behavior was concerned. We selected and slightly modified Academic Learning Time - Physical Education (ALT-PE; Siedentop, Tousignant, & Parker, 1980) because it includes mutually exclusive student behavior categories, is simple and easy to learn, and it has been largely accepted as a useful instrument by many teaching researchers.

The teacher behavior category system was more difficult. We have focused on teacher behavior for so long that the list of behaviors that have served as variables for research is endless. We began by listing all the teacher behaviors that might be relevent to instruction; we designed methods of recording these behaviors and recruited 15 students from the educational psychology department to experiment with various data collection schemes. Hoping that a set of reliable, mutually exclusive, and comprehensive behaviors would emerge from the morass of variables, we were sorely disappointed. It just seemed that any system we could establish was too complicated to be learned easily and interpreted in any meaningful way for students.

After abandoning that project, we sat in the stands during one of our clinics and began to make anecdotal records of what each teacher did during an instructional session. After several days of observation, it seemed that all teachers engaged in essentially 11 general behavior categories (Table 1). We recognized that many categories could be further subdivided but that to do so would render the instrument too complex to be useful in student feedback and too difficult to learn data collection easily. We were finally satisfied with our teacher behavior categories and were already pleased with the simplicity of ALT-PE. So, if any principle emerged from these experiences, it was this: Design category systems that are simple enough to be learned easily by data collectors and understood by students, yet specific enough to provide useful evaluative and research data (Principle 5).

In addition to being satisfied with the simplicity of the category systems, we found that they had other advantages. First, neither ALT-PE nor the teacher behavior system were so specific as to dominate either a student's or a teacher's personality. There are a multitude of ways to be "on task" (an ALT-PE behavior category) just as there are a multitude of ways to give "reinforcement" (a teacher behavior category). Thus, the category systems provided a framework that allows us to change behavior without drastically affecting an individual's personality. Principle 6 states: Design category systems that are flexible enough to allow useful information to be presented irrespective of the personalities being observed. A second advantage was that both category systems could be used in virtually any physical education setting. It's not that we would expect the same data profile in preschools as in high schools, but that meaningful information can be generated irrespective of the setting. Principle 7 emerges: Design the minimum number of category systems that generalize across the maximum number of settings.

The next step in the design process revolved around the observation format to be used in collecting data. With no deliberate intention of departing from the interval/time sample tradition, we decided to purchase two electronic behavioral data processors.[2] The primary disadvantages of selecting the electronic format involved cost and the inability to make valid data comparisons with popular interval data used elsewhere. We concluded, however, that the sheer capacity and versatility for collecting data using the electronic format outweighed its disadvantages. For instance, in any single observation session, for up to 20 behaviors,

---

[2]Datamyte® 801, Electro General Corporation, 14960 Industrial Road, Minnetonka, MN 55343.

Table 1
Teaching Behavior Code Definitions

Behavior	Definition
General observation (1)	Teacher watches student groups or individuals engaged in any category of student behavior. The teacher must not be engaged in any other category of teacher behavior in order to record "general observation." This category includes passive supervision, and there is no relationship of the observation to an instructional focus.
Encourage (2)	Teacher makes a verbal statement, the purpose of which is to enhance the students' perception of their ability to accomplish a subsequent task.
Reinforce (3)	Teacher makes a positive verbal statement or gesture following an appropriate student behavior (skill or organizational) clearly designed to increase or maintain such responses in the future.
Corrective/ punishment (4)	Teacher makes a negative or critical verbal statement or gesture following an inappropriate student behavior (skill or organizational) clearly designed to decrease such responses in the future.
Managerial (5)	Teacher is engaged in carrying out a non-subject matter task (setting up equipment, taking roll, collecting papers, etc.).
Instruction (6)	Teacher verbally describes to the students how to do a skill, or uses a verbal prompt to direct students in attempting a skill or activity.
Modeling (7)	Teacher demonstrates to students how to do a subject matter task, or participates with students in a subject matter task or activity.
Physical guidance (8)	Teacher physically guides students through a subject matter task or activity.
Non-task verbal (9)	Teacher talks to students about non-subject matter and non-managerial subjects.
Off task (10)	Teacher is not paying attention to what are clearly his/her responsibilities regarding the class at hand.
Specific observation (11)	Teacher watches one or more students engaged in a subject matter task for the purpose of providing feedback related to performance.

our processors can generate the following information: duration, frequency, mean duration, percent of total time, minimum duration for an occurrence, maximum duration for an occurrence, and duration and frequency data for up to 10 programmable sequences of behaviors. That kind of versatility, we believed, might allow us to see relationships in the data that simply would not be possible to see with interval formats.

In addition to its capacity, we believed the electronic processor had at least one other advantage. Since the instrument directly measures the duration of a behavior, it avoids problems of overestimation (as in partial interval systems) and underestimation (as in whole interval systems) (Powell, Martindale, & Kulp, 1975). Resulting data are not estimates based on a sample of any population of behaviors, but rather are direct frequency and duration measures as in event and duration recording with most of the advantages of a multiple behavior coding system. The validity of the coding system is thereby enhanced because the data are more clear representations of what actually occurred.

Table 2 lists the student (ALT-PE Learner Involvement) and teacher behavior categories along with the particular types of data that we enter into our computer subsequent to each observation. It is clear from the table that the amount of information available from any single observation is remarkable. The data base that we are developing should provide an outstanding foundation for an insightful program evaluation.

Pupil performance data

Just about the time we became satisfied with our evaluation design, it occurred to us that we hadn't planned to collect any data on perhaps the most important instructional variable: pupil performance outcomes. All the teacher time and student time measures that exist are of questionable validity unless relationships between those time measures and pupil learning are established (Coker, Medley, & Soar, 1980). The fact is, very little is known about those relationships, at least in physical education, which is all the more reason to collect those data. However, valid and reliable measures of pupil performance outcomes are difficult to find, and we certainly don't have any revolutionary solutions. Nevertheless, we concluded that a partial, temporary solution to the problem lay so close that we almost missed it. The vast majority of clinical experiences, including the microteaching, the public school elementary field experiences, and the on-campus clinics, utilize IPI systems for instruction in individual skills. All pupils have entry-level data, and performance outcome data are automatically generated from hierarchically sequenced activity programs. Although we are not completely satisfied with the validity of all the sequences, we nevertheless view these kinds of data as far better than no pupil performance data at all. So Principle 8 emerges: Don't overlook anything, least of all data that your program naturally generates, but which heretofore has not been recognized as data.

Table 2

Teacher and Student Categories and Data Types

Teacher categories	F	R	D	%
1. Observe	X		X	X
2. Encourage	X	X		
3. Reinforce	X	X		
4. Corrective/punishment	X	X		
5. Managerial	X		X	X
6. Instruction	X	X	X	X
7. Modeling	X	X	X	X
8. Physical guidance	X	X	X	X
9. Non-task verbal	X	X		
10. Off task			X	X
Sequences				
1. Instruct-observe-reinforce	X	X		
2. Instruct-observe-correct	X	X		
3. Model-observe-reinforce	X	X		
4. Model-observe-correct	X	X		
5. Physical guidance-observe-reinforce	X	X		
6. Physical guidance-observe-correct	X	X		
7. Instruct-reinforce	X	X		
8. Model-reinforce	X	X		
9. Physical guidance-reinforce	X	X		
Student categories				
13. Motor appropriate	X		X	X
14. Motor inappropriate	X		X	X
15. Motor supporting	X		X	X
16. Cognitive	X		X	X
17. On task	X		X	X
18. Off task	X		X	X
19. Interim	X		X	X
20. Waiting	X		X	X

Use of evaluation data in teaching and research

We must confess that, in spite of the centrality of evaluation to our training program, we are really more interested in teaching and research. Therefore, we began to look for ways in which our program evaluation data could be used for purposes other than program evaluation. We were pleasantly surprised. As far as our teaching interests are concerned, it was immediately clear that the data-based approach has a significant usefulness within the instructional setting. To a remarkable degree, the evaluation process becomes the instructional process. Just as evaluative data provide stimuli for program change, they also provide stimuli for student behavior change. We are not alone in believing that a great deal of learning takes place during the laboratories, microteaching, field experiences, and clinics precisely because the data are shared (Siedentop, 1976).

Another pleasant surprise involved the degree to which our program evaluation data led us down interesting paths as far as research is concerned. Using our electronic data processors in evaluation activities broadened our view of many teacher and student behaviors. During May 1982, for instance, we were conducting field tests to refine our category systems and evaluate our master teacher candidates. Instead of focusing on the duration of instruction, which we were taught was often a liability (teachers usually talk too much), we became interested in the frequency of instructional sessions, the ratio of instructional sessions to reinforcers, and the sequences of key teacher behaviors like instruct-observe-reinforce. This change of focus was a direct result of collecting program evaluation data. We observed (Hawkins, Wiegand, & Bahneman, Note 1) that teachers utilizing IPI systems often spent as much as 40% of their time instructing, far more than is recommended in some texts. However, most of the instructional sessions took place with individuals, were frequent, short in duration, and much of it seemed appropriate. When it was done well, the result was performance by the pupil and some kind of feedback by the teacher. Consequently, we are currently interested in the extent to which instructional sessions culminate in reinforcers, a key teacher behavior sequence that, to some degree, implies pupil learning.

Our final principle becomes apparent: Design program evaluations for a multiplicity of purposes, that is, don't just do one thing when you can do three things almost as easily. It should be noted that designing multi-purpose instruments is not by any means contrived. The reason why the evaluative, instructional, and research purposes can be served by the same instruments is that they are, or should be, intimately related. Research on teaching should have a direct impact upon program changes in teacher preparation institutions to a far greater extent than is currently practiced.

Summary

It cannot be emphasizd too strongly that our evaluation design emerged from a strong conceptual foundation supported by faculty concensus. Coherent intellectual foundations have the capacity to give birth to valid student performance outcomes. In addition, we have planned to collect data throughout our students' training experience, even into their professional careers. The data we are collecting include competency checklists, student and teacher behavior category systems, and pupil performance outcomes. The category systems we have selected include comprehensive and mutually exclusive behavior categories, are simple and straightforward, and generalize across instructional settings. Finally, we have designed and selected our instruments to serve a multiplicity of purposes, and have stressed the interrelatedness of instruction, research on teaching, and the evaluation of professional preparation programs.

Reference Note

1. Hawkins, A., Wiegand, R., & Bahneman, C. *Data based master teacher program*. Paper presented at the Teaching Research Workshop, The Ohio State University, Columbus, June 1982.

References

COKER, H., Medley, D., & Soar, R. How valid are expert opinions about teaching? *Phi Delta Kappan*, 1980, **62**(2), 131-134.

POWELL, J., Martindale, A., & Kulp, S. An evaluation of time-sample measures of behavior. *Journal of Applied Behavior Analysis*, 1975, **8**, pp. 463-469.

SIEDENTOP, D. *Developing teaching skills in physical education*. Boston: Houghton Mifflin, 1976.

SIEDENTOP, D., Tousignant, M., & Parker, M. *Academic Learning Time-Physical Education Coding Manual*. School of Health, Physical Education and Recreation, The Ohio State University, 1982.

SMITH, B.O. Pedagogical education: How about reform. *Phi Delta Kappan*, 1980, **62**(2), 87-90.

Teaching physical education— A competency-based approach to physical education teacher training. Results of a research project of the German Sport Federation

Herbert Haag
Christian-Albrechts-Universitaet

The actual process of teaching physical education in different settings inside and outside of the school is influenced by the socialization that physical education teachers have gone through in their professional study. Therefore it is reasonable to consider concepts and models by which the competency of teaching physical education is developed within the professional training. A research project sponsored by the German Sport Federation, "teaching physical education—a competency-based approach to physical education teacher training," will be analyzed in its process and product dimension. The presentation will be given in three steps: research design, research result; general concept and research result; teaching competency in the curriculum for physical education teacher training.

Research design

The research methodology implied in this study will be explained in three steps.

Necessity of the research project

Since 1945 there has been a rapid development in the training of physical education teachers in the Federal Republic of Germany. New aspects have been introduced, and curricula for professional training were changed. There was, and is, a constant challenge to redesign physical education teacher training curricula in order to improve school physical education. In 1973 the governing board of the German Sport Federation agreed on the necessity for some long range research on physical education teacher training, and assigned a group of researchers from six different universities and schools.

The group finished its research work in 1975 and published an extensive report (DSB [Hrsg.]: Sportlehrerausbildung. Analyse und Reform. Frankfurt 1975). A short English version followed in 1979, since the research report had received great recognition outside of Germany. This was most likely due to the fact that physical education teacher training often is regarded as unsatisfactory because it has been predominantly perceived as a practical introduction to the art of teaching.

The purpose of this research project, therefore, was to derive the aims and objectives of physical education teacher training from the facts and duties of the physical education teacher, and to develop a model of multi-competence-based physical education teacher training in which the competence to teach physical education is of central concern.

Hypotheses

One underlying hypothesis was the assumption that a review of existing concepts for physical education teacher training would reveal many weaknesses, especially as related to the necessary integration of different aspects of the training towards a teaching competency. It was therefore assumed possible to develop a valid concept for physical education teacher training that could be applied throughout Germany, and maybe even considered in foreign countries. The specific feature of the new approach to physical education teacher training should be competency-based, with teaching competency as the focal point in which other competencies should be integrated.

Research method/data collection/data analysis techniques

Basically, the descriptive research method was used within this research project. The written material analyzed in a descriptive way consisted of

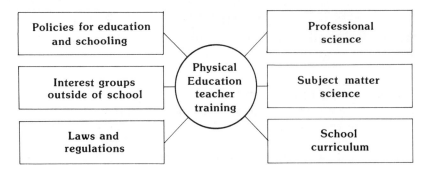

Figure 1—Aspects determining physical education teacher training.

literature on teacher training (general and physical education), existing study curricula for physical education teacher training, and literature on sport pedagogy. On this basis, theoretical inferences were drawn that led to the development of the concept for competency-based physical education teacher training.

The main technique of data collection was content analysis of the indicated literature. Furthermore, the validation of the concept through expert rating was secured. The innovative character of the project required much reasoning on the basis of the available material in order to reach a valid concept for physical education teacher training. The main technique of data analysis therefore was interpretation, drawing conclusions, making inferences, and developing logical relationships.

Research results: General concept

In order to arrive at a competency-based model for physical education teacher training, many aspects had to be considered that determine physical education teacher training as outlined in Figure 1. A further important requirement was to bring the different necessary competencies in a proper relationship, keeping in mind that teaching physical education is the central acting competency, based on other different competencies. The circle model in Figure 2 shows an adequate description of this relationship of sportive, scientific, political (social active), and teaching competency. The different acting competencies will be described in the following in more detail.

Sportive competency
Sportive competency is acquired through sporting action—that event in which a future physical education teacher does what his or her pupils (will) do, performing activities that are characteristic of the role of the pupil. In this sense, "sporting action" for the future physical education

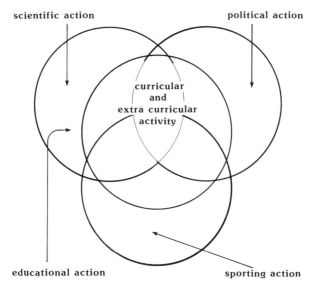

scientific action   political action

educational action   sporting action

Figure 2 — Dimensions of acting competency of the physical education teacher.

teacher means the self-experience of learning processes done by the pupils during sport instruction. This sporting action relates to the sport disciplines in a variety of ways, but also to the development of fundamental movement abilities as best described by words like agility, flexibility, coordination, balance, reaction, speed, strength, endurance. The importance of sportive competency as a necessary base to develop teaching competency resulted in the development of an entrance test for motor behavior at most sport science institutes.

Scientific competency

Scientific competency is a very complex construct. The word scientific/science, as used within this context, comprises the humanities, arts, social and natural sciences. It means the competency to understand, consume, and produce scientific results in a broad sense; it relates to all theory fields of sport sciences, from sport medicine to sport philosophy, and includes sport biomechanics, sport psychology, sport pedagogy, sport sociology, and sport history. Within the research project, four levels of scientific competency resulted from the investigation:

1. Scientific work is understood with the result that the student learns and retains statements that were the outcome of scientific research, and that were formulated in a way to give orientation to act in his or her profession.
2. Sport science literature also may contain results not exactly formulated for the field of physical education instruction. They are

then interpreted relative to the professional field beyond a mere reception of these results.

3. The third form of scientific action also may be called "genetic learning." Questions, conceptions, and methods of a scientific work are analyzed so that an evaluation of scientific statements is possible, through a knowledge and understanding of scientific theory, research methods, techniques of data collection, and techniques of data analysis.

4. Aside from knowing and understanding, there is need for personal application and practice. This fourth form enables a student to get to know science and to participate in the research process, for example, by writing a thesis.

Political (social active) competency

Within the research project, it was most difficult to determine political (social active) competency. The physical education teacher is exposed to multiple influences; as a teacher, he or she influences other persons (pupils, parents, colleagues, etc.). This teaching behavior itself is determined to a great extent by decisions, suppositions, demands, expectations, and conceptions that do not proceed from one's own plans, but instead from public or private institutions, organizations, and other people. Therefore, it is necessary to acquire a political (social active) competency. The political behavior of the physical education teacher has the pedagogical aim to make the pupil realize his or her responsibility. The teacher must enforce conditions for physical education teaching and the informal sport at school that enable him or her to meet the demands of the pedagogical task. Thus, it is necessary to know the political influences so that one can act politically in a proper way concerning pedagogical tasks.

Teaching competency

Based on the sportive competency, supported by scientific and political competency, the future physical education teacher must develop a central, integrated competency called "teaching." Teachers can only be called competent if they have basic experience in the subject matter (sporting action), and if they act in a scientific manner and with political responsibility. Educational action of the physical education teacher therefore has scientific, political, and sporting elements. Teaching competency — carrying out instruction — is only the realization of the educational action, which is central, and not be neglected, under the institutional conditions of the school and according to the definition of teaching tasks. Four phases are therefore distinguished for the teaching competency (instruction): (a) analyzing the preconditions; (b) planning the steps; (c) realizing the phases; and (d) evaluating the result of a teaching and learning process in physical activity. These qualifications in teaching competency can be gained by watching others teach, by being taught, and by teaching. In what follows, teaching competency will be explained in some detail, especially how it can be acquired within physical education teacher training according to the result of this research project.

Research results: Teaching competency in the curriculum for physical education teacher training

After defining the qualifications that a future physical education teacher should acquire, constructing the curriculum was the next step within the research process. It is important that the four competencies not be developed in isolation, but in constant mutual relationship within the study curricula, since this research project showed the need to integrate the four qualification areas within physical education teacher training. This idea is best expressed in the spiral model shown in Figure 3. This model relates to the principle that sequences concerning the curriculum content must follow in a certain order, always trying to integrate the development of the four competencies. As a second principle, it has been stated that certain training units have a common objective. The following segments are distinguished in the model-curriculum:

- introduction and orientation;
- age-specific instructional competency;
- specialization and enlargement;
- introduction to the profession;
- inservice training and continuing education.

The last aspect cannot be analyzed in detail, but it is quite obvious that due to fast changing life conditions, teacher competencies have to be renewed and changed periodically.

The following will analyze the development of teaching competency within the first four segments in order to provide further insight into this aspect of physical education teacher training.

Introduction and orientation

This first segment of the curriculum lasts for two semesters and aids in

1. furthering the experience in sport by one's getting to know more basic types of physical education such as throwing-back games, sports "against nature," endurance sports, and aesthetical sports as well as fundamental movement patterns, yoga, neuromuscular re-laxation, etc;

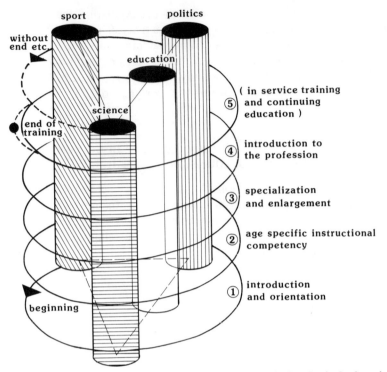

Figure 3 — Integration of the four qualification areas within physical education teacher training (spiral model).

2. acquiring experience with changes of sport, depending on the aims and objectives;

3. changing of the view of sport from the receiver to the responsible. This should be accomplished by observing instruction in different schools and school levels in order to base the decision for a certain teaching career at least partly on one's own perception.

During this first teacher training unit, development of the teaching competency cannot be the central aspect; but it is already included in introduction and orientation so that within the second teacher training unit it can serve as a starting point.

Age specific instructional competency

Teaching competency can be seen in a general dimension, but also in its relationship to certain age levels or school types. The main aspect of the second part of teacher training is the acquisition of teaching competency to teach at the school level chosen by the student. The aims and objectives of this training can be formulated on five different levels dealing with specific instructional competence, as shown in Table 1.

Table 1

**Parts of the Second Teacher Training Unit
"Age Specific Instructional Competency"**

Curricular conditions of school sport	Theories of instructional acting and instruction trials in the school levels	Subject-oriented practical work	Theory and practice in the various school levels	Introduction to areas of sport science research
2 hours	8 hours	4-6 hours	12 hours	8 hours

1. "Curricular conditions of school sport" make visible sport-related teaching situations and aspects of instructional theory, experienced in the first training unit, depending on curricular conditions.
2. "Theories of instructional acting and instruction trials in the school levels" help the student learn about the conditions of instruction given by the specific learning conditions and needs of pupils in a particular school level. Concepts of instructional theory are combined with teaching trials in the school levels in a parallel or mutual way, excellent example of integrating theory into practice.
3. "Subject-oriented practical work" means that the student learns to deal with sporting content and to transmit it in an adequate didactic way in the different school levels. The external functions of sportive competency become very important during the 4 to 6 weeks of practical work on the chosen school level.
4. "Theory and practice in the various school levels" means that the student deals with sport outside of the school, divided in sport disciplines, combined under variable aspects and related to aspects of education, instructional theory, and science.
5. "Introduction to areas of sport science research" implies that students gain insight into important problem-oriented research such as coaching, movement, recreation, health, instruction, curriculum, and play. It can be related to the acquisition of teaching competency by examining, for instance, the needs for sport and sport instruction and their possible realization. The development of teaching competency is of central concern within this second training unit.

Specialization and enlargement

After having been introduced to the school level chosen, the student can be introduced to the professional situation in its whole complexity. Two objectives are pursued, one being that each student should gain (in an exemplary manner by an independent scientific work with professionally relevant questions) insight into the improvement of scientific research results. The other objective is that each student should be qualified to competently realize special tasks in a special field. The scientific qualifications, as well as the special tasks, both admit the integration of teaching competency, even if the acquisition of this competency is not the central aspect of the third teacher training unit.

Introduction to the profession

This fourth teacher training unit, carried out after attending the university, occurs in so-called teacher training seminars. There is, however, a strong reform movement that this part should be integrated in the university study rather than follow as a relatively separate phase beyond the university. The first three teacher training units offer possibilities to orient oneself in limited aspects to the professional fields and to gain first instructional experiences. This practice in its simplification is still far away from the complexity of the real professional situation. By contrast, the fourth teacher training unit allows the future physical education teacher to confront, under guidance, the complex reality of his or her future profession.

Furthermore, one can learn to integrate acquired sporting, scientific, and political (social active) qualifications into educational action. This fourth teacher training unit, therefore, is very important to the whole teacher training concept because the development of the teaching competency is the central concern, based on the assumption that one is now able to integrate the three other acquired competencies into the teaching of sport and physical education.

Final remarks

The following mentions some aspects that are important in terms of further considerations after the main phase of the research project is finished, namely, the development of the curriculum concept for physical education teacher training. At present, different competencies are field tested for use in a concrete curriculum. Then, instructional materials are developed. According to the research strategy of curriculum research, the next step would be to revise the curriculum and material before field testing the whole physical education teacher training curriculum. The design of this evaluative research is accomplished, but it can only be partly realized due to concrete restrictions in the social context.

Despite these difficulties, however, it could be that some practical consequences are possible. This model could serve as an alternative as compared to existing physical education teacher training programs; it could serve as a guideline to improve the present status of physical education teacher training, even in certain aspects. The extensive report of this research project would in itself be of great value to future physical education teachers.

Within this research project, it was not possible to initiate investigations of physical education teachers, their personalities, teaching behaviors, etc. Since research results on the physical education teacher are very rare, such a direction may be necessary for future research. To a certain extent, the same is true about research on the student at different age levels. Both types of research are a necessary basis for curriculum and instruction research; so far, there is little evaluative research because its realization is very difficult. However, this again is an important part of a balanced curriculum and instruction research concept.

This research report presented an analytical view of four competencies required of future physical education teachers. The central competency, teaching, based on sportive and related to scientific and political (social active) competency, was presented in detail and in its curricular sequence. One major result of this research project is the fact that an integration of the four qualification areas within physical education teacher training is necessary in a spiral model, which must come to include even inservice training and continuing education. This means especially that the four competencies must be represented within all three phases of the study at the university and within the two phases beyond the university. Their implementations vary, however, and are not the same for every competency in every phase. The realization of this new model of physical education teacher training is somewhat difficult; it depends widely on the kind of personnel at institutions of higher learning who are responsible for physical education teacher training.

References

DIETRICH, K., Dassel, H., Haag, H., Kurz, D., Menze, C., & Wolf, N. *Sportlehrerausbildung. Analyse und Reform.* Frankfurt: DSB, 1977. (English edition: DSB [Ed.] *Training of physical education teachers. Analysis and reform.* Frankfurt: DSB, 1979).

HAAG, H. *Sport pedagogy: Content and methodology.* Baltimore: University Park Press, 1978.

HAAG, H. Development and structure of a theoretical framework for sport science ("sportwissenschaft"). *Quest*, 1979, **31**(1), 25-35.

HECKHAUSEN, H., et al. *Lehrer 1980. Lehrerbildung für die künftige Schule. (Teacher 1980. Teacher training for the future school.)* Düsseldorf, 1970.

RÜHL, J.K. (Ed.). *Das Studium der Sportwissenschaft. (The study of sport science).* Saarbrücken/Bamberg: Deutscher Sportlehrerverband, 1967.

Staff development
and the study of teaching

Frank N. Rife
The University of Massachusetts

It is clear that research on teaching in physical education has made impressive strides in the last 15 to 20 years (Locke, Note 1). We have established a small but impressive body of literature including first-rate research involving real teachers and real students working in their natural settings of gymnasia and playing fields (Metzler, Note 2; Pieron & Mathy, Note 3). Because of the nascency of our research beginnings, there are various degrees of the quality of that research but our sophistication is beginning to show. We are beginning to ask crucial and important questions, demonstrating fascinating insights, interesting research designs, incisive analyses, and some reasonable inferences about why things happen the way they do.

In addition, we've developed a language to describe and analyze teaching that is clear and understood by those who work in and around pedagogical research. We've seen bright pockets of programmatic research (Siedentop, 1981), and yearly arrivals of new and enthusiastic faces from graduate programs with varying degrees of any research tradition, all eager to try out their new skills.

It is clear that in some ways we are able to distinguish between good and bad teaching (Earls, 1981; Graham, 1981; Graham & Heimerer, 1981; Griffey, 1981), something about what teachers know and feel about their teaching (Rog, 1979), and how they plan for instruction (Placek, 1982). The list of our accomplishments in research on teaching could be extended, but it is important to remember that our efforts have been guided continuously by constructive criticism and legitimate caution (Graham, 1981; Graham & Heimerer, 1981; Locke, 1977; Siedentop, 1982). It is within this vein of constructive concern that I would like to direct my comments.

One area within our realm of teacher education and the study of teaching has not received as much systematic attention as have other professional pursuits. This concerns our relationships with our public school colleagues. In our haste to open up the black box of the gyms and playing fields in order to learn more about teaching, we have created a fishbowl, a veritable freeway from our own institutions into the field. Yet we've given precious little in relation to what we've received. Like those of us who enjoy the wilderness, we may create a delicate paradox. As we encourage our colleagues to come and partake of the wonders there, we must alert all to be careful or else we may lose our opportunities to return. Like all travelers to such areas, we should bring as well as take, all the while not damaging the functional and productive aspects of that environment.

Our colleagues conducting classroom research, however, have made a fine start in addressing the issues of problems regarding this relationship. In the past 10 years, practices of successful association with the public schools have centered around helping schools learn to help themselves (Bentzen, 1974), and doing so in a systematic manner encompassing a unifying theme of staff development and instructional improvement — from preservice undergraduates to inservice public school personnel (Bishop, 1976).

But lest my comments be misconstrued as a blanket indictment upon all of us who conduct research on teaching in physical education, let me quickly add that a few of our colleagues are showing signs of the same insights and sensitivity (Anderson, 1982; Knowles & Hord, 1981).

There have been several models of inservice activities for public school personnel (Rubin, 1978; Schmuck, Runkel, Arends, & Arends, 1977), with the more effective practices being verified by the same systematic research efforts that have identified successful educational practices in the classroom and the gym. Research into verifying effective staff development programs have identified the following characteristics ("Synthesis of Research on Staff Development," 1980):

1. They are concrete and aimed at specific skills.

2. They emphasize demonstrations and opportunities for staff to practice new skills and receive feedback (Joyce & Showers, 1982). Recent investigations about this "coaching of teaching" is revealing a powerful way to make changes in what teachers do (Brandt, 1982).
3. Effective programs are individualized to address the requirements of each participant and to relate to on-the-job needs.
4. They are ongoing, lasting throughout the school year.
5. The inservice offerings are held at school sites rather than elsewhere.
6. They include opportunities to observe other teachers who have mastered and are practicing the skills being taught.
7. Administrators should participate in staff development programs and demonstrate their knowledge and support, but teachers should have primary responsibility in choosing the program and acting as helpers and planners.
8. Local resource personnel make better trainers than do outside consultants. But many teachers would rather *not* be trained by local administrators, which suggests that staff members other than administrators should be the trainers and that the functions of evaluation and training should be separate.

An additional model of inservice to come out of the research on staff development is the notion of collaboration (Huling, Note 4) and the rewards of collaborative research efforts staffed by teams of researchers and practitioners (Tikunoff, Ward, & Griffin, 1979). Recent reports by Michigan State's Institute for Research on Teaching ("Teacher Collaboration," Note 5) indicate that teachers involved as collaborative members of a research team stated that they found research an efficient self-correcting tool, that it increased their self-confidence, and that it renewed their zest for teaching.

There are plenty of examples of first-rate research conducted by researchers and public school teachers (Ballard & Glenn, 1975; Buckingham, McLaughlin, & Hunsaker, 1978; Carnine, 1976; Hart & Risley, 1975; Poling, Miller, Nelson, & Ryan, 1978) and it is time we accepted the fact that our practitioner colleagues can provide more to our research efforts than simply allowing us in their classes. Bill Anderson (1982) offers some excellent advice for approaching inservice teachers when he says we "will need to devise new ways of working with inservice teachers that acknowledge the voluntary, collaborative and collegial nature of that relationship" (p. 16).

In Massachusetts, we have developed a model of inservice that incorporates several of the above characteristics. It is a three-phase model involving the collaborative efforts of the entire membership of the state association for health, physical education, and recreation entitled

"Teachers Helping Teachers" (Rife, 1982). This model for inservice support was conceived with the broad goal of being a resource for *all* physical education teachers in Massachusetts. In addition, it would not only serve the population of physical educators in the state, but also draw its resources and expertise from this same population. This objective of servicing the needs and utilizing the strengths of the same group is considered a key factor for the project's success. This network of support is *not* designed to be run and supported by a small group of physical educators from the college and university sector. Every teacher and agency within the Commonwealth of Massachusetts who has an interest in physical education is encouraged to contribute their expertise.

In order to better evaluate this project, the following objectives were established:

1. to publish the results of the initial needs assessment questionnaire and any succeeding questionnaire results to all MAHPER members;
2. to conduct evaluations of each regional workshop and inservice activity;
3. to publish a resource directory identifying individuals and agencies that can provide inservice support for teachers and programs for physical education.

A three-phase model

In order to accomplish these objectives, this collaborative model of inservice was divided into three phases.

Phase 1

With some seed money from The Council for Leisure Services of The Eastern District Association of AAHPERD and the state organization, the project began with several workshops conducted throughout the state during the school year 1980-81. In addition to the normal workshop offerings, a session was devoted to giving public school teachers and administrators an opportunity to speak out about concerns and problems they encountered in their jobs. These concerns were recorded and developed into an 18-item questionnaire that was mailed to the entire membership.

The purpose of the questionnaire was twofold: to rank the top concerns of the respondents so that inservice offerings could be developed, and to develop a resource directory of members willing to offer inservice support. The questionnaire was mailed and returned during the spring of 1981. Four weeks after the initial mailing, the questionnaire return rate was 25%. The final return was 51%. Results indicated that 64% of the respondents offered their skills as potential workshop presenters and leaders. Of this total, 54% were from the public school sector. The top 10 concerns on the returned questionnaire were reflected in the following ranking:[1]

1. how to improve the image of physical education in the school and the community;
2. how to obtain accurate, up-to-date information about alternative careers for physical educators;
3. how to develop curricula which encourage an active lifestyle;
4. how to change student attitude toward physical education;
5. how to work with limited facilities and equipment;
6. how to teach classes with a wide range of student skill;
7. how to improve the inservice offerings from colleges and universities;
8. how to develop accountability procedures for physical education programs;
9. how to teach special-needs students;
10. how to teach larger classes.

From the questionnaire items, respondents were asked to identify those areas they considered to be some of their strengths. By signifying their strengths, members became part of a resource directory, which meant they had some expertise in a certain area and could conduct a workshop or inservice offering on that subject. The top 10 items ranked as resource considerations were:

1. how to develop curricula that encourage an active lifestyle;
2. how to change student attitudes toward physical education;
3. how to improve communication with students;
4. how to work with limited facilities and equipment;
5. how to teach special-needs students;
6. how to teach classes with a wide range of student skill;
7. how to teach coed classes;
8. how to improve the image of physical education in the school and community;
9. how to teach larger classes;
10. how to improve communication with co-workers.

A Spearman Rank-Order Correlation (rho) of $+.13$ determined that the two complete sets of 18 items did not demonstrate a strong relationship. This suggested that for some of the concerns, resource people would have to come from outside the membership responding to the original questionnaire. The information from the mail questionnaire signaled the end of Phase 1 and provided the necessary information to begin Phase 2.

---

[1]The complete rankings of the 18 items are available from the author.

Phase 2

Phase 2 began in the fall of 1981. Its primary goal was to have the resource members offer workshops based upon the responses from the returned questionnaire. This workshop phase offered support through a variety of formats (workshops, seminars, etc.) at different regions around the state, with the members presenting and leading these inservice activities.

During and after these workshops, there was time for informal conversations so that workshop presenters and participants could discuss the information from the formal sessions, find out what occurred at sessions that participants were unable to attend, and meet with other practitioners to discuss similar concerns and topics related to their jobs. In evaluating that day's activities, participants were to provide formal feedback regarding their input about professional concerns, relevant topics for future inservice activities, and their availability as resource people for future inservice offerings throughout the state.

In order to assess any new concern or affirm original responses, participants were asked to rank the original questionnaire items in light of their current situations and to identify any additional problems that could be molded into sessions for future inservice activities.

The original questionnaire was redistributed and the results were determined. The top 10 rankings from the workshops were:

1. how to improve the image of physical education in the school and community;
2. how to improve school scheduling arrangements;
3. how to develop curricula that encourage an active lifestyle;
4. how to change student attitudes toward physical education;
5. how to develop accountability procedures for physical education programs;
6. how to improve communication with students;
7. how to teach larger classes;
8. how to improve communication with co-workers;
9. how to improve the inservice offerings from colleges and universities;
10. how to discipline larger classes.

In addition, we received feedback about the following: Would you prefer inservice support at a college/university or in your geographic area? Would you prefer the format of a summer school course, a night class, one-day workshop, a series of seminars, or a weekend seminar?

Phase 3

The third phase of our project has yet to begin, as this involves working with individual staffs and departments throughout the state. The key will be to follow the guidelines established by the research in this area as we narrow our inservice efforts and focus on a school or school system.

Staff development and the study of teaching

By establishing such inservice offerings, we can contribute to the study of teaching in five ways: (a) It will develop or maintain our access into the public school world of teaching and allow us to continue our research efforts. (b) It can provide for accurate assessment of teacher concerns and factors affecting their teaching. (Some of these items may be global and some may be situation-specific.) (c) By working with practitioners, in varying relationships, we can gain insights for analysis that only those people close to the situation can provide. (d) It will provide a substantial ground for theory generation as well as theory verification (Glaser & Strauss, 1967). (e) It should facilitate efforts for making collaborative change. Basing our staff development efforts on practitioner needs and concerns will certainly pave the way for experimental efforts in the study of teaching and teacher change (Siedentop, 1982).

As research on staff development has demonstrated an impact on practitioners, it will be important to expand such inservice offerings in order to redress our historical imbalance given to preservice education. Addressing the problems of public school programs and improving the teaching of physical education can be worthwhile goals as we continue our agenda for the study of teaching. Inservice education and staff development desperately need to be given higher priority. Such career counterparts of preservice education can provide for change, renewal, quality education, and professional competence, all worthy achievements our profession can add to its growing list of accomplishments.

Reference Notes

1. Locke, L.F. *Research on teaching physical activity: A modest celebration.* Paper delivered at the VII Commonwealth & International Conference on Sport, Physical Education, Recreation & Dance, Brisbane, Australia, September 1982.
2. Metzler, M. *Bibliography of academic learning time in physical education.* Unpublished bibliography, Virginia Polytechnic Institute and State University, 1982 (computer print-out). Available from the author at Memorial Gymnasium, VPI & SU. Blacksburg, VA 24061.
3. Pieron, M., & Mathy, J. *Study of teaching physical education: Teaching effectiveness, teachers, students interactions and related subjects.* Unpublished bibliography (computer print-out). Available from the author at The University of Liege, Belgium.
4. Huling, L. *Six-step guide to developing and implementing an interactive research and development project.* (A manual available from The Teacher Corps

Project, College of Education, Texas Tech University, Lubbock, TE 79409.)
5. Teacher Collaboration: What's in it for a Teacher? *Communication Quarterly*, 1982, **5**(1), 1-3. (A newsletter available from The Institute for Research on Teaching, College of Education, Michigan State University, East Lansing, MI 48824.)

References

ANDERSON, W. Working with inservice teachers: Suggestions for teacher educators. *Journal of Teaching in Physical Education*, 1982, **1**(3), 15-22.

BALLARD, K., & Glenn, T. Behavioral self-management in story writing with elementary school children. *Journal of Applied Behavior Analysis*, 1975, **8**, 387-398.

BENTZEN, M. *Changing schools: The magic feather principle.* New York: McGraw-Hill, 1974.

BISHOP, L. *Staff development and instructional improvement: Plans and procedures.* Boston: Allyn & Bacon, 1976.

BRANDT, R. On improving teacher effectiveness: A conversation with David Berliner. *Educational Leadership*, 1982, **40**(1), 12-15.

BUCKINGHAM, H., McLaughlin, T.F., & Hunsaker, D. Increasing oral responses in a special education student with a token program. *Education and Treatment of Children*, 1978, **1**(3), 19-25.

CARNINE, D. Effects of two teacher presentation rates on off-task behavior, answering correctly and participation. *Journal of Applied Behavior Analysis*, 1976, **9**, 199-207.

EARLS, N.F. Distinctive teachers' personal qualities, perceptions of teacher education and the realities of teaching. *Journal of Teaching in Physical Education*, 1981, **1**(1), 59-70.

GLASER, B., & Strauss, A. *The discovery of grounded theory: Strategies for qualitative research.* New York: Aldine, 1967.

GRAHAM, G. Research on teaching physical education: A discussion with Larry Locke and Daryl Siedentop. *Journal of Teaching in Physical Education*, 1981, **1**(1), 3-15.

GRAHAM, G., & Heimerer, E. Research on teacher effectiveness: A summary with implications for teaching. *Quest*, 1981, **33**(1), 14-25.

GRIFFEY, D. What is the best way to teach? *Journal of Teaching in Physical Education*, Spring 1981, pp. 18-24.

HART, B., & Risley, T. Incidental teaching of language in preschool. *Journal of Applied Behavior Analysis*, 1975, **8**, 411-420.

JOYCE, B., & Showers, B. The coaching of teaching. *Educational Leadership*, 1982, **40**(1), 4-11.

KNOWLES, C., & Hord, S. The concerns-based adoption model: Tools for planning, personalizing and evaluating a staff development program. *Journal of Teaching in Physical Education*, 1981, **1**(1), 24-37.

LOCKE, L.F. Research on teaching physical education: New hope for a dismal science. *Quest*, 1977, **28**, 2-16.

PLACEK, J. An observational study of teacher planning in physical education. (Doctoral dissertation, The University of Massachusetts, 1982.) *DAI*, 1982, 43/04, 1081-A. (University Microfilms No. DA8219838)

POLING, A., Miller, K., Nelson, N., & Ryan, C. Reduction of undesired classroom behavior by systematically reinforcing the absence of such behavior. *Education and Treatment of Children*, 1978, **1**(3), 35-43.

RIFE, F. Teachers helping teachers: The MAHPER State-wide in-service project. *Journal of The Massachusetts Association for Health, Physical Education and Recreation*, 1982, **29**(3), 6-8.

ROG, J. Faculty attitudes toward teaching: A descriptive interview-based study of three departments of physical education. (Doctoral dissertation, University of Massachusetts, 1979). *Dissertation Abstracts International*, 1979, **40**, 1348. (University Microfilms No. 79-20891A)

RUBIN, L. *The in-service education of teachers.* Boston: Allyn & Bacon, 1978.

SCHMUCK, R., Runkel, P., Arends, J., & Arends, R. *The second handbook of organization development in schools.* Palo Alto, CA: Mayfield, 1977.

SIEDENTOP, D. The Ohio State University supervision research program summary report. *Journal of Teaching in Physical Education*, Spring 1981, pp. 30-38.

SIEDENTOP, D. Teaching research: The interventionist view. *Journal of Teaching in Physical Education*, 1982, **1**(3), 46-50.

SYNTHESIS of research on staff development. *Educational Leadership*, 1980, **38**(2), 182-185.

TIKUNOFF, W., Ward, B., & Griffin, G. *Interactive research and development on teaching: A final report.* San Francisco: Far West Laboratory for Educational Research and Development, 1979.

Program development
and related research

Susan M. Schwager and William G. Anderson
Teachers College, Columbia University

For a number of years, research at Teachers College has focused on the description and analysis of teaching. Currently, in addition to studying teaching, our work is drifting in another direction as well. We are actively involved in trying to improve ongoing physical education programs in several school districts. We are also conducting research that is directly related to our work as facilitators of program development.

As the word "drifting" indicates, the work currently under way at Teachers College involving program development in several school districts evolved from studying teaching, and studying what is going on in physical education programs, to actively trying to change existing programs. The work began with one district in 1978. It expanded to two districts, and in the spring of 1980, resulted in the formation of the Physical Education Program Development Center with five affiliated school districts. The Center was not created to conduct research. Rather, its purpose was to improve the physical education programs in the affiliated districts. The research evolved from the early program development efforts and from the realization that our involvement in program development projects gave us a unique opportunity to study these projects.

The Physical Education Program Development Center

The Center provides the context in which program development and related research can take place. One of the five affiliated school districts donated space in its administration building for the Center office and resource library. The Center staff includes a director, an associate director, and a group of graduate students at Teachers College who serve as Center associates. The advisory council, composed of the director, associate director, and the directors of physical education for each of the affiliated school districts, assists in planning Center activities and advises the Center on policy. In addition to our five affiliated districts, we communicate with a regional network of districts, informing them about our activities. On occasion, these other districts join us on an ad hoc basis in connection with various projects. The Center is funded by Horace-Mann Lincoln Institute of Teachers College, the Department of Movement Sciences and Education of Teachers College, and annual dues from each school district.

The Center Staff encourages district teachers to evaluate their programs and classes, identify possible improvements, and implement one or more improvements every year. This change-oriented strategy recognizes the unique problems confronting different schools and different grade levels, and allows teachers to pursue projects they perceive as valuable. At the same time, the Center arranges for meetings of teachers within and across districts to identify mutual concerns and potential collaborative efforts. Once the direction for change is established, the Center staff does all it can to help keep the project moving ahead. We provide resource materials, call meetings to discuss progress, run workshops, visit programs to monitor progress and consult with teachers, get teachers to write brief reports on what they have done and distribute the reports to others, arrange for interschool and interdistrict visitation by teachers, and obtain release time for teachers to engage in joint program planning. A substantial number and variety of projects have been undertaken during the first 1½ years of the Center's operation and during the previous 2 years leading up to its formation. Some projects involved a single teacher working with selected classes; others involved teachers from all districts.

Related research

The idea that research in program development would be a significant part of our work was late in coming. In fact, we began with a commitment not to allow research to interfere with, or to corrupt, our program development efforts. We would not "use" the schools for our own research interests; so our initial efforts began without any intention of doing research. Doctoral students simply worked at the Center to gain experience and to assist with the program development projects.

We soon realized, however, that it would be extremely valuable to document the change process we were facilitating, and that we could do it in a way that did not interfere with the program development itself. The idea of studying our program development efforts emerged. Then, questions arose concerning who would conduct the research and how it would be done. We decided that doctoral students would study the program changes and that they could simultaneously coordinate and investigate these projects. That is, they could study their own curriculum development projects. We adopted this rather controversial approach, recognizing that we would sacrifice a certain amount of scientific objectivity, but felt that we might gain subjective depth and artistry. We also agreed that the doctoral students' work as facilitators of program development (in addition to studying the process) should count as part of their dissertation work. After all, it was professionally demanding and required extraordinary competencies in program development, which is precisely what we are trying to develop in our doctoral students.

Finally, with full understanding that some members of the scientific community would be appalled at the idea, we decided to consider this work in facilitating and studying program development as "research" because it: (a) utilizes an existing body of knowledge and theory to design and carry out the work; (b) deals with professionally significant problems; (c) employs a comprehensive array of appropriate data collection techniques; (d) yields a thorough descriptive account of events; and (e) provides for a responsible professional interpretation of those events. Of course, it does not confirm or reject any generic hypotheses. On the contrary, it yields information about a specific case — with all its complexities, idiosyncracies, and enigmas. Its value must derive from the value that one gains from learning about the particular case, and not from any universal generalizations that emerged.

The Competency-Based Physical Education Project

An overview
The project. The Competency-Based Physical Education Project exemplifies the type of program development activity sponsored by the Physical Education Program Development Center. This project brought together participants from the five affiliated districts to work toward improving existing programs. It was a year-long project, ending in June 1982, but we expect the program development activities to continue next year and, hopefully, beyond. In this respect, the project represents the Center's commitment to long-term program development.

The project focused on upgrading the elementary school physical education programs; competency-based education (CBE) was used as a structure to develop program segments. These segment topics were varied and included specific sport skills, fitness components, and skill or fitness-related concepts. The program development approach used was characterized by extensive involvement of participating teachers in planning and conducting all phases of the project. They were responsible for designing and implementing the competency-based program segments, and their input was sought on other activities such as the plans for workshop sessions and the timing of project directors' visits. The project directors (Schwager & Anderson) served as facilitators, planning and conducting workshop meetings and providing teachers with written resources, guidance, and encouragement.

Seventeen competency-based segments were designed and implemented by eight participating teachers. Some gains in student performance were noted, and the teachers' reactions to the different project phases were generally favorable. We decided on a competency-based approach to program development for very practical reasons. It provided a useful structure for designing program segments that emphasized consistency among goals, activities, and assessment procedures. Competency-based education was also considered an attractive focus by the district superintendents, who supported the project by approving inservice credit for participating teachers and by giving the participants release time to attend workshops.

The related research. The purpose of studying the project, during which Schwager served as investigator, was to document what happened and to assess the project's impact on existing school programs. By monitoring the project activities, some insights could also be gained about the successful aspects of this particular approach to program development that emphasizes teacher ownership and focuses on finding practical solutions to existing problems. A review of relevant literature was instrumental in determining the nature of the program development project and the methods used to study it (Anderson, 1982; Berman & McLaughlin, 1978; Cruickshank, Lorish, & Thompson, 1979; Huling, Trang, & Correll, 1981; Klausmeier, 1982; Lieberman, 1978; Tikunoff, 1979).

A variety of quantitative and qualitative data collection techniques were used. The quantitative data consisted of student scores resulting from the assessment procedures used for each competency-based program segment. In some instances, pre- and post measures were taken, while other segment assessment procedures provided post measures that were compared to criterion scores. The teachers themselves determined the assessment procedures for each program segment. Qualitative data were collected via interviews, questionnaires, teacher logs, field notes from observations of classes, and workshop critiques.

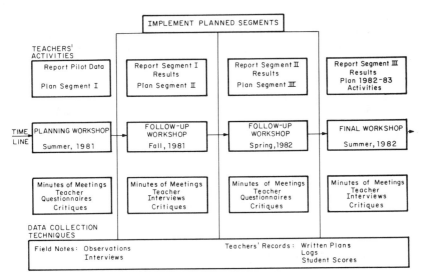

Figure 1—Competency-based physical education project.

The results of a study that relies so heavily on qualitative data collection techniques is difficult to summarize in a few pages. For a more detailed description of the project, and the procedures and results of the related study, see Schwager (1983).

Sequence of activities

A time line of the project provides a picture of its different phases and the data collection techniques used at each phase (Figure 1). The sequence of activities shows a pattern of periodic workshop meetings, which were typically spent sharing the results of previous program change efforts and planning for subsequent changes. The project directors aided the implementation efforts by visiting the teachers frequently to provide additional written resources and to offer suggestions and encouragement.

The investigator and an assistant took minutes during workshop sessions, interviewed participants after each workshop, and gave them post workshop questionnaires for the first and third workshops. The project directors, other Center staff members, and outside consultants conducted critiques of each workshop. Each teacher typically received at least three visits from the investigator during the competency-based segment. Field notes were taken during two class observations per segment, and the teachers were interviewed at the conclusion of each segment. The teachers also submitted logs and copies of student scores when each segment was completed. Each teacher was interviewed prior to the final workshop to review and assess the overall project.

Project scope

During the course of the project, 17 competency-based program segments were planned and implemented by eight elementary school physical education teachers from the five school districts, targeting more than 1,000 students. The teachers determined the specific skills or activities and the grade levels to be targeted, as well as the number of classes to involve in each segment. The teachers also designed and implemented their own segments; they decided on the focus, the goals, the activities (how to spend class time), and the assessment procedures to be used.

Program changes and student performance

In reporting the results of a study appraising a program development process, it is important not to overlook the obvious outcomes. Probably the most striking result of this study is that the 17 competency-based program segments were carefully planned and implemented by only eight teachers, targeting more than 1,000 students. Tables 1 and 2 summarize the results of the student assessment procedures used for the program segments. The assessment procedures for eight of the segments were based on pre/posttests of student performance. Table 1 shows the percent of students in each of these segments whose scores improved from pre- to posttests. The assessment procedures for the other nine segments consisted of posttests only. Table 2 shows the percent of students who achieved a predetermined criterion score for each of these segments. Since each segment was unique, it is difficult to summarize the results of these assessment procedures. Therefore, these figures are best analyzed in the context of the specific segments. It can be noted, however, that in some instances the segments in which pre/post measures were taken seemed successful at improving student performance. Those segments in which student posttest scores were compared to a criterion score showed some percent of the students' achieved minimum competence as defined by the criterion score.

The scores mainly gave teachers useful information about the impact of their program segments on the students' performance. The teachers made decisions to repeat or revise the program segments primarily on the basis of the results of the assessment procedures.

An emphasis on behavior management was an important aspect of the program changes that occurred. Discussions during the planning workshop brought out a common concern the participants shared about the social behaviors of students. The teachers were unanimous in their desire to encourage appropriate behaviors (e.g., good sportsmanship), and all said they wanted to do something to improve the behavior of their students. As a result of these early discussions, an outline for a segment entitled "Appropriate Behaviors in Physical Education" was compiled

Table 1

Activity Segment Results Student Assessment Pre/Posttest

Segment title	Grade level	Number of students	% students improved from pre- to posttest
Throw for accuracy	1	116	73.7
Volleyball serve	4	78	70.5
Gymnastics-tumbling	1	22	68
Power volleyball	6	21	67
Archery	4	26	65.4
Balance	1	109	49
Body mechanics/balance	5	23	48
Jogging	4	22	40.9

Table 2

Activity Segment Results Student Assessment Posttest

Segment title	Grade level	Number of students	% students achieved criterion score
Fitness concepts-soccer	4	22	87
Rope skipping	5	23	87
Fitness concepts-soccer	5	36	67
Fitness concepts-swimming	5	40	72
Arm strength	4	157	63
Basketball skills	4	17	63
Gymnastics	5-8	186	52
Nutrition concepts	K	37	40.5
Basketball skills	4	76	43.4

and distributed to all the teachers. The participants agreed to implement some form of the outline during the 1981-82 school year and report on their progress at workshop meetings. Although implementation of this segment did not strictly follow the competency-based format, it was an attempt to tackle the difficult problem of behavior management in a systematic fashion. It became an important part of the project, especially for some teachers.

The competency-based education framework

The teachers had mixed reactions regarding competency-based education as a tool for program development. Some of the typical responses obtained from interviews and teachers' logs reflected both advantages and disadvantages of the use of CBE: (a) Competency based education provided a useful structure and helped the teachers plan in a more organized fashion; (b) students' scores gave the teachers useful information for future planning; (c) the segment results demonstrated to the teachers that their programs made a difference; (d) the assessment procedures tended to be time-consuming, using up precious activity time.

A key feature of competency-based education that we wanted to encourage was systematic attention to student assessment. Before taking part in the project, the teachers said their assessments of student performance were made primarily through casual observation. Their objections to spending precious class time administering performance tests surfaced early, and we tried to address the problem during workshops by encouraging the use of efficient assessment procedures, for example, student self-monitoring and rotating stations. Teachers experimented with various techniques and reported back to the group. Eventually, all participants adopted reasonably efficient assessment procedures and record-keeping techniques.

In the judgment of the project directors and expert consultants, competency-based education as defined in the context of this project was very useful; it encouraged consistency among goals, activities, and assessment procedures in planning program segments. The use of a common approach to program development provided a context for workshop discussions within which the variety of specific segments could be reviewed. CBE also encouraged systematic assessment of student progress to a greater degree than the teachers had been doing prior to the project.

Assessment of project activities

Through interviews and evaluative questionnaires, we sought feedback from the teachers concerning the different project activities. These activities for facilitating the teachers' own program development efforts were of special interest to us. In particular, we sought teachers' reactions to the workshops and the frequent visits from the project directors during the course of the project.

Regarding the workshops, the teachers reacted quite favorably to the opportunity of meeting with their peers to discuss programs, teaching methods, and common problems. They looked forward to reporting on their progress, as well as to hearing about the implementation efforts of other teachers. They came to each workshop with samples of materials, charts, and visual aids used, and were prepared to present their segment results to the group. Also, there was ample evidence that information shared at workshops was used to develop subsequent segments.

The mid- and post workshop critiques were a valuable tool for reviewing the progress of sessions in light of plans versus reality, and in making necessary changes in planned activities for subsequent sessions. The critiques consisted of discussions among the project directors, other staff members attending the workshops and, on some occasions, outside visitors. The critiques were conducted during lunch breaks (mid-session) and at the conclusion of each session (post-session). For each workshop, the mid-session critique caused changes in plans for the afternoon meetings. At the post-session critiques, the workshop plans and recorded minutes were reviewed, and assessments were made concerning the workshop activities just completed. Numerous changes in subsequent workshop plans were suggested and eventually implemented as a consequence of these sessions.

Our frequent visits to the teachers during the implementation phases played a crucial role in the facilitation process. Based on the teachers' reactions during interviews, our presence served as a strong reminder that they were expected to follow through on the plans developed during workshop sessions. The individual attention paid to each teacher also seemed to serve as a reward for his/her past efforts and as an encouragement to continue. In several instances, the teachers said that our visits caused them to initiate or renew a segment that was being postponed or neglected.

Long-term commitment to program development

The project began in June 1981 and ended in June 1982. The major outcomes of its final workshop were that the teachers planned to continue program development activities, and the project directors agreed to continue their support. The teachers said they intended to continue using competency-based education as a structure for developing and refining program plans during the 1982-83 school year. The Physical Education Program Development Center staff will sponsor periodic workshop meetings to give the teachers opportunities to continue sharing progress and exchanging ideas.

The 17 segments planned and implemented by the participating teachers reflect the extent to which targeted programs have changed during the course of the project. The extent to which these changes persist, and whether the teachers continue to engage in program development activities next year, will provide additional insight into the effectiveness of this approach to program development.

We at Teachers College foresee a series of studies in the future that may yield a data bank of program development research. In any event, we intend to continue doing this kind of research; it is enormously challenging, thoroughly enjoyable, and offers the opportunity to deal with real-life problems of teachers and school administrators.

References

ANDERSON, W.G. A physical education program development center. *Journal of Health, Physical Education, Recreation and Dance*, 1982, **53**(5), 7-10.

ANDERSON, W.G. Working with inservice teachers: Suggestions for teacher education. *Journal of Teaching in Physical Education*, 1982, **1**(3), 15-22.

BERMAN, P., & McLaughlin, M. *Federal programs supporting educational change* (Vol. 8). *Implementing and sustaining innovation*. Report No. R1589/8-HEW. Santa Monica, CA: Rand Corp., 1978.

CRUICKSHANK, D., Lorish, C., & Thompson, L. What we think we know about inservice education. *Journal of Teacher Education*, 1979, **30**(1), 27-32.

HULING, L., Trang, M., & Correll, L. IR&D: A promising strategy for teacher educators. *Journal of Teacher Education*, 1981, **32**(6), 13-14.

KLAUSMEIER, H.J. Research strategy for educational improvement. *Educational Researcher*, February 1982, pp. 8-13.

LIEBERMAN, A., & Miller, L. The social realities of teaching. *Teachers College Record*, September 1978, **80**(1), 54-68.

SCHWAGER, S. *The planning, implementation and analysis of a program development project in elementary physical education*. Unpublished doctoral dissertation, Teachers College, Columbia University, New York, 1983.

TIKUNOFF, W., & Ward, B. *Interactive research and development on teaching study: Final report*. Report IR& DT-79-11. San Francisco: Far West Laboratory for Educational Research and Development, 1979.

Section five
Academic learning time in physical education

In the short time since its inception, a fairly extensive and consistent body of knowledge has developed about Academic Learning Time in physical education. Continued progress into ALT-PE research — involving all three categories in the research loop — is evident in the three papers presented here. Each one employs some multiple-system combination to assess student time-on-task as it relates to other phenomena within the physical education setting.

Patt Dodds presents a two-level analysis of teacher behaviors measured by the Tarp-Gallimore Coaching Behavior Observation Instrument compared directly to student behaviors measured by ALT-PE. The analysis yields 29 statistically significant correlations.

Michael Metzler combines Experimental Teaching Units (ETU) and ALT paradigms to show how student process behaviors can be used to analyze teaching effectiveness in terms of student achievement. Results suggest that little skill improvement can be expected when Motor ALT accrual is small, but Metzler concludes it is possible to organize instructional settings that promote higher Motor ALT accrual rates.

The third paper, by Victor Mancini, D.A. Wuest, E.K. Clark, and N. Ridosh, employs the Cheffers Adaptation of the Flanders Interaction Analysis System (CAFIAS), Academic Learning Time-Physical Education (ALT-PE), and the Maslach Burnout Inventory (MBI) concurrently to explore the relationships between teacher burnout levels and teacher-student interaction patterns. Differences in low-burnout teachers and high-burnout teachers were reflected in efficiency, organization of class activities, learning opportunities for students, and design of instruction.

Taken separately, these presentations illustrate the usefulness of the ALT-PE paradigm. Together they attest to its versatility and portend its future.

Relationships between academic learning time and teacher behaviors in a physical education majors skills class

Patt Dodds
University of Massachusetts

In its short history of 4 years, research on Academic Learning Time in physical education has matured to the point where some examples exist in all three categories of Rosenshine and Furst's (1973) loop model of descriptive-analytic, correlational, and experimental research. That progress toward understanding the operation of ALT-PE in gym classes has occurred through each of these basic paradigms is a tribute to the exciting nature of ALT-PE variables as phenomena worthy of study. It also is confirmation that a small but growing cadre of physical education/ teacher education researchers can explore the same topic without getting in each other's way and with some degree of collegiality.

The breadth of skills and interests represented among ALT-PE researchers has produced a remarkably extensive and relatively consistent

This paper is part of an ongoing research project by Patt Dodds, Frank Rife, and Shirley Shute, University of Massachusetts.

body of knowledge about student time-on-task variables in physical education. Reliable ALT-PE records now exist for elementary, secondary, and college students; traditional and movement education approaches to elementary physical education; and a representative variety of movement forms including team, individual, and lifetime sports, gymnastics, rhythms and dance, and fitness activities. Further ALT-PE data have been collected for students sampled from intact classroom groups, and for students sampled by particular characteristics, for example, special needs or disabilities, motor skills levels, and gender (Dodds, Rife, & Metzler, 1982).

Beginning with Metzler's (1979) initial foray into public school gymnasia to determine whether the original ALT instrumentation developed for use in the Beginning Teacher Evaluation Study (Fisher, Filby, Marliave, Cahen, Dishaw, Moore, & Berliner, Note 1) of classroom teaching could be used in physical education, descriptive-analytic researchers have methodically broadened subject populations and refined sampling techniques, observation protocols, and data analysis procedures. Regardless of differing technical details in separate studies, however, the findings provided by descriptive analysis show certain regularities. In general, the amount of successful movement time engaged with appropriate instructional tasks provided for most students is far less than commonly imagined, and much of the ALT produced in physical education is cognitive rather than motor. The structure inherent in the observation system captures this situation in a characteristic funnel effect, that is, successively decreasing amounts of Content-PE, Learner Engagement, and Successful Engagement lead to figures for Successful Motor Engagement, which are a small proportion of available class time.

Intervention/experimental studies have established a strong case that several relatively simple changes in what teachers do can increase ALT-PE over baseline levels. Techniques that work include increasing teacher feedback to students and reducing managerial time (Birdwell, 1980), using task cards for students and changing game rules and structures (Paese, Note 2), or applying behavior analysis strategies of timeout for disruptions of class and public posting of completed tasks as positive reinforcement (McKenzie, Note 3). Aufderheide, McKenzie, and Knowles (1982) found, in the only true experimental design reported in the ALT-PE literature, that significant differences in elementary students' ALT-PE existed between teachers who individualized and those who did not.

The only two correlational studies of ALT-PE (Keller, 1982; Young & Metzler, Note 4) confronted the cornerstone issue upon which ALT-PE research rests, that is, whether or not student learning time is a valid and reliable substitute for actual achievement. These researchers found only one significant, and disappointingly small, relationship (between Motor ALT and achievement scores) in an ETU protocol. Silverman (1982), using an observation instrument similar to ALT-PE, discovered that the characteristics of individual students greatly mediated the relationships found between Motor Engaged time and achievement in college level swimming classes. These three studies together indicate that the relationships between time-on-task measures and student achievement may be more complex than was previously imagined.

Locke (Note 5) has called for multi-dimensional research to examine concurrently several layers of complexity present in any education environment. ALT-PE researchers so far have neglected research designs for simultaneously examining other teaching-learning variables which may be related to ALT-PE. With two exceptions, they have concentrated instead on describing naturally occurring ALT-PE or on modifying only variables within the ALT-PE system. Birdwell (1980) added a fifth tier of teacher behavior observation to the original four-tiered ALT-PE system. This made possible interval-by-interval comparisons of teacher behaviors with student ALT-PE. Though Birdwell was then more interested in intervening with teacher management and feedback to increase ALT-PE, her data could be re-examined to determine exactly what the teacher was doing when students experienced high or low ALT-PE.

The second attempt at multi-level analysis of behaviors in the gym occurred when Aufderheide, Olson, and Templin (Note 6) triangulated the ALT-PE and OSIA-PE (Olson, 1979) observation instruments with ethnographic observation procedures. While providing three quite different perspectives on life in those particular gyms, the report did not include direct comparisons of data generated from each of the three sources.

Reacting to the relative stability of the ALT-PE data base, the ever present urge for physical educators to connect with classroom-based research on teaching and learning, and the need to unravel threads at multiple levels from the complexities of what goes on in gym, our research team designed the study reported here. This investigation described the actions of both teachers and students in a physical education setting indigenous to all professional preparation programs. Our study represents a first attempt to add a two-level analysis of what goes on in gym to the ALT-PE data base. The purpose was to discover the relationships which appear when student behaviors measured by ALT-PE I (Siedentop, Birdwell, & Metzler, Note 7) and teacher behaviors measured by the Tharp-Gallimore Coaching Behavior Observation Instrument (Tharp & Gallimore, 1976) are compared directly. This exploratory analysis centered on the following questions, which were intended to represent only a few of many possibilities:

1. What were typical class days like for students and teacher? (prose descriptions of overall ALT-PE and teacher behavior patterns)

2. What ALT-PE patterns appeared when class sessions were the unit of analysis? (graph for visual inspection)
3. What teacher behavior patterns appeared when class sessions were the unit of analysis? (graph for visual observation)
4. What are the direct relationships present between teacher behavior and student learning time when these events are considered together? (correlations)

Methodology and procedures

Subjects included an intercollegiate Division I varsity lacrosse coach and the 17 students in her physical education skill class. All students were undergraduate women majoring in physical education. Most were beginners at lacrosse, a few having had some lacrosse experience in high school. None were on the intercollegiate varsity team, but two played on the junior varsity. The teacher had nationally ranked field hockey and lacrosse teams each of her four years on the university faculty. Thirty-six observations were equally distributed across the 17 students during eight class sessions randomly dispersed across the whole semester.

Two observation instruments were chosen. Teacher behavior was event-recorded with the Tharp-Gallimore Coaching Observation Instrument (Tharp & Gallimore, 1976), comprising 12 categories: Instruction, Hustles, Positive Modeling, Negative Modeling, Praise, Criticism, Cue, Nonverbal Praise, Nonverbal Criticism, Alert, Question, and Other. Investigators audiotaped the code for each observed event during a class session and later transcribed the taped data onto a recording sheet.

ALT-PE I (original version, Siedentop, Birdwell, & Metzler, Note 7) was selected to record student learning time. In this system, four major categories (Setting, Content, Learner Move, and Difficulty Level) are each subdivided into actual coding categories (see Figure 1). ALT-PE observers, responding to a pre-cued audiotape with signals at 6-second intervals, wrote observations directly onto a recording sheet.

ALT-PE and teacher behavior data were not necessarily collected simultaneously on the same students. Thus, the class session was the unit of measurement as well as the unit of analysis.

At a later time, data from all recording sheets were keypunched for computer analysis by SPSS programs, the ALT-PE program being specially written by Silverman (Note 8). Descriptive statistics included frequencies and percentages totaled by class sessions for both instruments. Correlations were computed between observation categories in both instruments to determine what relationships existed between specific teacher behaviors and student learning time measures.

Three trained observers collected data together, one using the Tharp-Gallimore instrument, the second coding ALT-PE, and the third coding

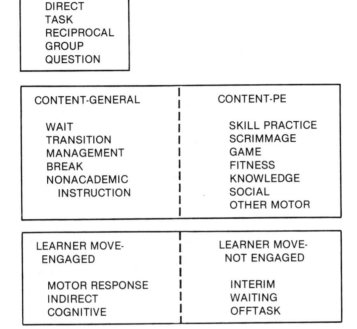

Figure 1—ALT-PE observation instrument categories.

with the others for InterObserver Agreement (IOA) checks at random throughout the semester. When not doing IOA checks, the third observer coded ALT-PE. Four students were coded by each ALT-PE observer during a class session. IOA checks affirmed that both observers saw and recorded the same events. When the third observer coded ALT-PE, eight students were observed in that class session, and IOA data were collected for a short time during which both ALT-PE observers attended to the same designated student.

Results and discussion

InterObserver agreement

The three observers met an IOA criterion of .90 on successive occasions prior to data collection, using the scored-interval method of calculation

(Hawkins & Dotson, 1975). Subsequent IOAs computed during the study ranged from .86 to 1.00 for ALT-PE, and from .77 to 1.00 for the Tharp-Gallimore instrument (lowest IOAs for Positive Modeling, highest for Hustle, Nonverbal Criticism, and Other). At the outset, then, observers saw and heard the same real world events, appearing not to drift from category definitions or from each other as data collection progressed.

Typical class days

Aggregating data from the ALT-PE and teacher behavior instruments across the whole semester gives a rough sketch of an average day for this lacrosse class. ALT-PE percentages (see Table 1) show that Content-PE (actual work in lacrosse) consumed 85% of class time, with Skill Practice taking 46% of the total and Knowledge taking 37% of the total. Students spent 35% of their time Cognitively, but only 16% in Motor Engagement. The 86% of class time spent on lacrosse included 21% Waiting, usually for a turn or a trial. Students were Engaged in lacrosse content 55% of class time, and engaged successfully (performing either Cognitive or Motor skills) 49% of the time. Only 11% of class time was spent in successful Motor performance, however. The teacher paced the class 80% of the time, most often during Knowledge presentations and starting and stopping drills, while students paced themselves in a practice style (Mosston, 1981) only 15% of the class time, mostly during Skill Practice.

The teacher was as active as the students (see Table 2). She emitted behaviors at high rates, ranging from 12 to 24 per minute. In an average class session, she emitted almost 600 Instructions, Cues, Praises, and other categories, while across the eight sessions observed she accumulated 4,626 total events: a third (1,546) delivered to individuals and two-thirds (3,080) to the class group. Three categories of teacher behavior accounted for most of the instructional moves made: Instruction, Praise, and Cue. Whether analyzed by percentages directed only to individuals, to the class group, or combined to both targets, these three verbal behaviors appeared most frequently. The other categories showed much smaller percentages.

In a word picture, students generally arrived individually, usually grabbing a ball to practice alone or with a partner, or standing around to chat until the teacher officially began class. No ALT-PE or teacher behavior data were recorded prior to the official start, because no specific tasks were set, nor were all students present. Following a short period of explanation or discussion when new rules, skills, positions, or strategies were presented, students usually were divided into two to four working groups for line drills. At times, drills involved motor activity for one student only (as in cradling), for two students working together (as in

Table 1

**Semester Summaries of ALT-PE Categories
in Mean Percentages of Total Class Time**

Setting	(100%)
Direct	80%
Task	16%
(rest 5%)	
Content-PE	(85%)
Knowledge	37%
Skill practice	46%
(rest 2%)	
Learner move engaged	(55%)
Cognitive	35%
Motor	16%
Difficulty level	
Easy (ALT units)	49%
Motor easy (ALT-PE units)	11%
Learner move not engaged	(31%)
Waiting	21%

Table 2

**Three Most Frequent Teacher Behaviors Delivered to Students
(Entire Semester Summary)**

Totals to class and individuals		Totals to class group		Totals to individuals	
Instruction	50%	Instruction	67%	Praise	36%
Praise	17%	Cue	8%	Cue	27%
Cue	15%	Praise	8%	Instruction	16%
(Rest = 4% or less)		(Rest = 5% or less)		(Rest = 6% or less)	

passing and catching), or for two students working in opposition (defensive positioning as an attack player feints and dodges).

The teacher moved from group to group during Skill Practice, continually talking to individuals, encouraging them, praising good efforts and skillful moves, offering specific feedback, cues, and demonstrations when she saw mistakes. Each drill continued until the teacher changed to a new activity. Each student was afforded at least two or three chances to perform the isolated game skills. When the teacher decided to move on, she called the class together, gave feedback to the group about their performance in the previous drill, presented new materials, and answered questions. This episode was generally followed by a different drill.

This pattern was typical throughout the semester, with more difficult skills being added and combined in drills, while the drills themselves in-

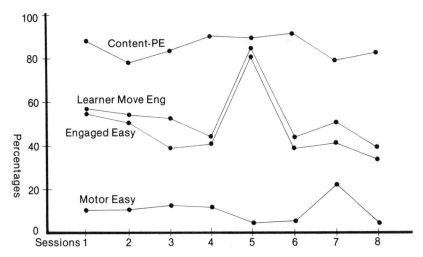

Figure 2—ALT-PE categories in percentages across class sessions.

creased in complexity and likeness to full game situations. The teacher generally talked through new skills, pointing out salient features as her assistant (a varsity All-American) demonstrated. Once a drill began, students were expected to continue, each group pacing itself, while the teacher roved and made comments to each student in the class.

Class session as the unit of analysis

When ALT-PE data were graphed by class session (Figure 2), the funnel effect was clearly present. Content-PE, Learner Move Engaged, Successful Engagement, and Successful Motor Engagement all neatly fell in place from high or low. The low portion of successfully executed motor practice trials provides a clear mandate that interventions to raise ALT-PE are desperately needed, even in college-level classes taught by excellent teachers to students specializing in sport activities.

The three most frequent categories of teacher behavior are graphed in Figure 3. The interdependence of Tharp-Gallimore categories (i.e., the fact that they are mutually exclusive, high levels of one necessitating low levels of others) is dramatically emphasized in Session 5. Heavily oriented toward instruction, this day was unusual because the class was inside, watching and listening to a lecture/demonstration on goalkeeping. Student opportunity to practice and therefore to receive praise, cues, or other teacher behaviors, was greatly reduced. These data highlight the need for thoughtful preclass preparations when teachers are concerned about maintaining high ALT-PE (Placek, 1982).

Correlations between teacher behavior and ALT-PE

Pearson product-moment correlation tables for teacher behavior

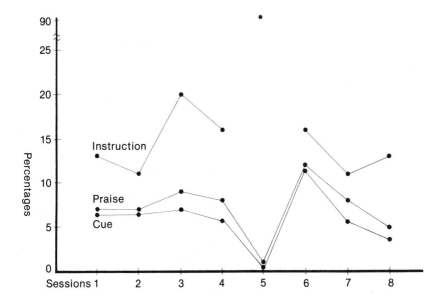

Figure 3—Season totals by class session for three most frequent teacher behaviors.

categories and selected ALT-PE measures yielded 29 statistically significant correlations, 19 at the .05 level, 7 at the .01 level, and 3 at the .001 level (by sessions). Only correlations significant at the .01 and .001 levels are reported in Table 3. Class session totals used for correlation were (a) mean ALT-PE I category percentages for students observed that day, and (b) total frequencies (combined for individuals and the whole class group) of each Tharp-Gallimore teacher behavior category.

All correlations in Table 3 are strong, indicating that some teacher behaviors appeared quite regularly at the same time as particular student behaviors. When learners were in a Content-PE Knowledge mode, the teacher instructed, criticized, and demonstrated mistakes, but was unlikely to praise. During Skill Practice, students performed motor skills while the teacher praised quite frequently, but did not often instruct, criticize, or demonstrate mistakes. Because Cognitive Engagement is so closely tied to Knowledge (note similar percentages in parentheses), it was not unexpected that the strength and direction of correlations in those categories approximated each other closely. When students worked on lacrosse motor skills, the teacher was likely to praise and give short, quick reminder cues about the actions being performed.

Table 3 shows that the teacher generally gave new or additional information or criticism, or demonstrated mistakes while students were unsuccessfully performing lacrosse skills. In contrast, when students Waited in lines for turns, the teacher did not engage in any of these three

Table 3

Pearson Correlations for ALT-PE Categories With Teacher Behaviors

ALT-PE categories		Teacher behaviors	r
Content-PE	(86%)		
Knowledge	(37%)	Instruction	.90
		Praise	−.83
		Criticism	.70
		Negative modeling	.63
Skill practice	(46%)	Praise	.82
		Instruction	−.81
		Criticism	−.73
		Negative modeling	−.63
Cognitive	(35%)	Instruction	.90
		Praise	−.80
		Criticism	.66
		Negative modeling	.58
Motor	(16%)	Praise	.64
		Cue	.64
Engaged easy			
(ALT unit)	(49%)	Instruction	.89
		Criticism	.69
		Negative modeling	.63
Not engaged	(31%)		
Wait	(21%)	Instruction	−.79
		Criticism	−.64
		Negative modeling	−.56

behaviors. Catching a student waiting between turns, particularly if that person just completed a learning trial, might provide an ideal moment for instructions, critical comments on skill performance, or a graphic display of an error. It would be interesting to experiment with this as a useful teaching strategy to make more efficient use of class time.

The correlational data confirm the data-based descriptions reported earlier in the paper. Readers are cautioned not to interpret these correlations as teacher actions causing student behaviors, or vice versa. The wise research consumer will use these 'r' values as indicators of potentially powerful variables to use in designing experimental studies, or as clues to use in designing more sophisticated multiple level descriptive-analytic studies. Through either approach we can discover more detail about naturally occurring events in complex learning environments.

ALT-PE intervention studies have not yet been designed, for example, to reduce instructional time in class so that more individual Skill Practice time accrues, or to induce criticism immediately followed by a retrial after a faulty practice trial. Both of these interventions, each suggested by strong correlations in the present exploratory study, might cause significant changes in ALT-PE. Questioning why Negative Modeling appears to be strongly related to five of the six ALT-PE categories could lead to an interesting descriptive-analytic investigation designed to tease out more detail and perhaps some causal hypothesis for this occurrence.

One bit of evidence confirming the complexities of teaching as related to learning (at least to student time engaged in learning) is that successful engagement with subject matter (ALT units) was related only to three of 12 teacher behaviors, and successful motor engagement (ALT-PE) did not appear at all in the table of significant correlations. There really *are* no easy answers for teachers who want to do the right things to produce high ALT-PE for their students.

This first attempt to correlate what teachers do when they teach—with what ALT-PE tells us students do when they learn—is a tentative step away from mainstream ALT-PE research. Although these results simply support common sense notions about what happens in skills classes, the study may serve an important purpose if it stimulates the design of other correlational studies linking student ALT-PE with teacher behaviors. By so doing, we can perhaps identify more readily the most potent variables for those confirmed interventionists to use in working directly to improve the teaching of physical education. Some day we can look forward to a multitude of ALT-PE studies in each loop of the Rosenshine and Furst model, all of which together can point the way toward better practices on the gym floors and playing fields of the real world.

Reference Notes

1. Fisher, C., Filby, N., Marliave, R., Cahen, L., Dishaw, M., Moore, J., & Berliner, D. Teaching behaviors, academic learning time, and student achievement: Final report of Phase III-B, *Beginning Teacher Evaluation Study*. San Francisco: Far West Laboratory for Educational Research and Development, 1978.
2. Paese, P. *The effect of feedback on ALT (PE Motor) in student teachers' classes*. Paper presented at the AAHPERD National Convention, Houston, 1982.
3. McKenzie, T. *ALT-PE in beginning swimming classes for children*. Paper presented at the AAHPERD National Convention, Detroit, April 1980.
4. Young, J., & Metzler, M. *Correlations between ALT-PE and student achievement in a novel skill ETU*. Paper presented at the AAHPERD National Convention, Houston, April 1982.
5. Locke, L. *Qualitative research in physical education: Theory and methods*. Teaching Behavior Research Workshop, Ohio State University, June 1982. (unpublished workshop materials)
6. Aufderheide, S., Olson, J., & Templin, T. *An integrated approach to the assessment of ALT-PE in a secondary level mainstreamed physical education class*. Paper presented at the AAHPERD National Convention, Boston, April 1981.
7. Siedentop, D., Birdwell, D., & Metzler, M. *A process approach to measuring*

teaching effectiveness in physical education. Paper presented at AAHPERD National Meeting, New Orleans, March 1979.
8. Silverman, S. *Using SPSS to analyze ALT-PE data.* Unpublished manuscript, University of Massachusetts, 1981.

References

AUFDERHEIDE, S., McKenzie, T., & Knowles, C. Effects of individualized instruction on handicapped and nonhandicapped students in elementary school physical education classes. *Journal of Teaching in Physical Education*, 1982, **1**(3), 51-57.

BIRDWELL, D. The effects of modification of teacher behavior on the Academic Learning Time of selected students in physical education (Doctoral dissertation, The Ohio State University). (Ann Arbor, MI: University Microfilms, 1980. No. 8022239)

DODDS, P., Rife, F., & Metzler, M. Academic Learning Time in physical education: Data collection, completed research and future direction. *AIESEP World Conference Proceedings*, 1982.

HAWKINS, R., & Dotson, V. Reliability scores that delude: An Alice in Wonderland trip through the misleading characteristics of interobserver agreement scores in interval recording. In E. Ramp & G. Semb (Eds.), *Behavior analysis: Areas of research and application.* Englewood Cliffs, NJ: Prentice-Hall, 1975.

KELLER, J. *Modification of a hockey/golf ETU.* Unpublished master's thesis, Virginia Polytechnic and State University, 1982.

METZLER, M. The measurement of Academic Learning Time in physical education (Doctoral dissertation, The Ohio State University). (Ann Arbor, MI: University Microfilms, 1979. No. 8008314)

MOSSTON, M. *Teaching physical education* (2nd ed.). Columbus, OH: Charles E. Merrill, 1981.

OLSON, J. Adaptation of the Observational System for Instructional Analysis (OSIA) for use in physical education (Doctoral dissertation, Ohio State University, 1979). *Dissertation Abstracts International*, 1979, **40-01**,11556-A. (University Microfilms No. 7916013)

PLACEK, J. *An observational study of teacher planning in physical education.* Unpublished, doctoral dissertation, University of Massachusetts, 1982.

ROSENSHINE, B., & Furst, N. The use of direct observation to study teaching. In R.M. Travers (Ed.), *Second handbook of research on teaching.* Chicago: Rand McNally, 1973.

SILVERMAN, S. *The relationships among student achievement, student engagement, and selected student characteristics in physical education.* Unpublished doctoral dissertation, University of Massachusetts, 1982.

THARP, R., & Gallimore, R. What a coach can tell a teacher. *Psychology Today*, 1976, **9**(8), 75-78.

Using academic learning time in process-product studies with experimental teaching units

Michael W. Metzler
Virginia Polytechnic Institute and State University

Those of us in physical education who actively engage in research on teaching can be rightfully accused of collectively following the leaders. The leaders in this case are mainstream educational researchers, who develop lines of inquiry and/or instrumentation for addressing empirical questions in the classroom. (A few of us have also followed another set of leaders — those applied behavioral analysis researchers from a variety of clinical and educational settings.)

Our *modus operandum* is strikingly similar in these instances — a new research concept, variable, instrumentation, or data analysis procedure is introduced to us in the context of classroom teaching research. We then attempt to comprehend and adopt that new work into our own unique context of teaching motor play skills and attitudes in the gymnasium and elsewhere. We usually carry over the basic assumptions of the work directly into our setting, while altering the instrumentation to reflect instructional behavior differences between the classroom and the gym. Once having done that, we then pursue a course roughly parallel to that of the original line of inquiry. Although numerous examples are available, the best illustration is the prolific CAFIAS work (Cheffers, 1972), extending from Ned Flanders' original.

Now this is not to imply that following the leaders is bad. On the contrary, such inventive adaptations as the one noted (and many more) have helped us to keep stride with the mainstream of inquiry, and to begin carving out a place for ourselves within it. Part of Siedentop's (1982) claim that "research on teaching in physical education has, or is about to come of age" is attributable to our abilities to identify promising empirical questions and concepts from other sources and subsequently develop instrumentation to pursue them in our own settings. From my own, mostly recent experiences, I can easily sense the pleasantly mild hints of surprise from other faculty members in the College of Education when they realize my familiarity with current methodological advances generated from their research leaders such as Berliner, Marliave, Peterson, Eisner, Rosenshine, and others. I suspect that others have experienced some of these same reactions since teaching physical education research has come of age.

In addition to the already noted CAFIAS and teacher expectations work, we have attempted to stay astride by adapting whole models of research along with current mainstream trends. Research models do not focus upon a single variable or even a set of variables, but rather attempt to address broad empirical questions within a single investigative paradigm—that by itself can be used to parcel out promising variables for study. Dunkin and Biddle (1974) identified several such research paradigms, including a "Process-Product" model that studies the relationship between observed activities in the learning environment (process) and subsequent student achievement (product).

The basic assumptions of this paradigm seem sound indeed, especially after a long, frustrating pursuit of the "Presage-Product" model (Dunkin & Biddle, 1974). This change marked a shift from looking at how the makeup of the cast of characters in the teaching/learning process affected achievement, to looking at how and what they do in class affects achievement, in the hope of better understanding the determinants of learning. Those first attempts at studying process-product relationships looked at a host of *teacher* instructional behaviors such as feedback, questioning, clarity, management, and directness (Dunkin & Biddle, 1974).

In line with our tendency to follow the lead of others, we in physical education also first pursued teacher instructional behaviors in our initial process-product studies, but at a much slower pace. This slower pace was a result of two constraints. First, we did not have enough reliable instruments for recording instructional behaviors in the gym and, secondly, we lacked valid product measures of achievement identifiable from process variables (Graham & Siedentop, 1978.) We found ourselves in a double bind for conducting process-product research in physical education because we had little or no technology for either aspect of the paradigm!

However, the late 1970s were highlighted by the design and implementation of many reliable instruments for measuring teacher and student behaviors in physical education. We successfully overcame the technological problems in identifying and measuring important instructional processes in the gymnasium and elsewhere. The CAFIAS instrument (Cheffers, 1972), the related instruments from the Video Tape Data Bank Project (Anderson, 1980), and the series of applied behavior analysis-based instruments from the Ohio State Teaching Research Program (Siedentop, 1981) are representative of our great accomplishments in observational technology in recent years.

Through all of this we did not address the product segment of the research model. We could say a lot about what was happening in physical education classes, but little about how those process variables affected student achievement. Part of the dilemma was caused by the lack of valid measures for relating immediate learning processes to delayed achievement indicators; we could attribute little of the influence of one day's instruction to student gain measures taken the next day, the next week, or later.

Once again, we were shown by mainstream educational researchers a model for reducing this seriously limiting problem. The resolution was in the form of Experimental Teaching Units (ETUs), developed during the BTES research project (Filby, 1972). An ETU is a standardized unit of instructional content presented to students in a short instructional period. The ETU "package" consists of pre- and posttests developed directly from the specific instructional content, a predetermined instructional time span, and stated instructional objectives. To reduce prior learning effects, the instructional task should be novel for the target subject group. Typically, teachers are free to choose their own instructional strategy, but dictating the pattern of teaching can add known constants to the instruction for certain research purposes. While the use of ETUs does not solve the larger methodological problem of long term process-product relationships, given our current lack of standardized curricula and achievement tests (Graham & Siedentop, 1978), they are certainly an acceptable alternative.

Indeed, the use of the ETU in physical education is already established. A host of them were designed in the Georgia PEETU Project (Graham, 1979). Beverly Yerg has used them quite widely (1982a; Note 1), and now they are being explored with the Academic Learning Time student process instrumentation (Keller, 1982; Young, 1981; Young & Metzler, Note 2).

But merely adapting the ETU research concept to study process-product relationships might not be enough. Perhaps we need to once again follow the lead of current educational research thought that the most important processes for determining student achievement gains are those of *student* in-class behaviors and not teacher behaviors. Specifically, attention is now turning to how students spend their time in class. Whether called academic engaged time (Rosenshine, 1978), academic focus (Berliner & Rosenshine, 1977), Academic Learning Time (Marliave, 1976) or any one of several other labels, the history of "time-on-task" and its relationship to student achievement is quite impressive and impossible to ignore. In a recent collation of reviews, Waxman and Walberg (1982) identified 11 such time-on-task variables under the aegis of "engagement" from 19 sets of data. All 11 engagement variables in those numerous studies were positively correlated with significant student gain scores. Only one *teacher behavior* variable had an equivalently impressive relationship — and that one was a major determinant of student engagement, namely, management.

The few initial efforts with ETUs in physical education seem to support the importance of looking to student process behaviors as better determinants of achievement than teacher behaviors. Recently, Beverly Yerg (1982a) concluded that several categories of teacher instructional behavior showed conflicting relationships with student gain scores in a cartwheel ETU. However, she did conclude in the same study that student engaged time was a powerful factor in student learning in the ETU. In a later, related paper, (Yerg, Note 1) she openly acknowledged that the "impact of the learner has been overlooked and needs to be examined."

This paper will offer additional support for the notion of focusing on student behavior in the teaching/learning process. While the data will not be used to contrast teaching process measures with student process measures directly, they will provide a look at what happens when teacher behavior is systematically ignored in the process-product paradigm and student behavior is analyzed independently from teaching behavior. This effort does not ignore the great impact of the teacher in the instructional process, but is intended to show how student process behaviors can be used to analyze teaching effectiveness in terms of student achievement.

Sources of data

The data to be shown here are a re-analysis from a master's thesis by Joe Keller, completed at Virginia Tech (Keller, 1982). The original purpose of the Keller study was to modify a hockey/golf skill ETU to make it more sensitive to real differences in student achievement scores within the ETU. An earlier study by Janice Young concluded that although contrasting teaching strategies resulted in differing engagement rates for students, the ETU task was too easy and did not allow differences in gain scores to emerge between students (Young, 1981).

Methods

The ETU in the Keller study was a slight modification of one developed in the Georgia PEETU Project (Graham, 1979). The instructional task consisted of hitting a tennis ball with a field hockey stick into a 36-inch hoop secured flat to the ground in the least number of "strokes." The ball had to come to rest in the hoop before the task was completed. The distance was 45 yards from the starting point to the hoop. Protocol for administering the pre- and posttests, conducting scoring, and implementing the ETU itself were all followed from the Georgia Project Handbook. The scoring was done by university students, not by the subjects themselves.

Subjects and setting
A total of 77 ($N = 77$) subjects from four Blacksburg area elementary schools participated in the study. All of them were fifth-graders, with a nearly equal number of boys and girls. The ETUs were taught at school sites away from all other classes. All efforts were made to maintain consistent features at each site in terms of terrain and weather conditions; several inclement days resulted in delaying the ETU at some sites until conditions were reasonably identical across sites.

Instructional groups
At each of three schools, the subjects were divided into two instructional strategy groups. One group was taught with a "reverse chaining" strategy that began instruction at the hoop with the flip shot. Instructional tasks were then sequenced with a gradual increase in distance from the hoop until they reached the starting point and hit drives. This group was never called together for teacher direction-giving and instruction but instead remained at their positions to receive this information. Students were instructed not to change their distance from the hoop until directed by the teacher.

The second group received a "lecture/demonstration" strategy for their instruction. All directions and demonstrations were given to the entire class group, requiring intentional relocation time in the ETU. This group started with a long direction-giving episode that covered all skills in the ETU. They then practiced the skills from the starting point to the hoop with repeated trials. In other words, they "drove" from the starting point, got the ball into the hoop, and returned to the starting point for another trial. This cycle was periodically interrupted by the teacher to bring the students together for tips and feedback.

The teachers in this study were two graduate students who were given predetermined lesson plans and a practice session before meeting their classes. They were coached by the researcher in their respective strategies and always taught the same strategy to their groups. The differing strategies were intended to produce variability in student engagement across groups, ultimately causing variability in Academic Learning Time accrual.

Length of ETUs

The ETUs were taught not only with different strategies, but also at three different lengths of allocated time. Each strategy was taught at 20 minutes, 30 minutes and 40 minutes. A final group, the control, received no instruction at all for 20 minutes between pre- and posttest trials. In all, seven groups of students took part in the study.

Measuring achievement

Each subject was given three pretest and three posttest trials to hit the ball into the hoop in the fewest number of strokes. The mean score from each set constituted their score in that phase. Achievement, or gain, was measured as the difference between mean scores in each phase. Because scoring in this skill is similar to that in golf, improvement is then reflected in *lowered* posttest scores from the pretest phase.

Observations

Each lesson in the study was videotaped to include all students in the picture, with a remote microphone on the teacher. The ALT-PE interval recording instrument (Siedentop, Birdwell & Metzler, Note 3) was then used to measure several student class time variables during the lessons. No sampling techniques were used; every student in every group was coded individually. The ALT-PE instrument was chosen because it reflects an assumption that looking at student process behavior is the best determinant of subsequent achievement gains.

Data analysis

This presentation will limit its focus to examining the relationship between accrued minutes of ALT-PE(M), or "Motor ALT," and student achievement in the ETU. Because of the varying allocated times in the ETUs, it is not possible to use the percentage of observed intervals of Motor ALT as the independent variable. Instead, all student ALT-PE(M) accrual was converted to units of time by multiplying the number

Table 1

Scored-Interval Reliability Percentages

Category	Mean Agreement %
Direct instruction	100%
Task instruction	100%
Transition	100%
Skill practice	100%
Not engaged, interim	80%
Engaged, motor	92%
Easy	100%
Medium	100%

of observed ALT-PE(M) intervals by the length of the interval recording cycle (24 seconds).

Related T-tests were used to analyze for significant differences between pre- and posttest scores in this presentation. A preset alpha level of ($p > .05$) was established for these analyses.

Reliability

The scored-interval method for estimating reliability was used in this study (Hawkins & Dotson, 1975). Three reliability checks were conducted on each observer during the course of videotape observations. Table 1 shows the results of the S-I reliability determinations — all of which are well within acceptable standards for the ALT-PE system (Metzler, 1979).

Results

Because the main purpose of this presentation is to examine the relationship between accrued Motor ALT minutes and student achievement, no data will be shown on the student time differences resulting from the contrasting instructional strategies. However, it should be noted that the reverse chaining strategy groups had significantly greater percentages of engaged time, motor engaged time, and ALT-PE(M). The lecture/demonstration strategy produced significantly higher percentages of instructional waiting time, management time, and cognitive engagement time. No difference was found in content-PE time between strategies.

The first question to be addressed prior to examining the relationship between ALT-PE(M) and achievement is that of the influence of allocated time on achievement. If student gains are simply a function of increased allocated time, then the ALT variables take on lesser importance.

Table 2

Student Gain Scores by Allocated Time Groups

Group	df	Mean Gain	T-Ratio	Level
Control (20 minutes)	16	– .60	1.26	NSD
20 minutes	21	– .62	1.36	NSD
30 minutes	21	–1.67	3.85	.001
40 minutes	15	–1.54	2.10	NSD

Table 2 shows the analysis of gain scores for the three ETU allocated time groups and the control group. The issue here is not the differences between instructional strategies, but rather differences in allocated time; so the sample was grouped according to allocated time, independent of instruction received. All four groups demonstrated lowered posttest scores from the pretest phase. Only one group, with 30 minutes of allocated time, had a statistically significant decrease (–1.67). The group with the most allocated time (40 minutes) did not demonstrate a significant drop despite a decrease of –1.54 strokes per trial. This finding suggests that improved performance in the ETU was not a direct function of increased allocated time for students. Note that the group receiving no instruction had a mean gain score almost identical to that of the 20-minute allocated time group.

Having addressed the influence of allocated time on student gain, the way is then cleared to examine better the relationship of Motor ALT to achievement. The variable of Motor ALT does not change across instructional situations; it is always that amount of time a student spends in relevant motor activities at an easy level of difficulty (Metzler, 1979). It is then capable of being analyzed independently from instructional time and teaching strategy. To illustrate this independency, the subjects from the Keller sample were placed in stratified groupings based on the amount of each student's accrued Motor ALT. Three groups are shown in Table 3, with varying amounts of Motor ALT between them. The first group accrued from zero to 1.9 minutes, the second group accrued from 2.0 to 6.9 minutes, and the third accrued over 7 minutes. This stratification allows for students from different allocated time and instructional strategy ETUs to be grouped according to similar Motor ALT accrual. In effect, it eliminates differences that could result from a student's original treatment group in the study.

The time cutoffs for each strata were established in this analysis to make roughly equal groups representing low, medium, and high accrual from the range in the sample. As an aside, I should note that the relationships in Table 3 will hold up under any of a variety of reasonable

Table 3

Gain Scores by Accrued Motor ALT Minutes

Accrual Group	df	Mean Gain	T-Ratio	Level
0 to 1.9 minutes	21	− .29	−2.95	NSD
2.0 to 6.9 minutes	25	−1.94	3.84	.001
7.0 + minutes	28	−1.49	5.84	.001

stratification criteria, including one based on standard deviations around the mean of accrued Motor ALT minutes in the sample. Those relationships seem quite clear: Students accruing less than 2.0 Motor ALT minutes barely decreased in their posttest means while both of the other groups showed mean decreases of −1.94 and −1.49 strokes per trial. Keep in mind that decreased scores represent improvement in this ETU skill. Of some interest is the fact that the group with the highest accrual actually had less gain than the medium group, even though both groups' gains were statistically significant ($p > .001$).

Table 4 shows a Duncan Multiple Range score analysis to determine significant differences between groups. This table confirms what could easily be surmised from visual analysis of Table 3 — that the lowest Motor ALT group was significantly different from the other groups and that the medium and high accrual groups were not significantly different from one another in their gain score means.

Discussion

The data analyses from this sample begin to lend empirical support to some groundwork previously established in an ALT-PE line of inquiry (Dodds, Rife, & Metzler, Note 4). The first question addressed here was that of the relationship between allocated time and achievement. These data suggest that just being in class longer does not guarantee greater achievement scores. This should come as no surprise to those familiar with the ALT-PE descriptive work and the noticeable "funneling effect" phenomenon (Metzler, 1979). For any number of reasons, students spend precious little meaningful learning time in the physical education classes studied so far. If so little time can be reasonably labeled as productive in terms of stated learning objectives, then merely adding more meaningless instructional minutes is clearly not the solution toward increased student learning.

The early descriptive ALT-PE work prompted several researchers to seriously question available student opportunity to learn skills when Motor ALT is critically low (Metzler, 1979; Placek et al., 1981). These present analyses support that notion and point out the real effects of

Table 4

Duncan Multiple Range Test
$(pr > .05)$

Grouping	N	Motor ALT Accrual	Mean Gain
A	21	0 to 1.9 minutes	− .29
B	25	2.0 to 6.9 minutes	−1.94
B	28	7.0 + minutes	−1.49

Groupings with the same letter are not significantly different from each other.

negligible Motor ALT accrual. Student scores in the lowest accrual group barely changed from the pretest mean — some of them despite 30 and 40 minutes of allocated time — supporting suspicions that very little skill improvement might be expected from very little Motor ALT accrual.

To the extent that generalizations can be made from this ETU task and student sample, one might be inclined toward optimism about how much Motor ALT is needed to promote skill gains of significant magnitude. These analyses suggest that such gains can be demonstrated with modest amounts of Motor ALT, easily and consistently attainable in any teaching setting. The strategy employed in this study to promote higher student ALT rates over the contrasting strategy contains no previously unknown class organizational scheme, and certainly nothing that every teacher could not incorporate into his or her daily class conduct.

This leads, then, to a bad news-good news situation. The bad news is that commonly occurring low accrual rates of Motor ALT can very possibly result in missed chances for students to acquire skills; on the other hand, the good news is that the path to accrual rates that *can* promote skill acquisition is at once more clear, and the organizing of instructional settings to promote accrual rates equivalent to this sample's medium and high groups is definitely attainable.

Of some interest is that the group with the highest accrual of Motor ALT (7 minutes, plus) showed gain scores somewhat lower than the medium accrual group. This might have been a result of the small sample in the study, but was most likely due to the simplicity of the ETU task itself (even when modified from the Young study). In effect, once a student accrued the Motor ALT minutes necessary for learning the task well, additional minutes would no longer set him or her apart from other students also accruing the necessary Motor ALT minutes. This potential ceiling effect raises some interesting questions for future ALT-ETU studies with more complex and demanding tasks.

As might be expected at the end of a research report such as this one, a call for additional study is sounded. Although many times such calls are hollow ringings toward wishful thinking that someone else will do it, I am convinced that focusing our process-product efforts on student behaviors in the context of Experimental Teaching Units will reap certain benefits in our understanding of how students acquire motor play skills in our schools' physical education settings.

Reference Notes

1. Yerg, B. *Relationship of specified instructional teacher behaviors to pupil gain on a motor skill task.* Paper presented at the AIESEP Annual Meeting, Boston, August 1982.
2. Young, J., & Metzler, M. *Correlations between ALT-PE and student achievement in a novel skill ETU.* Paper presented at the AAHPERD National Convention, Houston, April 1982.
3. Siedentop, D., Birdwell, D., & Metzler, M. *A process approach to measuring teaching effectiveness in physical education.* Paper presented at the AAHPERD National Convention, New Orleans, March 1979.
4. Dodds, P., Rife, F., & Metzler, M. *Academic Learning Time in physical education: Data collection, completed research and future directions.* Paper presented at the AIESEP Annual Meeting, Boston, August 1982.

References

ANDERSON, W.G. *Analysis of teaching physical education.* St. Louis: C.V. Mosby, 1980.

BERLINER, D., & Rosenshine, B. The acquisition of knowledge in the classroom. In R. Anderson & W. Montague (Eds.), *Schooling and the acquisition of knowledge.* Hillsdale, NJ: Lawrence Erlbaum, 1977.

CHEFFERS, J.T. *Validation of an instrument designed to expand the Flanders system of interaction analysis to describe nonverbal interaction, different varieties of teacher behavior, and pupil responses.* Unpublished doctoral dissertation, Temple University, 1972.

DUNKIN, M., & Biddle, B. *The study of teaching.* New York: Holt, Rinehart & Winston, 1974.

FILBY, N. *Plans for the future development of Experimental Teaching Units* (Tech. Rep. V-2, Beginning Teacher Evaluation Study). San Francisco: Far West Laboratory for Educational Research and Development, 1972.

GRAHAM, G. *Physical education experimental teaching unit project.* Unpublished manuscript, University of Georgia, 1979.

GRAHAM, G., & Siedentop, D. Developmental stages of teaching effectiveness: A stochastic model. In *National College Physical Education Association for Men Proceedings*, 1978.

HAWKINS, R., & Dotson, V. Reliability scores that delude: An Alice in Wonderland trip through misleading characteristics of interobserver reliability in interval recording. In E. Ramp & G. Semb (Eds.), *Behavior analysis: Areas of research and application*. Englewood Cliffs, NJ: Prentice-Hall, 1975.

KELLER, J. *Modification of a hockey/golf ETU*. Unpublished master's thesis, Virginia Polytechnic Institute and State University, 1982.

MARLIAVE, R. *A review of the findings of Phase II*. (Tech. Note l-2, Beginning Teacher Evaluation Study). San Francisco: Far West Laboratory for Educational Research and Development, 1976.

METZLER, M. *The measurement of Academic Learning Time in physical education* (Doctoral dissertation, The Ohio State University). Ann Arbor, MI: (University Microfilms, 1979. No. 8009314.)

PLACEK, J., Silverman, S., Shute, S., Dodds, P., & Rife, F. Academic Learning Time in a traditional elementary physical education setting. *Journal of Classroom Interaction*, 1981, **17**(2), 41-47.

ROSENSHINE, B. Academic engaged time, content covered, and direct instruction. *Journal of Education*, 1978, **160**, 38-66.

SIEDENTOP, D. The Ohio State University supervision research summary report. *Journal of Teaching in Physical Education*, 1981, pp. 30-38. (Introductory issue)

SIEDENTOP, D. Teaching research: The interventionist view. *Journal of Teaching in Physical Education*, 1982, **1**(2), 46-50.

WAXMAN, H., & Walberg, H. The relation of teaching and learning: A review of reviews of process-product research. *Contemporary Education Review*, 1982, **1**, 103-120.

YERG, B. The impact of selected presage and product behaviors on the refinement of a motor skill. *Journal of Teaching in Physical Education*, 1982, **1**(1), 38-46.

YOUNG, J. *The influence of Academic Learning Time on the acquisition of a novel motor task*. Unpublished master's creative component, Iowa State University, 1981.

A comparison of interaction patterns and academic learning time of low- and high-burnout secondary physical educators

V.H. Mancini, D.A. Wuest,
E.K. Clark, and N. Ridosh
Ithaca College

Teacher burnout is considered by some authorities as one of the most crucial problems in education today (McGuire, 1979; Sparks & Hammond, 1981; Truch, 1980). Teachers, confronted with unrelieved work stress, are leaving the profession in increasing numbers (Truch, 1980; Veninga & Spradley, 1981). Other burned-out teachers remain on the job, albeit reluctantly, coping with burnout by going on "active retirement" — teaching by simply going through the motions (Austin, 1981; Ricken, 1980; Veninga & Spradley, 1981). One way that physical educators go through the motions is by "throwing out the ball."

The problem of burnout among physical educators is a professional concern of the American Alliance of Health, Physical Education, Recreation and Dance (AAHPERD), as reflected in recent publications: "Alternatives to Teacher Burnout" (AAHPERD, 1980), "Combating Teacher Burnout" (AAHPERD, 1981), "The Teaching/Coaching Challenge" (AAHPERD, 1981), and *Managing Teacher Stress and Burnout* (Sparks & Hammond, 1981).

The potential consequences of job burnout are very serious for teachers as well as for the students and the school involved. Farber and Miller (1981) asserted that the most critical impact of burnout will be centered on the delivery of educational services. Within the realm of physical education, burnout can significantly affect the physical educator's job performance, resulting in behavioral inflexibility, inefficiency, and infrequent or careless planning of classes (Farber & Miller, 1981; Sparks & Hammond, 1981; Veninga & Spradley, 1981). Burned-out teachers may display impersonal or negative attitudes toward students as well as a detached or depersonalized manner (Maslach & Jackson, 1981). They may offer little sympathy, praise, encouragement, or reinforcement of students' efforts (Farber & Miller, 1981). Burned-out teachers may be critical of their students and give them minimum feedback (Sparks & Hammond, 1981; Veninga & Spradley, 1981). Lack of involvement, infrequent student interaction, and lowered expectations for students are also common (Farber & Miller, 1981; Maslach & Jackson, 1981; Veninga & Spradley, 1981).

A review of the literature on the effects of teacher burnout, both in physical education and academic areas, reveals that research has focused largely on defining burnout, characterizing the burnout syndrome, identifying the causes (i.e., teacher stress), describing the impact, and offering suggestions for remediation (AAHPERD, 1980, 1981; Farber & Miller, 1981; Sparks & Hammond, 1981). Little research has been undertaken within the realm of physical education to systematically assess the effects of teacher burnout, especially as it relates to teacher-student interactions and student learning. The impact of teacher burnout on teaching behavior, job performance, and students may be assessed through the use of descriptive-analytic techniques or systematic observation.

In the present study, two systematic observation instruments — Cheffers' Adaptation of Flanders' Interaction Analysis System (CAFIAS) (Cheffers, 1972) and Academic Learning Time-Physical Education (ALT-PE) (Siedentop, Tousignant, & Parker, 1982) — were used concurrently to address the following questions:

1. What is the relationship between different levels of teacher burnout and teacher-student interaction patterns?
2. Is there a relationship between teachers who exhibit different levels of teacher burnout and the amount of time their students spend on learning specific movement tasks in physical education classes?

Procedures

Three instruments were used in this investigation. The Maslach Burnout Inventory (MBI) (Maslach & Jackson, 1981) was used to determine the level of burnout. Cheffers' Adaptation of Flanders' Interaction Analysis System (CAFIAS) (Cheffers, 1972) identified the interaction patterns between the teacher and the students. The revised ALT-PE instrument (Siedentop et al., 1982) described the nature of the class activity and the involvement level of individual students.

Thirty certified physical education teachers from the Southern Tier section of New York served as subjects. After completing the informed consent form, each teacher was administered the MBI. Using the median split technique, the teachers were assigned on the basis of their MBI scores to either the low-burnout (LB) (N = 15) or high-burnout (N = 15) group. Ten teachers were then randomly selected to represent each group, but they were not aware of their designation as LB or HB.

The 20 teachers, wearing wireless microphones, were videotaped three times while teaching their previously planned regular classes. A total of 60 classes were videotaped, 30 from each group. CAFIAS data were obtained from an expert's coding of the three videotapes of each subject. Ratios and percentages of the CAFIAS variables and parameters were derived through computer analysis. Stability reliability for the CAFIAS coding was established at .95.

The videotapes were again viewed and coded for ALT-PE data by two coders experienced in descriptive-analytic techniques. Using the interval recording technique, three students were randomly selected from each taped class and were observed alternately using a 6-second observe, 6-second record format. Percentages and ratios for each ALT-PE category were computed manually. The scored interval method was used to determine reliability (Siedentop et al., 1982). Interobserver reliability for all ALT-PE categories ranged from .929 to 1.00. The average interobserver reliability was .957 for all ALT-PE categories.

Results

Interaction analysis

To ascertain whether significant differences in teaching behaviors and interaction patterns existed between the LB and HB groups, multivariate analysis of variance (MANOVA) was performed on the eight CAFIAS variables. The MANOVA revealed a significant difference in the teaching behavior between LB and HB teachers, $F(8, 11)$ = 75.37, $p < .05$. Discriminant function analysis identified the relative contributions of the variables to this between-group difference, with teacher use of verbal acceptance and praise (TVAP) accounting for 73.77% of the variability. When this was combined with student-suggested pupil verbal initiation (SSPVI) (12.65%) and teacher use of verbal questioning (TVQ) (8.81%), over 95% of the variability between the groups was explained.

Means and standard deviations for each of the eight CAFIAS variables were calculated. Through univariate ANOVA, two variables that independently contributed significant between-groups differences ($p < .05$) were identified. These variables were teacher use of verbal acceptance and praise (TVAP) and teacher use of nonverbal acceptance and praise (TNVAP). In each case, the HB teachers exhibited less acceptance and praise with their students than did the LB teachers. The HB teachers exhibited more teacher direction and criticism toward their students.

Descriptive data were gathered by calculating the mean percentage of occurrence of each of the 20 CAFIAS categories and the most predominant interaction patterns for each group. These calculations were based on 34,660 behaviors in the LB group and on 28,476 behaviors in the HB group.

Figure 1 shows that LB teachers displayed a greater percentage of verbal and nonverbal acceptance, praise, questioning, and information-giving. The HB teachers employed a greater amount of verbal and nonverbal directions and criticism than did their LB counterparts. Thus, LB teachers were more varied in their teaching behaviors, both in the manner in which they presented the material and gave feedback to their students. The LB teachers were more encouraging and supportive of their students as reflected by the amount of praise and acceptance, whereas the HB teachers criticized their students more frequently and were more restrictive in their behaviors.

Students taught by LB teachers gave slightly more verbal predictable responses and displayed a greater amount of nonverbal broad interpretation of teacher activities. Students taught by HB teachers gave more nonverbal predictable responses and slightly more verbal interpretation than did students taught by LB teachers. There was little student initiative in either group and this behavior occurred less frequently than did the previous types of student behaviors. Both groups exhibited large amounts of student-to-student verbal interaction.

The predominant interaction patterns were also identified. Extended student-to-student interpretive response and game playing (8 \ -10-8 \ ) was the dominant behavior pattern for both groups, occurring 21.0% in LB teachers' classes as compared to 31.5% in HB teachers' classes. The next highest pattern, exhibited 15.9% of the time by LB teachers, was teacher information-giving followed by student interpretive behavior followed by further information (5-8 \ -5); this occurred only 5.4% of the time in the HB teachers' classes. The HB teacher provided information in a different manner, spending 6.7% of the time giving extended information (5-5). The LB teachers spent 4.3% of their class time providing extended information to their students. This reflects differences in teachers' methods of imparting information, the LB teachers providing students with feedback information while the students were actively involved,

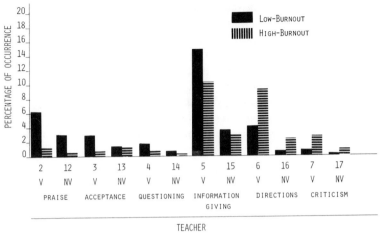

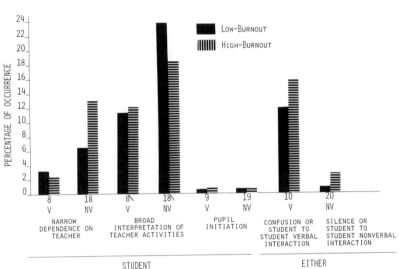

Figure 1—Mean percent of behaviors in each CAFIAS category.

whereas the HB teachers tended to give students information while they were inactive or passive.

Two other significant patterns that differentiated the groups were the amount of praise and acceptance exhibited by teachers to their students' interpretive ideas and actions. In the LB group, the pattern of student interpretive response followed by teacher praise followed by further student interpretive response $(8 \setminus -2-8 \setminus)$ occurred 9.0% as compared to 1.2% in the HB group. The pattern of student interpretation followed by teacher acceptance followed by further student interpretation $(8 \setminus -3-8 \setminus)$ occurred 4.2% in the LB group as compared to 2.4% in the HB group.

Students in LB teachers' classes also participated in more extended interpretation of teachers' activities (8 \ -8 \ ) than did students in HB teachers' classes (8.0% versus 4.5%).

While student interpretive response or game play (8 \ -10-8 \ ) was the most predominant pattern in HB teachers' classes, the next highest pattern was teacher direction-giving followed by student predictable, mechanical response followed by further teacher directions (6-8-6). This pattern occurred 10% of the time in the HB teachers' classes as compared to only 3.5% of the time in the LB teachers' classes, which indicates that in the HB teachers' classes a greater amount of time was spent on drills and activities more mechanical than interpretive in nature. The percentages for extended student predictable responses (8-8) were also higher in the HB teachers' classes than in the LB teachers' classes; this pattern occurred 5.3% for the HB group and 2.2% for the LB group.

ALT-PE

Percentages and ratios were calculated for all ALT-PE categories (see Table 1). These calculations were based on 2,204 observation intervals for LB teachers and 2,325 observation intervals for HB teachers. A total of 180 students were observed.

Comparison of the total percentages for the context level subdivisions—general content, subject matter knowledge, and subject matter motor—reveals only slight differences, less than 6%, occurred between the LB and HB teachers. However, the data for the categories within these major subdivisions reveals differences between the LB and HB teachers. The HB teachers' classes spent slightly more time in general content (29.7%), performing organizational details such as changing groups, getting equipment, or receiving directions from the teacher. The HB classes spent more time in transition (14.9%) and management (6.7%) than did LB classes (13.0% and 3.6%, respectively). Both LB and HB teachers' classes spent approximately 7% of their time in warm-up.

With respect to subject matter knowledge, the LB teachers' classes spent slightly more time focused on knowledge related to physical education content (9.5% versus 6.9%). HB teachers spent slightly more time instructing the class in technique (5.1% versus 4.1%); the LB teachers spent a greater percentage of time relating strategy and rules to the class (4.8% versus 1.5%). In both groups, no time was devoted to social behavior, and virtually no time was devoted to providing students with background information about the activities.

Most of the time in LB and HB classes was devoted to motor involvement and participation in physical education activities. The LB teachers' classes recorded a slightly greater percentage of time for subject matter motor than did the HB classes (66.7% versus 63.5%). HB teachers' classes spent a greater percentage of their time practicing specific skills

Table 1

Percent Occurrence of ALT-PE Categories
Low- and High-burnout Teachers

Category	Low-burnout	High-burnout
Context level		
General content (total)	23.8	29.7
Transition	13.0	14.9
Management	3.6	6.7
Break	0.0	.2
Warm-up	7.2	7.9
Subject matter knowledge (total)	9.5	6.9
Technique	4.1	5.1
Strategy	2.4	.8
Rules	2.4	.7
Social behavior	0.0	0.0
Background	.7	.3
Subject matter motor (total)	66.7	63.5
Skill practice	8.0	11.3
Scrimmage/routine	4.5	4.3
Fitness	11.3	2.8
Game	43.0	43.8
Learner involvement level		
Not motor engaged (total)	43.9	57.5
Interim	4.8	6.5
Waiting	7.0	17.6
Off task	3.8	10.9
On task	13.5	14.4
Cognitive	14.8	8.1
Motor engaged (total)	56.1	42.5
Motor appropriate	48.0	25.7
Motor inappropriate	7.6	16.6
Supporting	.5	.2

and performing drills as compared to the LB teachers' classes (11.3%
versus 5.8%). For both groups, approximately 4% of the time was spent
in scrimmage, refining skills, and 43% of the time was spent in game play
and application of skills. There was a large difference in the percentage
of time LB and HB teachers devoted to fitness activities. Fitness was the
emphasis for 11.25% of the time in LB classes as compared to 2.8% in
HB classes. These differences were due to the type of activities taught by
the teachers.

The greatest differences between the two groups were found in the
learner involvement level, both in the not-motor-engaged and in the
motor-engaged categories. Learners were not engaged in motor activity
for 43.9% of the time in LB teachers' classes, whereas lack of motor in-

volvement by learners in the HB teachers' classes accounted for 57.5% of the total class time. Students in HB teachers' classes spent twice as much time performing interim and off-task activities and waiting than did the students in LB teachers' classes. Similar percentages were recorded in both groups for learners' involvement in on-task activities such as performing a management, transition, or warm-up task. Cognitive behaviors such as listening to teachers' instructions or watching a demonstration occurred 14.8% in the LB group, compared to 8.1% in the HB group.

Students actively participated in motor activities for 56% in LB teachers' classes, whereas the students in HB teachers' classes were engaged in motor activity only 42.5% of the class time. The most pronounced differences between LB and HB teachers' classes were observed in the motor appropriate category reflecting the amount of Academic Learning Time-Physical Education (ALT-PE). Students in the LB teachers' classes were involved 48% of the time in the performance of motor appropriate activity (ALT-PE)—activity that contributed to lesson goals and that the learner could perform successfully. Approximately half as much time was recorded for ALT-PE in the HB teachers' classes (25.7%). In contrast to the findings for motor appropriate activity, twice the amount of inappropriate activity was recorded for HB students as compared to LB students (16.6% and 7.6%, respectively).

Discussion, conclusion, and recommendations

This study was an initial effort to explore the effects of teacher burnout on teacher behaviors, interaction patterns, and student learning (ALT-PE). There are few studies with which to compare the findings. Although teacher burnout has become increasingly prevalent, there is not enough research utilizing systematic observation, specifically CAFIAS and ALT-PE, to assess the impact of burnout on the aforementioned variables.

The results indicated that LB and HB teachers exhibited different teacher behaviors and interaction patterns. Specifically, LB teachers exhibited significantly more praise and acceptance of their students' ideas and actions and interacted more frequently with their students than did HB teachers. Secondly, there was a difference in the ALT-PE of students in classes taught by LB and HB teachers, with students in HB teachers' classes spending less time in ALT-PE than students in LB teachers' classes.

Interaction analysis

The CAFIAS data revealed a clear demarcation between LB and HB teachers'· behaviors and interactions with their students. Essentially, all behavior patterns occurred in the classes of LB and HB teachers. More varied behaviors — praise, acceptance, questioning, information-giving — were exhibited by the LB teachers. Not only did they provide their students with more information than did HB teachers, but they asked questions to clarify student understanding and to solicit student input on subject matter. Although game play predominated, the LB teacher also encouraged and provided for student interpretive behavior.

HB teachers employed less varied behavior, which tended to restrict student behavior by use of directions and criticism. Students in the HB teachers' classes engaged in more game play than did students in LB teachers' classes. However, other than game play, HB teachers provided less opportunity for student nonverbal interpretive behavior, and their students exhibited more nonverbal narrow responses (i.e., mechanical drills, calisthenics, etc.).

Not only were the behaviors of LB and HB teachers different but the sequencing of the behaviors — interaction patterns — varied as well. LB teachers interacted more frequently and were more personally involved with their students, and were frequently engaged in activity or game play with their students (i.e., 8 \ -3) rather than just observing student performance. In contrast, HB teachers were less involved and spent more time observing students' efforts.

Noticeable differences were found in the manner and nature of the feedback that LB and HB teachers provided to their students. Generally, LB teachers provided their students with concurrent feedback so that students could use this information to improve their skills while continuing to perform. LB teachers were also more responsive to students' ideas and actions, and used significantly more praise, acceptance, and encouragement both during and after students' efforts. If students are given praise in a selective manner and in concert with their performance, they are more likely to repeat the reinforced behavior patterns (Brophy, 1981). This acceptance and recognition of students' efforts assists teachers in establishing personal relationships with their students. These behaviors were not evident in HB teachers' interactions.

In the HB teachers' classes, teachers gave information in an extended manner while the students were passive or inactive. In comparison to the praise and acceptance given by LB teachers, the HB teachers directed more criticism, justification of their authority, and cynical remarks to their students. HB teachers offered little encouragement and seldom interjected feedback during student performance. Generally, student performance was extended and silently monitored, without suggestions or encouragement from the teacher, who assumed the role of the "silent observer." This detachment and distancing from the activity of the class may be categorized as "going through the motions" (Ricken, 1980; Veninga & Spradley, 1981) or "throwing out the ball."

The image of the burned-out teacher, as reflected in the CAFIAS data, is similar to that portrayed by other researchers (Austin, 1981; Farber & Miller, 1981; Ricken, 1980; Veninga & Spradley, 1981). Lack of involvement, detachment, infrequent use of encouragement, and coping with burnout by "throwing out the ball" were all characteristic of the HB teachers.

ALT-PE

The ALT-PE data indicated that teacher burnout has an impact on job performance, particularly on efficiency, organization of class activities, and on student opportunity to learn. Student learning can be enhanced when teachers carefully design instruction to provide a maximum amount of student engaged time (Berliner, 1979). Additionally, when teachers use efficient management techniques, the time allocated for instruction and active participation can be used to its fullest (Siedentop, 1976). LB teachers were more efficient in class management than were the HB teachers, who spent almost twice as much time in management than did LB teachers. As observed from the videotapes, HB teachers did not hurry to start class instruction; they spent more time in taking roll and in general conversation. When students were in transition, such as changing sides during a game or moving from station to station, the HB teacher observed the students without comment as they casually strolled about. The HB teachers did little to hustle students along so that instruction could continue; in fact, they frequently sauntered along with them. This casual approach to efficiency and management on the part of the HB teachers undoubtedly contributed to the greater amount of waiting and off-task behaviors by students.

Differences between LB and HB teachers were also reflected in the design of instruction. LB teachers provided their students with more varied cognitive information. While the HB teachers primarily related information about technique, the LB teachers discussed not only technique but also rules and strategy, this additional information giving their students broader exposure to the activity being taught.

Although LB and HB teachers' classes spent similar amounts of time in motor activity, student involvement within the activities differed. Motor activity in the LB classes was more motor appropriate and appeared to contribute to the achievement of the instructional objectives. If, as Berliner (1979) suggests, the ALT reflects students' learning, students in the LB teachers' classes had the opportunity to learn more.

In the LB classes, the pace of the class was more task-focused and the teacher seemed to be more intent on accomplishing the instructional objectives. Management and transition time was minimal; the instruction was designed so that students had more time to engage in appropriate motor behavior (ALT-PE). The LB teachers appeared to monitor student activity more closely to ensure that students were on task and appropriately engaged than did the HB teachers.

The differences revealed by the ALT-PE data substantiated the concern of researchers that burnout may have an impact on the educational delivery system — specifically on efficiency, planning, and student learning (Farber & Miller, 1981; Veninga & Spradley, 1981).

Conclusions and recommendations

The differences revealed by CAFIAS and ALT-PE were in congruence with those of other researchers relative to the impact of burnout on teacher behavior and job performance (Austin, 1981; Farber & Miller, 1981; Maslach & Jackson, 1981; McGuire, 1979; Ricken, 1980; Truch, 1980; Veninga & Spradley, 1981). The investigators would like to offer the following recommendation for future research on teacher burnout in physical education. If Ricken (1980) is correct in his perception that teacher burnout is a failure of the supervisory process and his assertion that preventing teacher burnout is the supervisory challenge of the 1980s, the next step would be to conduct intervention studies that use descriptive-analytic techniques as a feedback tool. Training in descriptive-analytic techniques has been found beneficial in changing teacher behaviors (Quinn, 1982; van der Mars, 1979). This approach may also be beneficial in mitigating the effects of teacher burnout. As of this writing, research using CAFIAS as an intervention technique with high-burnout secondary physical educators, and the effects of this feedback on teaching behaviors and ALT-PE, is being completed.

This study was the initial attempt to study the effects of teacher burnout on secondary physical educators using two descriptive-analytic techniques, CAFIAS and ALT-PE. Hopefully, it will offer some directions and provide the impetus for descriptive-analytic studies of teacher burnout in physical education.

References

AMERICAN Alliance for Health, Physical Education, Recreation, and Dance. Combating teacher burnout. *Journal of Physical Education, Recreation, and Dance*, 1981, **52**(9), 35-48.

AMERICAN Alliance for Health, Physical Education, Recreation, and Dance. The teaching/coaching challenge. *Journal of Physical Education, Recreation and Dance*, 1981, **52**(9), 15-25.

AMERICAN Alliance for Health, Physical Education, Recreation, and Dance. Alternatives to teacher burnout. *Journal of Physical Education and Recreation*, 1980, **51**(9), 53-60.

AUSTIN, D.A. The teacher burnout issue. *Journal of Physical Education, Recreation, and Dance*, 1981, **52**(9), 35-36.

BERLINER, D. Tempus educare. In P. Peterson & H. Wallburg (Eds.), *Research on teaching: Concepts, findings, and implications*. Berkeley, CA: McCutchan, 1979.

BROPHY, J. Teacher praise: A functional analysis. *Review of Educational Research*, 1981, **51**(1), 5-32.

CHEFFERS, J.T.F. *The validation of an instrument designed to expand the Flanders' System of Interaction Analysis to describe nonverbal interaction, different variables of teacher behavior, and pupil responses*. Unpublished doctoral dissertation, Temple University, 1972.

FARBER, B.A., & Miller, J. Teacher burnout: A psychoeducational perspective. *Teachers College Record*, 1981, **83**(2), 235-243.

MASLACH, C., & Jackson, S.E. *Maslach Burnout Inventory: Research edition manual*. Palo Alto, CA: Consulting Psychologist Press, 1981.

McGUIRE, W.H. Teacher burnout. *Today's Education*, 1979, **68**(4), 5.

QUINN, P.A. *The lasting effects of instruction and supervision in interaction analysis on the teaching behavior, effectiveness, and attitudes of inservice physical educators*. Unpublished master's thesis, Ithaca College, 1982.

RICKEN, R. Teacher burnout—a failure of the supervisory process. *NASSP Bulletin*, 1980, **64**(434), 21-24.

SIEDENTOP, D. *Developing teaching skills in physical education*. Boston: Houghton Mifflin, 1976.

SIEDENTOP, D., Tousignant, M., & Parker, M. *Academic learning time-physical education coding manual*. School of Health, Physical Education and Recreation, College of Education, The Ohio State University, 1982.

SPARKS, D., & Hammond, J. *Managing teacher stress and burnout*. Reston, VA: American Alliance for Health, Physical Education, Recreation and Dance, 1981.

TRUCH, S. *Teacher burnout and what to do about it*. Novato, CA: Academic Therapy, 1980.

van der MARS, H. *The effects of instruction in and supervision through interaction analysis on the relationship between perceived and observed teaching behavior of preservice physical education teachers*. Unpublished master's thesis, Ithaca College, 1979.

VENINGA, R.L., & Spradley, J.P. *The work stress connection: How to cope with job burnout*. New York: Ballantine Books, 1981.

Section six
Teaching styles in physical education

In several ways, the three presentations in this section are eclectic in nature. Indeed, each fits that classical definition and presents what appears to be the best from diverse sources, systems, or styles. Each looks at a different aspect of teaching in physical education and uses difficult lenses to study the phenomena. And the results of each are thought-provoking and useful.

Using Mosston's Spectrum of Teaching Styles as the theoretical statement, Michael Goldberger summarizes the first three studies in an ongoing program of research on teaching at Temple University. Teaching styles selected from Mosston's "direct cluster" (practice, reciprocal, and inclusion) were studied in order to establish positive relationships between specific teaching processes and selected learning outcomes in a hockey accuracy task. The practice style appears to consistently produce the best results. Further analyses are in process concerning ability groups, socioeconomic groupings, a second task, and self-concept groups.

Thom McKenzie reviews a series of four studies that examines the use of machines in pacing instruction, such as program boards, automatic light-cuing systems, and programmed audio cassette tapes. Dependent variables include work output (rate of performance), student attitudes toward machine-pacing, student active learning time, and quantity and quality of different teacher behaviors.

Results indicate that the devices allow more opportunities to learn by increasing motor response time, and by increasing the amount and quality of augmented feedback to students. McKenzie contends that the use of such devices will make a good teacher even better.

In his paper, Anthony Annarino juxtaposes the current findings of research in the teaching of physical education against a historical backdrop of the profession—its truths, knowledges, information, and the preparation of its leaders. He suggests that recent investigations about the physical education teaching-learning process validate many ideas of early leaders in the profession, and maintains that such cumulative evidence should lend direction to physical education instruction. Annarino presents an overview of his findings from recent visits to 47 public schools in six states, suggesting a problem-solving approach that might resolve the critical incidents he found.

Direct styles of teaching and psychomotor performance

Michael Goldberger
Temple University

This report will outline the program of research on teaching we've undertaken at Temple University and will summarize the results of our first three studies. Our goal in this research effort was to begin establishing data-based linkages between selected teaching styles and specific learning outcomes in the psychomotor domain. In planning such a research program, we confronted a number of decisions concerning the teaching processes and learning outcomes to be studied, the context within which these interactions were to be observed (including the characteristics of the children to be studied), and the research designs that would best provide useful information about these linkages. The first part of this report discusses these decisions and clarifies our points of departure. The report concludes with the summary of our first three studies, an assessment of this work, and a description of our next efforts.

Since this research program focused on teaching, it was logical to begin by identifying the teaching processes to be studied. In general, there appear to be at least two ways to approach this issue. The first, emanating from an empirical perspective, involves studying the behavior of real teachers in naturalistic classroom settings. This approach first specifies the desired learning outcomes, usually in terms of children's scores on standardized achievement tests. The researcher then identifies classrooms that demonstrate consistency in either going beyond or failing to reach expected performance norms on these standardized tests. The teachers in these classrooms who were either consistently successful or unsuccessful in bringing about desired learning outcomes are observed while teaching, and their teaching behavior is objectively recorded. The intent of this approach is to establish meaningful linkages between learner achievement and specific teaching behavior. As a number of well planned and executed studies conducted over the past decade have demonstrated, this approach has been useful in identifying some of these linkages (Brophy, 1979; BTES, 1980; Rosenshine, 1977; Soar, 1979; Stallings, 1980).

The second approach in identifying the teaching processes to be studied emanates from a theoretical perspective; the independent variable is drawn from a theoretical statement about the teaching process. The purpose of a research program emanating from this perspective is to systematically test aspects of the theory, to make modifications and refinements in its structure, and to build up a data base supporting the theory and its constructs. This approach requires one to begin with a theoretical statement about the teaching process. A number of candidates, including those proposed by Bennett, Jordan, Long, and Wade (1976), Flanders (1970), Joyce (1972), and Mosston (1981), would be useful for this purpose. These theoretical statements appear, in general, to offer alternative, and not conflicting, views of the teaching process.

For the research program at Temple University, we've adopted this second approach because it seems that in the long run this will prove to be the more productive strategy. Beginning a research program from a theoretical perspective makes both the formulation of research questions and the structuring of hypotheses more rational and systematic. The theoretical statement, if it is precise, helps to clarify both the internal structure of teaching style being studied as well as how this style relates to other styles. The theoretical statement makes it easier for the researcher to verify fidelity between the teacher's actual behavior and the theoretical teaching style being studied. Finally, it provides a framework for the synthesis of research findings, both those of the researcher and those of others in the field.

Mosston's *Spectrum of Teaching Styles* serves as our theoretical statement. This unified structure of alternative teaching/learning behaviors was developed during the early 1960s by Muska Mosston and first appeared in print in his 1966 book entitled *Teaching Physical Education*. Since its inception, the Spectrum has undergone continual refinement as Dr. Mosston and his associates have attempted to implement these ideas in the schools. Although the theoretical statement is more sophisticated today than it was two decades ago, it is based on the same foundation and principles as the original model.

The cornerstone of the Spectrum is a decision-making model called "the anatomy of any style." Within the anatomy, each decision about the teaching/learning transaction is categorized as to whether it is made before (pre-impact), during (impact), or following (post-impact) the interaction between teacher and learner. Actual teaching styles emerge by identifying who, teacher or learner, makes which decisions. As can be seen in Figure 1, what evolves is a theoretical framework of alternative teaching/learning role models, all anchored in and connected by the anatomy and contained within the limits of complete teacher decision-making (Style A) and complete learner decision-making (Style H). Between these theoretical limits exist a number of structurally pure "landmark" styles of teaching and an infinite variety of other styles of teaching that fall under the "canopies" of these landmark styles.

The principal value of any teaching style lies in the conditions for learning that it provides. An analysis of the conditions for learning provided by each of the landmark styles reveals that styles with common characteristics appear to form loosely organized "clusters" of styles along the Spectrum. For example, Styles F and G seem to cluster together in that both of these landmark styles call upon the learner to exhibit higher than recall levels of cognitive behavior. In other words, the learners must think either logically (Style F) or expansively (Style G) when participating in these styles. Likewise, Styles A through E appear to form a cluster in that in each of these five landmark styles of teaching, learners are expected to reproduce the specific content or skills prescribed by the teacher. Learners are expected to practice and master the tasks designed and prescribed by the teacher. The teaching behavior associated with these five styles represents, in general, the kind of teaching Rosenshine (1977) has called "direct instruction."

The processes

The styles of teaching we selected to initiate our research program were chosen from this so-called "direct cluster," this decision being based primarily on two factors. It is clear that the most prevalent teaching currently practiced in classrooms and gymnasia across this country falls under the canopies of the styles within this direct cluster. Secondly, almost all of the major research on teaching conducted over the past 10 years has focused, in general, on the kind of teaching found within this direct cluster. It was therefore decided to begin our work with teaching styles selected from this direct cluster and to build upon existing knowledge in an area of widespread application.

The Anatomy of Any Style		(T)	(T)	(T)	(T)	(T)	(T)	(T)	(L)	
	Pre-Impact	(T)	(T)	(T)	(T)	(T)	(T)	(T)	(L)	
	Impact	(T)	(L)	(d)	(L)	(L̸)	(T/L)	(L≶)	(L)	
	Post-Impact	(T)	(T)	(o)	(L)	(L)	(L/T)	(L)	(L)	

Teacher Maximum Decision Making	A	B	C	D	E	F	G	H	Teacher Minimum Decision Making
Learner Minimum Decision Making									Learner Maximum Decision Making
	Command Style	Practice Style	Reciprocal Style	Self-Check Style	Inclusion Style	Guided Discovery	Divergent Style	Learner Designed Program	

Figure 1 — The spectrum of teaching styles.

A brief description of each of these styles, namely Styles B, C and E, is necessary to better understand the nature of these teaching/learning models and to appreciate how the dependent variables were selected. Under Style B conditions, the teacher designs and assigns specific tasks for the learners to complete. While the learners are practicing these single-standard tasks, the teacher circulates around the area and periodically provides feedback to each learner as frequently as possible. This particular style represents, in general, the most prevalent teaching found in classrooms and gymnasia today.

Style C, the second style we studied, is similar to Style B, but rather than periodic feedback being provided by the teacher, the feedback is provided both during and after each practice trial by a peer. This is accomplished by having the children form pairs, and as one partner performs the tasks the other partner observes the performance and provides immediate feedback based on criteria supplied by the teacher. After the first partner has completed the tasks, they switch roles and reciprocate. The teacher is available to the observer for assistance.

Under Style E conditions, each learner assesses his or her own performance on the tasks based on criteria supplied by the teacher. In other words, this style enables the learners to test themselves. In addition, the teacher provides alternative levels of difficulty within each task; that is, the same tasks but each with multiple levels of difficulty. This arrangement allows each learner to select the level of difficulty for each task which is most appropriate for his or her ability at the time. The learner may switch to a less or more difficult level at any time. The implications of this kind of arrangement for learning are obvious particularly for students of high and low ability. The teaching behavior associated with Style E represents, in general, the kind of teaching found in "individualized instruction" programs. In summary, we began our research program by studying the effects of Styles B, C, and E, "direct cluster" styles that represent, in general, the kind of teaching found in most schools today.

The products

As noted earlier, the intent in this kind of research is to establish meaningful relationships between specific teaching processes and selected learning outcomes. These learning outcomes can be identified in at least two ways. In most of the major studies mentioned, the dependent variables were children's scores on standardized achievement tests. These widely used tests, considered to reflect academic achievement in the basic content areas of the school curriculum, were selected because they represent agreed-upon products of schooling. In other words, products can be identified arbitrarily based on their current popularity or emphasis in the curriculum.

In a research program such as ours, in which the teaching processes to be studied were selected from a theoretical statement about teaching, the product, the dependent variables, could and should be identified in a more rational manner. Each teaching style being studied should be analyzed in terms of the conditions for learning it produces; then the anticipated learning outcomes — the products — can be identified logically by envisioning the probable effects of such conditions on the learner's intellectual, psychomotor, and social/emotional development. For example, the conditions produced by Style B suggest that in terms of intellectual development the learners would be engaged in memory-type cognitive behavior. Or, if Style C were the focus, the arrangement in which learners work as partners to help each other learn the task at hand, it seems logical to hypothesize that these children would improve on selected social skills associated with giving feedback to and receiving it from a peer.

Since we were primarily interested in the effects of these teaching styles on psychomotor performance, we decided to select a psychomotor task which would meet the following criteria. It would need to be:

1. unique and novel to the children;
2. representative of the kinds of tasks found in school physical education curricula;
3. learned easily and independently of the child's fitness level;
4. amenable to control of the operational differences among the three styles of teaching under study;
5. easily transported and stored.

The psychomotor task selected was a hockey accuracy task adopted from Skinner (1974) that requires the children to shoot hockey discs, using a street hockey stick, under a screen and into a target area calibrated to yield scores ranging from 0 to 20. This algorithmic motor task (Goldberger, 1980) met all the criteria listed above and in several pilot studies proved to be both feasible and appropriate.

In addition to psychomotor performance, a number of other dependent variables primarily from the affective domain were selected for study
in this program of research. These are described below during the discussion of the specific studies. Identification of these variables was based on
the same kind of analysis of the conditions produced by the independent
variable under study, as was the case for the psychomotor variable.

Design and contextual considerations

The subjects for these studies were fifth grade children in local schools,
who were randomly selected from a larger pool of volunteer subjects and
randomly assigned to the treatment groups.

To control for as many of the contextual factors as possible that would
likely affect the influence of the teaching styles on learning, it was decided to conduct the first study in a controlled, laboratory type setting.
An empty room near the gymnasium in the school we were using was prepared as our training area and was equipped with the motor task appara-
tus and equipment, the data recording equipment, and other necessary
materials. At scheduled times, pairs of children reported to this room for
training and testing.

The teachers in these studies were the regular physical education
teachers in these elementary schools. All were well trained in the theory
and were experienced in its application. Throughout these studies, they
were observed to assure fidelity to the theoretical model being implemented.

Most of the process-product studies to date used a correlational approach in attempting to link teaching styles with learning outcomes. But
this approach was not used in our studies for two reasons. The landmark
styles we were studying are not typically found in naturalistic settings
because, to date, the Spectrum has found only limited application in
practice. In addition, where they are found, they are not in their pure
landmark form. Secondly, the experimental approach we adopted is a
stronger research design in attempting to establish cause and effect relationships.

The first study

In the first study of this series (Goldberger, Gerney, & Chamberlain,
1982), 96 fifth-grade children from a suburban elementary school were
randomly selected from a larger pool of volunteer subjects and randomly
assigned to either the Style B, Style C, or Style E treatment groups, and
were taught the psychomotor task described above. Motor performance
data were collected prior to, midway through, and following training.
The data were analyzed within each group to determine if performance
improved over the course of training, and across the three groups on the
posttest to examine the relative effectiveness of these teaching styles.

Table 1

**Means for the Pre-, Mid-, and Posttest Trials for the
Three Treatment Groups and the Control Group over the Three Studies**

Study treatment		Pretest means*	Midtest means*	Posttest means*
First study	Style B	45.0	53.5	57.0
(N = 96)	Style C	43.0	52.5	55.0
	Style E	41.5	49.5	51.5
Second study	Style B	44.5	56.0	57.5
(N = 136)	Style C	45.0	52.5	56.0
	Style E	46.5	55.5	56.5
	Control	43.5	42.0	45.0
Third study	Style B	43.0	53.0	57.0
(N = 96)	Style C	43.5	51.0	52.0
	Style E	40.5	52.5	58.0
	Control	46.0	45.0	46.0

Note: These means are based on standard scores and not raw scores.

A 3 (treatment) X 3 (sets of trials) ANOVA, with repeated measures on the trials factor, yielded a significant main effect due to blocks of trials ($F = 58.84$, df $= 2/186$, $p < .01$). As can be seen in Table 1, all three treatments facilitated improvement in performance over the course of training. It was also revealed (see Figure 2) that most of the gain was attained during the early stages of learning.

It was hypothesized that in terms of social development the conditions provided by Style C would enhance positive interaction between the performer and the observer. To measure the effects of training on the children's social behavior, the children in the Style B and Style C treatment groups were asked to learn the same hockey task using the nonpreferred hand immediately following the posttest trials. The children in both groups were asked to "help your partner learn this skill." The interaction between the pair was recorded using a low inference coding system (the Reciprocal Coding System). Significant differences were clearly evident between these two groups in terms of the amount of feedback exchanged, the quality of the feedback, and the affect established. The children trained in Style C offered significantly more feedback more often. Perhaps more importantly, they were more empathetic and positive when compared to their Style B counterparts.

In this initial study, various analyses revealed that: (a) all three treatment groups significantly improved their performance equally well; (b) the Style C group, in which learners worked in pairs, was found to have significantly enhanced their social skill development; and (c) Style E, the

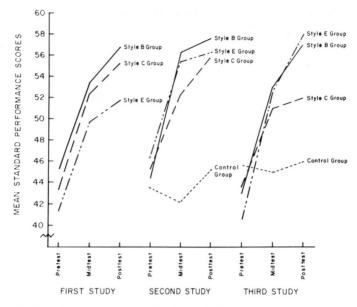

Figure 2 — Learning curves across the three studies.

teaching style that provided the most individualized instruction, was not found to be particularly effective with low ability children as had been hypothesized.

The second study

The major purpose of the second study was to replicate the first study, to check our initial findings, and to shed some light on the following question. What is the effect of a child's background, ability, and self-concept on the potential effects of these treatments on motor performance?

This study (Goldberger, Gerney, & Dort, Note 1) also employed an experimental design in which equal numbers of fifth-grade boys and girls from two elementary schools, one serving children from low socioeconomic status (low SES) backgrounds and the other serving children from relatively high socioeconomic status (high SES) backgrounds, were randomly selected and randomly assigned to one of the three treatment groups or to the control group. The study involved 80 children from the high SES setting and 56 children from the low SES setting. The task to be learned was an adaptation of the same psychomotor accuracy task used in the first study. Training for the treatment groups consisted of 60 practice trials under the conditions for learning provided by the different teaching styles. Again, pre-, mid-, and posttest trials were administered under control conditions during the training. Treatments and testing protocols were identical to the first study.

A 4 (treatment) X 2 (setting) X 3 (blocks of trials) ANOVA, with repeated measures on the trials factor, revealed a number of significant findings. Most importantly, significant interactions were found between treatments and blocks of trials (F = 3.30, df = 6/256, $p < .01$) and treatments and setting (F = 6.68, df = 3/128, $p < .01$). As can be seen in Table 1, all three treatment groups again significantly improved their performance over the course of training ($p < .01$) and all three groups had posttest means significantly higher than the control group ($p < .01$). Concerning the treatment by trials interaction, although all three treatments effectively promoted a significant improvement in performance, as was found in the first study, the Style B group again appears to have profited the most from their training (see Figure 2). As can be seen in Table 1, the Style B group improved their score by about 13 points, as compared to 11 and 10 points for the Style C and Style E groups respectively.

In comparing children from the low SES setting with their high SES counterparts, it can be seen in Table 2 that although significant differences were found between the posttest means for both the Style C group (F = 7.74, df = 1/32, $p < .01$) and the Style E group (F = 7.83, df = 1/32, $p < .01$), these differences appear to be a function of the lower pretest scores of the low SES children and do not reflect the effects of training. In comparison with their high SES counterparts, these children generally started out with lower scores and maintained this relative position throughout their training. It should be noted that the conditions provided by Style B appear to have been particularly helpful to the low SES children. This observation is consistent with the findings of Brophy (1979) and others concerning the impact of Direct Instruction.

In the first study, we hypothesized that the conditions for learning in Style E, which provides the most individualized learning conditions of the teaching styles being studied, would be particularly useful to children with exceptional ability; our data did not support this contention, however. The present study addressed this issue again. Low, average, and high ability groups were formed a posteriori based on each child's pretest mean score. Children in the high ability group (N = 42) had pretest means at least one half a standard deviation above the overall pretest mean, and children in the low ability group (N = 40) had pretest means at least one half a standard deviation below the overall mean. Of course, the average group (N = 54) were those children between a half a standard deviation above and below the overall pretest mean.

For the high ability group significant differences were found between the posttest means of each of the treatment groups and the control group (F = 19.73, df = 3/38, $p < .01$), as shown in Table 2. The differences among the treatment groups were not significant. For the average ability group the only significant difference found was between the Style B

Table 2

Raw Posttest Mean and Pre-Post Change Scores for Both the Low and High SES Groups and the Low, Average, and High Ability Groups (Second Study)

| | Treatment groups | | | | Significant Across-group Differences |
	Style B	Style C	Style E	Control	
Overall (N)	(34)	(34)	(34)	(34)	
Posttest mean	9.91	9.24	9.58	6.83	
Change score	3.14	2.36	2.38	0.41	B,C,E/Control
Low SES group (N)	(14)	(14)	(14)	(14)	
Posttest mean	9.40	8.21	8.33	7.61	
Change score	2.71	2.01	1.88	1.14	NSD
High SES group (N)	(20)	(20)	(20)	(20)	
Posttest mean	10.27	9.96	10.45	6.28	
Change score	3.45	2.60	2.73	−0.11	B,C,E/Control
High ability gp. (N)	(11)	(11)	(11)	(9)	
Posttest mean	11.55	10.10	10.77	4.62	
Change score	1.57	0.42	0.57	−4.24	B,C,E/Control
Avg. ability gp. (N)	(10)	(14)	(16)	(14)	
Posttest mean	10.06	8.66	9.06	7.06	
Change score	3.25	1.94	2.32	0.55	B/Control
Low ability gp. (N)	(13)	(9)	(7)	(11)	
Posttest mean	8.41	9.09	8.89	8.34	
Change score	4.39	5.38	5.38	4.03	NSD

group and the control group ($F = 4.13$, df $= 3/50$, $p < .01$). Among the low ability children, it is clear that all three treatments had a positive effect on performance; yet the low ability control group also improved significantly, rendering the differences between each of the treatment groups and the control group nonsignificant.

We found in the first study that children trained under Style C conditions displayed significantly more "helpful" behavior when asked to help a fellow student learn a new task, compared with their Style B counterparts. In the present study, we wanted to build upon this finding. Instead of observing the social interaction immediately following training, as we had done in the first study, we delayed this phase of the investigation a week in order to examine these effects over time. Each pair of children in both the Style B and Style C groups reported back to the training room at times scheduled one week after their initial training. At this time they were asked to "help your partner to learn this new task," a simple dart-throwing activity. While the pair worked together on the task, their behavior was video-taped for later analysis.

Tapes were analyzed using the same 14-category low inference coding system (the Reciprocal Coding System) as had been used in the first study. Fifteen ratios were developed to capture such social interaction as the type of feedback, its frequency, how the feedback was used, the effect of the interaction, and degree of reciprocation. In our first study differences on these 15 ratios were extraordinarily evident between the two groups. In this later study, with the week between the training and the testing, there were virtually no differences between the two groups.

The third study

We conducted the third Spectrum Study to see if we would get similar results in a naturalistic as opposed to a laboratory type setting. In addition, a second task was included to see if these findings would persist across different areas of psychomotor content.

This study employed the same basic experimental design and protocols as the second study. Forty-eight fifth-grade children from a high SES setting and 48 children from a low SES setting served as subjects. Children were randomly selected and randomly assigned to one of the three treatment groups or the control group. We used the same hockey accuracy task but moved it into the gymnasium. We also included a balance beam task involving three positions on the beam.

As can be seen in both Table 1 and Figure 2, the results of this study were similar to those of our first two studies. All three treatment groups significantly improved their performance over the course of training. Significant differences were found between each of these groups and the control group. However, in comparing these three treatment groups on their posttest means, no significant differences were found among them. Although Style E subjects improved the most over the course of training, the difference between their improvement and Style B's was not significant.

At this writing the analyses concerning the ability groups, the SES groups, the second task, and the self-concept groups are not yet completed. These should be forthcoming shortly and may be obtained from us at Temple University.

Summary and conclusions

As can be seen clearly in Figure 2, all three treatments were found to consistently facilitate learning of this type of algorithmic motor task. Style B, the teaching style which most approximates the "direct instruction" model (Rosenshine, 1977), appears to consistently produce the most effective results. This consistent effectiveness of Style B was apparent across both SES settings and across the three ability groupings.

In terms of social development, it appears that children can be taught through Style C training to become more productive in social interactions with their peers. It appears also, however, that without opportunities to practice these behaviors any changes in social development are short-lived.

It is clear that data-based linkages can be established between selected teaching styles and specific learning outcomes. We have tested aspects of Spectrum theory and have begun to systematically build data bases supporting the theory.

For the next few studies, we want to continue limiting ourselves to styles of teaching within this direct cluster, build upon what has been done, replicate our work whenever feasible, and continue using the same basic experimental approach. Our next study will focus on determining the best sequence of episodes to use in teaching a new motor skill. We are also interested in studying the long-term effects of these styles in naturalistic settings. We want to look at differences, if any, across teachers using the same styles. Actually, as this research program continues, it appears to be generating more research questions than answers. They say this is the way it is supposed to be.

Reference Notes

1. Goldberger, M., Gerney, P., & Dort, A. *The effects of direct teaching styles on the psychomotor performance of high and low SES children of varying ability levels.* Paper presented at the Annual Meeting of the American Alliance of Health, Physical Education, Recreation, and Dance, Houston, 1982.

References

BEGINNING Teacher Evaluation Study. In C. Denham & A. Lieberman (Eds.), *Time to learn.* Sacramento, CA: Commission for Teacher Preparation and Licensing, 1980.

BENNETT, S.N.,Jordan, J., Long, G., & Wade, B. *Teaching styles and pupil progress.* Cambridge, MA: Harvard University Press, 1976.

BROPHY, J.E. Teacher behavior and its effects. *Journal of Educational Psychology*, 1979, **71**, 740-741.

FLANDERS, N.A. *Analyzing teacher behavior.* Reading, MA: Addision-Wesley, 1970.

GOLDBERGER, M. *A taxonomy of psychomotor forms.* (Occasional Paper No. 35). East Lansing, MI: Institute for Research on Teaching, 1980.

GOLDBERGER, M., Gerney, P., & Chamberlain, J. The effects of three styles of teaching on the psychomotor performance and social skill development of fifth grade children. *Research Quarterly for Exercise and Sport*, 1982, **53**, 116-124.

JOYCE, B.R., & Weil, M. *Models of teaching*. Englewood Cliffs, NJ: Prentice-Hall, 1972.

MOSSTON, M. *Teaching physical education*. Columbus, OH: Charles E. Merrill, 1966.

MOSSTON, M. *Teaching physical education* (2nd ed.). Columbus, OH: Charles E. Merrill, 1981.

ROSENSHINE, B. Review of teaching variables and student achievement. In G. Borich (Ed.), *The appraisal of teaching: Concepts and process*. Reading, MA: Addison-Wesley, 1977.

SKINNER, R. *The decision process during the acquisition of a complex motor skill*. Unpublished doctoral dissertation, Columbia University, 1974.

SOAR, R.S., & Soar, R.M. Emotional climate and management. In P.L. Peterson & H.J. Walberg (Eds.), *Research on teaching*. Berkeley, CA: McCutchan, 1979.

STALLINGS, J. Allocated academic learning time revised, or beyond time on task. *Educational Researcher*, 1980, pp. 11-16.

Machine-paced instruction: Innovations for improving teaching in physical education

Thomas L. McKenzie
San Diego State University

Classroom management has been defined as involving "the provisions and procedures necessary to establish and maintain an environment in which instruction and learning can occur" (Duke, 1979, p. xii). Although classroom management is considered important enough to justify an entire NSSE yearbook (Duke, 1979), there is a limited body of empirical research on the topic of class management in physical activity settings.

Class management is a daily fact of life for every physical education teacher and student. Research indicates that extraordinary amounts of time are spent on managerial tasks both indoors and outdoors and at all educational levels. Studies on classroom management by Kounin (1970) and his colleagues revealed that an important part of preparing for effective management was preparing for effective instruction. That is, Kounin found that effective managers used instructional techniques that prevented student disruption instead of responding with desist techniques after behavior problems occurred.

Because response repetition is necessary for learning motor skills, effective instruction in physical education demands that teachers be able to arrange and direct efficient drills. In managing activities where repetition is a goal, the pacing of instruction is an important factor. Pacing not only affects the number of responses a student makes in a given amount of time, but it also controls the number of opportunities a student has to receive feedback and reinforcement during that time. The pacing of transition periods from one activity to another is also important because it enables high rates of student-engaged time to occur.

Teachers spend a great deal of time and energy pacing students through drills and other repetitive activities, commonly referred to as directing or cadence calling functions. Unfortunately, cadence calling such as that which occurs while directing dance, fencing, and karate drills, is a monotonous chore that prevents a teacher from providing instruction, giving feedback, and interacting personally with students. Automated machines or other hardware can be devised for cadence calling and other routine management tasks. If these machines can contribute to learning while at the same time be acceptable to students, preferred by teachers, and be reasonably inexpensive, then they should be considered for widespread use.

Using machines to enhance instruction is certainly not a new idea. Pressey and his colleagues at The Ohio State University were researching the effectiveness of machines in presenting material to students as early as the 1920s (Lumsdaine & Glaser, 1960). In general education, teaching machines have been designed not only to pace instruction but to present antecedent stimuli clearly, reduce irrelevant responses, provide reinforcement, and to gain mastery of material (Skinner, 1968).

In physical education, machines and instructional devices have been used quite frequently (Siedentop, 1976). Some have been used to restrict the scope of a learner's response, for example, such as when an archer wears an eye patch or covered eyeglass lens to inhibit aiming with the nondominant eye. Others have been used to provide feedback, such as mirrors and indicator lights in fencing. A few, such as ball-pitching machines for baseball and tennis, have been used to increase the number of attempts a learner gets per unit of time, but their effectiveness in large classes has not been reported.

This paper will review the findings of a series of four studies designed to examine the use of machines in pacing instruction. Three different teaching machines were studied: program boards, an automatic light-cueing system, and programmed cassette tapes. Dependent variables included work output measured in rate of performance (laps per minute), student attitudes toward machine pacing, student active learning time, and quantity and quality of different teacher behaviors.

The first of these studies, published several years ago in the *Journal of Applied Behavior Analysis*, illustrated the effectiveness of self-recording task completion as a procedure to increase work output in a competitive age-group swimming team (McKenzie & Rushall, 1974). The pacing equipment consisted of four 2- × 3-foot homemade program boards, over 500 program unit cards, and a wall clock. A transparent pocket along the top edge of each board held the work-unit cards that indicated segments of a training program (e.g., pull 4 × 100 freestyle). The cards were inserted and positioned over permanently marked columns. The work program could easily be altered by changing the cards. Horizontal lines divided the board into a number of rows. The top row, labeled "laps," indicated the cumulative total of laps that would be completed when the workout program was followed sequentially. The remaining rows were assigned to individual swimmers who entered their names at the left. As a swimmer completed a work unit, a checkmark was entered in the appropriate square with a grease pencil attached to the board by a string. The checkmark indicated the portion of the training program the swimmer had just finished and the total number of laps that he/she had completed that practice session.

The effectiveness of the program boards was studied over 74 practice sessions and follow-up. In short, during program board conditions, the work output of the swimmers increased by 27.1 percent. This was equivalent to an additional 619 yards of swimming for each individual during each 55-minute practice session.

Under program board conditions, the swimmers did not have to depend upon coaches for their pacing, as is the case in traditional swim practices. Rather than waiting for others to finish and for a coach to direct them to begin again, the swimmers initiated a new work unit as soon as they had reached their target heart rate (e.g., 24 beats in 10 seconds). Such a procedure radically changed the behavior of the coaches. Since they were relieved of the time-consuming duties of practice director and supervisor, they could attend to more individual coaching tasks and provide more specific form training for the swimmers.

The second study took place in a fencing environment. It was designed to examine how students reacted to a machine-controlled drilling system compared to a traditional system in which the instructor called cadence (Williams & McKenzie, 1978). Fencing was selected because routine pattern drills form a standard part of its instructional process. The machine used for controlling drills, called an "autopacer," consisted of four sets of light bulbs mounted on both sides of the fencing salle under the control of a Dual Interval/Repeat Cycle timer. With this instrument, lights could be flashed automatically at regular intervals, much like a metronome but with a wider range of intervals. A "Gray Lab" Universal control timer was used with the autopacer to control the duration of drilling periods, thus freeing the instructor from having to constantly watch the clock.

Students were taught to react to a flashing light by using their peripheral vision. Consequently, with the autopacer they learned to respond to visual cues as they would in bouting rather than to verbal cues from the instructor. In addition, since the delivery of cues could be altered precisely in steps as small as 0.1 seconds, the rhythm and pace of skill moves could be shaped more systematically. As classes progressed, students were required to move faster by reducing the time between cues.

Although students had to work in unison during teacher-paced drills, they could work independently during machine-paced drills. For example, in an "advance-extend-lunge-recover" drill, some students would be advancing while others would be extending, lunging, or recovering, all being cued by the same flashing light. Other advantages of the machine-paced drilling system were that the instructor was liberated from cadence calling and the salle became quieter. The instructor was now able to circulate among learners, at times interacting quietly on an individual basis and at times providing pertinent instruction to everyone. Throughout the semester the instructor used both teacher- and machine-paced drills. No attempt was made to measure skill or fitness gains under the two conditions.

One hundred and three university students in six co-ed fencing classes responded to an 11-item questionnaire concerning their opinions of the class, the instructor, and the methods of drilling. The responses were anonymous and were machine scored on a five-point Likert-type scale. In brief, the students favored being paced by the machine and considered the quality of the machine-paced drills to be better than that of drills paced by the instructor. They also perceived the instructor to be a competent teacher and were sensitive to his/her concurrent presence during machine pacing.

While this second study examined student attitudes toward machine pacing in fencing, the third and fourth studies looked at opportunities for students to learn under different drilling conditions. The pacing instrumentation for these two studies consisted of a tape recorder and programmed cassette tapes, the latter being programmed to direct students in sustained, purposeful, and repetitive practice drills. Fencing movement patterns, such as basic footwork drills for advancing, retreating, and lunging, were recorded on a series of tapes. The tapes were designed in a manner that would advance students systematically from simple to more complex movements, from slow to fast responses, and from easy workouts to those demanding greater endurance.

In fencing there are no established product standards, such as those found in archery, bowling, and golf; and there are no official rating scales like those for gymnastics, diving, and ice skating. Because valid product measures were not obtainable, process measures in terms of student behavior and teacher behavior were selected for study.

Data for Study 3 were collected at a large state university during two sections of beginning fencing classes. A modification of the Academic Learning Time-Physical Education-Teacher Behavior Observation system, developed by Siedentop and his students, was used to code how students spent their time in class and to concurrently code teacher behavior into 16 different categories. Three students were selected randomly from each section and were observed alternately using a 6-second observe/record format. All 56 classes were taught by the same experienced instructor, who wore a remote wireless microphone but was naive to the exact student and teacher behaviors under study.

When the data were analyzed to compare student behavior during machine-paced and teacher-paced drilling (Clark, McKenzie, & McKenzie, 1982, p. 77), it was evident that the percent of time spent actively engaged at an appropriate level of difficulty was slightly higher during machine pacing. That is, when the tape recorder was used to direct drills, students had more opportunities to respond. Additionally, when paced by the recorder they received almost twice as much augmented feedback from the teacher (51.6% of intervals cf. 25.4% during teacher-paced drilling).

Besides increasing the rates of teacher feedback, use of the tape recorder modified the occurrence of other teacher behavior categories. For example, giving directions (3.4% cf. 48.4%) and modeling (0.6% cf. 13.3%) were reduced when the machine was used, whereas maintenance (3.6% cf. 0.6%), answering student questions (1.7% cf. 0.9%), and behavior praise (2.0% cf. 0.9%) categories were increased. An advantage of the system for this particular teacher was that it established an environment that promoted student accountability. During machine-paced drilling, the teacher was free to evaluate the skill performances of students for feedback and grading purposes, thus completing an important task not possible under teacher-paced drilling (15.2% cf. 0.0%).

Since feedback from a teacher is such an important instructional behavior, a fourth study was devised (McKenzie, Clark, & McKenzie, Note 1), which examined not only the quantity of feedback but its quality as well. Data for this study were collected at a junior college throughout a semester of advanced fencing. The observational system used was similar to the one used in Study 3, except that subscripts were added to obtain qualitative measures on the augmented feedback provided by the teacher.

Results indicated that during this advanced class, the instructor gave feedback almost six times more frequently during machine-paced drilling than during teacher-paced drilling (41.4% cf. 7.0%). In addition, under machine-paced conditions the feedback was more specific (95% cf. 88%), more corrective (76% cf. 58%), and directed more toward individuals (96% cf. 79%). For this particular age group and skill level, feedback during machine-paced drilling was of better quality than it was during teacher-paced drilling.

The data for studies 3 and 4 support the use of a tape recorder to pace drilling in fencing. With the recorder, students had higher motor engagement rates and were able to receive increased amounts of feedback of higher quality from a teacher who was now liberated from traditional directing functions. But these data provide only part of the rationale for using programmed tapes. Tapes can be designed, as they were in these fencing classes, to promote interval training — by ensuring that students have activity for a specific amount of time at a specific level of intensity. In addition, tapes can be used for management purposes. Pauses can be programmed onto the tapes to provide rest periods for students and to allow the teacher time to give instruction and group feedback. With pauses programmed for appropriate lengths, instructors can limit the amount of time they spend talking to students and can thus ensure that high amounts of practice time are provided. With tapes, teachers can also monitor the amount of practice time each learner gets. For example, in partner drills the specific time each learner drills while the other responds is controlled without the teacher having to attend to a stop watch. A cue on the tape indicates when partners are to change roles. Transition time can also be kept low; for example, the changing of partners will occur quickly when the next drill is programmed to begin 10 seconds after the cue to find a new partner is given.

In summary, three automated devices designed to pace drilling periods in physical education — program boards, a light cueing system, and programmed tapes — were examined in the four studies. Results indicate that these devices provided more opportunities for students to learn by increasing their motor response time and by increasing the amount and quality of augmented feedback they received. These three machines were more than acceptable to students and preferred by the teachers, and they stood the test of time — all three being currently in use several years after these studies were completed.

Although none of these studies was conducted in a public school setting, the instrumentation used to pace instruction is directly suitable for use in such an environment. The program boards were first used with adolescents on a competitive swimming team, but have subsequently been used during instructional classes with children and adults. The tape recorded drilling system for fencing has also been used with diverse populations, from beginning junior high school students to intercollegiate state champions.

For practical or philosophical reasons, some educators are opposed to using machinery for instructional purposes. Space does not permit a thorough response to their arguments. However, machine-paced instruction does seem to be affordable. The program board and the tape recording systems in the studies reviewed here each cost less than a leather basketball. Meanwhile, most gymnasiums already have a built-in pacer: The stop clock that is used only for Friday night ball games can easily be adapted to manage classes. Machine pacing is not likely to lead to technological unemployment. While mechanical devices will eliminate some of the drudgery of a teacher's work, they will not necessarily shorten the amount of time the teacher is in contact with students. Philosophically, from a control point of view, the use of machines provides students with greater opportunities to develop independence. When the teacher gives up the directing function, students are forced to become more autonomous and self-directed.

For the most part, physical educators work hard at a difficult job. Unfortunately, many of the instructional procedures we use are inefficient, and burn-out rates for the profession are high. Realistically, many teaching functions can be performed either by a human or by a machine. The need to overcome instructional inertia is great. Physical educators should be developing, producing, and researching labor-saving devices that will enable them to be more effective teachers—to make their instructional environments more productive and more pleasant. To this end, it should be remembered that program boards, flashing lights, and tape recorders are not substitutes for a good teacher. They are devices that enable a good teacher to be better or, as said in fencing circles, "to be a touch above the rest."

Reference Note

1. McKenzie, T.L., Clark, E.K., & McKenzie, R.E. *Quantity and quality of augmented feedback observed in fencing classes: Relationship to instructional style.* Paper presented at the annual convention, California Association for Health, Physical Education, Recreation, and Dance, Monterey, April 1982.

References

CLARK, E.K., McKenzie, T.L., & McKenzie, R.E. Instructional strategies: Influence on teacher behavior and student motor engagement rates in university fencing classes. *Research Papers: 1982 AAHPERD Convention.* Reston, VA: AAHPERD, 1982. (Abstract)

DUKE, D.L. (Ed.). *Classroom management: The seventy-eighth yearbook of the National Society for the Study of Education.* Chicago: The University of Chicago Press, 1979.

KOUNIN, J.S. *Discipline and group management in classrooms.* New York: Holt, Rinehart, & Winston, 1970.

LUMSDAINE, A.A., & Glaser, R. (Eds.). *Teaching machines and programmed learning.* Washington, DC: National Education Association, 1960.

McKENZIE, T.L., & Rushall, B.S. Effects of self-recording on attendance and performance in a competitive swimming training environment. *Journal of Applied Behavior Analysis*, 1974, **7**, 199-206.

SIEDENTOP, D. *Developing teaching skills in physical education*. Boston: Houghton Mifflin, 1976.

SKINNER, B.F. *The technology of teaching*. New York: Appleton-Century-Crofts, 1968.

WILLIAMS, D., & McKenzie, T.L. Student responses to machine-paced skills in physical education. *TAHPER Journal*, Fall 1978, pp. 10-11; 60-61.

The specter of teaching styles: Realities and dilemmas

Anthony A. Annarino
Purdue University

As a neophyte teacher educator in the early 1950s, my concerns and questions were: How do you prepare, educate, and train a physical educator to be an effective teacher? What is the best information available that can be used for this task? Since then, have my concerns and questions changed? Has the profession changed? Has the available information changed?

What was truth in the 1950s and 1960s? What was known by the profession? How were physical educators prepared? What was the best information available? What did Wood, Bancroft, Williams, Cowell, Hetherington, Cureton, McCloy, Staley, Steinhaus, Oberteuffer, Nash, and many others contribute to that area of the body of knowledge called Pedagogy?

John Dewey has said, "History is the past of the present." We can understand the present more completely if we examine it both in retrospect and in prospect—in its relationship to the possible future. For example, the following are a few selected quotes from early leaders in the profession:

It is essential to go as rapidly as possible from one exercise to the next, and to make individual corrections without interrupting the work of the entire class. This individual work implies a cultivation of the teacher's own powers of observation, which have to be accustomed to this new field. When the teacher has acquired the power to observe these things, individual corrections can be made while the whole class is at work, by directing glance, commands, and incidental remarks to the pupils who most need them. (Bancroft, 1903, p. 27)

A teacher is judged by what the children are doing. Is time wasted in getting ready for the physical education period? Do they report at the gymnasium or play field promptly? Is changing of squads made quickly? Are the children so organized that all are taking part in the same activity? Does the teacher analyze and tell the children just what is wrong and right? (Wood & Cassidy, 1927, pp. 325-327)

The causes of inefficiency in instruction in physical education are many. Efficiency means the saving of time from unproductive activity. The teacher should study the causes of waste and eliminate them as soon as possible. The causes of waste in class organization are: failure to have equipment ready, lack of proper plans for roll taking, useless floor formations, absence of procedure for controlling the class, slowness in changing the activity, poor explanations, improper grouping, badly planned programs. To maintain maximum efficiency in the class period should be the ideal of every teacher. Each pupil should be busily engaged in the activity at hand and of course the activity should be worthwhile. Are all of the children busy most of the time and most of the children busy all of the time? Are the activities in which they are busy worthwhile; i.e., do they lead the participants onward and toward the goals set up as objectives? (Williams, Dambach, & Schwendener, 1932, p. 108)

These ideas and those of many others constituted truth—that was the basis for teaching physical education in the 1950s and 1960s. Contrast and compare truth in the 1960s with the findings of research in the teaching of physical education today. A synthesis of these findings is:

1. That the selection, organization, managing, and monitoring of effective learning experiences are critical problems in the day-to-day teaching of physical education (Annarino, Note 1).
2. That different types of teacher interventions can positively or negatively affect student engaged and waiting time (Costello & Lanbach, 1978).
3. That certain teaching styles produce varying types and degrees of objective achievements (Graham & Heimerer, Note 2).
4. That teaching behaviors and managerial skills can be modified to produce more positive teacher-student interactions in an educational setting (Mancini, Doenges, & Morris, Note 3).
5. That the scope of activity offerings and objectives to be achieved

must be considered in planning, due to limitations of time constraints in school programs (Annarino, Note 1).

6. That a well-designed observational system can more objectively
   describe what is happening in a class (Siedentop, 1983).

7. That process variables and types of instruction have been identified
   and analyzed as to their effect on student achievement for other
   disciplines. Even though their specific impact on physical education
   instruction and types of student achievement needs to be further investigated, there are implications to consider. They are:

   a) That the quality and quantity of time a student spends in a motor
      activity affects achievement (Berlinger, 1979; Rosenshine, 1979).

   b) That direct instruction (teacher-directed, content-focused, and
      sequenced) yields higher rates of learning time (Rosenshine,
      1979).

   c) That to be effective, teachers must consider and plan for the
      quantity and quality of time allotted for specific content, student
      time engaged on class content, the time that a student is engaged
      in relevant content at an appropriate task level, and the type of
      teaching behaviors that affect the learning environment climate
      (Siedentop, Birdwell, & Metzler, Note 4).

8. That a knowledgeable and sensitive teacher can develop an effective
   instructional strategy for desired outcomes by planning and selecting the appropriate teaching-learning process variables (Annarino,
   Note 1).

9. That the teaching-learning process is a complex multi-interrelated
   variable phenomenon that will continue to challenge teacher educators in their pursuit for truth (Annarino, Note 1).

A comparative analysis would indicate that recent investigations
related to the physical education teaching-learning process validate many
ideas proposed by early leaders. The cumulative evidence should provide
a focus and direction for physical education instruction.

However, the results of systematic descriptive observations in many
school physical education classes indicate a lack of relationship between
teaching behaviors, teacher-learner interactions, content, and the known
criteria for student achievement. In addition, there is a lack of systematic
and coordinate planning between grade divisions within the same school
system. Why do these problems exist? Why is there a gap between
theory—what we know, and practice—what we do? What are the
realities? What are the dilemmas? Can the gap be closed and, if so, how?

In attempting to find answers to these questions, last year I visited 47
public schools in 6 states. I observed 123 physical education classes (72
secondary, 34 junior high, and 17 elementary) taught by 119 different
teachers.

Data were obtained by an observational system that had been designed, refined, and modified over a period of years to observe specific class functions: (a) managerial and organizational, (b) waiting time, (c) teacher talk, and (d) engaged motor time. Data were analyzed for these functions for teaching modes, activities, teacher type, class type, school size, class size, school grade divisions, quality and quantity of practice trials, and frequency, type, and quality of instructional feedback.

In addition, a questionnaire was designed and used for personal interviews with teachers, administrators, and students. Data were obtained specific to curriculum practices and school demographics, the duties, responsibilities, problems, and life styles of teachers, and reactions of students and administrators to physical education.

My findings replicate, with some variations, the results of other investigations within the research on teaching in physical education school settings. Sufficient evidence is available to establish some basic generalizations about curriculum and instruction practices that exist in physical education school settings:

1. That the selection, organization, managing, and monitoring of appropriate student learning experiences are critical problems in the day-to-day teaching of physical education in school settings.
2. That the responsibility for a student's learning experience and achievement is the primary function of the physical education teacher.
3. That learning experience problems can be minimized or resolved by effective teaching-planning.

Can these results and research findings from other subdisciplines of physical education be effectively used to minimize and/or resolve the critical incidents that occur? One alternative approach is a problem-solving strategy that should be an integral part of professional preparation pedagogy classes and in-service training programs for teachers. An example of a proposed strategy is shown in Table 1.

Implementation of the strategy involves students and teachers by:

1. Identifying and classifying curriculum and instructional critical incidents by the objective domains.
2. Analyzing the critical incidents as to cause and effect.
3. Reviewing the research literature and formulating principles and concepts that apply to the incidents.
4. Developing specific and practical alternatives.
5. Implementing the most effective and feasible alternative based upon identified criteria imposed by specific school settings.
6. Evaluating.

In addition, other affectors and effectors directly or indirectly causing critical incidents such as socioeconomic conditions, teacher burnout,

Table 1

Critical Incident Analysis Strategy

Critical Incidents	Analysis	Principles	Alternatives
		Physical Domain	
Typical class exercise program consists of low intensity command style calisthenics for 2-3 minutes.	If fitness qualities—strength, endurance, flexibility and leanfat ratio are to be improved, why are low intensity, short duration, and minimal repetition type exercise activities used? To what degree does this type of program, intensity, and duration contribute to the components of physical fitness?	Muscle strength and endurance are developed by exercise programs with progressively increased load, repetitions, and duration. Cardiovascular endurance is developed by working heart, lungs, and blood vessels to a high level of capacity and progressively increasing the work intensity. Flexibility is improved by a slow, steady, over-stretching of the joint. Leanfat ratio is changed by diet and exercise.	Every class period should include a high intensity conditioning activity for a minimum of 10 minutes. (e.g., stretching exercises combined with either circuit training, interval training, or aerobics). One class period per week should be devoted to vigorous fitness evaluations, activities, and discussion of exercise principles.
		Psychomotor Domain	
Every activity is allotted the same amount of learning time. Learning objectives are too difficult or too easy for the class.	Activities vary in complexity as to specific learning demands and requirements.	Learning situations should be appropriate for the abilities of the student and the complexity of the activity.	Use a station organization with ability grouping that permits time variances for individual rates of learning and task difficulty. Segment objectives into smaller learning tasks.

Student physical inactivity (30-50%) due to waiting, rotated out of games, and inefficiency in the use of equipment and space. (e.g., in a 55 minute gymnastics class, a student performs five practice trials - two vaulting, one on the parallel bars and two on the side horse. No feedback.)	Student inactivity, inappropriate learning tasks, and lack of direction as to what is to be learned affects learning and results in student apathy and boredom. Teacher intervention is not evident.	The amount and efficiency of practice affects the quality of learning. Instructive feedback minimizes learning errors. Develop multiple activity areas that utilize all available space and equipment. Provide correlated activity learning tasks for total class participation at multiple activity areas, either verbal or written (e.g., major activity: badminton). Correlated activities: rope skipping, interval running, agility drills, and balance activities.

Cognitive Domain

Factual information is given by lecture that is lengthy and too extensive for students to process.	Concepts and principles are not integrated in learning experiences.	Cognitive development is the ability to memorize and recall information, comprehend, apply, analyze, synthesize, and evaluate. The level of cognition must be appropriate to the student's developmental stage. Design written tests that measure different levels of cognition.
Teacher-made written tests are superficial and primarily test rote memory of factual information.	Learning experiences primarily involve a stimulus-response rather than problem-solving experiences. Only low levels of cognition (memory and recall) are evaluated.	Use guided discovery and problem solving techniques that require students to explore, discover, and apply self-learned information either through verbal or motor response. Integrate "Basic Stuff Series" concepts and principles. Assign outside readings for factual information.

Table 1 cont'd

Critical Incident Analysis Strategy

Critical Incidents	Analysis	Principles	Alternatives
		Affective Domain	
Students: excessive absenteeism, apathy, boredom, lack of enthusiasm, and not involved in planning or decision making.	The result of teacher apathy, boredom, lack of enthusiasm, poor managerial and planning skills, autocratic leadership, and burnout.　　These incidents are related to incidents for the other domains.	Affective outcomes must be considered in planning and instruction.　　The abstract and intangible terms that define the affective domain are difficult to assess.　　The teacher can be the most effective force for the development of student behaviors.	Involve students in planning and decision-making.　　Use teaching behaviors that praise and encourage student performance, be sensitive to and respect individual feelings, and listen to student ideas.　　Provide experiences for students to do well and feel good.

teacher-coach role conflicts, and types and behaviors of students, must be identified and considered in the strategy.

This strategy, recommended as *one* viable way to change the behaviors of students and teachers by making them more aware of the types, causes, and effects of critical incidents prevalent in the planning and teaching of physical education, can expand their knowledge of the best information available from research studies. They can develop the problem-solving ability that should resolve present and future critical incidents.

Reference Notes

1. Annarino, A. *Status of curriculum and instructional practice.* Manuscript in preparation, 1983.
2. Graham, G., & Heimerer, A. *Research on teaching effectiveness: A summary with implications for teaching.* Paper presented at the meeting of the AAHPERD, Detroit, April 1980.
3. Mancini, V., Doenges, R., & Morris, H. *The use of elementary age students as modifiers of physical education teacher behavior.* Paper presented at the meeting of the MAHPER, Roxbury, MA, 1978.
4. Siedentop, D., Birdwell, D., & Metzler, M. *A process approach to measuring teaching effectiveness in physical education.* Paper presented at the meeting of the AAHPERD, New Orleans, March 1979.

References

ANDERSON, W.G., & Barrette, G.T. What's going on in the gym: Descriptive studies of physical education classes. *Motor Skills Theory and Practice Monograph*, 1978, **1**.

BANCROFT, J.H. *School gymnastics free hand.* New York: D.C. Heath, 1903.

BERLINGER, D.C. *Research on teaching: Concepts findings and implications.* Berkeley, CA: McCutchan, 1979.

COSTELLO, J., & Laubach, S. Student behavior. What's going on in gym: A descriptive study of physical education classes. *Motor Skills and Theory Monograph*, 1978, **1**.

EARLS, N.F. Distinctive teacher's personal qualities, perceptions of teacher education and the realities of teaching. *The Journal of Teaching in Physical Education*, 1981, **1**(1), 59.

ROSENSHINE, B. Content, time and direct instruction. *Research on teaching: Concepts, findings and implications.* Berkeley, CA: McCutchan, 1979.

SIEDENTOP, D. *Developing teaching skills in physical education.* Palo Alto, CA: Mayfield, 1983.

WILLIAMS, J.F., Dambach, J., & Schwendener, N. *Methods in physical education.* Philadelphia: W.B. Saunders, 1932.

WOOD, T.D., & Cassidy, R.F. *The new physical education.* New York: MacMillian, 1927.

Section seven
Research on teaching in physical education settings

The papers in this section represent some facet of research on teaching in physical education settings, and also indicate varied positions in the loop model of descriptive-analytic, correlational, and experimental research. While it is apparent that much has been done in recent years, on the other hand it is obvious that in some areas the research process has just begun. Given the quality and sophistication of the works presented here, the future seems bright.

Janice Olson and Judith Rink have taken descriptive-analytic procedures beyond the common practice of describing single behavior frequencies and percentages. Each describes a different technique used in the continuing search for effective teaching behaviors. Olson presents the results of her searches for relevant instructional configurations. She uses pattern analytic techniques to identify chains of three or more behaviors, and discusses how to extend these probes and determine their relevancy in particular situations.

Rink uses content analysis procedures to describe the stability of the teaching behaviors of three instructors over an entire unit of instruction. She discusses results showing teaching behaviors concerning content development, the utilization of class time, management, presentation of information, and feedback. Finally, she presents ideas about stability and instability of teaching behaviors for specific behavioral dimensions and their relationship to teacher effectiveness.

In his paper, Neal Earls looks at research on the immediate effects of instructional variables on the motoric responses of children. Using instructional variables such as teacher actions and factors in the setting, he discusses investigations that show how these variables elicit progression and regression of movement quality in children's skill practices. From his studies in laboratory settings and in elementary schools, Earls concludes that teachers can improve their effectiveness by evaluating the effects of such variables on student movement response patterns.

Several studies in this section have used various modifications of the experimental research paradigm in research on teaching in physical education settings. Bernard Oliver's paper deals with the area of direct instruction that seems to represent the most universally accepted protocol resulting from process-product research on teaching. Oliver surveys the development of direct instruction, reveals the different definitions of the concept, and cites the paucity of research in this area of physical education. He then focuses on a direct instruction model derived from a large scale naturalistic process-product study, found to account for much of the variance in posttest achievement, attitude, and skill measures. Oliver speaks of information, play, and feedback processes, discusses the pattern that emerges from these results, and suggests appropriate steps for further investigation.

One of the newest areas of process-product research within physical education is that of Aptitude Treatment Interaction. David Griffey's study of ATIs investigates the possibility that pupil aptitudes interact differently with instructional styles that vary the amount of student choice. He reports that convincing mediating effects were found to be associated with initial ability, gender, and student style. No significant ATIs were found for other aptitudes, however, and further investigation is recommended.

Another alternative from within the process-product research design in physical education is the mini-ETU (experimental teaching unit) format. George Graham and Beverly Yerg both offer up-to-date information on the use of this paradigm. Graham presents material from five mini-ETU studies, comparing the design characteristics of each: task, length and number of lessons, number and characteristics of students per class, and number of teachers and the number of classes taught by each one. He compares the findings on utilization of time and teacher feedback, and relates his conclusions to the credibility of the mini-ETU format and the generalizability to teaching in the gymnasium.

Yerg compares two process-product studies, both of which employ the ETU approach with upper elementary grade students. The Teacher Behavior Observation System (TBOS) was used to analyze teacher behavior during instruction. A comparison of two regression models (full and reduced) was used to analyze the data in each study and to permit isolation of the effects of the teacher behavior variables. Somewhat conflicting results about practice and feedback are presented. Also presented and discussed is a proposed revised paradigm for research on teacher effectiveness in physical education.

The final two papers in this section deal with experimental designs and new methods and applications of previously introduced techniques. In his consideration of the appropriate unit for analysis, Steve Silverman uses data from a study focusing on the relationship between student engagement and achievement in physical education. For both descriptive and process-outcome data, class means and individual students were compared as analysis units. Silverman's results indicate that greater insight is gained about the structure of the data when both units are used. He discusses the probable ramifications of using the student as the unit of analysis, indicating that in some instances it is a viable option but in others it is not.

Hal Morris concludes this section with a paper that contrasts true and natural experimental designs and looks at discriminant analysis as a model for analyzing data from a natural experiment. This technical paper will interest those whose research on teacher effectiveness in physical education has diversified to the point that their analysis of data requires nontraditional statistical procedures.

The papers in this section represent the state of the art in research on teaching in physical education settings. The reader will undoubtedly find the ideas to be both interesting and worthwhile.

Review and implications of physical education experimental teaching unit research

George Graham
University of Georgia

One of the strongest designs a researcher can employ to document teacher effectiveness is the process-product design (Dunkin & Biddle, 1974). Student learning is typically used as the *product* or outcome measure of teacher effectiveness. Teacher behaviors, documented through systematic observations, serve as the *process* or independent variables.

Several large scale process-product studies have been conducted in education (Brophy & Evertson, 1976; McDonald, 1976; Rosenshine, 1976) over a period of many months with relatively large numbers of teachers. The frequency with which these studies are cited in the literature on teaching effectiveness suggests that they have had a substantial impact. Studies of this magnitude, albeit valuable, are nevertheless expensive to conduct — both in terms of time and financial costs.

One alternative to long term, large sample process-product research designs has been the Experimental Teaching Unit (Arehart, 1979; Berliner & Tikunoff, 1976; Gage, 1976; Gall, 1977; Popham, 1971). An Experimental Teaching Unit (ETU) is a brief series of lessons on a topic of general interest to the grade level of students to be taught by the teachers in the experiment. Ten lessons have been a typical classroom ETU length. All the teachers in an ETU study teach the same content and are typically provided with a rationale for the unit, specific performance objectives, pretests for students, sample posttest questions, and a variety of instructional materials.

Physical education experimental teaching units

Researchers in physical education have used a mini ETU format (Yerg, 1981a) in studies employing a process-product research design. These mini ETUs have typically been shorter and have been taught to smaller classes than the classroom ETU studies cited above. Five mini ETU studies have been completed in physical education (Graham, Soares, & Harrington, 1983; Keller, 1982; Yerg, 1977, 1981a, 1981b; Pieron, Note 1; Young & Metzler, Note 2). Four more are in progress (Paese, Note 3; Salter, Note 4; Silverman, Note 5; Woodford & Cross, Note 6). The five completed studies have used closed rather than open skills as the content of the ETU (Figure 1). Three of the studies employed a novel golf task (Graham et al., 1983; Keller, 1982; Young & Metzler, Note 2). Yerg (1977, 1981a, 1981b) used a cartwheel as the topic of her ETU. Pieron (Note 1) also had his teachers teach a gymnastics skill, the handstand rollover.

The most common length of the physical education ETUs has been a single 20-minute lesson. Pieron's ETU required two 9-minute lessons. Keller (1982) varied the length of the time for the single lesson in his ETU between 20, 30, and 40 minutes.

Ten physical education major student teachers served as the teachers for Pieron's ETU. Yerg (1977, 1981a, 1981b) also used undergraduate physical education majors (N = 40) as teachers in her ETU. Two graduate students served as teachers for Keller's (1982) study. Eleven credentialed teachers taught the ETU lesson in the study by Graham et al. (1983) and two credentialed teachers taught the ETU lessons in Young and Metzler's study.

The classes ranged in size from 3 to 30. In Yerg's study (1977, 1981a, 1981b), each class consisted of three children ranging from third to sixth grade. The class sizes in the studies by Young and Metzler and Graham et al. (1983) averaged approximately 30 fourth- and/or fifth-grade children. Fifth-grade children also served as students in Keller's study, in class sizes ranging from 8 to 14. The only ETU that did not use children as subjects was Pieron's study, in which four freshman physical education majors served as students for the ETU lessons.

Table 1

Mini ETU Physical Education Design Characteristics

Author(s)	Task	Length of lesson(s)	Number of Lesson(s)	Characteristics of students	Number of students per class	Number of teachers	Number of lessons taught by each teacher
Yerg (1977, 1981a, 1981b)	Cartwheel	20 minutes	1	3rd-6th graders	3	40 undergrad. P.E. majors	1
Pieron (Note 1)	Handstand rollover	9 minutes	2	Freshmen P.E. majors	4	10 P.E. student teachers	2
Young & Metzler (Note 2)	Novel "golf" task	20 minutes	1	Fourth graders	c.30	2 - one experienced and one inexperienced	1
Keller (1982)	Novel "golf" task	20,30,40 minutes	1	Fifth graders	8-14	2 graduate students	3-4
Graham, Soares, & Harrington (1983)	Novel "golf" task	20 minutes	1	4th-5th graders	14-30; average 27	11 experienced teachers	1

Results

As one would expect, the design of the five physical education ETU lessons varied considerably within the parameters of the ETU paradigm. It is possible to draw some generalizations from these studies, however, because the product and process variables were similar in several studies.

Utilization of time

The variable that can be classified as utilization of time served as a process variable in each of the five studies (Table 2). Although the variable was defined and measured differently in four of the five studies, the analysis of time in each of the studies was similar enough to permit generalization.

The most obvious and expected finding was that the physical education teachers' utilization of time correlated with student learning. Students who learned more had teachers who provided them with more time to practice the criterion skill. Students who learned less spent more time waiting, listening, managing, and organizing than their counterparts. This trend, clear in all five of the studies, is extremely important because it corroborates the finding from the classroom process-product studies — more successful teachers involve their students with the appropriate materials more of the time than do less successful teachers (Graham & Heimerer, 1981).

Teacher feedback

Three of the five physical education ETU studies included teacher feedback as a process variable with differing results (Table 3). Pieron (Note 1) reported that students in classes characterized by higher learning received more teacher reactions to skill attempts and particularly more *specific* reactions to skill attempts. Yerg (1977, 1981a, 1981b) found that teacher feedback was not significantly related to student achievement and that, in fact, teacher feedback may detract from actual practice time without correspondingly enhancing student learning. She found an inverse relation between teacher feedback and the guidance and support of practice by the teachers.

In the study by Graham, Soares, and Harrington (1983), teacher feedback was classified into one of six categories utilizing the Feedback Diversity Classification System. Affective feedback was the most common type of feedback and was used similarly by both the more effective and the less effective groups of teachers. There were no substantial differences between each group's employment of teacher feedback.

Other process variables

Two other process variables were also examined in two of the physical ETU studies. Yerg (1977, 1981a, 1981b) found no relation between the

Table 2

Utilization of Time

Author(s)	Definition	Observation System Employed	Findings
Yerg (1977, 1981a, 1981b)	Amount of time teachers provided for practice	T.B.O.S.	Positive relationship between time provided for practice and student achievement.
Pieron (Note 1)	Motor activity - engaged time; criterion time-on-task; frequency of criterion trials	OBEL/ULg	Students in more effective teachers' classes spent 22.1% of lesson practicing criterion task, total of 514 criterion trials. Students in less effective teachers' classes spent 7.7% practicing criterion task, total of 163 criterion trials (significant difference), NSD for engaged time, practice of noncriterion task, e.g., handstand without rollover.
Young & Metzler (Note 2)	Time spent on physical education content; engaged in cognitive and motor tasks	ALT-PE	Motor ALT-PE averaged 16.03%, whereas general ALT-PE averaged 42.34%; correlation between Motor ALT-PE and student achievement was significant at .05 level.
Keller (1982)	Time spent on physical education content; engaged in cognitive and motor tasks	ALT-PE	Below 2 minutes of M-ALT significantly different from above 2 minutes of M-ALT; NSD between 2-7 and above 7 minutes.
Graham, Soares & Harrington (1983)	Time majority of class spent in activity, management, waiting, and instruction	Duration recording	More effective teachers averaged 654 seconds of activity time, 26 seconds of waiting time. Less effective teachers—389 seconds of activity time, 482 seconds of waiting time (NSD).

Table 3

Teacher Feedback

Author(s)	Definition	Observation System Employed	Findings
Yerg (1977, 1981a, 1981b)	Feedback classified by task relatedness and level of specificity	T.B.O.S.	Not related significantly to student achievement, inversely related to guiding and supporting practice.
Pieron (Note 1)	Teacher reaction to skill attempts	OBEL/ULg	Students in classes characterized by higher learning received more teacher reactions to skill attempts (they had significantly more skill attempts) and particularly more specific reactions to skill attempts.
Young & Metzler (Note 2)	—	—	—
Keller (1983)	—	—	—
Graham, Soares & Harrington (1983)	Feedback classified as: evaluative, descriptive, comparative, explicative, prescriptive, affective	Feedback Diversity Classification System (FDCS)	No significant difference between more effective and less effective teachers' usage of feedback —by amount or type.

teachers' knowledge and performance of cartwheels and student learning. Keller (1982) utilized a semi-programmed format requiring the teachers to employ one of two approaches—lecture demonstration or reverse chaining. Neither of these approaches was found to be more effective in promoting student learning. Both approaches, however, were significantly more effective than no instruction, the condition imposed upon the control group students who practiced on their own—a comforting thought for physical education teachers.

Implications

Prior to drawing any implications, it is important to reemphasize the rather limited nature of the five process-product studies conducted thus far, because this is not a substantial number of studies from which to posit unqualified generalizations. One would do well to keep in mind Cuban's (1982) statement in a recent article related to the high school classroom:

> Equating the concept of effectiveness with a narrow set of student outcomes that are assumed to be linked to what teachers do in classrooms—in the absence of any persuasive body of evidence linking teacher behavior with student performance—is as ambitious, if not as misguided, as a medieval alchemist trying to extract sunshine from cucumbers. (p. 118)

On the other hand, it seems too easy to simply dismiss the five process-product studies that have been completed thus far in physical education as too few or too brief. The relative strength of an ETU is limited when compared with full scale process-product studies. Professors Lawrence Locke and Daryl Siedentop addressed this very point in a discussion on the topic of research on teaching physical education:

> Locke: The ETU (is) one alternative that needs to be tested out. Siedentop: Exactly. Any kind of small scale process-product simulations. We could get enough of those, using somewhat different models, and if they tended to produce confirmatory results, we would have to assume that it would be that way too if we mounted a full-scale effort. (Graham, 1981, p. 13)

We do not have enough process-product studies as yet to provide a "persuasive body of evidence." We do, however, have a body of literature from which it seems reasonable, bearing the above statements in mind, to begin drawing some cautious implications about teaching physical education.

1. Just as in the large scale classroom process-product studies, the amount of time students spent practicing the criterion task was consistently related to student learning. More successful teachers, in the

classroom and the gymnasium, not only provide their students with more opportunities to practice the appropriate tasks but their students actually spend more time practicing the criterion skills.

2. The influence of teacher feedback has yet to be documented through process-product research in physical education. Conventional wisdom continues to suggest that it is an important teaching skill but we probably need studies of greater length before we can either verify or discount the amount and types of feedback that enhance student learning. Open skills, as well as closed skills, must also be employed as the content for longer process-product studies before we can document the relationships of teacher feedback and student learning. Based on the five physical education ETU studies completed up to this time, it is logical to suggest that teacher feedback that severely inhibits opportunities to practice will restrict rather than enhance student learning, regardless of the type or quality of the feedback.

3. Positive relationships between a particular method, or a teacher's knowledge or skill about a topic, and student learning were not found in the two studies that included them as process variables (Keller, 1982; Yerg, 1977, 1981a, 1981b). Keller did find, however, that teaching, of whatever type, was superior to no teaching. The implication is obvious; hopefully, this finding will be replicated in future studies of physical education teaching.

Conclusion

The major outcome of the five mini ETU studies conducted to date in physical education has been the corroboration of the classroom process-product research related to student utilization of time. For students of the literature on research on teacher effectiveness, this is not startling. The significance of this finding for physical educators, however, is that mini process-product physical education studies have yielded similar results to the lengthier, larger, and better-funded classroom research studies. This is significant for two reasons. First, it suggests that certain findings from classroom research on teaching can be generalized to teaching in the gymnasium. Second, it adds credibility to the mini ETU format as a valid, albeit limited, design for process-product research in physical education.

Reference Notes

1. Pieron, M. *Research on teacher change: Effectiveness of teaching a psychomotor task study in a micro-teaching study.* Paper presented at the AAHPERD National Convention, Boston, April 1981.

2. Young, J., & Metzler, M. *Correlations between ALT-PE and student achievement in a novel task experimental teaching unit.* Paper presented at the AAHPERD National Convention, Houston, April 1982.
3. Paese, P. Southwest Texas State University, personal communication, July 7, 1982.
4. Salter, W. University of Georgia, personal communication, October 1982.
5. Silverman, S. Louisiana State University, personal communication, October 1982.
6. Woodford, R., & Cross, T. University of Oklahoma, personal communication, September 1982.

References

AREHART, J.E. Student opportunity to learn related to student achievement of objectives in a probability unit. *Journal of Educational Research*, 1979, **72**, 253-258.

BERLINER, P., & Tikunoff, W. The California beginning teacher evaluation study: Overview of the ethnographic study. *Journal of Teacher Education*, 1976, **27**, 24-30.

BROPHY, J.E., & Evertson, C.M. *Learning from teaching.* Boston: Allyn & Bacon, 1976.

CUBAN, L. Persistent instruction: The high school classroom, 1900-1980. *Phi Delta Kappan*, 1982, **64**(2), 113-118.

DUNKIN, M.J., & Biddle, B.J. *The study of teaching.* New York: Holt, Rinehart & Winston, 1974.

GAGE, N.L. A factorially designed experiment on teacher structuring, soliciting and reacting. *Journal of Teacher Education*, 1976, **27**(1), 35-38.

GALL, M. The importance of context variables in research on teaching skills. *Journal of Teacher Education*, 1977, **28**(3), 43-48.

GRAHAM, G. Research on teaching physical education: A discussion with Larry Locke & Daryl Siedentop. *Journal of Teaching in Physical Education*, 1981, **1**(1), 3-15.

GRAHAM, G., & Heimerer, E. Research on teacher effectiveness. *Quest*, 1981, **33**(1), 14-25.

GRAHAM, G., Soares, P., & Harrington, W. Experienced physical education teacher's effectiveness with intact classes of fourth and/or fifth grade classes: An ETU study. *Journal of Teaching in Physical Education*, 1983, **2**(2), 3-14.

KELLER, J.G. *Modification of a physical education experimental teaching unit.* Unpublished master's thesis, Virginia Polytechnic Institute and State University, 1982.

MCDONALD, F. Report on phase II of the beginning teacher evaluation study. *Journal of Teacher Education*, 1976, **27**(1), 39-42.

POPHAM, James W. Performance tests of teaching proficiency: Rationale, development and validation. *American Educational Research Journal*, 1971, **8**(1), 105-117.

ROSENSHINE, B. Recent research on teaching behaviors and student achievement. *Journal of Teacher Education*, 1976, **27**(1), 61-64.

YERG, B.J. Relationships between teacher behavior and pupil achievement in the psychomotor domain. (Doctoral dissertation, University of Pittsburgh, 1977). (*University Microfilms*, 1980, No. 77-21, 229)

YERG, B.J. Reflections on the use of the RTE model in physical education. *Research Quarterly for Exercise and Sport*, 1981, **52**(1), 38-47. (a)

YERG, B.J. The impact of selected presage and process behaviors on the refinement of a motor skill. *Journal of Teaching in Physical Education*, 1981, **1**(10), 38-46. (b)

Research on the immediate effects of instructional variables

Neal F. Earls
University of Wisconsin-Madison

Time-on-task and academic achievement have been found to be significantly related in the research on classroom teaching of children in particular subjects. Time-on-task, however, provides a minimal and temporal indication of student engagement in learning. Research by Pieron (1981) suggests that the frequency of practice events (student trials) may better indicate teaching effectiveness than do time-based data.

The quality of learning experiences is also important. Researchers using the ALT-PE system (Siedentop, Tousignant, & Parker, 1982) address the concern for quality by noting the difficulty of the learning experience in terms of the student success rate.

Another indicator of the quality of learning opportunities in physical education is the type of movement pattern a student utilizes. The research reported here assumes that it is desirable for a child who has not developed an optimal movement pattern to practice the most advanced movement pattern in his or her movement repertoire at that time. It is hypothesized that a child's regression to the practice of a less advanced movement pattern is not generally conducive to motor development.

Observable changes in children's movement patterns can be viewed as immediate effects of instruction if the changes occur in response to instructional variations within the lesson. Such process outcomes represent the "observable changes in pupil behavior" (p. 39) in Dunkin and Biddle's (1974) model for research on classroom teaching. This element of their model is important in researching teacher effectiveness since long-term product measures of learning cannot be closely linked to instructional variables due to the intervention of variables that are beyond the researchers' assessment or control. The length and complexity of instructional treatments confound the identification of specific aspects of instruction that may have contributed to student progress. The fewest variables mediating the effects of instruction are found between teacher actions and the immediate responses of individual students.

Purpose

This paper reports procedures and results from a series of studies examining children's immediate motoric responses to instructional variations. Instructional variables were teacher actions (e.g., verbal emphasis or use of demonstration) and other factors such as the characteristics of the task and equipment. The investigations, initiated at the University of New Hampshire and continuing at the University of Wisconsin, were designed to increase understanding of the role of instructional variables in eliciting progression and regression of the quality of movement pattern practice of children. Selected procedures and hypotheses are presented here to partially illustrate the application of this new research strategy throughout the past 5 years of research.

Procedures

The research occurred in two types of settings. In the first setting, a university movement laboratory program, children of ages 3 to 10 were observed in play-like situations. The second setting was in elementary physical education classes of first- through fifth-grade children. Descriptive studies were conducted initially in both settings in order to identify relevant variables for experimental manipulation and control, while experimental studies were conducted in the movement laboratory and, subsequently, in the elementary schools.

In the movement laboratory experiments, instructional variables were isolated and recorded in a simple format involving event coding and narrative descriptions. For the elementary school studies, a system for describing instructional variables was developed and refined. This system was developed from a synthesis of several established teacher behavior research systems and from principles of instruction in motor learning and motor development literature.

Subject _____ Age _____ Sex _____
Observer _____ Object/size _____
Level & nature of task:

Observation #1   2   3
Observable Response Components   Date:_____

A. Hand-arm action
  1. None (no responses to object arrival)
  2. Trapping (arms and/or body)
     a. Basket trap (arms flex upward to chest)
     b. Encircling trap (arms close around ball)
  3. Tentative hand catch (hands used with reliance on arms or body)
  4. Definite hand catch (hands only)
  5. Hand catch with giving action

B. Head-eye action
  1. Protective reaction (head turns well before object arrives, eyes may close)
  2. Late avoidance (slight turning away and/or eyes closing when object arrives)
  3. Continued focus (eyes focus on object receipt)

C. Tracking response
  1. None (hands stationary)
  2. Premature (reaction to early trajectory)
  3. Complete (adjustment to latter portion of object flight)

D. Grasping
  1. None (no response)
  2. Untimely
     a. Late closing
     b. Early closing
  3. Timely

Figure 1—Movement pattern and quality scale—(catching).

Children's movement pattern responses were classified according to criterion-referenced developmental scales (Earls, Note 1; Roberton & Halverson, 1977). These scales were used because they are based on longitudinal research and are structured by a component approach that can describe a child's movement pattern more accurately than can the conventional total body classification schemes (Roberton, 1978). Figure 1 presents a movement pattern scale with developmental steps hypothesized within each of four components of a catching performance. A profile can be obtained for each response by classifying the observed movement response for each component. In this research, students were observed to determine how their response profile changed in different contexts. Changes in the instructional situation were recorded and analyzed in relation to corresponding changes in the student's movement response profile.

An early experiment is portrayed in Figure 2. This subject provides a simple illustration since it was a rare instance where only one component changed in the movement profile. Two variations of ball size and two variations of verbal emphasis were examined for their possible effect on the child's movement pattern responses. With ball size held constant, the quality of hand-arm action *regressed* from a tentative hand catch to a trapping action when the verbal emphasis on results was imposed. After the verbal emphasis was removed and a medium-sized ball was used, the child's hand-arm action *progressed* to Pattern 4, a definite hand catch. If this pattern of effects was expected to remain consistent, then hand-arm action might be predicted to regress to tentative hand catch (Pattern 3) in the fourth experimental condition. An interaction effect appeared, however, as the movement pattern response by this particular child was immediately and consistently representative of hand catching, with a pronounced "giving" action to absorb the force of the ball.

Performance results were also recorded in the experiments. The child in the experiment in Figure 2 was always "successful" in each of the four experimental conditions and was never close to losing control of the ball. Because of such clear results and an intriguing interaction effect, additional experiments were designed. Responses were not always so clear, nor were the movement pattern responses as consistent. Fewer incidentally varied factors were permitted, and especially powerful variations (e.g., point of object arrival in catching) were controlled or the experiment was deleted from data analyses. The two-by-two design prevailed in experiments, although one-by-three designs were used when more than two variations of a factor were desired for experimentation.

Descriptive studies and experiments were captured on 8 mm film or videotape. Frequently subjects were unaware that they were being filmed because a zoom lens was used. Data were obtained from the films by means of slow-motion and stop-action analysis of movement patterns. The film records also allowed verification of the consistency of factors such as speed of object travel, point of object arrival, and trajectory.

Numerous instructional tasks and movement patterns were the focus of experiments with the greatest attention given to interventions involving catching, throwing, kicking, jumping, landing, and striking pattern responses. Interventions involved experimental manipulation of factors such as those listed as experimentally controlled or incidentally varied in Figure 2. Additional verbal cues and other aspects of instructional conditions were tested.

Data were collected to capture the movement responses of students immediately following instructions from the teacher; the camera remained

Catching experiment #780409: Teacher verbal emphasis and size of object

Subject: Boy (SEJ), age 9.5, advanced catching skills (hand-arm = 5/6, head-eye
= 3, tracking = 3, grasping = 3)

Experimentally varied factors
Factor A : Verbal emphasis by teacher
    A1: No verbal emphasis (just "play catch")
    A2: Verbal emphasis on quantitative results ("catch as many as you can
    in a row; make certain the ball does not touch the floor")

Factor B : Size of object
    B1: Large playground ball, 13" diameter (red)
    B2: Medium rubber ball, 7" diameter (blue)

Experimentally controlled factors
    Point of object arrival; performer movement; weight, resilience, and density of
    objects; hardness and compression; speed of object travel; flight trajectory;
    background and contrast; extension via implements (none were used); and
    distance.

Incidentially varied factors
    Texture of object, grainy large ball and smooth medium ball; color of object;
    subject's color preference, not determined; choice of object, no choice given.

	Size of Object			
Verbal	Large ball (B1)		Medium ball (B2)	
Emphasis	Pattern	Results	Pattern	Results
None (A1)	Hand 3 Head 3 Track 3 Grasp 3	8 of 8 (1)	Hand 4 Head 3 Track 3 Grasp 3	8 of 8 (3)
Results (A2)	Hand 2a/2b Head 3 Track 3 Grasp 3	8 of 8 (2)	Hand 5 Head 3 Track 3 Grasp 3	8 of 8 (4)

Figure 2 — Teacher verbal emphasis and size of object.

focused on students who had just been the subject of teacher intervention. Several strategies for videotaping were field-tested, and three acceptable procedures evolved. All require an active camera operator because wide angle recording is needed when the teacher instructs large
numbers of students, and the zoom lens is needed to capture student
movement following teacher interactions with individuals or small
groups.

Interim results

Tentative results are discussed here as hypotheses regarding the relationship between instructional variables and the movement responses of learners across skills in this research. Findings are reported elsewhere (Earls, Note 2) for the particular skill of catching. Future research reports will present specific evidence and statistical analyses on which to evaluate the merit of the following observations.

The early years in this series of investigations revealed that many common instructional and curricular practices induce regression in student practice of movement patterns. Variance was noted, however, and the movement pattern responses were context-specific. In general, for both the laboratory and field experiments, quantitative movement results varied less frequently and less strongly in conjunction with experimental variations than did the movement patterns of students. The experiments clearly demonstrated that the quality of students' movement pattern practice can be changed considerably by varying teacher actions, environmental factors, and the characteristics of tasks. The researchers and collaborating teachers willfully influenced both progression and regression of movement pattern practice without commenting to students about *how* they should move their body parts.

Instructional objectives and teacher actions

A theory of teaching should relate to a set of purposes, both short- and long-term, or there is nothing relevant against which to evaluate the theory. A delimitation of these field studies was the singular focus on one effect of teaching—the movement pattern responses of students. It became apparent that effects on movement patterns were not the implicit purpose of teacher actions in most settings. While a researcher's imposition of a particular focus can be justified, the research is more likely to be informative and contextually valid if data are collected regarding the teacher's explicit and implicit intentions. Observations regarding two types of teachers from this phase of the research will highlight the need for a broad and flexible perspective in assessing the effects of instruction.

Teachers who used *conventional* strategies and behaviors often explained and demonstrated an idealized movement pattern in their initial instructions to students. Subsequent teacher actions, however, often were not consistent with the initial attention to the objective of improving student movement form. Much of the teachers' feedback during student practice and game play was directed toward the results of student performance rather than toward the quality of the movement pattern he or she practiced. When a teacher addressed the specifics of how a student moved the body, a positive effect was seldom noted. Frequently a student did not receive another performance trial following teacher intervention, or considerable time elapsed before the student's next performance.

The purposes of teachers who used a *nonconventional* and movement-oriented approach were reflected in strategies and actions that were not well accounted for by the initial techniques in this research. It is no solace that most of the research on teaching that has purported to include "movement education" teachers has similar shortcomings. Since the immediate effects these teachers often sought were changes in the effort qualities of movement, the effects of their teaching could not not be adequately examined by the initial tools in this research.

A more sophisticated analysis revealed that in subtle ways the nonconventional teachers intentionally varied the task characteristics, environmental factors, and verbal interactions to gradually improve the quality of movement pattern practice. Many of these teachers' actions were congruent with the desirable variations identified in the movement laboratory experiments of this research.

Effects of conventional instruction

There is little evidence that conventional instruction is positively related to the learning and development of motor skills for most students. This statement is based on an analysis of published research, the research reported herein, and a recent 3-year study (unpublished) of the progress of elementary school children in terms of movement patterns without the benefit of a physical education program. The latter research raises sobering questions about using student gains on skill tests to indicate instructor or program effects.

There appears to be few teachers who really make a difference in skill development for many of their students, due partially to the amount of nonteaching that exists in physical education. Teacher-coach role conflict (Massengale & Locke, Note 3), teacher burnout, and the "athletics syndrome" (Earls, 1981) may contribute to the frequency of nonteaching as well as to poor teaching. Additionally, physical education teachers generally demonstrate little practical understanding of the motor development of children and adolescents. There seems to be a large gap between what stage of development the students are at and the response capabilities presumed by many physical education teaching practices.

Explanation and demonstrations by the conventional teachers in this research had little immediate effect on the motor performance of students. Many students cannot, or at least do not, follow the ideal model their teachers present. Subsequent experiences in conventional lessons seldom elicit the desired movement pattern. If any effect is noted, it is likely to reflect regression of the quality of movement practice as the student changes from individual and partner practice to more complex and challenging drills and conventional lead-up games.

Many practice situations used in classes are not appropriate because most of the students are *developing* skill patterns. The same practice drills are perhaps more appropriate for after-school teams since many of the athletes are *refining* skills. This mismatch of learning experiences with learner readiness may also be related to the teachers' implicit or explicit intentions. The actions of most physical education teachers observed in this research convey the message that their main goal is to engage students in traditional game playing. After inadequate time or poor quality of work in progressive skill development, students are placed in competitive games where the primacy of results and the complex demands of performance almost insure that most of them will substitute less desirable movement patterns. A child's readiness is frequently violated by the leap from simple drills to complex games.

Motor learning researchers, coaches, and teachers have long recognized that performance results are likely to be worse for a while if a change, however mechanically sound, is made in a performer's movement pattern. In physical education, however, conventional teachers do not seem to realize that instructional conditions that aid in achieving short-term results do not necessarily produce qualitative gains in movement pattern. The instructional variables that seem to aid in immediate achievement of quantitative movement results often have a reverse effect on the students' quality of movement pattern habits.

Figure 3 depicts a sequence of changes in student movement responses that illustrate how frequently the movement practice quality regresses. Early in the class, a child was observed kicking a stationary ball with Pattern 2 of knee action and Pattern 1 of hip action. The teacher facilitated the child's movement pattern progress by simply encouraging the child to "kick harder." Immediately following that verbal emphasis, the child increased the preparatory cocking of one leg rearward. His movement pattern practice thus progressed as the ensuing kicks reflected the utilization of Pattern 3 of knee action and Pattern 2 of hip action (see Figure 2). The child's task was then changed so that he had to kick a ball that was rolling directly toward him. He "succeeded" in making contact consistently, but his movement pattern regressed regularly to Pattern 2 of knee action and Patterns 1 and 2 of hip action. Noting the student's "success," the teacher continued the preplanned progression of tasks. The child was challenged to move laterally and kick an oncoming ball. On the first attempt, the child kicked too late and missed the ball. The next attempt probably reflected an overcompensation since he kicked too early and the ball struck the bottom of his foot. On the fourth attempt and thereafter, the child adjusted by keeping one foot close to the ground most of the time and kicking primarily with slight knee flexion. "Successful" in making contact, he continued to practice kicking with knee action of Pattern 1 and hip action of Pattern 1. This complete regression to the least

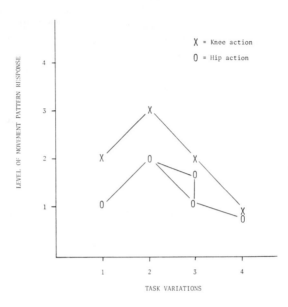

Figure 3 — A sequence of movement responses to instructional task variations for kicking.

desirable movement pattern occurred in instructional conditions of increasing task complexity and was not reflected in the results produced by the child' efforts through observations of the frequency of contact or the distance the ball traveled. Table 1 outlines a framework for examining generic occurrences of the preceding phenomenon and suggests the importance of encouraging teachers to observe the movement patterns of students, rather than the quantitative results only.

Research questions

Teachers may improve their effectiveness by evaluating the effects of their actions on the quality of student movement response patterns. Future research and theorizing may be improved by attending to the following questions and comments as well as others raised by this series of studies.

If a teacher's intent is to change how a child moves in performing a motor task, does the child's movement change in the desired direction? If not, then what is the explanation or implication? Was the teacher intervention ineffective due to being "out of touch" with the child's developmental readiness, or was the intervention designed to achieve its effect over a longer term? If the latter is true, then how do we research the long-term effects in a meaningful and useful way, given the many intervening variables that mediate effects and confound interpretation? The answers

Table 1

A General Sequence of Student Movement Responses in a Progression of Tasks with Teacher Focus on the Results of Movement

Task	Student responses: Movement results and pattern	
1	"Successful" quantitative movement results Initial movement pattern	(baseline)
2	Continued successful results Movement pattern improves	(progress)
3	Continued successful results Movement pattern same as in second task	(stability)
4	Continued successful results Movement pattern regresses to the pattern used in first task	(regression)
5	Unsuccessful results initially; success follows student adjustment of movement pattern Movement pattern is worse than that used in first task	(additional regression)
6	Obviously unsuccessful results; teacher has student return to task 5 Movement pattern still worse than in first task	

may depend more on improving our impoverished theoretical base than on improving research tools. Aristotle suggested that the mark of an educated person is to seek precision in each class of things just so far as it remains practical and just so far as the nature of the phenomenon permits.

Reference Notes

1. Earls, N.F. *Movement pattern and quality scales.* Unpublished materials, University of New Hampshire, 1977-1981.
2. Earls, N.F. *Effects of teacher actions and environmental variables on the movement pattern practice of children.* Paper presented at the International Symposium on Research in School Physical Education, Jyväskylä, Finland, 1982.
3. Massengale, J.D., & Locke, L.F. *The teacher/coach in conflict: Perceived and experienced dysfunction within the occupational role.* Paper presented at the national convention of AAHPER, Milwaukee, 1976.

References

DUNKIN, M.J., & Biddle, B.J. *The study of teaching.* New York: Holt, Rinehart & Winston, 1974.

EARLS, N.F. Distinctive teachers' personal qualities, perceptions of teacher education and the realities of teaching. *Journal of Teaching in Physical Education*, 1981, **1**(1), 59-70.

PIERON, M. From interaction analysis to research on teaching effectiveness. *International Journal of Physical Education*, 1981, **18**(4), 16-21.

ROBERTON, M.A. Stages in motor development. In M. Ridenour (Ed.), *Motor development*. Princeton, NJ: Princeton Book Co., 1978.

ROBERTON, M.A., & Halverson, L.E. The developing child—His changing movement. In B. Logsdon (Ed.), *The child in physical education: A focus on the teaching process*. Philadelphia: Lea & Febiger, 1977.

SIEDENTOP, D., Tousignant, M., & Parker, M. *Academic learning time—Physical education, 1982 revision, coding manual*. Columbus, OH: School of Health, Physical Education and Recreation, Ohio State University, 1982.

Hunting the elusive ATI: How pupil aptitudes mediate instruction in the gymnasium

David C. Griffey
The University of Texas at Austin

A typical ATI

Aptitude-treatment interactions (ATIs) are present when individuals near the end of a range of some human ability or characteristic are affected differentially by alternate instructional interventions. Simply stated, an ATI is present when persons high in some aptitude profit most from one kind of instruction, while persons low in that aptitude profit from a different kind of instruction. An ATI is characterized in Figure 1 where best fit regression lines represent two groups that have received different kinds of teaching, method A and method B. The lines have different slopes, indicating that pupil performance was not merely a function of the kind of teaching but also a function of the aptitude. This is particularly true in method A, the treatment with a steeper slope.

Point X' is the point of intersection of the regressions and prescribes the decision rule for instructional intervention. That is, students above X' in the aptitude should receive method A and those below that point will profit most from method B.

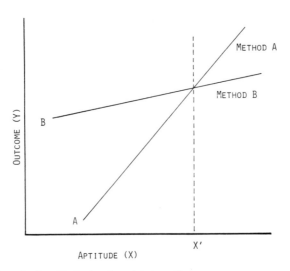

Figure 1 — A typical aptitude-treatment interaction.

The aim of interaction research

While good teachers may conceptualize teaching in ways that result in their altering instructional interventions according to the pupils at hand, and I believe they do, aptitude-treatment interaction research has been conducted in an effort to develop a unified theory of the teaching/learning process, not to effect an immediate improvement in the quality of instruction in schools. That is not to say that technologically notable findings have not resulted from ATI research, but that has not been the main intent of the effort. ATI studies have been undertaken within a critical science orientation. That is, the development of an elegant theory of learning and instruction has meant moving beyond "minimum assumption," main effects models of instruction.

Thus, ATI research has differed philosophically from the positivistic orientation that has characterized research on teaching physical education to date. Generally, we have been aiming at descriptions and inferences that aid in the immediate improvement of efficiency or effectiveness of instruction in the gym. Such a positivistic orientation, while extremely valuable, is very different from theory building. So, too, with the ethnomethodologies that have recently gained in popularity among us. These phenomenological investigations are concerned with the meaning of events for the participants, not with a theory of instruction in any direct sense.

Siedentop's (1982) recent question, "Does anybody really believe that the investigation of ATI's and such interaction effects will somehow render less important what we already know about *main effects*?" (p. 47) has, therefore, three possible answers depending on the philosophic orientation and assumptions of the investigator. (a) Positivistically, the answer is no. The exigencies of teaching 30 students, with the limited resources and time available for the task, makes hope for an interactional instructional technology seem dim at this time. Such a technology seems incompatible with the *present* organizational structure of physical education classes. (b) Phenomenologically, the answer is maybe. It seems logical that the quality of the instructional experience, as perceived by the participants, will be significantly altered when interventions are tailored to individuals' needs, interests, styles, and abilities. Students' satisfaction and sense of achievement are almost certainly altered under different instructional regimens. (c) And, from a critical science orientation, the reply is yes. Learning has been found to vary considerably as a function of the nature of the task, the teaching method, the instructional materials, the context of learning, and the character of the learner (Calfee & Hedges, Note 1). Now, an interactional theory of teaching could probably never be made parsimonious enough to be of great cognitive or technological use. However, it is clear that, in any but the most totalitarian environment, individual differences and the ways that those differences relate to various kinds of teaching can add a great deal to understanding the mechanisms operating within instructional interventions.

Learning models

Research on alternate models of learning can be characterized by the assumptions made about the factors that affect student learning and cognition. The simplest class of models—minimum assumption models—assume that learning occurs as a function of the amount of time spent in study and practice. Little else can be stated about the nature of the learning process or the factors affecting learning (Calfee & Hedges, Note 1).

A second class of models of learning and instruction pays attention to the input factors that influence learning. We know that learning varies as a function of the nature of the task, the teaching method, the instructional materials, the context of learning, and the characteristics of the learner. Early research in this vein consisted of A-B comparisons with one group assigned to an experimental treatment and the other group designated as control. The ATI concept provided a way to incorporate individual differences into the input factor research, permitting a more thorough description of the learning process and a means of resolving contradictory results of main effects investigations.

The third class of models, those currently receiving the most attention in subject areas other than physical education, is "process models." Recently, information processing models have been developed that are theoretically quite elegant. These models attempt to explain cognition and learning as a series of steps, each step carrying out a particular cognitive function. These models hold the potential to represent performance in a variety of skilled tasks. Additionally, they provide a comprehensive theoretical framework for ATI research — for the study of individual response to instruction. In sum, ATI work aims at the long range goal of describing the complex nature of instruction.

Choosing aptitudes

Throughout education's subject matters, the most consistently observed ATIs are associated with general mental ability (G). As the instructional method places more information processing demands on learners, those with less ability to structure, form relationships, and visualize are at an increasing disadvantage. Now, G has no apparent relationship to performance in a sport or human movement environment — the correlation between them being at or near zero. G_v, the ability to visualize spatial relationships (after Cattell, 1971), however, has been shown to be an important aptitude in learning some types of motor skills. Fleishman (1966) found in his studies on pilot selection and training that certain spatial abilities accounted for a large part of the between-person variance in the performance of a psychomotor task. This was particularly true during early learning trials. We suspect that G_v might interact with different teaching styles as those styles place more responsibility on the learner to visualize the movement pattern and the means to performing it. In other words, direct styles may place fewer information processing demands on individuals and thus favor low G_v persons.

Task specific abilities are a second kind of variable that hold potential for ATI research. Cronbach and Snow (1977) summarize the relationship: "We see [persons with high initial ability] doing better when given greater freedom to proceed in their own manner, when thrown more upon their own resources. And we see regression slopes becoming flatter when more of the intellectual work is done for the learner" (p. 503).

Additionally, task specific abilities have been shown to account for more variance in learning psychomotor skills than have measures of general motor ability (Marteniuk, 1969). So, a pragmatically straightforward place to look for ATI would seem to be among the initial abilities of learners at the instructional tasks.

A third class of aptitudes holding potential for ATI research, and one that perhaps most teachers spend a great deal of time considering when planning pedagogical acts, is pupil personality. Of particular theoretical interest is student anxiety, as it is increased or decreased by the instructional environment. Many teachers have been perplexed at a set of student evaluations of their instruction — some reporting a rewarding, valuable experience while others in the same class recount one of the worst classes in their long educational careers.

That students' personality aspects can enhance or interfere with optimal functioning in different instructional environments has been shown in a number of studies (Domino, 1968, 1971; Dowaliby & Schumer, 1973; Peterson, 1977). Specifically, more teacher demand for conformance and a high degree of structure in lessons have been shown to benefit anxious students. Less anxious students appear to be more comfortable in settings that permit independence and contain less structure than those that benefit high anxiety students.

Domino (1968, 1971) found that students who scored high on the achievement via conformance scale (AC) and low on the achievement via independence scale (AI) of the *California Psychological Inventory* (Gough, 1957) performed significantly better in courses that permitted considerable choice in structuring learning activities, compared to their high AC, low AI peers. He also found the converse to be true. Low AI, high AC students performed significantly better than did their high AI, low AC peers in courses where the instructor provided strict requirements and structured the learning activities.

Finally, student gender appears to be an important characteristic to consider in ATI research. Oliver (1978) and Griffey (1980) have found steeper regression slopes for females than for males within instructional treatments — regardless of the treatment. Females with low initial ability have repeatedly been observed to score lower on product measures than males with similar low initial ability. And, high initial ability females have scored higher on product measures than their male counterparts. Some characteristic associated with gender, therefore, appears to be an important consideration in ATI research.

In summary, initial task-specific ability, general spatial ability, student style (or anxiety), and gender are aptitudes that seem to hold potential for adding to our understanding of how instruction in the gym is mediated by individual characteristics.

The study

We have explored the possibility that these pupil aptitudes interact differentially with instructional styles that varied in the amount of choice that students were permitted during class sessions. The treatments were Mosston's (1966) command, a teacher-centered style with teachers making all decisions, and task, with students being permitted choice in structuring in-class activities (see Griffey, 1980, for a description of treatments). The treatments are seen as requiring different amounts of information processing, visualizing, and structuring of students, with the task style being more demanding in these areas.

Volleyball skills of forearm passing and overhead serving were taught to 145 high school students during a 2-week study. Students were tested on initial ability at the two tasks using the Russell-Lange Volleyball test (Russell & Lange, 1940). Additionally, student spatial ability (G_v) was assessed using the paper folding and embedded figures tests from the French Kit of Reference Tests (French & Ekstrom, 1963), and students' preferred style for instruction was assessed using the achievement via conformance and achievement via independence subscales of the California Psychological Inventory (Gough, 1957). Following instruction under either the command or task styles, students were retested on the volleyball skills.

Results

In a number of cases the ATIs we expected to find were present, and in others they were not. A significant interaction was observed for males and females between initial ability and the two styles of instruction for forearm passing. Task instruction was found to have a steeper slope. High initial ability students were found to have higher posttest scores when taught with task instruction than with command. In the lower range of initial ability, command instructed subjects performed better than their task instructed counterparts.

This finding is consistent with ATI studies on cognitive learning. Subjects with sufficient initial ability appeared able to structure their own learning more successfully than the teacher was able to do (see Wittrock, 1974, for a discussion of generative learning).

No ATIs were found between initial serving ability and the two instructional styles. In fact, very little improvement occurred in students' serving ability during the study. A significant main effect was found among female subjects; those who were task instructed had higher posttest scores across the range of initial ability than did their command instructed peers.

The results of analyzing "learning style" were not consistent with the hypothesized outcomes in all cases. Domino's (1968, 1971) results were replicated in three of the four analyses performed. The number of students who could be dichotomized into either high on achievement via conformance and low on achievement via independence (HIAC-LOAI), or low on achievement via conformance and high on achievement via independence (LOAC-HIAI) was quite small, however, making inference difficult.

Of the 145 subjects in the study, 16 and 20 HIAI-LOAC subjects exhibited higher posttest passing and serving scores in conjunction with task treatment. The effect size for passing was $.54s_x$ and that for serving was $.51s_x$ (Table 1).

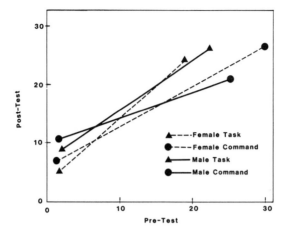

Figure 2 — Best-fit linear regression lines of posttest on pretest passing scores by sex and treatment (*n* = 145).

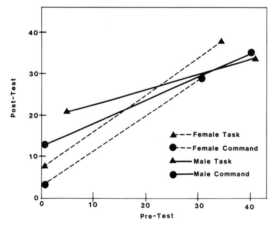

Figure 3 — Best-fit linear regression lines of posttest on pretest serving scores by sex and treatment (*n* = 145).

The mean for LOAI-HIAC subjects for passing was higher in the command instruction group than for the task group. The effect size for this difference was $.82s_x$. Means for serving ran counter to the prediction showing higher scores associated with the task style in the LOAI-HIAC group with an effect size of $.46s_x$.

Spatial ability
The analysis of the relationship of the spatial measures (paper folding and embedded figures) with posttest performance on passing and serving

Table 1
Interactions of Student Style With Treatments

HIAI-LOAC

		Low initial ability	High initial ability	Overall
Passing	Command	11.67, $S^2 = 29.87$, n = 6	14.00, $S^2 = 28.67$, n = 4	12.60, $S^2 27.60$, n = 10
	Task	13.33, $S^2 = 16.33$, n = 3	17.33, $S^2 = 25.33$, n = 3	15.33, $S^2 21.47$, n = 6
				$\epsilon S^2 = 25.71$, $\epsilon S = 5.07$, $\Delta = 2.73$, ES $= .54\sigma X$
Serving	Command	9.40, $S^2 = 82.80$, n = 5	23.00, $S^2 = 132.0$, n = 4	15.44, $S^2 142.3$, n = 9
	Task	16.33, $S^2 = 145.9$, n = 6	27.40, $S^2 = 147.8$, n = 5	21.36, $S^2 165.5$, n = 11
				$\epsilon S^2 = 132.3$, $\epsilon S = 11.5$, $\Delta = 5.92$, ES $= .51\sigma X$

LOAI-HIAC

		Low initial ability	high initial ability	Overall
Passing	Command	10.00, $S^2 = 2.00$, n = 5	17.86, $S^2 = 20.14$, n = 7	14.58, $S^2 28.08$, n = 12
	Task	9.36, $S^2 = 11.65$, n = 11	22.00, $S^2 = 0$, n = 1	10.42, $S^2 23.90$, n = 12
				$\epsilon S^2 = 25.71$, $\epsilon S = 5.07$, $\Delta = 4.16$, ES $= .82\sigma X$
Serving	Command	16.20, $S^2 = 127.2$, n = 5	21.00, $S^2 = 32.86$, n = 8	19.15, $S^2 67.47$, n = 13
	Task	16.20, $S^2 = 201.7$, n = 5	30.00, $S^2 = 70.0$, n = 6	23.73, $S^2 167.62$, n = 11
				$\epsilon S^2 = 132.3$, $\epsilon S = 11.5$, $\Delta = 4.58$, ES $= .40\sigma X$

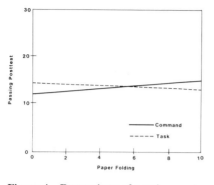

Figure 4 — Regressions of passing posttest performance onto paper folding scores by treatment group ($n = 145$).

Figure 5 — Regressions of passing scores onto embedded figures scores by treatment group ($n = 145$).

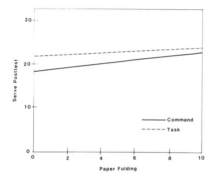
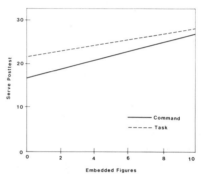

Figure 6 — Regressions of posttest serving scores onto paper folding scores by treatment group ($n = 145$).

Figure 7 — Regressions of serving posttest scores onto embedded figures scores by treatment group ($n = 145$).

suggested that no connection existed between these abilities. Regressions of posttest passing scores onto paper folding resulted in slopes that were not significantly ($p < .05$) different from zero. The regressions of posttest passing scores onto embedded figures scores showed a slightly better fit but no appreciable interaction (Figures 4 & 5).

Regressions of posttest serving scores onto paper folding and embedded figures tests were all nonsignificant ($p < .10$). Therefore, no significant ATIs were found for the aptitude of spatial ability as measured with the french-kit tests and the volleyball skills under study (Figures 6 & 7).

In summary, we have observed convincing mediating effects associated with initial ability, gender, and student style. These results, however, are tentative and inconsistent, and seem to call for further investigation.

Future research

If we are to come to a finer understanding of the instruction process, we must conduct research on how student aptitudes mediate the spectrum of teaching styles. These preliminary findings suggest that teaching styles designed to allow for individualization may actually handicap some individuals when compared to more direct methods.

Many serious theoretical, pragmatic, and methodological issues attend interactional approaches to the study of teaching physical education. Methodologically, ATI studies are usually conceived as experiments. They are expensive in time and resources. Most researchers use designs that are fully crossed; all aptitudes and treatments are applied to all subjects. There is the possibility of reducing expense by using fractional factorial designs, but this has not been widely explored (Calfee, 1975).

An additional methodological problem with studies that look at instructional style is ensuring that teachers conform to a treatment specification (style). Each teacher has evolved his or her individual style of teaching. Many have difficulty putting aside their own preferences and beliefs for even a short time. The experimenter must constantly monitor teachers and be prepared to cajole them back into conformance to a treatment when they wander off.

A second area of concern centers on theory. It is difficult to build a theory of instruction without considering the purposes of the curriculum and the nature of the learning process. Interactional research on teaching cannot progress far without the simultaneous investigation of the discrete processes involved in motor learning and philosophic exploration of curriculum issues.

We have had to borrow heavily from research on cognitive subject matters in identifying aptitudes that might mediate instruction in the gymnasium. The absence of developing process theories of motor learning has made this necessary. We do know that the aptitudes related to motor skill performance vary as people master a skill. It remains to systematically relate those aptitudes to instructional styles. And, it remains to identify discrete processes in motor learning that might mediate instruction.

Building theories about effective instruction also requires some acknowledgement of, if not consensus about, the outcomes of physical education. The dependent variable in experiments on teacher effectiveness is by definition some product of instruction; attitude, knowledge, or motor performance. It is not optimal to talk about effective teaching in generalities. Results of research on teaching must be interpreted relative to the outcomes that are valued, which requires dialogue about the goals of physical education.

A third theoretical issue centers on the description of treatments. What is the full range of teaching styles and what are the dimensions that can be used to describe them? Mosston (1981) has described a spectrum of styles along the continuum of teacher-student choice in curriculum, instruction, and evaluation. Joyce and Weil (1980) have described styles of teaching as members of families that have different educational goals; information processing, personal development, social development, or behavior modification. And, Broudy and Palmer (1965) have chronicled famous teachers from the past. Certainly the issues of economics, teacher preference, and other idiosyncracies associated with specific school sites must be considered.

Finally, many pragmatic issues must be considered in evaluating the potential technological importance of an interactional theory of instruction. Many people persist with the notion that there is a one best way to teach. We don't know much about how teachers arrive at decisions while instructing, nor even while they plan for instruction. It may be that teachers do not plan for instruction or make decisions in a rational way. They appear to proceed in an incremental fashion, staying with an instructional decision as long as students remain engaged in an activity (Griffey & Housner, Note 2). We don't presently know if teachers can accomodate to and use practical ATIs in their instructional repertoire.

In sum, the tools for systematic inquiry into the relationships between the spectrum of teaching styles, the characteristics of learners, and purposes of education and training exist. It remains for us to use them in our search for understanding about instruction.

Reference Notes

1. Calfee, R.C., & Hedges, L.V. *Independent process analyses of aptitude treatment interactions.* Unpublished manuscript, Stanford University, 1978.
2. Griffey, D.C., & Housner, L.D. *Interactive decision making in student teachers.* Paper presented at the annual meeting of the American Alliance for Health, Physical Education, Recreation and Dance, Houston, 1982.

References

BROUDY, H.S., & Palmer, J.R. *Exemplars of teaching method.* Chicago: Rand McNally, 1965.

CALFEE, R.C. *Human experimental psychology.* New York: Holt, Rinehart & Winston, 1975.

CATTELL, R.B. *Abilities: Their structure, growth, and action.* Boston: Houghton-Mifflin, 1971.

CRONBACH, L.J., & Snow, R.E. *Aptitudes and instructional methods.* New York: Wiley, 1977.

DOMINO, G. Differential predictions of academic achievement in conforming and independent settings. *Journal of Educational Psychology*, 1968, **59**, 256-260.

DOMINO, G. Interactive effects of achievement orientation and teaching style on academic achievement. *Journal of Educational Psychology*, 1971, **62**, 427-431.

DOWALIBY, F.J., & Schumer, H. Teacher-centered versus student-centered mode of college instruction as related to manifest anxiety. *Journal of Educational Psychology*, 1973, **64**, 125-132.

FLEISHMAN, E.A. Human abilities and the acquisition of skill. In E.A. Bilodeau (Ed.), *Acquisition of skill*. New York: Academic Press, 1966.

FRENCH, J.W., Ekstrom, R.B., & Price, L.A. *Kit of reference tests for cognitive factors* (1963 Revision). Princeton: Educational Testing Service, 1963.

GOUGH, H. *Manual for the California Psychological Inventory*. Palo Alto, CA: Consulting Psychologists Press, 1957.

GRIFFEY, D.C. *A study of aptitude x treatment interactions associated with student decision making in physical education classes*. Doctoral dissertation, Stanford University, 1980. (University Microfilms No. 81-03, 514)

JOYCE, B., & Weil, M. *Models of teaching*. Englewood Cliffs, NJ: Prentice Hall, 1980.

MARTENIUK, R.G. Generality and specificity of learning and performance on two similar speed tasks. *Research Quarterly*, 1969, **40**(3), 518.

MOSSTON, M. *Teaching physical education* (2nd ed.). Columbus, OH: Merrill, 1981. (Originally published, 1966.)

OLIVER, B. *The relationship of teacher and student presage and process criteria to student achievement in physical education*. Unpublished doctoral dissertation, Stanford University, 1978.

PETERSON, P.L. Interactive effects of student achievement and attitude. *Journal of Educational Psychology*, 1977, **69**(6), 779-792.

RUSSELL, N., & Lange, E. Achievement tests in volleyball for junior high school girls. *Research Quarterly*, 1940, **11**, 33.

SIEDENTOP, D. Teaching research: The intervention view. *Journal of Teaching in Physical Education*, 1982, **1**(3), 46-50.

WITTROCK, M.C. Learning as a generative process. *Educational Psychologist*, 1974, **11**(2), 87-95.

The student as the unit of analysis: Effect on descriptive data and process-outcome relationships in physical education

Stephen Silverman
Louisiana State University

The question, "For this study, what is the appropriate unit for analysis?" is often asked by those doing research on teaching. If a researcher were to pursue this question by investigating the literature, a variety of answers would appear. The possibilities include the use of aggregate units such as school or class means, within group analysis, and the individual student as the unit of analysis. Other possibilities and permutations of the three above might arise and offer an even greater variety of possible units for analysis.

Most discussions on the appropriate unit of analysis surround the assets and liabilities of those possible units mentioned above (i.e., means, within group analysis, and the student). In most every case the unit of *measurement*, as opposed to the unit of *analysis*, is the individual student. The question, therefore, revolves around whether to combine students by class or some other characteristic within classes, or to use the individual student as the unit of analysis.

The underlying issue in selecting the appropriate unit of analysis is the independence or interdependence of observations. Independence is an assumption of many of the well-known experimental and quasi-experimental statistical models.

One way to think about independence in a learning situation is to imagine a gymnasium full of activity during a physical education class. This class is one of a number of classes participating in a study of teacher effectiveness in physical education. The janitor is mowing the grass outside the gymnasium. Students who hear the lawnmower have this in common, whereas students in the other classes do not share this experience (Cronbach, 1976).

If the lawnmower distracts many students in a similar way, then the students in this class have something in common that may preclude them from being independent of one another. This lack of independence should be of concern to the researcher studying this class. However, if the effect of the lawnmower was independent across the students in the class (i.e., each student had an individual reaction to the lawnmower) then there is little concern for the event's effect on the independence of the sample.

We can think of the effect of the teacher on individual students in the class in a similar way. If the teacher arranges the learning situation so that each student in the class is having the same experience, then the student observations are likely to be interdependent. On the other hand, if learning of the skill is individualized, it is unlikely that students in the class will be interdependent. In all situations where some experience is shared, there will be some degree of interdependence. How you interpret the level of independence is a matter for each researcher to confront.

This paper compares data from a study focusing on the relationship between student engagement and achievement in physical education. Class means and individual students are compared as analysis units for the type and scope of information derived from each unit. This is done for both descriptive and process-outcome data.

Methods

Students (N = 102) enrolled in university intermediate swimming classes were the subjects of this study. The students were pretested, received instruction, and were posttested on the breaststroke.

Skill evaluation

An investigator-designed instrument was used to evaluate skill level for the pretest and posttest. Each student was rated on the five parts of any swimming skill: body position, arm action, leg action, breathing, and coordination (Brawnwarth, 1981). Three evaluators rated each part of the skill from 0 to 5 and recorded this information on an evaluation sheet. The skill evaluators were trained to use behavioral anchors to reliably rate the skill among themselves. In order to ensure that all instructors were familiar with the skill rating criteria, each instructor was trained in the criteria and procedures for rating the skill.

On the day of the skill evaluation, the skill was modeled for the class prior to testing. One at a time, students were evaluated by three raters positioned at the side of the pool. Skill levels for each student were calculated by summing the scores for each of the five parts of the stroke and taking the mean for the three raters' scores.

Instruction

Instruction consisted of four 15-minute classes. Each instructor taught breaststroke only during these time periods, and no guidelines for teaching the skill were provided. All instructors were reliable raters of the breaststroke and therefore were familiar with the evaluation criteria.

Instruction was videotaped using two cameras feeding a special effects generator. Elapsed time was superimposed on the split-screen image as the class was being recorded. Individual students were identified in subsequent coding of the videotapes by wearing white swim caps, each marked with a unique geometric shape.

Engagement coding

Two 1-minute periods were randomly selected for coding of student engagement from each third of the 15-minute instructional period. Thus, each student was coded for a total of 6 minutes in each class. Students missing any of the instruction or testing were dropped from coding and subsequent data analysis.

The videotapes were coded for the actual time that students spent in motor engagement, cognitive engagement, and the nonengaged categories of management, waiting, and off-task behavior. Basic definitions and a decision log were developed for coding within these exclusive and nonoverlapping categories. Total time that students spent in each category was summed for each class and then summed over the four classes. Greater detail on engagement coding, instruction, and testing is available elsewhere (Silverman, 1982).

Data analysis

Data analysis was performed both with class means and the individual student as the unit of analysis. When students were the unit of analysis, analyses were performed for subgroupings of initial skill level, previous experience level, and sex. Initial skill levels of high, medium, and low were based on pretest scores. Students were categorized as high, medium, or low previous experience based on their relative score on an investigator-designed questionnaire. Sex of the student was indicated on this questionnaire.

Mean percentage of class time was calculated for the amount of time students spent in motor engagement, cognitive engagement, and the nonengaged categories of management, waiting, and off-task behavior for both units of analysis. With the individual student as the unit of analysis, regression analysis was performed to determine if students with different initial skill levels, previous experience levels, or sex were engaged, managed, waiting, or off-task at significantly different rates. Each coded time variable separately was regressed on each student characteristic, using binary or "dummy" coding for the student characteristic to obtain an F ratio (Cohen, 1968; Draper & Smith, 1981).

To determine process-outcome relationships, regression analysis again was performed. The posttest score was the dependent variable, and the effect of initial ability was removed by entering pretest score into the equation as the first variable. Individual regression analyses were then performed for posttest on motor engagement, posttest on cognitive engagement, and posttest on all engagement (the total of motor and cognitive engagement). The above procedure is analogous to studying part correlations (Kerlinger & Pedhazur, 1973) since the effect of the third variable (in this case, initial skill) is removed from only one of the two variables being examined. The procedure was performed for class means, and with the student as the unit of analysis for the entire group, and for each subgrouping of the three student characteristics.

The results from all procedures will be presented and discussed in light of the information obtained using the different units of analysis.

Results

When means were calculated from aggregates (means) of all students (N = 47 after attrition) 25.76% of total class time was spent in motor engagement, 28.62% in cognitive engagement, and most of the time remaining was spent waiting (26.20%). Means on the entire sample, calculated from individual students, were similar (within 0.2% for all categories) to those calculated above from class means.

As indicated in Table 1, when means were calculated for the various subgroupings of students there is variability within each of the categories. In fact, there is a significant difference (p < .05) among students in the three previous experience levels for the amount of time spent in all three nonengaged categories (management, waiting, and off-task behavior). When overall mean is the only statistic calculated, these differences are obscured.

When class means for the three engagement variables were used in regression analysis to determine process-outcome relationships, cognitive

Table 1

**Percentage of Student Time
in Engagement/Nonengagement Categories**

	Motor engagement	Cognitive engagement	Management	Waiting	Off-task
Total sample (means)	25.76	28.62	12.97	26.20	5.81
Initial skill level					
High	23.26	27.89	11.81	31.25	5.85
Medium	26.81	27.51	12.65	27.99	4.89
Low	28.03	30.58	14.93	19.50	6.70
Previous experience level[a]					
High	24.78	27.95	10.88	31.60	4.89
Medium	25.14	30.64	14.38	20.33	7.59
Low	27.47	26.65	12.52	28.74	4.38
Sex					
Male	25.89	28.52	13.25	26.48	5.70
Female	25.64	28.72	12.73	25.95	5.91

Note. Significance levels were determined by binary coding of student characteristics and regressing on percentages in each engagement/nonengagement category to obtain an F value.

[a]Significant differences ($p < .05$) among the previous experience levels were found for the categories of management, waiting, and off-task behavior.

engagement was the only variable that was a significant addition to the equation. Cognitive engagement had a negative relationship with posttest score after accounting for initial ability.

As indicated in Table 2, when the student was the unit of analysis, both positive and negative relationships were found within the various subgroupings of students. Of particular note are the subgroupings within initial skill level, where all engaged time had a positive relationship with adjusted posttest score for high skilled students, and a negative relationship for medium skilled students. Cognitive engaged time had a negative relationship with adjusted posttest score for low skilled students. As can be seen in Table 2, analyses of various subgroupings with the student as the unit of analysis provides insight into significant relationships, which might otherwise not be seen if subgroup analyses were not performed.

Discussion

It is apparent from contrasting the information provided by the two units of analysis employed in this study that greater insight into the structure of the data is derived when both units are used. The use of class means or

Table 2

**Direction of Significant Relationships
between Achievement and Engagement**

	Motor engagement	Cognitive engagement	All engagement
	Aggregate units		
Class means		−	
	Student units		
All cases			
Initial skill level			
High			+
Medium			−
Low		−	
Previous experience level			
High			+
Medium			
Low			
Sex			
Male		−	
Female			

Note. + indicates a positive relationship between the engagement variable and achievement.

− indicates a negative relationship between the engagement variable and achievement.

The direction of a relationship is indicated only in instances where the addition of the engagement variable to the equation was statistically significant ($p < .05$).

a single mean for obtaining all descriptive statistics does not allow the researcher or those reading the research report to know what really occurred within classes or subgroupings of the sample. In this study there is variability, particularly in the nonengaged categories, among students who vary on a characteristic. The overall mean, while providing some description of the data, does not provide as rich a composite of what is happening. The richness is based, of course, on viewing the data from a variety of perspectives based on the student characteristics.

Page (1975) has suggested that "when the class is reduced to an "average" we seem to have reached analytical impoverishment" (p. 342). We may not be completely impoverished when class means are used, but with only aggregate unit statistics we are certainly far from being well off.

Again, we are provided with a much more complete understanding of the data when we look at process-outcome relationships for subgroups with the student as the unit of analysis. When adjusted posttest score was regressed on class means for the engagement variables, cognitive engagement was a negative predictor of adjusted posttest score. When we looked further and used the student as the unit of analysis, we saw that cognitive and all engaged time were negatively related to adjusted posttest score for low and medium students, respectively. For high skilled students, however, a different relationship emerged. This may suggest other or more involved conclusions than those based solely on relationships from group means.

Brophy (1975) has urged use of the individual as the unit of analysis in process-product research. When class means are used, it is impossible to evaluate slope interactions or test hypotheses based on learner characteristics (Hopkins, 1982). In addition, one or a small number of deviant scores may change a mean statistic and, therefore, not really reflect the central tendency of the majority of the class (Fletcher, 1968).

Many investigators have found no significant relationships based on class means, and those means may have served to obscure significant relationships based on student characteristics. A number of process-product studies in physical education (Oliver, 1979; Taylor, 1976; Yerg, 1977) have found few if any significant relationships based on class mean analysis. Even if significant relationships are found, the use of mean statistics may obscure important subgroup differences and will provide little insight into possible interactions occurring in physical education classes.

Cronbach (1976) has suggested one other beneficial aspect of using students as analytical units. When class means are used as the unit of analysis, the number of classes required to detect significance is large. This may make the study financially infeasible in most instances where teacher effectiveness paradigms are used. Since students are the unit of measurement in most studies, and if 30 classes were needed to provide the appropriate power, as many as 900 students would have to be measured. When the purpose of the study is to explore what relationships exist and for whom, using the student as the unit of analysis is a viable option for future process-product research in physical education.

The reader should be aware, however, that although Cronbach (1976) suggests a variety of levels of analysis based on what question is being asked, he and others (Earls, 1982; Griffey, 1981; Peckham, Glass, & Hopkins, 1969; Raths, 1967) warn against using the student as the unit of analysis when experimental studies are being conducted. For the most part, within group or nested groupings seem to be the method of choice when experiments or quasi-experiments are being analyzed.

The student as the unit of analysis may provide richer and fuller information when used with certain teacher effectiveness paradigms. However, it is not appropriate in all instances. Perhaps Glass, Peckham, Percy, and Sanders (1972) provide the advice that everyone doing research on teaching should keep in mind when planning and analyzing a study. That advice is, the researcher must weigh the facts and then make what seems to be the most appropriate decision on the unit of analysis and significance tests. This author would add that some might find fault in whatever unit of analysis is selected, but the decision should be well-reasoned and intentional.

References

BRAWNWARTH, A. A system for analyzing the teaching of swimming (Doctoral dissertation, Columbia University, 1980). *Dissertation Abstracts International*, 1980, **41**, 1473A. (University Microfilm No. 80-22,098)

BROPHY, J.E. *The student as the unit of analysis*. Austin, TX: University of Texas, 1975. (ERIC Document Reproduction No. 147-273)

COHEN, J. Multiple regression as a general data-analytic system. *Psychological Bulletin*, 1968, **70**(6), 426-443.

CRONBACH, L.J. *Research on classrooms and schools: Formulation of questions, design, and analysis*. Stanford, CA: Stanford Evaluation Consortium, School of Education, Stanford University, 1976.

DRAPER, N.R., & Smith, H. *Applied regression analysis* (2nd ed.). New York: Wiley, 1981.

EARLS, N. The need for within-class analysis of learner characteristics. *Journal of Teaching in Physical Education*, 1982, **1**(2), 40-43.

FLETCHER, H.J. Possible interpretive problems in analysis using group means as experimental units. *Psychological Bulletin*, 1968, **69**(3), 157-160.

GLASS, G.V., Peckham, P.D., Percy, D., & Sanders, J.R. Consequences of failure to meet assumptions underlying the fixed effects analysis of variance and covariance. *Review of Educational Research*, 1972, **42**(3), 237-288.

GRIFFEY, D.C. What is the best way to teach? *Journal of Teaching in Physical Education*, 1981, **1**, 18-24.

HOPKINS, K.D. The unit of analysis: Group mean versus individual observation. *American Educational Research Journal*, 1982, **19**(1), 5-18.

KERLINGER, F.N., & Pedhazur, E.J. *Multiple regression in behavioral research*. New York: Holt, Rinehart & Winston, 1973.

OLIVER, B.L. The relationship of teacher and student pressage and process criteria to student achievement in physical education (Doctoral dissertation, Stanford University, 1978). *Dissertation Abstracts International*, 1979, **39**, 5395A-5396A. (University Microfilm No. 79-05,955)

PAGE, E.B. Statistically recapturing the richness within a classroom. *Psychology in the Schools*, 1975, **12**, 339-344.

PECKHAM, P.D., Glass, G.V., & Hopkins, K.D. The experimental unit in statistical analysis. *Journal of Special Education*, 1969, **3**(4), 337-349.

RATHS, J. The appropriate experimental unit. *Educational Leadership*, 1967, **25**(3), 263-266.

SILVERMAN, S.J. The relationships among student achievement, student engagement, and selected student characteristics in physical education (Doctoral dissertation, University of Massachusetts, 1982). *Dissertation Abstracts International*, 1982, **43**, 1082A. (University Microfilms No. 82-19,849)

TAYLOR, J.L. Development and use of the physical education observation instrument (PEOI) for rating patterns of teacher behaviors in relationship to student achievement (Doctoral dissertation, Stanford University, 1976). *Dissertation Abstracts International*, 1976, **37**, 2615A. (University Microfilms No. 76-26,009)

YERG, B.J. Relationships between teacher behaviors and pupil achievement in the psychomotor domain (Doctoral dissertation, University of Pittsburgh, 1977). *Dissertation Abstracts International*, 1977, **38**, 1981A. (University Microfilms No. 77-21,229)

Catenas: Exploring meanings

Janice K. Olson
Purdue University

The need to conduct research on teaching behavior so that antecedent and consequent variables are identified and measured has been recognized (Doyle, 1979; Medley & Mitzel, 1963). Some see the real meaning of any behavior in its dynamic relationship to subsequent events (Martin, 1976), consider the study of behavior patterns in the classroom essential for establishing teacher effectiveness (Smith, Note 1), and maintain that effective teaching requires a synthesis of skills into complex and sometimes subtle patterns of behavior (Brophy, 1976). However, data analysis techniques have not kept pace with data collection systems, and these closely linked series of behaviors or *catenas* have been totally ignored in conventional frequency measures and only slightly accounted for in the more sophisticated matrix analyses (Shymansky, Penick, & Wortman, 1976).

Background and rationale for the study

Use of multi-stage chains of analysis in education
A few observational studies have successfully preserved proximity relations among more than two neighboring events. One of the earliest and

perhaps more elegant of these resulted in a system by Bellack, Davitz, Kleibard, and Hyman (1966) in which teacher-student verbal interactions were analyzed as pedagogical moves, sequences of which form teaching cycles. Bellack et al. identified 21 different cycles, patterns initiated by soliciting or structuring moves.

Other research efforts have echoed the sentiments of Bellack that studying teacher effectiveness in terms of isolated teacher variables is futile in view of the indivisible character of the teaching-learning process. Nuthall and Church (1972) constructed flow-charts of sequential classroom patterns. Prokop (1974) has suggested a method for processing sequential verbal interaction data using the Flanders system.

Campbell (Note 2) proposed a "macroanalysis" technique that utilized chains of three or more tallies to focus on sequences of classroom behavior. Shymansky, Penick, and Matthews (1975) refined the technique (now termed MACROanalysis) so that all series of repetitive behaviors are collapsed into single units when isolating longterm patterns. MACROanalysis has been used to look at teacher behavior patterns, student performance at various levels, the effects of different teaching strategies on student behavior, and detailed profiles of broad instructional strategies (Penick & Shymansky, 1977; Shymansky & Matthews, 1974; Shymansky et al., 1975, 1976; Shymansky, 1978).

Another system, the Observational System for Instructional Analysis (OSIA) (Hough & Duncan, with Belland & Siders, 1975, 1980) allows for monitoring chains of events as well as for collapsing repetitive behaviors. Ebro (1977) used OSIA to study instructional behavior patterns of distinguished university faculty and identified 10 patterns that all used.

Use of multi-stage chains of analysis in physical education
In physical education the use of systematic observation techniques has lagged far behind other education areas (Locke, 1977). Sherman (1978) has addressed our lack of attention in studying sequential patterns of behavior:

> While descriptive-analytic studies of teacher behavior have confirmed what we always wanted to know but were afraid to ask, they have left many stones unturned. They have identified the elements of teaching but have not shown how the elements fit together. Surely, teaching is greater than the sum of its parts! Future research should focus on the antecedents and consequences of discrete events and construct flow charts to illustrate how single moves merge into cycles, how cycles merge into episodes, and how episodes merge into models. (p. 28)

Fortunately, the physical education field is not completely devoid of attention to this problem; a few investigators have attended to the sequential patterning of instructional events. Nygaard (1975) identified a pattern (silence and/or confusion, lecture, silence and/or confusion) in his analysis of verbal interaction in physical education classes. Using the OSIA instrument, Pieron and Drion (1977) found the pattern (activity, lecture, demonstration, directions, activity) in classes they observed. The interaction pattern observed by Cheffers and Mancini (1978) involved: extended teacher information-giving and demonstration, narrow student response, teacher information-giving, extended teacher direction, and narrow student response. Morgenegg (1978) used an adaptation of the Bellack system to study cycles of teacher and student behaviors in 40 physical education classes.

Using an adaptation of the observational system for instructional analysis for physical education (OSIA-PE), Olson (1979) found the instrument to be a useful tool in isolating different chains in diverse and varied settings. Extended general and specific feedback chains occurred with greater frequency at elementary levels. Teacher solicitation-student response, and teacher solicitation-student response-teacher corrective feedback bahaviors were more prevalent at higher grade levels. The presence (or absence) of these particular behaviors were not in themselves sufficient to allow global judgments about physical education instruction at the grade levels involved. It was suggested, however, that related chains or catenas show great promise for illuminating the dynamic nature of instruction in physical education.

It was the purpose of this study to initiate a probe that would begin to identify and reveal relevant instructional configurations and multistage chains of behavior or catenas in the physical education environment.

Data analysis

The OSIA-PE instrument

The OSIA-PE instrument (Olson, 1979, 1982a) is a 13-category observation system for the classification of classroom (gymnasium-related) instruction. It is designed to collect information about instruction where instruction is defined as "the process of arranging human, material and temporal resources with the intention of facilitating the learning of self and/or others" (Hough et al., 1975, 1980, p. 1).

The 13 categories of behavior in the instrument are:

1. Thinking,
2. Sensing,
3. Manipulating artifacts,
4. Initiating,
5. Responding,
6. Soliciting Clarification,

7. Soliciting,
8. Positive Feedback - general,
9. Positive Feedback - specific,
10. Corrective Feedback,
11. Negative Feedback - general,
12. Negative Feedback - specific,
13. Instructionally Nonfunctional.

One of the most important features of OSIA-PE is that the same categories available for classifying teacher behavior may be used for student behavior as well. Other conventions permit focusing on the teacher or student, on the whole class, groups, dyads or individuals, on substantive and managerial situations, on events during activity and instruction time, on communication modes, and on specific subscripted events. The system can be made as simple or as inclusive as the researcher desires or the situation demands.

Continuous (event) recording with a convention to code those events lasting longer than 5 seconds at a fixed 5-second interval pace is the recording system used with the OSIA-PE instrument.

Procedure

The OSIA-PE instrument (Hough et al., 1975, 1980; Olson, 1979, 1982b) was used to analyze 24 videotapes of elementary, junior high, and senior high (eight at each level) physical education classes. Elementary classes were one each of a first, second, and fifth grade, two third grades, and three fourth grades. Junior high tapes were made in seventh and eighth grade classes, and high school tapes in grades nine through 12. Elementary school activities included track and field, ball skills, fitness, agility, strength circuits, striking skills, movement education, and frisbee. Activities covered in junior high were softball, basketball, soccer, hockey, tennis, and matball. High school activities observed were softball, volleyball, soccer, badminton, and canoeing. Twelve teachers of each sex were videotaped.

Tapes were coded by the investigator. The Cohen k coefficient (Frick & Semmel, Note 3) was used to determine intra-coder reliabilities, which were .86 or higher in every case.

Analysis

A computer program developed by Siders (Hough et al., 1975, 1980) for use with OSIA was used to analyze the data. The sequential ordering of the information collected provides a record of the interactive nature of the instructional events in which antecedent and consequent occurrences are retained. However, the program is not as yet set up to locate sequences and chains automatically; it only stores them.

Table 1

Sample Chains of Behavior by Category Set

Category set	Chain		
4 Initiating	T4	Teacher initiation	
	T7	Teacher solicitation	
	S5	Student responding	
5 Responding	S5	Student response	
	T8	Teacher positive feedback - general	
	T7	Teacher solicitation	
6 Soliciting clarification	T6	Teacher solicitation of clarification	
	S5	Student response	
	T7	Teacher solicitation	
7 Soliciting	T7	Teacher solicitation	
	S5	Student response	
	T4	Teacher initiation	
8 Positive feedback general	T8	Teacher positive feedback - general	
	T7	Teacher solicitation	
	S5	Student response	
9 Positive feedback specific	T9	Teacher positive feedback - specific	
	T7	Teacher solicitation	
	S5	Student response	
10 Corrective feedback	T10	Teacher corrective feedback	
	T7	Teacher solicitation	
	S5	Student response	

Identifying stored chains involved lengthy trial and error work. It seemed appropriate to begin by searching in the logical places in the instructional setting — places where sequences seemed likely to exist and places where a high frequency of a particular behavior had been observed. The search began by looking for chains beginning with these three behaviors: T4, Teacher Initiation; T7, Teacher Solicitation; and S5, Student Responding. Some chains of at least three behaviors did appear in the initial probe. Different "sets" of possible chains then were designed beginning with each category in the system that had produced frequencies of behavior in the first computer run. Sample chains of behavior identified for each category set are shown in Table 1. Six additional computer runs were necessary to search for 530 different chains of behavior. A total of 12,720 separate records of chains were produced for the 24 videotaped lessons.

Results

The total number of patterns located in the 24 videotapes was 4,048. These were distributed in sets of chains from Category 4 through 10. The

Table 2
Number of Different Patterns and
Collapsed Chains Found in Each Category Set

Pattern beginning category	Chains produced	Number of chains after collapsing
4	66	11
5	55	10
6	36	6
7	80	9
8	36	6
9	10	2
10	12	2
	295	46

number of different patterns and collapsed chains in each category set is shown in Table 2.

The total number of chains produced from Category 4 through 10 was 295. The total number of three- or four-event chains after collapsing was 46. Shymansky (personal communication, July 23, 1982) has stated that in all of his work with MACROanalysis, only rarely has an analysis yielded more than 50 chains of three or more behaviors with frequencies greater than one. There appears to be considerable agreement on this point between the work of Shymansky and results produced in this study.

The greatest number of different chains were found to begin in categories 4, 5, 6, and 7. These may well correspond to the structuring, responding, and soliciting cycles reported by Morgenegg (1978). At least two differences exist between findings in studies using the Bellack system and those reported here: (a) some cycles in the Bellack system consist of a single behavior, and (b) cycles in the Bellack system must begin with a structuring or a soliciting move. In these respects at least, catenas reported in this study are different.

No chains were found to begin with Category 2, Sensing. One should not generalize that such chains do not exist in these data, however. As will be noted in other tables, chains containing the Sensing behavior did appear. Sensing *was* taking place; chains beginning with that behavior simply were not revealed through the probings accomplished in this investigation. Others have found patterns beginning with and containing Sensing (or monitoring) to be present (Anderson & Barrette, 1978; Ebro, 1977; Shymansky et al., 1974, 1976).

Three- and four-stage chains, shown in Table 3, are presented within each category set in order of frequency. Some significant comparisons can be made using these data. Whereas the greater number of different chains were found to begin with Category 4, Initiation, the largest

Table 3

Chains in Order of Frequency by Category Sets

Category set	Stage behavior	Chain	Frequency
4 Initiating	3	T4T7S5	577
		T4S6T5	87
		T4S4T4	69
		S4T4S4	10
	4	T4T7S5T4	171
		T4T7S5T7	128
		T4T7S5T8	66
		T4T7S6T5	24
		T4T7S5T10	22
		T4S6T5S6	14
		T4S7T5T4	5
			1173
5 Responding	3	S5T8T7	186
		S5T6S5	96
		S5T10T7	77
		S5T8T4	51
		S5T8T2	35
		S5T2T8	18
		S5T10T4	16
		S5T9T7	10
		S5T10T2	3
		S5T9T2	1
			493
6 Soliciting, clariiating	3	T6S5T7	106
		T6S5T4	96
		S6T5T4	77
		S6T5T7	77
		T6S5T8	13
		T6S5T10	7
			376
7 Soliciting	3	T7S5T4	380
		T7S5T8	306
		T7S5T10	160
		T7S5T2	155
		T7T4T7	118
		T7S6T5	82
		T7S5T9	26
		T7S5T11	17
	4	T7S5T4T7	198
			1442
8 Positive feedback general	3	T8T7S5	220
		T8T4T7	62
		T8T2T7	40

Table 3 cont'd

Chains in Order of Frequency by Category Sets

Category set	Stage behavior	Chain	Frequency
		T8T8T8	6
		T8T2T4	3
	4	T8T4T7S5	37
			331
9	3	T9T7S5	24
Positive feedback		T9T9T9	8
specific			
			32
10	3	T10T7S5	143
Corrective feedback		T10S6T5	21
			164
		TOTAL	4048

number of occurrences of a set of chains appears in the Category 7 set, those beginning with Solicitation. Differences can be noted also in the number of different chains found beginning in Categories 9 and 10 and the number of times these chains were used. The number of collapsed chains located in Category sets 9 and 10 was the same, two chains. However, Category 10 chains, Corrective Feedback, were used 164 times, while Category 9 chains (Positive Feedback - specific) occurred only 32 times. Chains of behavior that included giving positive feedback to students with information were used sparingly by these teachers.

The only chain associated with negative feedback that appeared during this entire search was that of Category 11, Negative Feedback - general, and it was found as a part of the T7S5T11 chain that occurred 17 times throughout the study. The Category 2, Sensing, behavior mentioned earlier can be seen in four chains in Category Set 5, once in Category Set 7, and twice in Category Set 8. The chains in which it appears occurred with some frequency; however, chains beginning with Sensing have yet to be identified.

The 10 most frequent chains found were used a total of 2,496 times (see Table 4). This equals 61.66% of the total number of chains found (4,048). The most common 3-stage chains found made up 40.42% (1,636 of 4,048) of those used. The 4-stage chains comprised 16.4% (665 of 4,048) of the total number used.

Clearly not all teachers in this study used the same patterns. However, when a chain was found to exist for a teacher during one part of a lesson,

Table 4

Most Frequent Chains

10 Most frequent chains		Most frequent 3-stage chains per set		Most frequent 4-stage chains	
T4T7S5	577	T4T7S5	577	T7S5T4T7	198
T7S5T4	380	T7S5T4	380	T4T7S5T4	171
T7S5T8	306	T8T7S5	220	T4T7S5T7	128
T8T7S5	220	S5T8T7	186	T4T7S5T8	66
T7S5T4T7	198	T10T7S5	143	T8T4T7S5	37
S5T8T7	186	T6S5T7	106	T4T7S6T5	24
T4T7S5T4	171	T9T7S5	24	T4T7S5T10	22
T7S5T10	160			T4S6T5S6	14
T7S5T2	155			T4S7T5T4	5
T10T7S5	143				
TOTAL	2496		1636		665

for example, activity, it was likely to appear also for the same teacher during instructional and managerial portions of the same lesson.

Discussion

It is generally accepted that good teaching involves more than a command of a few isolated behaviors. Therefore, it is logical that the search for effective instructional strategies would involve an examination of teaching patterns. Shymansky (1978) regards pattern analytic techniques as potentially significant from several viewpoints. First, patterns can be identified through the use of highly reliable observation schedules for data collection. They are identified post hoc by the computer, not by the observer. The need for higher inference observation schedules is eliminated; instrument and observe reliabilities are thereby enhanced.

A second major feature of the pattern data is the information made available through use of the time scores it provides. No pattern overlaps itself, and every code signifies a predetermined time interval (in this study, 5 seconds). Within an observation, then, real time scores can be calculated for each pattern and summed across matching patterns. These time scores enable comparisons across observations and direct comparisons across observation sets. This can be accomplished by focusing on patterns identified *a priori* for their significance in particular situations.

Pattern analysis data can be used to better define and describe teaching strategies. For example, it may be possible to define catenas associated with direct or individualized instruction. Strategy behavior profiles would then be possible to ascertain, and independent variables in dynamic teaching situations could be validated and monitored. Teacher education and research in physical education would both benefit from such procedures.

Perhaps one of the most promising areas of application may be in associating catenas with Academic Learning Time. Locating and defining those teaching behaviors associated with high levels of student ALT would allow formation of an ALT teacher profile. Using pattern data to establish and maintain teacher behavior levels as the independent variable in a study of ALT teaching and non-ALT teaching strategies, while monitoring relationships to student ALT, is one example of a possible application of pattern analysis techniques in this area.

Recommendations

It is recommended that the work continue in attempts to find additional catenas, chains not only of sequential but also of related events. Considerations should be made of differences, if any, in the occurrences of chains at different school levels. Insight may be gained about teaching behavior by further studying those chains and the instances where they are used during substantive and managerial, and during activity and instruction time. Attempts should be made to find extentions of the chains that have been located already. Also, probing should continue in order to identify chains across different classes with different activities taught by the same teacher, and in classes of the same activity taught by different teachers. These steps may help us move toward Sherman's hope for research on teaching in physical education — an emerging model that will reveal its dynamic nature.

Reference Notes

1. Smith, B.O. Teaching: Conditions of its evaluation. In *The evaluation of teaching*, a report to the second Pi Lambda Theta Catena, Washington, DC, 1967, pp. 65-84.
2. Campbell, J.R. *Pattern analysis - A macroscopic development for interaction analysis.* Paper presented at annual meeting of the National Association for Research in Science Teaching, Detroit, March 1973.
3. Frick, T., & Semmel, M.I. *Observational records: Observer agreement and reliabilities.* Paper presented at annual meeting of the American Psychological Association, Chicago, April 1973. (ERIC Document Reproduction Service No. ED 097 375)

References

ANDERSON, W.G., & Barrette, G.T. (Eds.). *What's going on in gym? Descriptive studies of physical education classes.* (A special monograph of Motor Skills: Theory into practice. Newtown, CT) 1978.

BELLACK, A.A., Davitz, J.R., Kleibard, H.M., & Hyman, R.T. *The language of the classroom*. New York: The Institute of Psychological Research. Teachers College, Columbia University, 1966.

BROPHY, J.E. Reflections on research in elementary schools. *Journal of Teacher Education*, 1976, **27**(1), 31-34.

CHEFFERS, J.T.F., & Mancini, V.H. Teacher-student interaction. In W.G. Anderson & G.T. Barrette (Eds.), *What's going on in gym? Descriptive studies of physical education classes*. (A special monograph of Motor Skills: Theory into practice, Newtown, CT) 1978.

DOYLE, W. Making managerial decisions in classrooms. In D.L. Duke (Ed.), *Classroom management: Seventh-eight yearbook of the national society for the study of education*. Chicago, IL: University of Chicago Press, 1979.

EBRO, L.L. *Instructional behavior patterns of distinguished university professors*. Doctoral dissertation, The Ohio State University, 1977.

HOUGH, J.B., Duncan, J.K., with Belland, J., & Siders, W. *The Observational System for Instructional Analysis*. Draft papers, number one to seven, Columbus, OH: Faculty of Curriculum and Foundations, The Ohio State University, 1975, 1980.

LOCKE, L.F. Research on teaching physical education: New hope for a dismal science. *Quest*, 1977, **28**, 2-17.

MARTIN, J. Developing category observation instruments for the analysis of classroom behavior. *Journal of Classroom Interaction*, 1976, **12**(1), 5-17.

MEDLEY, D.M., & Mitzel, H.E. Measuring classroom behavior by systematic observation. In Gage, N.L. (Ed.), *Handbook of Research on Teaching*, Chicago: Rand McNally, 1963.

MORGENEGG, B.L. Pedagogical moves. In W.G. Anderson & G.T. Barrette (Eds.), *What's going on in gym? Descriptive studies of physical education classes*. (A special monograph of Motor Skills: Theory into practice. Newtown, CT) 1978.

NUTHALL, G., & Church, J. Observation systems used with recording media. *International Review of Education*, 1972, **18**, 491-505.

NYGAARD, G.A. Interaction analysis of physical education classes. *Research Quarterly*, 1975, **46**, 351-357.

OLSON, J.K. Adaptation of the Observational System for Instructional Analysis (OSIA) for use in physical education (Doctoral dissertation, The Ohio State University, 1979) *DAI*, 1979, **40-01**, 11556-A. (University Microfilms No. 7916013)

OLSON, J.K. The Observation System for Instructional Analysis for use in physical education (OSIA-PE). In P.E. Darst, V.H. Mancini, & D.B. Zakrajsek, (Eds.), *Systematic observation instruction for physical education*. West Point, NY: Leisure Press, 1982. (a)

OLSON, J.K. Catenas: A probe for relevant, instructional configurations in physical education settings. In M. Pieron & J. Cheffers (Eds.), *Studying the teaching of physical education.* Liege, Belgium: Association Internationale des Ecoles Superieures d' Education Physique, 1982. (b)

PENICK, J.E., & Shymansky, J.A. The effects of teacher behavior on student behavior in fifth-grade science: A replication study. *Journal of Research in Science Teaching, 1977,* **14**(5), 427-432.

PIERON, M., & Drion, C. Analyse de L'interaction entre le professeur et ses élèves en education physique, par le système de hough. *Revue de l'Education Physique*, 1977, **17**, 27-37.

PROKOP, M. A method for true sequential processing of verbal interaction analysis data. *Classroom Interaction Newsletter*, 1974, **10**(1), 45-50.

SHERMAN, M.A. Paradigms for research on teaching physical education. *AAHPER Research Consortium Symposium Papers: Teaching Behavior and Sport History*, 1978, **1**(1), 26-33.

SHYMANSKY, J.A., & Matthews, C.C. A comparative laboratory study of the effects of two teaching patterns on certain aspects of the behavior of students in fifth grade science. *Journal of Research in Science Teaching*, 1974, **11**(3), 157-168.

SHYMANSKY, J.A., Penick, J.E., Matthews, C.C., & Good, R.G. Using macroanalytic techniques to study teacher behavior patterns. *Journal of Research in Science Teaching*, 1975, **12**(2), 221-228.

SHYMANSKY, J.A., Penick, J.E., & Wortman, J.D. A computer program designed to identify behavior patterns in observational data. *Journal of Classroom Interaction*, 1976, **12**(1), 83-88.

SHYMANSKY, J.A. Assessing teacher performance in the classroom: Pattern analysis applied to interaction data. *Studies in Educational Evaluation*, 1978, **4**(2), 99-106.

Direct instruction:
An instructional model
from a process-product study

Bernard Oliver
The University of Texas at Austin

Over the past several years, classroom researchers utilizing the process-product paradigm have finally produced some tenable conclusions about teacher effectiveness research. Several substantial reviews exist that illustrate the nature of the classroom relationships in process-product research, that illustrate the nature of methodological problems associated with process-product research, and that outline problems in the conceptualization of process-product research (Berliner, 1976; Brophy, 1979; Doyle, 1978; Dunkin & Biddle, 1974; Gage, 1978; Good, 1979; Peterson & Walberg, 1979). More recently this line of inquiry has focused on the importance of student characteristics in determining teacher effectiveness, the importance of time allocations in learning and instruction, and the effectiveness of direct versus indirect instruction or teacher-centered versus learner-centered learning (Clark, 1979; Denham & Lieberman, 1980; Good, 1979; Peterson, 1979a; Peterson & Walberg, 1979). This paper will discuss the pattern of instruction labeled direct instruction, which owes much of its current popularity to the methodological, conceptual, and philosophical issues raised by the process-product research paradigm (Berliner & Rosenshine, 1977; Doyle, 1978; Fenstermacher, 1978; Shavelson & Dempsey, 1976; Winne & Marx, 1977).

Direct instruction

The pattern of effective teaching labeled direct instruction is not a new concept. (Richard Anderson first used the notion of teacher- vs. learner-centered in 1959.) However, the recent research on teacher effectiveness has led to the increased use of and research on direct instruction in explaining student achievement. Increasingly in the research community, this instructional pattern is consistently showing strong relationships with affective and achievement variables over a variety of studies and subject areas (Brophy, 1979; Carnine, 1979; Good, 1979; McDonald, 1976; Rosenshine, 1979).

Like many educational concepts, direct instruction has come to mean different things to different people. For example, Rosenshine (1979) suggests that the critical aspects of direct instruction are: a focus on academic goals, promotion of extensive content coverage that is teacher-centered, a task-oriented environment, the use of large groups rather than small groups, and feedback that is immediate and academically oriented. Defined by Good (1979), direct instruction is seen as active teaching in which the teacher sets and articulates the learning goals, actively assesses student progress, and frequently illustrates how to do the assigned work or tasks. The Direct Instruction Program at the University of Oregon, for example, is based on the interaction between the learner and the classroom environment. This more comprehensive view focuses on increased teaching time (e.g., utilizing paraprofessionals, small group instruction, and providing for more planning time), carefully designed curricula, direct teaching strategies (i.e., pacing, feedback, cuing, and reinforcing), quality control and accountability (i.e., using criterion referenced testing, monitoring student progress, using preservice and inservice training progress, and using preservice and inservice training modules), and parent involvement (see Table 1 for other conceptual definitions).

Empirical support for the direct instruction model can be found in the extensive reviews by Horwitz (1979) and Peterson (1979). These authors reviewed several studies that compared outcomes in open versus traditional instruction, and looked at the size of significance effect in these two approaches (traditional classrooms used in the previous studies refers to direct instruction in an indirect sense and includes many of the components mentioned earlier in this paper). In general, these authors found that students under direct instruction perform slightly better in achievement measures but lower on creativity measures, attitudes toward

Table 1

Characteristics of Direct Instruction

Author	Characteristics
Rosenshine (1979)	Academic focus, grouping students for instruction, teacher-centered focus, little student choice for activity, use of factual questions and controlled practice.
Good (1979)	Active teaching . . . a teacher sets and articulates learning goals, actively assesses student progress, and frequently makes class presentations illustrating how to do assigned work.
Powell (1978)	Not a set of prescriptive rules but a conceptual orientation that values active involvement in instructional tasks, expository learning, focused learning, accountability, allocating instructional time, and assigns instructional tasks in such a way that students have opportunities to learn all skills, with a high rate of success.
Berliner (1979)	Goal setting/structuring by the teacher, lack of absence from school, focus on time spent in class, coverage of content, monitoring student work, factual concrete questions, academic feedback, and a classroom environment characterized as warm, democratic, and convivial.
Graham & Heimerer (1981)	Instruction and feedback, grouping, praise, questioning, structuring, student choice, task-oriented, businesslike, warmth, and teacher expectancy comprise the direct instruction concept.
Carine (1979)	Increased teaching time, various teaching techniques, quality control procedures, and parent participation . . . the instructional patterns are teaching in a simplified context; practice on new skills is initially massed; teacher prompts are gradually faded; initially teacher feedback is immediate; overtising/covertising problem solving; and a shift from the teacher as a source of information.
Mosston (1967)	Organizational patterns are well executed; any command is followed by physical motion; teacher offers group/individual corrections; teacher command stops the lesson; role of the student is minimal.

school, and problem-solving measures. Two other reviews, by Stallings & Kaskowitz (1972) and Gage (1978), concluded that structured classrooms, persistency in academic tasks, and teacher involvement with students result in higher achievement gains.

Additional support for the direct instruction model is derived from several large scale field studies. Inman (1977), Bennett (1976), Stallings and Kaskowitz (1972), and McDonald (1976) all report that formal structured teaching, or teaching that increases direct instructional time in content areas, tends to result in increased learning gains. Several other studies investigating individual components of the direct instruction model (such as academic learning time, engaged time, small group vs. large group, etc.) provide further support for the effectiveness of direct instruction in increasing achievement gains in pupils (Anderson, Evertson, & Brophy, 1978; Crawford & Stallings, 1978; Good & Grouws, 1979). In all, these studies infer that teachers who are trained in direct instructional principles can have a significant impact on student achievement.

However, as the Peterson review (1979b) notes, researchers should be cautious about accepting the results of the direct instruction research carte blanche. Several studies cited in the Peterson review investigated the influence of student characteristics on the direct instruction model. These studies yielded inconsistent and conflicting results concerning students' ability level, personality, aptitudes, and motivation to learn in open versus traditional classrooms. Furthermore, the effectiveness of the direct instruction model seems to be dependent on the students' locus of control orientation, or the way they make sense out of the classrooms through what we know as causal attributions (Arlin, 1975; Janick, 1979; Wright & DuCette, 1976). In sum, these latter studies support Doyle's (1978) concept of students being mediating factors in teacher effectiveness research.

In general, effective teaching seems to involve a more structured or formal set of instructional principles that seemingly affect the learning of certain basic skills. However, as Peterson (1979b) suggests, the choice of direct instruction over an alternative model clearly depends on the type of learner and the educational outcomes desired.

Direct instruction in physical education

To date, only a few investigators have engaged in process-product research in physical education (Oliver, 1978; Taylor, 1976; Yerg, 1977). The paucity of research in this area leaves little hope for describing tenable relationships between teacher behavior, classroom variables, and student achievement in the gym. We do have some interesting and enlightening work on ALT, teacher thinking, expectations, etc., but we don't have the number of process-product studies that could lead us to conduct meta analysis and other vote-counting procedures to fully understand teacher-student relationships. This clearly points to the need for more study on process-outcome occurrences in the gym to bring teacher effectiveness research up to the conceptual level that permeates classroom research studies.

Although current writers have discussed the concept of direct instruction in physical education (Graham & Helmerer, 1981) and some of the characteristics of the model, they haven't really looked at teacher behavior. Moreover, the work of Mosston (1966) and Nixon and Locke (1973) has given researchers in physical education a conceptual framework of instructional processes in the gym that highlight some major components of direct instruction. Although few researchers have capitalized on the process-product paradigm and the conceptualization provided by the previous researchers, the work of Oliver (1978) and Taylor (1979) has provided some initial process-product data that support the impact of direct instruction on student achievement and attitude in the gymnasium. However, focusing on the results of a few studies rather than the results of many will obviously fail to portray the accumulated state of knowledge about teacher effectiveness research.

Empirical support for the direct instruction model in physical education can be inferred from the literature on motor learning. Singer and Pease (1977) conclude that, in learning initial motor tasks, guided instruction is more effective than discovery learning. Additional support for the effectiveness of guided instruction over other instructional approaches can be found in the work of Scott (1967), Prather (1971), and Singer and Gaines (1975). However, like other research in the teacher effectiveness arena, a few studies suggest that guided instruction does not lead to increased skill performance over other instructional models (see for example Howard, 1960; Thaxton, Rothstein, & Thaxton, 1977).

In general, the paucity of research studies on process-product occurrences in physical education makes it difficult to arrive at any generalizations for learning motor skill in physical education classes. Accordingly, this paper will focus on a direct instruction model derived from a large-scale naturalistic process-product study conducted in physical education.

Method

Subjects
Thirty secondary physical education teachers of a coed volleyball unit took part in this study (15 male and 15 female). They averaged 12 years of teaching experience and had varied skill abilities and knowledge about volleyball (see Oliver & Taylor, 1980, for more description). The students in this study (442 females and 379 males) were enrolled in grades 9 through 12.

Instrumentation
The classroom behavior of teachers and students was recorded by a version of the Physical Education Observation Instrument (PEOI)

developed by Taylor (1976). The classroom behaviors for this instrument were derived from research and the instructional model posited by Nixon and Locke (1973) and Hoffman (1971).

Student behaviors in this study consisted of student demonstration, individualized instruction, information receiving, organizing time, organizing movement, active engagement, disengagement, inactive behavior, and warmup. Teacher behaviors for this study consisted of managerial activity, explanation, demonstration promoting practice, feedback, observing, and individual instruction. (For more description, see Oliver & Taylor, 1980.)

Observers were trained in the use of the observation instrument through videotaped recordings of teaching episodes. An inter-observer reliability coefficient of .94 was obtained using the formula of Boehm and Weinberg (1977). The intra-observer reliabilities computed were well above the .80 level (for more information, see Taylor, 1979; Oliver & Taylor, 1980).

Procedures

Students were given a questionnaire to assess background characteristics, two skill tests to measure achievement in volleyball, a knowledge test, and an attitude measure during the first 3 days of instruction in coed volleyball. After 6 weeks of instruction, posttests were administered in the previous areas. Observers recorded the frequency of teacher-student behaviors at 15-second intervals on five occasions for the entire class period.

Results

The means and standard deviations of teacher-student behaviors were computed by day. As Table 3 illustrates, teacher behaviors that were seemingly related to direct instruction occurred more frequently at the beginning of the unit. That is, students initially spent more time listening to the teacher's explanation (goal setting/structuring), receiving feedback about their performance, and being provided a drill focus and practice time than in later parts of the unit (Table 2).

To further understand the relationship of some of the teacher-student behaviors, a factor analysis was used to organize those behaviors into a clearer picture of the direct instruction model. The new factor constructs depict a recognizable pattern of classroom behavior that is seemingly characteristic of the direct instruction model described earlier.

Factors

Information process. This new construct represents the extent to which teachers present and demonstrate tasks to enhance student learning. The

Table 2

Means of Teacher and Student Behaviors
for Five Classroom Observations

	Day				
Variable	1	2	3	4	5
1. Managerial activity	16.567	16.906	17.633	17.460	16.367
2. Explanation	19.233	15.267	14.500	10.400	6.000
3. Teacher demonstration	3.233	4.100	3.200	1.300	2.133
4. Student demonstration	1.533	.667	1.267	.433	.133
5. Feedback	9.600	7.600	8.433	8.533	6.467
6. Promoting practice	50.833	35.967	38.067	23.700	22.300
7. Observing	35.467	52.267	53.600	63.967	72.500
8. Individualized instruction	5.433	3.333	3.467	.600	.800
9. Inactive behavior	13.700	13.700	13.833	13.333	12.200
10. Information processing	18.300	18.300	13.300	9.667	4.933
11. Organizing time	10.800	8.300	8.967	9.267	7.633
12. Organizing movement	41.433	41.433	32.633	16.267	18.800
13. Active engagement	41.033	41.033	54.433	73.600	79.133
14. Student disengagement	2.433	2.433	2.033	1.967	4.400
15. Other	3.167	3.167	3.533	10.567	10.400
16. Exercise	6.333	6.333	7.200	8.400	7.667

Table 3

Factor Analysis of Teacher-Student Behaviors

Factor name	Variables	Weights
Information processing[a]	Explanation	.96
	Teacher demonstration	.82
	Student demonstration	.61
	Promoting practice	.37
	Observing	−.56
	Organizing time	.55
	Information processing	.94
Disengaged process[b]	Student disengagement	.84
	Other	.86
Play process[c]	Exercise	−.60
	Active engagement	.89
Feedback process[d]	Feedback	.82
	Other	−.37

[a]eigenvalue = 6.45; variance accounted for = 47%
[b]eigenvalue = 2.17; variance accounted for = 16%
[c]eigenvalue = 1.59; variance accounted for = 12%
[d]eigenvalue = 1.54; variance accounted for = 11%

highest loadings in this variable were explanation, teacher and student demonstration, promoting practice, observing, organizing time, and information processing.

Play process. This new factor construct is characterized by active engagement, which esentially represents the notion that students are provided content time to utilize their previously learned skills.

Feedback process. The last factor construct indicative of the direct instruction model is teacher feedback.

In the initial analysis of this process-product study, these three factors accounted for significant portions of the variance in posttest achievement, attitude, and skill measures after partialing out entering ability and the sex of the teacher and student (see Oliver, 1980 & Note 1 for further discussion about the relationship of these factors).

Discussion

A fairly consistent pattern emerges from the results of the process-product study discussed in this paper. The decreasing trend in certain teacher-student behaviors over the duration of the unit seemingly characterizes the direct instruction model posited by Carnine (1979). That is, students are first taught simple skills, after which the practice of the new skills is massed and has a group focus. The teacher then initially prompts (promoting practice) students and then fades, gradually decreasing feedback over the duration of the unit. Finally, the shift of information from teacher to student can be observed as students actively engage in playing the game.

The results of the factor analysis coincides with Good's (1979) notion that direct instruction is a multidimensional concept and cannot be viewed as a set of prescriptive rules. The three new factor constructs underscore the fact that direct instruction represents a conceptual continuum that changes as students become more proficient in acquiring motor skills.

Although the quality of time factors in this study does not rival those found in earlier direct instruction work, direct instructional time and engaged time tend to be associated with student achievement. One pitfall in measuring time factors in this line of research is the uncertainty about what constitutes a moderate level of task difficulty, and knowing if students are academically engaged. Similarly, the importance of content covered or opportunity to learn can be inferred from the trend in the descriptive statistics of the teacher-student behaviors. That is, teachers spend considerable time giving students the opportunity to learn by providing not only drill and practice, but explaining the nature of the task and allowing students to spend time acquiring skill in the context of game-like activity. As the students' repertoire of skill increases, teachers seem to allow students considerable time to play, with much less of a focus on active instructional strategies.

The impact of direct instruction behaviors on the achievement and attitudes of students warrants further investigation. Although the initial interpretation of the data in this study illustrated significant relationships with student achievement and attitude variables, the findings must be viewed in a tentative light until we have more research on direct instruction variables and other factors affecting the acquisition of motor skills in the gym.

In sum, a few caveats are in order concerning the notion of direct instruction and teacher effectiveness in the gymnasium. The direct instruction behaviors discussed in this study do not take into account the perspective of the student. For example, if students do not perceive the importance of time parameters in physical education as representing a time to learn or having an academic focus, chances are that they will approach instruction in the gymnasium with less than positive attitudes about acquiring ball skills. This concern about students' perceptions is eloquently stated in Doyle's notion of "mediating processes" and Weinstein's student perception paradigm in the teacher effectiveness arena. These mediating process approaches are focused directly on the implicit human processes that mediate between instructional stimuli and learning outcomes. Furthermore, these previous notions suggest that the overt and covert behaviors and processes that typically characterize educational research seem to represent relatively gross measures for describing student learning.

In addition to student perceptions of direct instruction and classroom events, we have not with any certainty determined what type of students are likely to benefit from direct instruction and under what context it is likely to be effective (team vs. individual sports, indoor vs. outdoor, etc.). Further exploration of process-product relationships and Doyle's mediating processes in physical education will yield valuable information for teacher effectiveness researchers. If we are to make sense of and understand teacher thinking/planning, and if we are to tell teachers how to teach effectively from process-product research, we have to fully understand what mediates instructional outcomes in the gymnasium. Telling teachers how to teach with rules derived from research is not an effective way to build bridges between research on teaching and *teaching practices*. We need evidence from the results of research that will test practitioners' beliefs about their work, and a schemata to help us see a phenomenon and a way to think about it (Fenstermacher, 1981). In the words of Erickson, we need a way to tell the story of teaching in the gymnasium.

Reference Note

1. Oliver, B. *Male teachers, student achievement and attitude in coed classes.* Paper presented at the annual meeting of the American Alliance of Health, Physical Education, Recreation and Dance, Boston, April 1981.

References

ANDERSON, L., Evertson, C., & Brophy, J. An experimental study of effective study of effective teaching in first-grade reading groups. *Elementary School Journal*, 1978, **79**, 193-223.

ANDERSON, R.C. Learning in discussions: A résumé of the authoritarian-democratic studies. *Harvard Educational Review*, 1959, **29**, 201-215.

ARLIN, M. The interaction of locus of control, classroom structure, and pupil satisfaction. *Psychology in the Schools*, 1975, **12**, 279-286.

BENNETT, N. *Teaching styles and pupil progress.* Cambridge, MA: Harvard University Press, 1976.

BERLINER, D.C. Impediments to the study of teacher effectiveness. *Journal of Teacher Education*, 1976, **27**.

BERLINER, D.C. Tempus educare. In P. Peterson & H.J. Walberg (Eds.), *Research on teaching: Concepts, findings and implications.* Berkeley, CA: McCutchan, 1979.

BERLINER, D.C., & Rosenshine, B.U. The acquisition of knowledge in the classroom. In R.C. Anderson, R.J. Spiro, & W.E. Montague (Eds.), *Schooling and the acquisition of knowledge.* Hillsdale, NJ: Erlbaum Press, 1977.

BOEHM, A., & Weinberg, R. *The classroom observer: A guide for developing observation skills.* New York: Teachers College Press, 1977.

BROPHY, J. Teacher behavior and student learning. *Educational Leadership*, 1979, **37**, 33-38.

CARNINE, D. Direct instruction: A successful system for educationally high-risk children. *Journal of Curriculum Studies*, 1979, **11**, 29-45.

CLARK, C. Five faces of research on teaching. *Educational Leadership*, 1979, **37**, 29-32.

CRAWFORD, J., & Stallings, J. *Experimental effects of inservice teacher training derived from process-product correlations in the primary grades.* Stanford, CA: Center for Educational Research, Stanford University, 1978.

DENHAM, C., & Lieberman, A. (Eds.), *Time to learn.* Washington, DC: National Institute of Education, 1980.

DOYLE, W. Paradigms for research on teacher effectiveness. In L.S. Shulman (Ed.), *Review of research in education.* Itasca, IL: F.E. Peacock, 1978.

DUNKIN, M., & Biddle, B. *The study of teaching.* New York: Holt, Rinehart, & Winston, 1974.

FENSTERMACHER, G. A philosophical consideration of recent research on teacher effectiveness. In L. Shulman (Ed.), *Review of research in education* (Vol. 6). Itasca, IL: F.E. Peacock, 1978.

GAGE, N.L. *The scientific basis of the art of teaching.* New York: Teachers College Press, Columbia University, 1978.

GOOD, T. Teacher effectiveness in the elementary school. *Journal of Teacher Education,* 1979, **30**, 52-64.

GOOD, T., & Grouws, D. Teaching and mathematics learning. *Educational Leadership,* 1979, **37**, 39-45.

GRAHAM, G., & Helmerer, E. Research on teacher effectiveness: A summary with implications for teaching. *Quest,* 1981, **33**, 14-25.

HOFFMAN, S.J. Traditional methodology: Prospects for change. *Quest,* 1971, **15**, 51-57.

HORWITZ, R.A. Effects of the "open classroom." In H.J. Walberg (Ed.), *Educational environments and effects: Evaluation, policy, and productivity.* Berkeley, CA: McCutchan, 1979.

HOWARD, S. *A comparison of two methods of teaching ball handling skills to third grade students.* Unpublished doctoral dissertation, State University of Iowa, 1960.

INMAN, W. *Classroom practices and basic skills: Kindergarten and third grade.* Division of Research, North Carolina State Department of Public Instruction, 1977.

JANICK, T.C. *Aptitude-treatment interaction effects of variations in direct instruction.* Unpublished doctoral dissertation, University of Wisconsin-Madison, 1979.

McDONALD, F. Report on phase II of the beginning teacher evaluation study. *Journal of Teacher Education,* 1976, **27**, 39-42.

MOSSTON, M. *Teaching physical education.* Columbus, OH: Charles E. Merrill, 1966.

NIXON, J.E., & Locke, L. Research on teaching physical education. In R. Travers (Ed.), *Second Handbook of Research on Teaching.* Chicago: Rand McNally, 1973.

OLIVER, B. *The relationship of teacher and student presage and process criteria to student achievement in physical education.* Unpublished doctoral dissertation, Stanford University, 1978.

OLIVER, B., & Taylor, J.L. Teacher characteristics and classroom behavior. *Journal of Classroom Interaction,* 1980, **16**, 11-18.

PETERSON, P. Direct instruction: Effective for what and for whom? *Educational Leadership,* 1979, **37**, 46-48. (a)

PETERSON, P. Direct instruction reconsidered. In P. Peterson & H.S. Walberg (Eds.), *Research on teaching: Concepts, findings, and implications.* Berkeley, CA: McCutchan, 1979. (b)

PETERSON, P., & Walberg, H.J. (Eds.), *Research on teaching: Concepts, findings and implications*. Berkeley, CA: McCutchan, 1979.

POWELL, M. Educational implications of current research on teaching. *The Educational Forum*, 1978, **43**, 27-38.

PRATHER, D.C. Trial-and-error versus errorless learning: Training, transfer, and stress. *American Journal of Psychology*, 1971, **84**, 377-386.

ROSENSHINE, B.U. Academic engaged time, content covered, and direct instruction. *Journal of Education*, 1978, **161**, 380166.

ROSENSHINE, B.U. Content, time, and direct instruction. In P. Peterson & H.F. Walberg (Eds.), *Research on Teaching: Concepts, findings, and implications*. Berkeley, CA: McCutchan, 1979.

SCOTT, R.S.A. A comparison of teaching two methods of physical education with grade one pupils. *Research Quarterly*, 1967, **38**, 151-154.

SHAVELSON, R., & Dempsey, N. Generalizability of measures of teaching behavior. *Review of Educational Research*, 1976, **44**, 265-291.

SINGER, R.N., & Gaines, L. Effect of prompted and trial-and-error learning on transfer performance on a serial motor task. *American Educational Research Journal*, 1975, **12**, 404-408.

SINGER, R.N., & Pease, D. A comparison of discover learning and guided instructional strategies on motor skill learning, retention, and transfer. *Research Quarterly*, 1977, **47**, 788-796.

STALLINGS, J., & Kaskowitz, D. *Follow through classroom evaluation*. Office of Education, Publication No. 100. Washington, DC: U.S. Government Printing Office, 1972.

TAYLOR, J.L. *Development and the use of the physical education observation instrument (PEOI) for rating patterns of teacher behavior in relationship to student achievement*. Unpublished doctoral dissertation, Stanford University, 1976.

TAYLOR, J.L. Development of the physical education observation instrument using generalizability study theory. *Research Quarterly*, 1979, **50**, 468-481.

THAXTON, A.B., Rothstein, A.L., & Thaxton, N. Comparative effectiveness of two methods of teaching physical education to elementary school girls. *Research Quarterly*, 1977, **48**.

WINNE, P., & Marx, R. Reconceptualizing research on teaching. *Journal of Educational Psychology*, 1977, **69**, 668-678.

WRIGHT, R.J., & DuCette, J.P. *Locus of control and academic achievement in traditional and non-traditional educational settings*. Glenside, PA: 1974. Beaver College (ERIC Document Reproduction Service No. ED 123203).

YERG, B. *Relationships between teacher behaviors and pupil achievement in the psychomotor domain*. Unpublished doctoral dissertation, University of Pittsburgh, 1977.

Re-examining the process-product paradigm for research on teaching effectiveness in physical education

Beverly J. Yerg
Florida State University

The Research on Teaching Effectiveness (RTE) movement has grown and waned, has been criticized and modified, and yet there continues to be a search for ways in which the outcome of teaching can be enhanced. In physical education, we are constrained by the relatively few researchers and institutions addressing this issue, by the complexity of expected learning outcomes, and perhaps by the indifference to the real meaning of "physically educated." The knowledges, skills, and attitudes that facilitate the adoption of a physically active lifestyle rank with those of reading, writing, and computation in providing for quality of life. And so the search goes on.

This paper, like the "Unfinished Symphony," will end without closure. The intent is to stimulate possibilities rather than provide explicit answers. Two similar studies using the process-product paradigm yielded dissimilar results and emphasized the need for further refinement in the study of the teaching-learning interaction in physical education. A summary of those studies is provided, followed by possible avenues of recourse to alleviate some of the deficiencies.

Table 1

Comparison of Contexts of the Two Studies

Aspect compared	1977	1982
Criterion task (product)	Cartwheel	Balance beam skills
Assessment on criterion task	Film analysis	Rating scale
N of instructional sessions	40	32
Learners per session	3	4
Duration of lesson	20 minutes	15 minutes
Process analysis	TBOS	TBOS
Pre- to posttest comparison	$p < .001$	$p < .000$

Comparison of two process-product studies

The studies compared both used a modified experimental teaching unit (ETU) approach with upper elementary grade learners. The somewhat conflicting results provide impetus for modification of the usual process-product paradigm. The first study (Yerg, 1977) involved 40 preservice physical education majors each teaching a 20-minute lesson on the cartwheel to three learners from grades three through six. The second study was 32 instructional sessions of 15 minutes' duration in which four learners from grades four through six were taught beginning balance beam skills by physical education majors with varying levels of experience in teaching physical activities (Yerg, 1982). The comparison of the contexts is presented in Table 1.

Analysis of teacher behavior during instruction was made, using the Teacher Behavior Observation System (TBOS) to time-sample the video-taped sessions for 5 seconds of every 20-second interval. The TBOS utilized three generic teacher behavior categories: task presentation; providing for practice; and providing feedback, with a fourth category, other, for those behaviors not covered in the first three. Subcategories in each generic category described communication mode, target audience, time of delivery, intent of behavior, and specificity of the behavior or communication. (For greater detail on TBOS, see Yerg, 1977, 1981a.)

Data analysis in each study utilized simultaneous multiple regression analysis where the full model included the group mean on the final performance of the criterion task as the dependent variable. The group mean on initial performance of the criterion task and the teacher behavior composite variables from the TBOS frequencies served as independent variables. The reduced model used the final performance group as the dependent variable, with the initial performance mean as the sole independent variable. A comparison of the two regression models permitted the isolation of the effects of teacher behavior

Table 2
Multiple Regression Data for the Reduced Model

Multiple R = 0.87 Source of variance	df	Sum of squares	R² = 0.75 Mean square	F*
Regression	1	1509.56	1509.56	114.60
Residual	38	500.55	13.17	

Data from Yerg, 1977.
*p < .001.

Table 3
Multiple Regression Data for the Reduced Model

Multiple R = 0.55 Source of variance	df	Sum of squares	R² = 0.31 Mean square	F*
Regression	1	10.59	10.59	13.16
Residual	30	24.13	.80	

Data from Yerg, 1982.
*p < .001.

variables. Results of the 1977 study, as presented in Table 2, indicated that 75% of the variation in final performance was explained by learner entry behavior. In the 1982 study, the impact of the entry behavior was 31% as presented in Table 3. This was a striking difference from the earlier study. The full model regression analysis for the 1977 study, presented in Table 4, indicated that an additional 2% of the variation in final performance was accounted for by the teacher behavior variables, for a total 77% explained variation. In the 1982 study, presented in Table 5, the full model accounted for 42% of the total variation explained by the independent variables of initial performance and teacher behavior. That means that 11% was attributed to teacher behavior effects; however, this was not statistically significant, nor was the 2% variation attributed to teacher effects in the 1977 study. In examining the data on the full model in each study, the order of input and the sign of the weighting is of interest. Entry behavior enters first in both studies as the most potent factor influencing outcome; however, the order and sign of the impact of the other variables was quite different. In the 1977 study, the practice component, followed by teacher knowledge and performance component, positively influenced the outcome, whereas task presentation and providing feedback negatively affected the final performance.

Table 4

Multiple Regression Data for the Full Model

| Multiple R = 0.88 | | | R² = 0.77 | |
Source of variance	df	Sum of squares	Mean square	F
Regression	5	1547.46	309.50	22.74*
Residual	34	462.65	13.61	

Variables in the equation	B	S.E. of B	F
Pretest scores	0.774	0.08	91.95*
Practice composite	0.114	0.20	0.37
Teacher knowledge/skill	0.488	0.48	1.04
Feedback composite	−0.114	0.13	0.70
Task present. composite	−0.137	0.35	0.16
(Constant)	15.930		

Data from Yerg, 1977.
*$p < .001$

Table 5

Multiple Regression Data for the Full Model

| Multiple R = 0.65 | | | R² = 0.42 | |
Source of variance	df	Sum of squares	Mean square	F
Regression	4	14.53	3.63	4.86**
Residual	27	20.19	.75	

Variables in the equation	B	S.E. of B	F
Pretest scores	1.076	0.27	16.23*
Practice composite	−0.012	0.01	4.45***
Task present. composite	0.006	0.01	.27
Feedback composite	0.011	0.02	.24
(Constant)	0.912		

Data from Yerg, 1982.
*$p < .001$; **$p < .004$; ***$p < .04$.

In the 1982 study, the practice component again followed the pupil entry behavior as a powerful factor in final performance, but it had a negative effect on that outcome. The other two composite variables, task presen-

Table 6

Percent of Time Spent in Generic Category Teacher Behavior

Category	1977 study	1982 study
Task presentation	23	20
Providing for practice	38	56
Providing feedback	17	6
Other	22	17

tation and providing feedback, had a positive effect on the outcome variable.

The data in Table 6 present a comparison of the percent of time spent in the generic categories across the studies. While time spent in task presentation and 'other' was somewhat reduced in the 1982 study, considerably more time was spent in the practice mode and significantly less time was spent in providing feedback. The use of time during instruction has been shown to be a factor in learning outcome.

Discussion

The results of the 1977 study raised speculation on several issues. It appeared that pupils were not uniformly ready for learning the task and that they needed ample practice time to get an idea of the skill to be performed. These students were not at a level of learning on the task where they could benefit from the feedback given. Thus, feedback inhibited the use of practice time, resulting in lower levels of performance. It was also noted that teacher competence on the skill had an effect on teacher behavior in the practice and feedback phases.

In the 1982 study, the teachers allotted more practice time while giving little feedback. The practice component was negatively related to pupil achievement on the task. Without feedback to guide subsequent performances, the learners did not progress even though the task was not complex. Teacher competence was not measured, but it appeared that the allotting of practice time may have been a "default option"; that is, the teachers did not know what feedback to give and thus remained silent observers. It seems to follow that to be effective, the teacher must understand the learners, the tasks, and the learning process in order to appropriately provide practice and feedback in facilitating learning.

Future directions

The somewhat conflicting results regarding practice and feedback, as well as the extent of the unexplained variation, lead to a further examina-

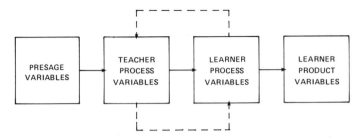

Figure 1 — Revised model for RTE in physical education.

tion of the paradigm. It becomes clear that additional facets of the interactive teaching phase must be studied.

Learner behavior during instruction ultimately affects final performance on the criterion task. Those behaviors associated with increased levels of performance should be identified, as well as those associated with decreased levels of performance. Then the teacher behaviors that facilitate or inhibit those specified learner behaviors are identified. It has been found that the negative impact of certain teacher behaviors was more powerful than the impact of positive or facilitatory ones (Yerg, 1981b), and it might be assumed that the same would hold true for learner behaviors. From the 1977 study, it was shown that some of the teacher behaviors during instruction were different for those with varying levels of knowledge and skill on the criterion task. Therefore an additional component, that of teacher competence both in knowledge and skill on the criterion task, should be considered in the overall paradigm.

Influenced by Doyle's (1978) critique on the process-product paradigm for use in studying teacher effectiveness, a proposed revised paradigm for RTE in physical education is presented in Figure 1. Presage variables would include learner input with respect to the criterion task, teacher knowledge, and teacher skill on the criterion task. Teacher process variables would be those aspects thought to have an impact on the student behaviors identified through previous research. Variables such as those already used from the TBOS, as well as climate and managerial components, would be appropriate. Learner process variables are those identified as being related to anticipated outcome such as receiving information, using feedback, and utilizing practice time. The product or outcome variables would be those of the specified criterion task, the expected learning outcomes.

Analysis for this expanded paradigm would require an approach such as path analysis which examines relationships and the strength of those relationships in the interactive paradigm. Models would be built hypothesizing the sequence of events based on past research and empirical judgment, and then mathematical techniques would be applied to correlations among all variables in the model (Gage, 1978). These tech-

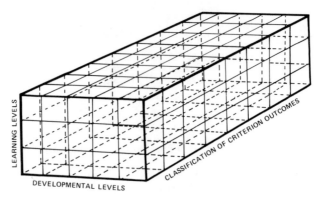

Figure 2 — Schema for identifying instructional parameters.

niques result in path coefficients that indicate the strength of the hypothesized relationship.

A final consideration in refining the teacher effectiveness approach in physical education is to provide some schema for defining the learner, the learning stage, and the criterion task on which the analyses are to be made. The complexity of the physical education environment with the myriad of contexts in which instruction takes place precludes generalization across all instruction. However, three aspects of the milieu seem to be pertinent. The developmental level of the learner dictates certain opportunities and limitations for instruction. The stage of learning, whether it is beginning, intermediate, or advanced, affects the teaching and learning strategy; and finally, the task itself dictates certain instructional strategies that will facilitate skill acquisition. If a model can be developed for instructional/research use that identifies the context for instruction in these three facets, then research on a specified cell of the model will isolate the factors being studied and permit generalization of results to that particular context. Figure 2 represents the beginnings of such a schema. Input is needed from motor development, motor learning, instructional design, curriculum, and teaching specialists to complete the model. Cells within the framework might be of greater focus in the study of teaching in physical education. In any case, identifying the cell of focus when initiating research would define the parameters for the study so that studies using the same cell would begin to provide a basis for generalization and more useable information for practitioners.

It was stated at the outset that this paper would not have closure. It is presented as a challenge to move forward, to further define and refine the processes by which we search for the answers to the question, "What is effective teaching in physical education?"

Acknowledgments

Appreciation is extended to Patricia Francis for her assistance in preparing the material for this manuscript and presentation.

Reference Note

1. Yerg, B.J. *Relationship of specified instructional teacher behaviors to pupil gain on a motor skill task.* Presentation to Association Internationale des Ecoles Superieres d'Education Physique World Convention, Boston, August 1982.

References

DOYLE, W. Paradigms for research on teacher effectiveness. In L.S. Shulman (Ed.), *Review of research in education* (Vol. 5). Itasca, IL: Peacock, 1978.

GAGE, N.L. *The scientific basis of the art of teaching.* New York: Teachers College Press, 1978.

YERG, B.J. Relationships between teacher behaviors and pupil achievement in the psychomotor domain (Doctoral dissertation, University of Pittsburgh, 1977). *Dissertation Abstracts International*, 1977, **38**, 1981A. (University Microfilms No. 77-21,229)

YERG, B.J. Reflections on the use of the RTE model in physical education. *Research Quarterly for Exercise and Sport*, 1981, **52**(2), 38-47.

YERG, B.J. Teaching-learning process factors related to pupil achievement on a psychomotor task. *Resources in Education*, October 1981. (ERIC Reproduction Documents SP 017 942 ED 202 815)

The stability of teaching behavior over a unit of instruction

Judith E. Rink
The University of South Carolina

The study of teaching in physical education is a relatively new area of investigation. Most of the research conducted so far has relied heavily on observing teaching behavior for relatively short periods of time. Usually the single lesson is used as a representative of teaching behavior. The validity of such a sample rests with the assumption of stability of the observed behavior over time. Stability of teaching behavior has been considered a critical dimension of reliability (Frick & Semmel, Note 1). Questions concerning the stability of the observed behavior over time are questions relative to the generalizability of the data (Rowley, 1974).

Studies done by Lombardo and Cheffers (1980) in physical education, as well as a mounting number of studies from classroom research, conclude that some behaviors are stable and some are not. Variability of teaching behavior in teaching effectiveness research is a critical issue (Rowley, 1974; Soar, 1972; Frick & Semmel, Note 1; Cohen, Note 2).

The purpose of this study was to investigate the stability of teaching behavior in physical education over a 15-lesson middle school volleyball unit. Observational data using the Observation System for Content

Development (OSCD-PE) (Rink, 1979) were analyzed for three teachers for each of the 15 lessons in the unit. The stability of teaching behavior for each of three teachers over the unit was described.

Method

Subjects
Three teachers from the same middle school in a low middle-class area of Columbia, South Carolina, were selected for the study, two males and one female. All three had been at the same school at least three years and had had previous teaching experience. Teachers were selected from this school primarily because the school's program had a good reputation, the teachers were supportive about having their behavior studied, and the school's location made travel feasible for the investigators.

Procedures
Each teacher was asked to teach a volleyball unit of 15 lessons (three weeks) to a group of his/her choice within his/her schedule. Conditions were that all teaching would be audiotaped, using a micro-cassette recorder and auxillary microphone worn by the teacher. Teachers were free to teach the unit for any outcomes they felt desirable as long as they worked independently of each other. Additional conditions were set as part of a more comprehensive study on effectiveness of teaching behavior.[1]

Class size ranged between 29 and 31 students, all classes being co-ed. One class was predominantly eighth grade, one class predominantly seventh grade, and one class was a mixture of seventh- and eighth-grade students. Students were given questionnaires to assess their previous experience with volleyball. Only a few had had previous instruction in volleyball, as it had not been part of the elementary or middle school curriculum for these students.

The middle school physical education program used the gymnasium facilities of a nearby recreational center. Equipment for volleyball included enough regulation size or nerf volleyballs for each student. There was no net, but teachers made use of a large rope strung across the length of the gymnasium. Actual class time ranged from 30 to 45 minutes, depending on whether teachers had students dress for activity and the time it took to walk to the facility.

---

[1]Comprehensive pre- and post-measures on students were taken in the cognitive, affective, and psychomotor areas. In addition, two lessons per week were videotaped for additional process data. The results of this larger study are being analyzed.

Data collection

Audiotapes were collected successfully on 13, 13, and 14 full lessons, respectively. All the lessons were coded by the experimenter, using OSCD-PE. Intra-observer reliability was determined at .91, using percentage of agreement on two of the 40 tapes. Inter-observer reliability was not considered a factor in this study since the instrument designer was the principal coder. One lesson was coded by a different trained observer, and inter-observer reliability was determined to be .86, using percentage of agreement.

The Observation System for Content Development-Physical Education is a multidimensional category system that sorts instructional events into mutually exclusive and inclusive categories.[2] The observational record preserves both the scope and sequence of events simultaneously recorded on five dimensions. Major constructs of the system are listed in Table 1.

Data analysis

Frequency counts and percentages of total behavior within a dimension were determined for each lesson and each teacher. The range, mean, and standard deviation for behaviors were determined for the unit of instruction for each teacher using lesson summaries. Stability of an instructional behavior was determined by the range and standard deviation for each teacher over the unit. The relationship of lack of stability to the unit of instruction was determined by analyzing the changes in the behavior over the 15 lessons.

Behaviors that tended to change in the same direction over the 15 lessons were considered to be a function of the unit for a teacher. Behaviors that tended to change from lesson to lesson with no apparent relationship to the unit were considered a function of the lesson. Behaviors that showed little change through the 15 lessons were considered stable behaviors for a teacher.

Results and discussion

The teachers studied in these units could each be called a good teacher. The data would support the facts that:

1. Activity time was greater than the average for physical education lessons;
2. Behavioral problems with students were almost nonexistent;
3. At least 20 percent of teaching behavior was spent improving the quality of student performance;

---

[2]The Observation System for Content Development-Physical Education is available from the author.

Table 1
Percent of Teacher Behavior for Lessons in the Unit

Behavior	Teacher A			Teacher B			Teacher C		
	X	S.D.	Range	X	S.D.	Range	X	S.D.	Range
Informing (total)	29	6	16-38	32	17	12-64	35	14	25-55
Solicit	4	7	1-10	5	3	1-8	7	3	3-19
Respond	4	2	1-7	3	3	1-7	2	2	—
Initiate	7	4	1-13	14	9	3-29	17	10	1-32
Appraise	4	3	1-8	5	3	2-10	13	22	3-10
Refining (total)	31	5	14-45	21	7	9-29	22	13	3-25
Solicit	13	4	5-20	7	5	2-15	11	5	2-22
Respond	3	2	1-6	1	1	0-4	0	0	0
Initiate	7	4	5-19	7	3	2-11	9	7	2-23
Appraise	8	4	4-19	4	7	1-5	5	2	1-8
Extending (total)	4	6	1-3	2	1	1-3	0	0	0
Solicit	1	2	—	1	0	0-1	0	0	0
Respond	—	—	—	—	—	—	—	—	—
Initiate	1	.01	0-2	2	1	1-3	1	1	1-4
Appraise	—	—	—	—	—	—	—	—	—
Applying (total)	10	6	2-22	12	13	1-43	15	23	0-64
Solicit	3	2	0-6	4	4	0-11	5	5	0-3
Respond	2	1	0-4	4	3	1-9	2	3	0-7
Initiate	5	4	1-11	6	7	0-11	11	16	1-42
Appraise	—	—	—	—	—	—	—	—	—

Conduct (total)	5	5	2-8	6	3	10-12	4	2	0-8
Solicit	2	1	0-4	3	2	1-5	2	1	4-13
Respond	—	—	—	2	1	1-3	—	—	—
Initiate	1	1	1-3	2	3	0-4	11	16	0-3
Appraise	—	—	—	—	—	—	—	—	—
Organization (total)	20	5	11-30	25	9	15-40	19	4	11-29
Solicit	12	3	9-17	14	4	10-22	10	5	6-13
Respond	2	1	1-3	1	1	1-3	2	1	1-3
Initiate	5	2	2-9	10	6	3-21	8	3	5-15
Appraise	2	5	0-2	2	1	0-3	—	—	—
Use of time[a]									
Beginning class	22	15	0-43	27	4	8-78	90	28	50-139
Activity time	58	11	46-85	46	13	25-75	51	11	35-74
Task time	25	10	8-39	24	15	9-57	69	31	24-117
Observing	10	10	1-16	23	17	0-55	8	7	0-18
Off-topic comments	4	3	0-13	—	—	—	—	—	—
Transition time	6	5	3-19	21	14	9-58	24.6	15	1-52
Demonstration	6	7	0-19	17	13	0-34	11	15	0-48
Use of time[a]									
Length of feedback	4	2	3-7	3	1	2-4	4.	2	2-7
Verbal interaction (teacher initiated)	26	18	3-44	9	8	2-25	7	6	1-17
Verbal interaction (student initiated)	11	6	3-20	7	6	0-21	7	4	1-18

[a] Use of time variables are given in terms of the number of 5-second intervals in each lesson.

4. Less than average amounts of time were spent in organization;
5. Feedback was highly specific;
6. All three teachers made attempts to individualize.

Because these teachers did not have managerial problems, the conditions under which the stability of teaching behavior was studied were somewhat more ideal than for a real world setting. The stability of behavior should have reflected differences in the approach of individual teachers to the content of the unit for their students.

The three teachers represented a spectrum of approaches toward the content. Teacher A stayed with the forearm pass and overhead pass the entire unit, building only to modified four on four-game play. Material was developed with very gradual changes in conditions and focuses of practice. Teacher B was more eclectic in approach, building skills in a similar way to Teacher A but including the serve and regulation game play as part of the unit. Teacher C's approach was the most traditional. The sport was presented with an emphasis on rules and was developed with fairly traditional drills. Skills included the dig and the spike, and students spent the final lessons in regulation game play.

Results for major variables are described in Table 1; space does not permit a discussion of all variables. Several dimensions of teaching behavior have been selected for discussion.

The utilization of class time

Activity time. Time allotted for motor activity that is content-related (activity time) is illustrated in Figure 1a. Differences between the teachers were clear, as was the trend for all three teachers to increase the amount of time allotted for activity as the unit progressed from beginning to end. These differences were only partially explainable by increased game-like play. Some of the higher levels of activity time occurred in lessons involved primarily with individual skills. This behavior through the unit averaged 43 percentage points for these teachers and would not be considered a stable teaching behavior. The beginning lesson and last lessons seemed to affect stability the most.

Task time. The average amount of time each teacher allowed students to work on each task before stopping the class and changing the focus of the task was determined. Figure 1b illustrates both the differences between teachers and their trend to increase the average activity time allotted to each task as the unit progressed. Teacher A had the highest activity time but not the highest average time for a task. Teacher C had the lowest activity time and the highest time allotted for each task. The behavior had an average range of 57 intervals (285 seconds) for these teachers over the unit and would not be considered a stable behavior. Again, the beginning and the last lessons had the most effect on stability.

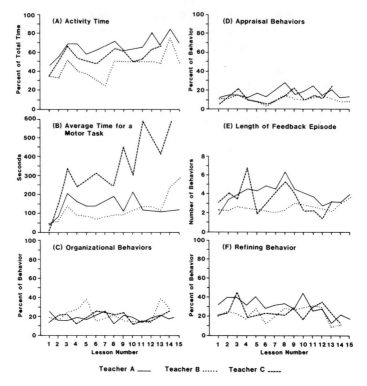

Figure 1 – Teaching behaviors over the fifteen lesson unit.

Lesson beginnings. Lesson beginning time is real time before the first motor task of a lesson. Teacher A averaged 1.8 minutes, Teacher B, 3.3 minutes, and Teacher C, 7.4 minutes. Even though the relative position of the teachers in respect to this variable remained fairly constant, the range for each teacher was great. Lesson beginning time is not considered a stable behavior for any of these teachers and does not seem to be a function of the unit.

Transition time. Transition time is the average of time spent between motor tasks in a lesson. The relative position of teachers with each other was similar to beginning time for this variable. The wide range for each teacher over the unit is indicative of a very unstable behavior with no apparent relationship to the position of a lesson within a unit.

The teacher as a manager

Management behaviors were the most stable behaviors studied within the unit, with no apparent relationship to the position of the lesson in the unit. Two dimensions of management are part of OSCD-PE. One dimension, conduct, identifies those behaviors that structure, direct or reinforce the conduct of students. A second dimension of management structures, organization, directs or reinforces the organizational arrangements of people, time, space, or equipment of a lesson.

Conduct. Conduct behaviors of the teacher consumed little class time for all three teachers, their range averaging only five percentage points throughout the unit. Conduct behaviors that were recorded were primarily solicitations for the attention of students (soliciting-conduct). Conduct was considered a stable behavior across the unit of instruction for all three teachers.

Organization. Organizational behaviors were fairly stable, with increases primarily occurring during the introduction of full game play in the unit (Figure 1c). Although teacher averages were similar (20%, 25%, and 19%), the specific organization behaviors were different. Teacher B broke down organizational tasks for students by having them perform one aspect at a time. Other teachers tended to give directions all at one time. The result was that teacher B had slightly more organizational time. Teachers A and C required more attention to organization during activity. Patterns of organizational procedures remained consistent for the three teachers.

The teacher as an informer

Teacher behaviors of communicating information about content to learners were not stable, and were associated only to a small degree with the lesson's position within a unit of instruction. Teacher C demonstrated a clear trend to decrease these behaviors as the unit progressed. The trend is not as consistent for Teacher B, and is nonexistent for Teacher A, whose behavior was the most stable.

Initiating. Initiating behaviors, related to informing behaviors, are structuring moves that do not require a response from the student. This behavior is usually contrasted with the soliciting behaviors, which are teacher directives to act. Except for the beginning lesson, these behaviors were fairly stable for the three teachers. The relative position of one teacher to another remained fairly constant through the unit.

Verbal questioning. Teacher-initiated verbal questioning was used by Teacher A more than Teachers B and C. All the teachers showed some trend to decrease the use of verbal questioning as the unit progressed. The behavior itself seems more related to the individual teacher. The teacher (A) who used verbal questioning used it consistently except for lessons at the end of the unit.

Use of demonstration. The number of demonstrations being used (not during activity time) were determined. Great fluctuations from lesson to lesson were observed for all teachers. When Teacher B and Teacher C entered game play, the use of demonstration stopped. Lessons prior to the end of the unit showed no trend toward an increase or decrease in the use of demonstration. Increases were primarily attributable to the introduction of new skills for most of the teachers.

The feedback of the teacher

The three teachers used high levels of specific skill feedback, with 75% of Teacher A's feedback being specific as opposed to general. Teacher B's specific feedback was 48%, and Teacher C's was 52%. In all cases feedback was more corrective than evaluative. The specificity of teacher feedback remained a relatively stable behavior through the unit.

Figure 1e illustrates the length of time teachers stayed with one student to give feedback, usually called a feedback episode. This behavior was quite stable for Teacher B but very unstable for Teachers A and C, who stayed with students at times for seven 5-second intervals of behavior.

Figure 1f illustrates refining behavior for the three teachers for the unit. Refining behavior seeks to qualitatively improve performance through corrective feedback, providing information on how to improve performance and evaluating performance specifically. Refining behavior as a total dimension was a relatively stable behavior for all three teachers, with a decrease toward the end of the unit when the emphasis was on game play.

The development of content

Constructs related to the development of content describe the way in which the teacher uses the processes of refinement (qualitative), extension (change in complexity or difficulty), and application (competitive) to develop the content with students. These processes appear as task focuses, feedback focuses, or in any content communication with students. The three teachers used all three focuses in developing their lessons and units, but not in the same way. Each teacher's approach to development did, however, remain fairly stable through the unit.

The task focus. Figure 2 describes the task focuses of the first four days of each unit for the three teachers. The obvious difference between the teachers is the number of different tasks presented in each lesson. This characteristic remains stable for a teacher through the unit. Another difference more clear in the analyses for 15 lessons is the number of different skills presented between teachers A and B, and Teacher C. This characteristic remained stable through the skill presentation of the unit. For teachers B and C, changes in task focuses stopped when students entered game play.

A less obvious difference between the teachers in the development of content was Teacher C's lack of tasks with a refining focus and the delay of application tasks until the end of the unit. Teachers A and B spaced both refining and application tasks throughout the development of all the skills taught.

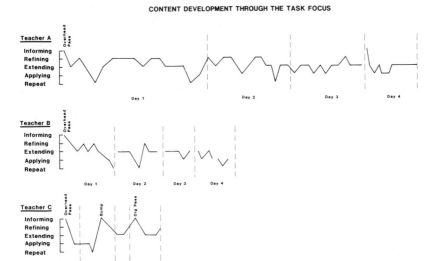

Figure 2 — Content development through the task focus.

Extension tasks characterize practice of skills under more complex and difficult conditions. After a skill was explained and the form communicated, Teacher C used only a few extension tasks before moving on to the next skill. Teachers A and C developed fewer skills with more changes in practice conditions. The use of refining, extending, and applying tasks does seem to be stable through the individual skill development part of a unit for these teachers. Teacher A developed game play in a similar way to the development of individual skills. Teachers B and C moved quickly through modifications of game play to more regulation game play. The end of the unit was characterized by tasks with only an application focus for Teachers B and C.

Summary and conclusions

Teaching behavior over a 15-lesson volleyball unit was analyzed to determine the stability of behavior over time. The results described behavior that was stable over the 15 lessons for one or all teachers, unstable behavior that seemed to be related to a lesson's position in the unit, and unstable behavior that could not be explained in terms of the lesson's position in the unit.

Some unstable teaching behavior not attributable to the progression of the unit is most likely attributable to specific events within a lesson. The investigator has been able to account for much of the variation in terms of lesson-specific events, although there are still peaks and valleys in the unstable behaviors that cannot be attributed to any specific event. In these instances, a teacher who normally responds in a certain way to a set of conditions does not respond in a predictable way. For instance, a teacher who normally is active, giving specific feedback to students during skill practice, becomes inactive.

Unstable teaching behavior will continue to be a problem in teaching research because of the unique events portion of each lesson. The teachers in this study were good managers; the management dimension of their behavior was very stable, which allowed the investigator to attribute the instability of many behaviors to unit and lesson events. In cases where management behaviors are not stable, it is unlikely that any real stability in any behaviors will be discerned. It is also unlikely, under conditions of management instability, that few changes in behavior can be attributed to lesson or unit events.

Instability in the unit of instruction for many behaviors was most acute for the beginning and the end of the unit. For two of the teachers studied, active teaching behavior declined considerably during game play. The teacher having the most stable behavior for all dimensions (Teacher A) was considered by the investigator to be the best teacher on the basis of known dimensions of teacher effectiveness. The idea that stability of teaching behavior for specific behavioral dimensions may be related to effectiveness is a new concept that needs further investigation.

Reference Notes

1. Frick, T., & Semmel, M.I. *Observational records: Observer agreement and reliabilities.* Paper presented at the annual meeting of the American Psychological Association, Chicago, April 1974. (ERIC Document Reproduction Service No. ED 097375.)
2. Cohen, S.J., & Bengston, J.K. *A psychological investigation of factors affecting teacher-observers' judgment.* Paper presented at the annual meeting of AERA, Washington, April 1975.

References

LOMBARDO, B.J., & Cheffers, J.F. Observing physical education teachers for variability, *Bulletin of the Federation Internationale D' Education Physique*, 1980, **50**(1), 31-35.

RINK, J. *Development of a system for the observation of content development in physical education.* Unpublished doctoral dissertation, Ohio State University, 1979.

ROWLEY, G. *The reliabilities of classroom observational measures.* Unpublished doctoral dissertation, Ontario Institute for Students in Education, 1974.

SOAR, R. Teacher behavior related to pupil growth. *International Review of Education*, 1972, **18**, 508-526.

Quasi experimentation and discriminant analysis in research on teaching in physical education

Harold H. Morris
Indiana University

A variety of paradigms have been used by scholars concerned with research in teaching physical education. That such a diversity of methods has been used testifies to the complexity of the topic (Locke, 1975). Nevertheless, scholars in teaching effectiveness, as with all disciplines, must search for new methods and new applications of previously introduced techniques if progress is to be continuous. With that premise in view, this paper will present a contrast of the true and natural experimental designs and an overview of discriminant analysis as a model for analyzing data obtained in a natural experiment.

The "true" experiment requires that the relationship between two variables be observed under conditions that permit the researcher to deliberately produce a change in one, the independent variable, while noting whether this alteration produces a change in the other, the dependent variable (Anderson, 1966). To insure that the change in the dependent variable can be explained only by the change in the independent variable, the investigator must control all other sources of variation.

While the control of all extraneous sources of variation would be impossible to accomplish in a physical manner, it may be achieved via probability. Thus, a characteristic of the true experiment is the random assignment of subjects to the various treatment conditions and the application of treatments individually to each experimental unit. The underlying assumption is that the groups will differ, prior to the administration of the treatments, only within the limits of sampling error. Therefore, significant differences among the groups will be attributed to the variation in the treatment effect. Failure to randomly assign forfeits control over the numerous inter-individual sources of variation that can confound the treatment effects. Failure to administer the treatments individually can introduce an unknown effect to one treatment group and not to others.

While the true experiment is a very powerful model that has had a great impact on science in the 20th century, it cannot be used in all research endeavors. For example, geologists and astronomers find little use for the true experimental model. In most problems in these disciplines, the scientists cannot manipulate the independent variable (Anderson, 1966). Similarly, researchers concerned with teaching cannot always manipulate the variable of interest. Teachers are either non-tenured or tenured, and either male or female. The students entering the class are either high or low in ability. The schools in a sample have specific facilities; one cannot randomly assign a swimming pool to a school that doesn't have one. Thus, like scientists in astronomy, oceanography, and geology, researchers concerned with teaching often must use the "natural experiment" as the model for their investigations. This is not to suggest that the true experiment model does not have application within the area of research on teaching, but that the natural experiment is frequently a more appropriate model. At least at this time in the development of research in teaching, the true experimental designs are often incompatible with the administrative and environmental constraints that are placed on such investigations.

In contrast to the true experiment, a natural experiment is one in which the differing characteristics or attributes of the subject represent the levels of the independent variable. "Nature" might represent a wide range of individual differences from those that are primarily hereditary such as sex, height, weight, and eye color to those that are operationally defined on the basis of experience, level of competence, or certification, such as tenure status or level of teaching expertise. The primary difference between the true and natural experiment models is that subjects with one particular attribute cannot be randomly assigned to another level of the independent variable. It is obvious the subjects who have been classified as novices, with regard to their teaching experiences and competencies, cannot be randomly assigned to the group of teachers classified as expert. Thus, in the natural experiment the researcher establishes, on the basis of some operational definition, that the groups of subjects differ. The groups are then compared on the dependent variable or variables, which implies that these variables are being tested as to whether they can discriminate between the levels of the independent variable.

To summarize the contrast of the true and natural experimental models, one might consider the questions that each model addresses. In the true experiment the research question is, "do the treatments cause a change in the value of the dependent variable," whereas in the natural experiment the question is, "are the dependent variables sensitive to the differences in the groups." Also, researchers should be aware that the natural experiment has a limitation. Since the individual subjects have not been randomly assigned to the treatment condition, the relationship between the independent and dependent variables may be either causal or casual. This implies that an observed difference between two levels of the independent variable may be due to another unidentified source of variation that affects both the independent and dependent variables. Notwithstanding this limitation, the natural experiment has an important place in scientific methodology (Anderson, 1966).

A statistical procedure known as discriminant analysis may be effectively used to analyze data recorded in a natural experiment. Discriminant analysis refers to those statistical procedures that focus on the differences between two or more groups of sampling units (usually subjects) with reference to an optimized combination of several predictor variables. Discriminant analysis is often used to achieve one of two research objectives, namely interpretation or classification (Klecka, 1980). In each case, the procedures require the calculation of a linear function of the predictor variables that correlate highest with a vector of code that identifies group membership.

To use discriminant analysis, the sampling units must be such that they permit classification into one of two or more mutually exclusive groups. For example, Rencher, Wadham, and Young (1978) classified individuals as tenured-outstanding, tenured-poor, first year, and teacher assistants. Thus, a given teacher could meet the operational definition of one and only one group. Another assumption of discriminant analysis pertains to the distributions of the underlying populations. The assumption is that the populations have a multivariate normal distribution. To reduce feelings of uneasiness concerning the assumptions, researchers should refer to the work cited in Lachenbruch (1975), which generally concludes that discriminant analysis is robust with regard to moderate violations of the assumption of multivariate normality. Failure to meet the assumption of the multivariate normality results in a reduction in the accuracy of classification.

To use the simplest mathematical procedures, an assumption is made that the covariance matrices, calculated within the various populations, are equal. In other words, this assumption requires that the correlations among the predictor variables be the same within each of the populations. Failure to meet this assumption results in the calculation of canonical discriminant functions that fail to maximize the distance between the groups and results in classification functions that are less effective in predicting the classification of the individual sampling unit. Nevertheless, if a significant discriminant function is found that produces a high percentage of correct classifications, the researcher can be assured that any violations of these assumptions has been minimal (Klecka, 1980).

Additional precautions should be expressed to the initial user. Discriminant analysis is a multivariate procedure that uses computational algorithms based on matrix algebra. Consequently, the set of predicting or discriminating variables, as they are sometimes referred to, may not contain a variable that is a linear combination of two or more of the other variables. In the simplest case, for example, the use of the variables "teacher talk" and "student talk" would preclude the simultaneous inclusion of the variable "total talk" if the latter were merely the sum of the two. Similarly, two variables that are perfectly correlated will prevent the calculation of the canonical discriminant function. The use of linear combinations or variables that are perfectly correlated result in a singular matrix that cannot be inverted, a primary operation in matrix algebra.

To introduce discriminant analysis, the fundamentals of multiple regression analysis will be reviewed. This was done because the discriminant analysis of two groups is a special case of multiple regression.

Discimination between two groups

Multiple regression is a procedure that maximizes the relationship between a single classification variable and a series of predictor variables. This is accomplished by determining a set of partial regression coefficients that are used as weights for the independent variables. In multiple regression analysis, the dependent variable as well as the independent variables are usually measured continuous values. It has been shown, however, that dichotomous "dummy coding" vectors can serve as the predictor variables (Cohen, 1968; Darlington, 1968; Knapp, 1978).

In the application of discriminant analysis, the predictor variables are continuous and measured, but the classification variable is a vector of code that labels group membership. Such an arrangement is shown in Table 1. Note that the classification vector, identified by Y, contains only ones (1's) and zeros (0's). Recall that the objective of multiple regression analysis is to maximize the relationship between the set of indepen-

Table 1

**A Data Set Identifying Group Membership
with Vector Y and Discriminating Variables X_1 and X_2**

Subject	Group Y	Discriminating Variables X_1	X_2
1	1	16	9
2	1	13	8
3	1	13	7
4	1	11	9
5	1	13	5
6	0	9	3
7	0	7	5
8	0	5	1
9	0	7	2
10	0	4	1

dent variables and the dependent variable. This same objective holds in the case of discriminant analysis. By maximizing the relationship between the set of predictor variables and the coding vector that represents group membership, discriminant analysis separates the groups as far as possible along a continuum called the discriminant function.

As can be seen in Figure 1a, the group labeled F is somewhat superior to the group labeled M on the vertical axis while the reverse is true on the variable represented on the horizontal axis. A simple illustration of the discriminant function is shown in Figure 1b, for line C, which bisects the area of overlap of the ellipses and is shown to be perpendicular to the discriminant function depicted as C'. It is apparent that the groups are separated on the discriminant function to a greater extent than they were on either of the original variables.

Thus, the discriminant function represents a continuum along which the groups are maximally separated. This function is formed by procedures that are, in essence, like those used in multiple regression analysis. Recall from multiple regression analysis the equation:

$$Y' = b_1X_1 + b_2X_2 + \ldots b_kX_k + a$$

where Y' represents the predicted score, X_1 to X_k represents the independent variables, b_1 to b_k represents the regression coefficients, and (a) represents the intercept of the Y axis. The discriminant function is identical to the above equation with the exception that the value Y' would represent a value along the discriminant function rather than a predicted

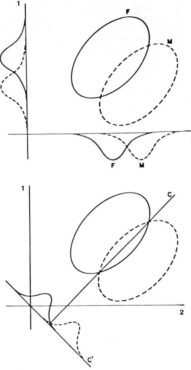

Figure 1—In 1a (above) the centroids of distribution F and M, formed from variables 1 and 2, are illustrated. In 1b (below) the discriminant function, C′, is shown. Note that this function is located at an angle that maximizes the distance between the two distributions.

score on a criterion or dependent measure. Various matrix algebra procedures are used to determine the vector of b weights, or unstandardized canonical discriminant coefficients as they are appropriately labeled in these procedures. The unstandardized coefficients are used to multiply the raw scores of the discriminating variables. These coefficients are unstandardized because the raw scores of the various discriminating variables do not have the same means and variances. The unstandardized coefficients are useful in classification analysis but are of little interpretative value.

To determine the relative contribution of each of the discriminating variables to the canonical discriminant function, attention should focus on the standardized discriminant coefficients. Like Beta weights in regression analysis, the standardized discriminant coefficients are used to multiply the standard scores rather than the raw scores of the discriminating variables. By considering the absolute sizes of the standardized coefficients, a researcher can determine the contribution of each of the variables to the discriminant function. Nevertheless, researchers are cautioned about deleting variables from further analysis when they have low standardized weightings because the discriminant function is subject to distortions due to multicollinearity and suppression among the discriminating variables (Cohen & Cohen, 1975). Researchers are advised to examine the structure coefficients when attempting to label the discriminant function or when attempting to identify variables that might be deleted in subsequent analyses. The structure coefficients are zero-order Pearson product-moment correlations between the variable and the discriminant function. Klecka (1980) provides a succinct contrast of the standardized coefficients and the structure coefficients.

> Structure coefficients tell us something quite different from what is communicated by the standardized coefficients. The standardized coefficients give us the variable's contribution to calculating the discriminant *score*. This is one way of looking at the variable's importance, but it has a serious limitation. If two variables share nearly the same discriminating information (i.e., if they are highly correlated), they must share their contribution to the score even if that joint contribution is very important. Consequently, their standardized coefficients may be smaller than when only one of the variables is used. Or, the standardized coefficients might be larger but with opposite signs, so that the contribution of one is partially canceled by the opposite contribution of the other. This is because the standardized coefficients take into consideration the simultaneous contributions of all the other variables.
>
> The structure coefficients, however, are simple bivariate correlations so they are not affected by relationships with the other variables. (p. 33)

Discrimination among three or more groups

When three or more groups of subjects have been classified, discriminant analysis may be considered a special case of canonical correlation analysis. A canonical correlation is an index of the relationship between two sets of variables. In multiple discriminant analysis, the use of more than two classifications or groups requires the use of more than one coding vector to represent group membership. Recall that one coding vector was sufficient to identify membership in either of two groups (cf. Table 1). It may be generalized that one less coding vector than classifications or groups will be required to identify group membership. An example of a data set using three groups is shown in Table 2.

In the case of three or more groups, additional discriminant functions can be calculated. The number of possible discriminant functions is equal to the number of discriminating variables or to the number of groups minus one, whichever is smaller. The additional discriminant functions are calculated to maximize the distance among the groups, subject to the constraint that each function is orthogonal or uncorrelated to

Table 2

**A Data Set Identifying Group Membership
with Vectors Y$_1$ and Y$_2$ and Discriminating Variables X$_1$ and X$_2$**

Subject	Group		Discriminating Variables	
	Y$_1$	Y$_2$	X$_1$	X$_2$
1	1	0	9	11
2	1	0	8	9
3	1	0	7	10
4	0	1	6	10
5	0	1	6	8
6	0	1	4	9
7	0	0	3	7
8	0	0	2	8
9	0	0	1	9

those functions that have been previously solved. Therefore, the first discriminant function will maximize the distance among the groups using all of the information available from the discriminating variables. The second discriminant function will maximize the distance among the groups using the residual variance that remains, following the calculation of the initial discriminant function. Thus, each successive discriminant function will be calculated on the residual variance of all functions that have been previously determined. It is understandable that the first discriminant function has the greatest statistical importance, as it has been calculated using all of the information from the independent variables, and that each successive function will be less effective in separating the groups.

Various tests of significance, including Wilks' Lambda, have been used to test the significance of the discriminant functions. In most applications where more than three groups are considered, the researcher tests the initial discriminant function. If that function is significant, further tests are completed to identify the significance of a second function. If that function is significant, the third is tested, and so on, until either a function is declared to be nonsignificant or the entire set of functions has been tested.

Classification

Discriminant analysis may be used to classify individual subjects into the different groups. Various procedures have been developed for individual classification. Klecka (1980) presents an overview of classification procedures developed independently by Fisher and by Mahalanobis. Fisher's (1936) procedure requires the researcher to compute a separate classification function for each individual for each group. The function associated with the group that produces the largest predicted value is the group into which the individual is classified.

The generalized distance measure (D^2) is the squared distance from the point of the individual case to the centroid of the group. A D^2 statistic is calculated for each group and the subject is classified into the group with the smallest D^2 value. The probability of membership in the various groups can be tested using chi-square.

The proportion of correct classifications of the individuals in the original data set is spurious. This is due to the fact that canonical discriminant function and the various classification functions were developed on the optimum separation of the groups formed with these subjects. Therefore, it is essential that a second set of data be used to cross-validate the various equations. Caution should be taken when analyzing the proportion of correct classification (Morrison, 1969). A tau statistic has been proposed by Klecka (1980) as the appropriate interpretation of the classification matrix. The tau statistic represents a proportional reduction of error, which is the improvement over a completely chance classification.

Application

Data from a variety of research questions in the areas of teacher preparation and teacher effectiveness can be analyzed using discriminant analysis. For example, samples of teachers who have been classified as outstanding can be contrasted with those who have been rated as marginal, using various classroom behaviors as the discriminating variables. Students who have attained the behavioral objectives of a course can be contrasted with those who have not. Students who complete the field experiences and become certified teachers might be contrasted with those who withdraw from the teacher preparation program. Groups of students who attain various levels of final achievement could be contrasted using student attributes, student behaviors, teacher behaviors, and various environmental parameters.

Discriminant analysis might be used to identify teachers that were misclassified for purpose of further study. Teachers rated as outstanding but classified as marginal by the discriminant function may be worthy case studies.

Discriminant analysis can be used to provide evidence that a particular assessment technique or measurement instrument has relevance. A teacher behavior observation system that will accurately classify a large number of teachers into the appropriate groups must be valid for that purpose.

Summary

Research on teaching effectiveness in physical education has diversified to include a variety of models that hold promise for future directions in this area. This diversification has required that various nontraditional statistical procedures be used in the analysis of the data.

Discriminant analysis seeks to maximize the distance among two or more groups of subjects and is suggested as an appropriate method for analyzing data that is obtained in answering some of the questions in the area of teaching behavior/effectiveness. In using discriminant analysis, the researcher can identify those variables that contribute greatest to the separation of the groups. Additionally, discriminant analysis can be used to classify individual subjects, on the basis of the observed variables, to one of the predetermined groups. Thus, subjects who are misclassified can be identified for further study on a case by case basis.

References

ANDERSON, B.F. *The psychology experiment*. Belmont, CA: Brooke/Cole, 1966.

COHEN, J. Multiple regression as a general data-analytic system. *Psychological Bulletin*, 1968, **70**, 426-443.

COHEN, J., & Cohen, P. *Applied multiple regression/correlation analysis for the behavioral sciences*. New York: John Wiley & Sons, 1975.

DARLINGTON, R.B. Multiple regression in psychological research and practice. *Psychological Bulletin*, 1968, **69**, 161-182.

DARLINGTON, R.B., Weinberg, S.L., & Walberg, H.J. Canonical variate analysis and related techniques. *Review of Educational Research*, 1973, **43**, 433-454.

FISHER, R.A. The use of multiple measurements in taxonomic problems. *Annals of Eugenics*, 1936, **7**, 179-188.

KLECKA, W.R. *Discriminant Analysis*. Beverly Hills, CA: Sage Publ., 1980.

KNAPP, T.R. Canonical correlation analysis: A general parametric significance-testing system. *Psychological Bulletin*, 1978, **85**, 410-416.

LACHENBRUCH, P.A. *Discriminant analysis*. New York: Macmillan, 1975.

LOCKE, L. The ecology of the gymnasium: What the tourists never see. *Proceedings of SAPECW*, spring, 1975 (ERIC Document Reproduction Service).

MORRISON, D.G. On the interpretation of discriminant analysis. *Journal of Marketing Research*, 1969, **6**, 156-163.

RENCHER, A.C., Wadham, R.A., & Young, J.R. A discriminant analysis of four levels of teacher competence. *The Journal of Experimental Education*, 1978, **3**, 46-51.

Paradigms for research on
teaching and teachers

Hal A. Lawson
University of British Columbia

> It is not inadequate teaching which bedevils us, it is mindless teaching; the non-teaching teacher. How to keep the teacher alive and struggling with the problem of doing good work, is now and will continue to be the question from which any great leap forward must begin. (Locke, 1977, p. 13)

Evolutionary stages in the histories of scientific and scholarly disciplines are often marked by a few, important conferences, such as this one. It is like the advent of adolescence for a field of inquiry which has remained for too long in its infancy. Therefore, there is every reason to celebrate.[1]

At the same time, there is also cause for critical self-appraisal. For as a field of inquiry matures, its requirements for academic rigor (cf. Locke, 1977) assume much more importance. So long as the field remained in its infancy, these requirements could be relaxed occasionally. During this early stage, some merit could be found in every investigation that was directed toward previously unexplored questions. Now that a more ad-

---

[1]Thanks are due to Gary Sinclair and Joan Vickers; both provided useful literature on research on teaching.

vanced stage has been reached, the absence of rigor can no longer be excused. From this point on, the quest must be for quality even if this means reducing the quantity of research.

Increased quality stands to result from a number of improvements, one of them being methodological advances. The proper questions for inquiry must also be identified to ensure economy of effort, and this requires more prerequisite attention to the development of better theories. In addition, scholars must become more reflective and reflexive in their work; not only must they critically and continuously review pet assumptions and methods but, also, when confronted with major anomalies, they must be willing to forsake their "pets" for more suitable counterparts (after Kuhn, 1975). And finally, quality will increase when there is a better differentiation between the kinds of scholars and the kinds of work that they perform. All these improvements are easier to implement when an appropriate communal structure exists. This structure may be called a paradigm, and it differs from Kuhn's (1975) paradigms.[2]

Used here, a paradigm refers to a disciplinary community. It consists of colleagues who have undergone the same kind of education and training, contribute to the same literature, embrace similar values, and direct their work toward the same goals. In some instances, colleagues also share the same exemplar, but in others they adopt competing exemplars. The metaphor of the puzzle serves to illuminate this relationship between a paradigm and an exemplar.

If a paradigm defines the structure and parameters of the puzzle, then its exemplars represent ways in which solutions to it are sought. An exemplar, an accepted way in which research may proceed, consists of "law, theory, application, and instrumentation together" (Kuhn, 1975, p. 10). It includes the rules for the conduct of inquiry as well as the criteria that are employed to determine the worth of the results. It is a means for puzzle solving; just as there are in principle many ways to solve any puzzle, so, too, is it possible to locate a number of exemplars within a given paradigm. The paradigm brings structural and communal harmony to the efforts of colleagues at the same time that its exemplars allow them useful diversity in their approaches to common questions.

To reiterate, then, quality in scholarship stands to increase when appropriate communal structures — paradigms — are established. For paradigms facilitate methodological advances as well as the construction and testing of theory, make it easier for colleagues to become more reflective

---

[2]Kuhn (1975), of course, made it clear that his discussion was not aimed at the social and behavioral sciences (pp. ix-x), let alone physical education. I have used his work, then, as a point of departure and do not intend to force-fit it on the questions addressed here. On the other hand, and despite his disclaimer, others in the social sciences and humanities have used Kuhn's work (cf. Gutting, 1980).

and reflexive, and provide the necessary distinction between different kinds of colleagues and their equally different kinds of work. Consequently, the question to address is: What are the appropriate paradigms for this area of inquiry in physical education? At this stage in the field's evolution, two such paradigms appear necessary, one for research on teaching and one for research on teachers. The ensuing analysis has been framed to clarify and support this observation.

Research on teaching

Since the bulk of the early research has been understandably directed toward improving instructional effectiveness in the gymnasium, it is appropriate to start with research on teaching and the colleagues who perform it. The intent in this connection is threefold: to begin distinguishing between the two paradigms, to offer constructive criticism and, in turn, to stimulate reflective and reflexive actions from colleagues.

A good definition is always the first step toward clarification. Research on teaching physical education, following Locke's (1977) and Graham's (1981) definitions, "includes only studies which employ data gathered through direct and indirect observation of instructional activity" (Locke, 1977, p. 10). Locke observed correctly that this definition effectively excludes other kinds of inquiry such as research on teachers and students in noninstructional contexts, surveys unrelated to behaviors in the gymnasium, and, all in all, any investigation in which less appropriate methods of data collection are substituted for observations by the investigator (pp. 10-11).

The paradigm for research on teaching

Such a definition also provides the foundation for a paradigm, not just because it specifies what research on teaching *is*, but more importantly, because it states what it is *not*. The commonalities among colleagues who do this research provide the social cement for this paradigm.

There is always a direct relationship between the kind of education and training that colleagues receive and the paradigm in which they enjoy membership. No less is the case here. During the 1970s, several new doctoral programs emerged, most notably at The Ohio State University, The University of Massachusetts, Teachers' College of Columbia University, and Boston University. Others have followed more recently. The primary purpose in each case has been to prepare young scholars for research on teaching. Despite institutional uniqueness and differences among their senior mentors, these young scholars even today have a great deal in common.

Beginning with their formal preparation and continuing with their subsequent research, their perspective has been colored by psychology and informed directly by educational psychology. Like their colleagues in these behavioral sciences, these scholars in physical education remain committed to establishing their own science—namely, a science of teaching physical education (Graham, 1981; Locke, 1977; Siedentop, 1982), or to what some prefer to call pedagogy. Moreover, their work is directed toward the same vexing and important question. Although early work began appropriately with global questions such as what is going on in the gymnasium, the driving question has always been: What is the best way to teach physical education?[3] Thus, in addition to establishing a science of teaching, a common goal is to derive from it a usable technology or set of technologies that act simultaneously to improve instructional effectiveness and to ease the burdens of teachers.

Other commonalities can be derived from the achievements of these young scholars together with their senior mentors. They have successfully published their work in psychological and educational journals, presented laudable papers at meetings of the American Educational Research Association, added the descriptor, instruction, to their professional association's curriculum academy, started their own journal, the newly ordained *Journal of Teaching in Physical Education*, and sponsored workshops and conferences. Even more to the point, they have been successful in creating an ever expanding market in the universities for colleagues who specialize in research on teaching (Graham, 1981). These achievements have resulted from common efforts, and at the same time have contributed to a greater unity among colleagues.

There also appears to be some unison in values. Drawing upon their own experiences as public school teachers, these researchers on teaching have remained sensitive to the questions that confront schoolteachers and have targeted for change the adverse, instructional conditions of the gymnasium. Time and again they have voiced their concern over the effectiveness of teacher education programs in light of the realities of teaching (cf. Locke, Siedentop, & Mand, 1981). And, amidst all of this activity, they have continued to endorse the virtues and values of a sports and games curriculum. It is in this latter connection that one of their common value orientations is most apparent. They are most concerned with finding the answers to "why" and "how" questions that surround effective teaching, instead of "what" questions of curriculum (that are taken as givens). As a group, they are concerned with problem solving rather than problem setting, and this orientation helps to distinguish

---

[3]Others have raised this question somewhat differently as: What makes good teachers of physical education? The criterion of "goodness," however, remains teaching effectiveness; thus, this question still points toward research on teaching.

them from other colleagues who are interested in research on teachers.

Thus, it is possible to conclude that researchers interested in teaching display commonalities that double as indicators of a unique paradigm. From definitions advanced to clarify their work, to the education and training they have received, to their approaches to research, to their notable achievements, and to the values they embrace, these colleagues possess commonalities that supercede in importance and effect the differences residing in their respective exemplars. It is in this connection that this Big Ten Conference constituted a milestone, giving evidence that research on teaching physical education has moved from a preparadigmatic stage to one where a unique and important paradigm has emerged. This in itself stands as an important and meritorious achievement for scholars committed to research on teaching.

Exemplars for research on teaching

There are a number of competing exemplars within this paradigm, their surface marked by now familiar descriptors for different approaches to research on teaching. These descriptors include interaction analysis, academic learning time, aptitude treatment interaction, process-product measures, and descriptive-analytic approaches to teaching and its ecological context. Other important differences exist beneath these familiar descriptors.

These differences begin with competing assumptions about the determinants of teaching and learning and the relative importance assigned to the behaviors or characteristics of teachers and learners. For example, students' time on task and the teacher's ability to keep them there are the single most important factors in studies of academic learning time, whereas in interaction analysis, importance is accorded to indirect teaching methodologies that are presumed to increase the amount of interaction between students and teachers.

There are also competing assumptions about the extent to which research in classrooms can be used to guide and explain the observable behaviors of teachers and students in gymnasia, and the extent to which theories of learning promise to illuminate the way to effective teaching. Differences such as these can be attributed in part to the varying amounts of confidence that scholars have in the state of existing knowledge and the methods by which it was created. Those with more confidence in this knowledge and its attendant methodologies are able to take as given what others view as problematic. This is a reason why they choose different exemplars.

These exemplars also differ in the extent to which they include a formalized, theoretical framework. For example, the studies of academic learning time are informed by the early work of Carroll (1963) and the later work of Bloom (1976) on mastery learning; whatever one's orientation toward this exemplar might be, the fact remains that an identifiable theoretical framework is in place. By contrast, much of the descriptive-analytic inquiry has been conducted without an adequate theoretical framework; this is not to suggest, however, that this work is forever destined to be *atheoretical*. Rather, current work is appropriately *pretheoretical*, but as such it is different than in other exemplars.

A third difference stems logically from differences in assumptions and in theoretical frameworks. In working toward the common goal of a science of teaching, scholars have identified different independent variables, dependent variables, and treatments or interventions. This is a mixed blessing. While it is useful and important to pursue a variety of avenues toward solving the same puzzle, problems arise when colleagues try to synthesize the divergent results into usable guidelines for the practicing school teacher (Graham & Heimerer, Note 1). This observation leads to a fourth and final difference.

Different purposes are associated with these exemplars. Some, such as that for process-product research, are oriented to description and explanation in the name of scientific understanding, whereas others, such as that for interaction analysis, are oriented toward changing the behaviors of teachers. Still others, as revealed in some studies of academic learning time, attempt to do both—describe and prescribe. Here, then, are exemplary differences between basic science and "action science" (Argyris, 1980; Siedentop, 1982; Susman & Evered, 1978) that help to identify competing exemplars.

Having acknowledged major differences among these exemplars for research on teaching, one should recognize some of the important similarities attesting to their compatibility within the same paradigm. First, all are consistent with the accepted definition of research on teaching; they involve formal, systematic, and usually direct observations and measures of teachers and learners in gymnasia.

Secondly, all involve the application of models and approaches that are accepted *a priori* by the investigators. This, too, is a mixed blessing. On the one hand, the investigator can be thoroughly attuned in advance as to what to look for, whereas on the other, such selective attention means that certain events, behaviors, and characteristics have been ignored in the research on teaching physical education (after Kyriacou & Newson, 1982). For example, sociological variables such as the socioeconomic status of students, the commitments and occupational timetables of teachers, and the ethos of different schools have been ignored in the research on teaching physical education.

Thirdly, all the exemplars place more emphasis upon quantitative measures than upon qualitative changes in teachers and students (Kyriacou & Newson, 1982; Clark, Note 2). Such an emphasis upon data that can be counted, presented on graphs, and analyzed statistically reflects a fourth and final commonality.

All of these exemplars have been conceived of and utilized in connection with a science of teaching physical education; this fact alone brings common criteria for assessing the results of inquiry (Graham, 1981; Locke, 1977; Siedentop, 1982; Clark, Note 2). The criterion for excellence appears to be the replication of initial findings in subsequent studies. Replication is also important because of the quest for generalizability; investigators search and research for laws or law-like statements about the relationship between teacher behavior and student achievement (Clark, Note 2). Finally, there are twin concerns for the validity and utility of the findings. This means an attendant emphasis upon direct observation, quantification and, above all, research designs that allow the investigator to capture the actions and interactions of teachers and students in the social life worlds of elementary and secondary school gymnasia.

Thus, although there are demonstrable differences among the exemplars for research on teaching physical education, there are also similarities. In the face of both, it seems safe to conclude that a paradigm for research on teaching physical education provides structural harmony and a communal harbor for the colleagues who endorse and utilize these exemplars. That this paradigm differs from its counterpart for research on teachers will become even more apparent as the latter is analyzed.

Research on teachers

The best way to start an analysis of research on teachers is to preview its differences from research on teaching. To begin with, teaching is an act and teachers are actors. Research on teaching, with its reductional requirements for operationalizing only selected parts of teaching and learning, often severs these acts from the actors; research on teachers begins with the actors and then attends secondarily, if at all, to their teaching. Exemplars for research on teaching, aimed toward a science, are dominated by a psychological perspective and employ some variation of the investigative model of the natural sciences. Exemplars for research on teachers usually reject this investigative model and use a sociocultural as well as a psychological perspective. Furthermore, research on teaching is framed by a perspective on problem solving, whereas research on teachers is framed by a perspective on problem setting. Differences such as these become even more apparent when the results of research are used to inform policy for teacher education programs and practice in the schools. That the policy alternatives often compete is not at all surprising, given the competing value orientations of scholars and the different paths to policy alternatives that each provides.

A paradigm for research on teachers

Research on teachers examines them in their twin capacities as professionals and people. It does not include criterion measures of their teaching effectiveness. Yet, there is more to add to the definition.

Research on teachers attends to their characteristics, needs, interests, and problems.[4] It includes psychological and socio-psychological investigations that are directed at teachers' cognitive characteristics and processes such as their intentions, schemata (Minsky, 1975; Simon, 1979),[5] and the heuristics that characterize their decision-making (Kahneman, Slovic, & Tversky, 1982; Shavelson & Stern, 1981). But teachers are also social beings, and so a sociocultural perspective is used to address other important questions. These begin with familiar questions surrounding the organizational expectations for teachers, as informed by role theory (cf. Bain & Wendt, in press; Chu, 1981; Locke & Massengale, 1978). Also included are less familiar questions surrounding teachers' career contingencies, occupational timetables, career aspirations, commitments, mobility patterns, and their professional subcultures. Above all, research on the dynamics of the socialization of teachers is part of this definition, including the ways in which teachers are shaped by social organizations and, in turn, the ways in which they shape these organizations (Lawson, in press). Since socialization is a lifelong process, research on teachers includes investigations of their childhood biographies and their formal education and training, as well as work during their formal careers. Research on teachers is attuned appropriately to observable behaviors and phenomena, but it is also designed to make explicit and understandable the teachers' often tacit models for work (cf. Argyris, 1980, 1982; Argyris & Schon, 1974, 1978; Polanyi, 1958).

Although such a definition covers a great deal of conceptual territory, it differs from an earlier definition for research on teaching. Research on teachers need not be conducted in the social life worlds of school gymnasia, need not include the investigators' direct observations, and need not include criterion measures for teaching effectiveness. Indeed, it is safe to use such measures as a basis for classification. When student

---

[4]Examples are in order. Characteristics include phenomena such as attitudes, personalities, and levels of physical and emotional fitness; needs include avenues and approaches to continuing learning, stress reduction, and professional interaction in the workplace; interests include things such as sport preferences that are work-related and those that are part of their leisure and lifestyle; problems include phenomena that stand to impair the well-being of teachers, such as the pressure of lateral roles (e.g. father, mother), economic constraints that accompany teaching as work, and knowledge obsolescence.

[5]The term schemata is used to refer to the conceptual and perceptual maps of teachers which inform their behavior. Others prefer labels such as conceptual archetypes, scripts, conceptual networks, or cognitive structures.

achievement is a dependent variable and teaching methods are either dependent variables or interventions, then it is research on teaching, not research on teachers, that has been discovered. Without such measures, one may safely assume that the interest is in teachers as professionals and people, quite apart from their immediate effectiveness with students.

Scholars who are interested in research on teachers share commitments to the questions that comprise it more than they share a common kind of education and training. This implies that, in comparison to scholars who perform research on teaching, this is a more diverse group of colleagues. This diversity is attributable to two related factors. In the first place, there has been less interest in physical education writ large in research on teachers, and this has meant a scarcity of researchers on teachers.[6]

In the second place, there are no specialized doctoral programs in physical education for preparing researchers who are interested in teachers; those colleagues who have performed this work have either planned their own doctoral programs in less familiar degree-granting institutions in teacher education, or have managed to maintain such an interest in programs that are directed toward research on teaching. Consequently, diversity is a logical outcome, with some researchers steeped in facets of psychology while fewer colleagues have embraced either functionalist sociology or classical social science. This kind of diversity will clearly remain until there is more interest in research on teachers and specialized doctoral programs are established accordingly.

On the other hand, this diversity does not mean that the basis for a common paradigm cannot be identified. Despite some differences in their education and training, these colleagues can still understand each other. Their differences are more in degree than in kind. In addition, their common goal is to learn as much as possible about teachers and their work. Whereas colleagues interested in research on teaching assume that the best procedure is to locate the most effective ways to teach, researchers in the paradigm for research on teachers attach importance to the understanding of teachers. This understanding then serves as the basis for changing teachers and the conditions that surround their work. In this latter perspective, everything in work and the workplace is open to question, including questions surrounding the curriculum and the role of physical education in the culture of the school. It is in this connection that scholars share a common value orientation. As a group they are oriented toward problem setting, whereas teaching researchers are oriented more toward problem solving. Researchers on teachers are interested in "what" and "why" questions more than in "how" questions.

---

[6]Clearly the mere fact that most teacher educators, who complete the bulk of the research on teaching and teachers, were themselves former teachers helps to explain this tendency. Yet there remain needs for research on these researchers.

The inherent assumption is that even the best teaching methods, once discovered, will not solve all of the problems confronting teachers; nor will these methods yield all that needs to be known about physical educators, their programs, and the organizations in which they are found.

Thus, there is a basis for asserting that a separate paradigm *should* be established for research on teachers. Having acknowledged this fact, it must also be granted that this paradigm is not nearly as visible or well developed as its counterpart for research on teaching. This observation becomes even more apparent in the face of this paradigm's wide array of exemplars.

Exemplars for research on teachers

There are few commonalities among these exemplars for research on teachers. There is, of course, the common goal to understand more about teachers as professionals and people. In addition, these exemplars do not attend to teaching effectiveness. The commonalities stop here.

A major explanation for the presence of so few commonalities in these exemplars doubles as a way to classify them on the basis of their differences. At a most fundamental level, these exemplars differ in the extent to which they embody the assumptions and approaches that accompany the investigative model of the natural sciences, and a host of other differences stem from this one. In this light, the differences among the exemplars for research on teachers follow distinctions among their counterparts in the parent disciplines of psychology, sociology, and anthropology.

For example, behaviorist psychologists and functionalist sociologists are committed to a science of human behavior and a science of society, respectively. Although this commitment does not by itself distinguish them from their colleagues, the way in which they endeavor to honor it does. These psychologists and sociologists believe that a true science is possible only when the investigative model of the natural sciences is borrowed completely for the exemplars of the behavioral and social sciences. The same belief can be found among some researchers on teachers, who believe that the investigative model of the natural sciences must be part and parcel of their exemplars for research on teachers. For this reason, these colleagues may be philosophically attuned with the logical positivists because they also endorse the assumptions of logical positivism. Thus, their exemplars may be classified as examples of positivist social or behavioral science.

It is worth examining selected assumptions that underlie the positivist approach because other exemplars for research on teachers can be classified by the varying degrees to which these assumptions are accepted as givens. To begin with, there are the twin assumptions about order in the universe and the ability of scientists to detect it. It is assumed that the world exists *a priori* as a unified and causally ordered system and that data about the structure and parts of this system can be inferred from empirical observations of scientists. Furthermore, it is assumed that these data can be logically constructed into laws and that, because these laws correspond to the real world, they may also be used for valid descriptions, explanations, and predictions. It is also assumed in this framework that humans, like other objects in nature, are *determined* by the systems of nature, and the doctrine of causality is accordingly labelled Determinism. In addition, not only is it assumed that the methods of science are value-neutral, but also that human values and other "mentalistic" constructs are denied ontological status because they do not lend themselves to empirical observation and verification. Finally, it is assumed that science and its cumulative results will reach an advanced stage in which an idealized denotative language will replace its less desirable connotative counterpart that is now used in everyday life.

To return to the earlier point, functionalists in sociology and behaviorists in psychology, as well as their counterparts who conduct research on teachers, endorse these assumptions and their corollaries. Here, then, are two exemplars utilized to perform research on teachers; there are numerous others. Rather than identify each, it is more important to turn to a classificatory basis for them.

There have been penetrating criticisms of positivist social and behavioral science and the assumptions that form its foundation. Some such criticism is directed only toward selected parts, whereas other criticism attends to the entire positivist framework. Colleagues have met these criticisms with mixed reviews; some have accepted them at face value but others have added modifications. In either case, either partially or completely different exemplars have resulted. Because these criticisms shed light on these different exemplars, it is useful to identify them briefly. For analytical purposes, critiques may be classified under the headings foundational, methodological, and epistemological.

A familiar foundational critique attends to the static conception of science that accompanies positivism; critics argue that science is a dynamic process in which the task of gaining knowledge is neverending (Bronowski, 1979). Other critiques are directed toward three major dichotomies present in the positivist platform, as well as to a necessary one that is missing.

The missing dichotomy, or distinction, is the one between society and nature. Critics of positivism argue that the failure to make this distinction will lead investigators astray. These critics grant that nature exists *a priori* as a causally ordered and unified system; it was there before humans. By contrast, society is a human product that, paradoxically enough, may react to shape its creators. It is therefore imperative to distinguish between investigations of society and of nature, and these distinctions should be reflected in the exemplars that are used to attend to both (cf. Giddens, 1976). Also in this light, the three already present and problematic dichotomies contained in positivism are singled out for criticism.

Proponents of positivist science automatically endorse three dichotomies: that between object and subject, that between an ideal language and the language of everyday life, and that between fact and value. The subject-object dichotomy can be illuminated in another light. By embracing Determinism, positivists deny humans the capacity for voluntarism because they assume that teachers are always shaped and can never act as shapers. They are part of nature, like objects. By contrast, critics suggest that teachers are knowing subjects who act purposefully in society and who act to shape society and be shaped by it.[7] These critics further suggest that while some actions are intentional and observable, others are unacknowledged and still others are unintended. Therefore, investigations into humans and their society must attend to actions beyond those that are empirically observable and verifiable. In this connection, the language of everyday life becomes an important analytical pivot; so, too, do the values embodied in acts of speech become more important than positivists assume. For positivists separate facts from values because values are not empirically observable. They can only entertain *is* statements, dismissing *ought* statements out of hand because the latter are not empirically verifiable.[8] Critics argue that *ought* statements, as expressions of values, are crucial to an understanding of the repeated divergence between acts of intention, such as planning, and the actual consequences of behavior. Here, then, are dichotomies that can be derived from foundational critiques (cf. Bernstein, 1976; Giddens, 1979; Susman & Evered, 1978) and that stand as point of departure for alternative assumptions and exemplars.

As might be expected, the methodological critiques emanate logically from those that are foundational. They assert that the investigative model of the natural sciences is inappropriate for the study of humans and their society, and they include suitable alternatives. Some, such as discussions of case studies (Yin, 1981), ethnographies (Sanday, 1979),[9]

---

[7]See Giddens (1979) for a discussion of what he calls "a recovery of the subject without lapsing into subjectivism" (p. 44).

[8]As Bronowski and Mazlish (1975) have shown, historical circumstances contributed to this posture. Specifically, in its early stages, science was formulated as the antithesis of religious doctrines and rationalism.

[9]Although I recognize that many colleagues have used presumed ethnographic methods to complete research on teaching, I have misgivings about these efforts. So do others (cf. Fetterman, 1982). Aside from the fact that the methodological requirements for good ethnographics are not met (cf. Sanday, 1978), there are conceptual difficulties.

and ethno-methodologies (Garfinkel, 1967) are very specific. Others are more general (Heron, 1981) and include approaches such as "action science" (cf. Argyris, 1980; Susman & Evered, 1978). Yet there are two other lines of criticism, one pertaining to the extent to which positivist scientists do in fact follow their own norms (Merton, 1973) and rules. It has been suggested that scientists do not always play the game of science by their rules (Kuhn, 1975; Mitroff, 1972, 1974), and therefore these rules and norms should not serve as methodological standards for colleagues such as those interested in research on teachers.

A second line of methodological criticism in launched by the analytic philosophers and is directed at the uses of language in investigations (Bernstein, 1976). At issue here is the extent to which an ideal language can ever be achieved in research and whether the constructs and concepts of scientists, in fact, correspond to reality. A familiar example illustrates the point. What scientists call intelligence, which they endeavor to measure by means of their carefully constructed tests, may not correspond at all to the intelligence of humans. Critics of this facet of the methodology of positivist science suggest that this happens more frequently than scientists may recognize. They question the very construct validity that scientists take as given.[10]

Thirdly, there are epistemological critiques that are related in some ways to their foundational and methodological counterparts. There appear to be two kinds, the first attending to other types of knowledge and other ways of knowing. Critics of positivist science do not waive its products away, but point to it as just one of many paths to truth instead of the only one (Giddens, 1979; Holzner & Marx, 1979). They elevate to an equal position knowledge derived from the personal accounts of humans that fits into epistemological categories such as common sense, experiental knowledge (Heron, 1981), and tacit knowledge (Bowers, 1981; Polanyi, 1958). This acceptance of other forms of equally valid and important knowledge serves as a springboard to exemplars that may secure a better understanding of these forms of knowledge.

Ethnographies have their origins in anthropology and are designed to describe entire cultures; all acts, actors, and the like are to be situated in such a cultural framework. The investigator, it is presumed, is immersed in a *new* culture, armed with an understanding of cultures and their dynamics. In this light, a focus on acts of teaching alone, by researchers who are familiar with schools and have teaching experience, serves to render these "ethnographies" less valid.

Ethnographies have great promise. But this promise appears to reside in research on teachers, or research on school cultures, conducted by people who have never taught (cf. Kyracious & Newson, 1982).

[10]Kuhn (1975) endeavors to explain such a tendency by analyzing the socialization of scientists. His claim that many scientists are engaged in "mopping up" operations leads to the conclusion that at least some do not engage regularly in critical self-appraisal.

The second kind of epistemological critique addresses the application and utilization of knowledge. Because positivist science separates facts from values and dismisses all *ought* statements, critics (cf. Polanyi & Prosch, 1975) have charged that it results in moral bankruptcy when human decision-makers rely solely on it. In the positivist framework, statements such as "we *ought* not to commit murder" do not enjoy a privileged ontological status because only *is* statements are accepted. Consequently, the desirability of murdering one's neighbor is in principle no different from loving the same person, and according to critics, this is surely the basis for moral bankruptcy. Others such as Argyris (1980) have followed suit by arguing that positivists, with their preoccupation with *is* statements, conduct research that only serves to reinforce the status quo. This, too, is seen as a limitation in the uses of knowledge.

Another criticism surrounding the application and utilization of knowledge marks as well a return to the foundations of positivist science. Whereas positivists assume that a nomothetic science is desirable, a science in which laws are generalizable to all teachers and schools, critics argue that there are *de facto* differences among teachers and schools that render efforts toward such a nomothetic science to be impossible. These critics suggest that any such science will be more idiographic than nomothetic. In making this judgment, they entertain different assumptions about the characteristics of teachers and their schools as well as about the extent to which any knowledge gained in research has lasting, cumulative, and generalizable values. Criticisms such as these stimulate the quest for competing assumptions by critics and also inform their quest for methodological alternatives.

To summarize, there are foundational, methodological, and epistemological critiques of positivist social and behavioral science. Not only are these critiques related in some instances, but differential acceptance of them and their resultant alternatives by colleagues has resulted in different exemplars for the study of teachers. And, although there are significant differences among the exemplars used for research on teachers, colleagues enjoy commonalities. They share the common goal of understanding teachers as professionals and people, do research that does not address teaching effectiveness, and are interested in problem setting more than problem solving. These commonalities act to unite colleagues who utilize different exemplars, and support the contention that researchers on teachers can form a common paradigm.

Further, their paradigm differs from that for colleagues interested in research on teaching. For research on teaching remains at least close, if not true, to the assumptions, norms, and rules of positivist science. This means that colleagues interested in research on teaching will search for *causes* while colleagues in a paradigm for research on teachers may be satisfied with *reasons* (cf. Bowers, 1981); researchers on teaching will look for generalizable laws derived from replicated findings, while researchers on teachers will look for time-bound forms of understanding that are often situation- and person-specific; researchers on teaching may be in pursuit of a true science, while researchers on teachers may be content with good scholarship, only some of which is scientific. The list of differences could go on. These differences are ultimately reflected at the level of policy for teacher education and practice. An illumination of the competing policy choices stemming from the two paradigms also calls attention to the value of both paradigms.

Paths to policy from the two paradigms

Policymaking in any endeavor is always a political process in which the participants engage in claims-making activities (Rein & Peattie, 1981), and policies for teacher education and practice are no exception. As the term claims-making suggests, policymaking places the participants in positions of advocacy; they must argue in favor of their views, often to the point that reasoned positions based upon personal and professional values outstrip the available data from research.

In the case of teacher education and school practice, there are a variety of participants: researchers, other teacher educators, parents, school boards, practicing teachers, and bodies that certify teachers and accredit programs. The mere fact that so many diverse people are involved further emphasizes the importance of values and implies that there will be less direct utilization of research. The impact of research in the policymaking process is further diminished when advocates recognize that few findings are beyond debate. Any discussion of the import of the paradigms for research on teaching and teachers for policymaking must be framed against this backdrop.

Yet, some policy implications stem predictably from the two paradigms, and they are often at odds with one another, as Zumwalt (1982) has demonstrated recently. The reasons are understandable. Different kinds of data are generated in the two paradigms, and this is largely attributable to the different interests and value orientations of the investigators. Blend in the other parts of the policymaking process, and the result is an interesting mixture of data and values in the claims-making activities of the participants.

Zumwalt (1982) suggests that two orientations can be located, a technological orientation and a deliberative orientation. The former is tied to research on teaching, while the deliberative orientation can be linked to research on teachers.[11] Each merits a capsulized summary.

---

[11]Zumwalt does not make the distinction between research on teaching and teachers but, in my view, it is implied in her discussion. Nevertheless, any interpretive or translative errors are my own.

Colleagues in the paradigm for research on teaching display a commitment to problem solving, and the technological orientation that emerges at the policymaking level reveals this commitment. The rule of thumb is relatively straightforward. By means of research, find good teachers and determine how they elicit student achievement. However separately investigators may sing these verses in their personal research, at the policy level their chorus is the same: "Let's teach would-be, new, and experienced teachers to teach and otherwise act like the good teachers we studied" (after Zumwalt, 1982). Such a translation of research findings into generalizable policies usually occurs systematically. The results range from teacher "should" lists (Zumwalt, 1982) to comprehensive approaches for teacher education and teacher evaluation, as in the case of the competency-based movement. The intent is appropriate and understandable, and it may be sketched as follows: If the behaviors that really count can be identified, then teacher educators, and their in-service counterparts in their efforts to train teachers, can emphasize them accordingly while eliminating content that may be of little value (after Zumwalt, 1982, p. 226). Thus, there is a drive toward efficiency in means and this emphasis is revealed in the policies emerging from the paradigm for research on teaching. Once implemented, these policies promise to improve the skills of individuals while reproducing other institutionalized practices (after Giddens, 1979).

Colleagues in the paradigm for research on teachers are more concerned with problem setting than problem solving, and their policymaking activities reveal this bias. Theirs is a deliberative orientation, so named because they view good teaching as resulting ultimately from the good deliberations and subsequent actions by teachers (after Zumwalt, 1982, p. 226). There is less interest here in "should" lists and competencies, and a much greater commitment to research perspectives that prompt analytical self-awareness. Instead of viewing teachers as mindless, the advocates of the deliberative orientation view them as mindful. That is, teachers are given due credit for their twin abilities to make intelligent decisions and take appropriate actions in their organizational context. Therefore, while their colleagues from the paradigm for research on teaching employ the vocabulary of training, advocates of the deliberative orientation talk about the features of an education in which teachers may learn to deliberate and then act as the contingencies so warrant. According to advocates of this orientation, teachers must learn to decide *"when, where, with whom, to what degree*, and under *what conditions* to take certain critical actions"* (Zumwalt, 1982, p. 241). In addition to the immediate actions of teaching, these acts may also be aimed at changing a curriculum and altering the conditions that surround teaching as work. Advocates of this position assume that there is so much complexity in the interactions of teachers, their students, and others in the work organization that it is both impossible and inappropriate to offer hard-and-fast, generalizable rules for all teachers in every situation. It is further assumed that teachers, in their deliberations and notions, may act as agents for institutional transformation (after Giddens, 1979).

There are, then, differences between the two orientations to policy-making. The ways in which they are tied to their respective paradigms is now more apparent and, in the face of paradigmatic differences, competing policies are all but inevitable. For paradigms are selective in the attention they give to phenomena and in the persons they harbor, and no less is this the case in the policies their members endorse. Having granted this, it is necessary to emphasize that colleagues in both paradigms perform useful work. To wit: Few persons would argue that teachers should not be skilled performers, as suggested in the technological orientation, or that teachers should not be able to engage in reasoned decision-making in their organizational contexts, as suggested by the deliberative orientation.

Thus, one conclusion is inescapable. Both paradigms are needed and both policy orientations stand to make contributions to improved practice. It is in this light that the differences between colleagues in the two paradigms ought to be embraced and made explicit, rather than be glossed over or denied. A more thorough understanding of these differences and their root assumptions stands to make dialogue among members of the two paradigms more meaningful and constructive. This same understanding serves to unite members of a profession, especially in instances where membership in separate paradigms might otherwise sever their relationships.

A concluding observation

And, lest the obvious point be missed, the increasing specialization that allows the establishment of two paradigms can have divisive effects. Indeed, as research becomes more plentiful and sophisticated there may well be needs for more paradigms, which by definition are founded on even greater degrees of specialization.[12] If so, there are even greater possibilities for divisiveness. If splintering is to be avoided, then at least two requirements must be met. The first, which has been the target in the preceding analysis, is the cultivation of both an understanding of and appreciation for paradigms and exemplars other than one's own. The second question, which has not been discussed here, is more difficult.

Who will synthesize for practitioners the results of research from these two paradigms and the others that exist in physical education? While this

---

[12]Another alternative exists, at least in principle. A single, grand paradigm may dominate the field. Kuhn (1975) suggests that this occurs only in mature fields, however, and I agree with him.

question points the way for future work, it only gains importance when there is a sufficient amount of research waiting to be synthesized and applied. In this light, this second question is welcome because it stands as testimony to the increasing maturity of an important area of inquiry.

Reference Notes

1. Graham, G., & Heimerer, E. *Research on teaching effectiveness: Implications for the real world teacher.* Paper presented at the AAHPERD National Convention, Detroit, April 1981.
2. Clark, C. *Five faces of research on teaching.* Occasional paper No. 24, College of Education, Michigan State University, 1979.

References

ARGYRIS, C. *Inner contradictions of rigorous research.* New York: Academic Press, 1980.

ARGYRIS, C. *Reasoning, learning, and action: Individual and organizational.* San Francisco: Jossey-Bass, 1982.

ARGYRIS, C., & Schon, D. *Theory in practice: Increasing professional effectiveness.* San Francisco: Jossey-Bass, 1974.

ARGYRIS, C., & Schon, D. *Organizational learning: A theory of action perspective.* Reading, MA: Addison-Wesley, 1978.

BAIN, L., & Wendt, J. Undergraduate physical education majors' perceptions of the roles of teacher and coach. *Research Quarterly for Exercise and Sport,* in press.

BERNSTEIN, R.J. *The restructuring of social and political theory.* London: Methuen & Co., 1976.

BLOOM, B.S. *Human characteristics and school learning.* New York: McGraw Hill, 1976.

BOWERS, K.S. Knowing more than we can say leads to saying more than we can know: On being implicitly informed. In D. Magnusson (Ed.), *Toward a psychology of situations: An interactional perspective.* Hillsdale, IL: Lawrence Erlbaum Associates, 1981.

BRONOWSKI, J. *A sense of the future.* Cambridge: M.I.T. Press, 1979.

BRONOWSKI, J., & Mazlish, B. *The western intellectual tradition.* New York: Harper Colophon, 1975.

CARROLL, J. A model of school learning. *Teacher's College Record,* 1963, **64,** 723-733.

CHU, D. Functional myths of educational organizations: College as career training and the relationship of formal title to actual duties upon secondary school employment. *NAPEHE Annual Conference Proceedings,* 1981, **II.**

FETTERMAN, D. Ethnography in educational research: The dynamics of diffusion. *Educational Researcher*, 1982, **11**(3), 17-29.

GARFINKEL, H. *Studies in ethnomethodology*. Englewood Cliffs, NJ: Prentice-Hall, 1967.

GIDDENS, A. *Central problems in social theory: Action, structure, and contradiction in social analysis*. Berkeley: University of California Press, 1979.

GIDDENS, A. *The new rules of sociological method*. New York: Basse Books, 1976.

GRAHAM, G. Research on teaching physical education: A discussion with Larry Locke and Daryl Siedentop. *Journal of Teaching in Physical Education*, 1981, **1**(1), 3-15.

GUTTING, G. (Ed.). *Paradigms and revolutions: Applications and appraisals of Thomas Kuhn's philosophy of science*. Notre Dame, IN: University of Notre Dame Press, 1980.

HERON, J. Philosophical basis for a new paradigm. In P. Reason & J. Rowan (Eds.), *Human inquiry*. New York: John Wiley & Sons, 1981.

HOLZNER, B., & Marx, J. *Knowledge application: The knowledge system in society*. Boston: Allyn & Bacon, 1979.

KAHNEMAN, D., Slovic, P., & Tversky, A. *Judgment under uncertainty: Heuristics and biases*. New York: Cambridge University Press, 1982.

KUHN, T. *The structure of scientific revolutions*. Chicago: University of Chicago Press, 1975.

KYRIACOU, C., & Newson, G. Teacher effectiveness: A consideration of research problems. *Educational Review*, 1982, **34**(1), 3-12.

LAWSON, H. Toward a model of teacher socialization in physical education. *Journal of Teaching in Physical Education*, in press.

LOCKE, L.F. Research on teaching physical education: New hope for a dismal science. *Quest*, 1977, **28**, 2-16.

LOCKE, L.F., & Massengale, J. Role-conflict in teacher-coaches. *Research Quarterly*, 1978, **71**, 27-40.

LOCKE, L., Siedentop, D., & Mand, C. The preparation of physical education teachers: A subject-matter-centered model. In H. Lawson (Ed.), *Undergraduate physical education programs: Issues and approaches*. Washington: AAPHERD, 1981.

MERTON, R. *The sociology of science: Theoretical and empirical investigations*. Chicago: University of Chicago Press, 1973.

MINSKY, M. A framework for representing knowledge. In P.H. Winston (Ed.), *The psychology of computer vision*. New York: McGraw Hill, 1975.

MITROFF, I. Norms and counter-norms in a select group of Apollo moon scientists: A case study of the ambivalence of scientists. *American Sociological Review*, 1974, **38**, 579-595.

MITROFF, I. *The subjective side of science: A philosophical inquiry into the psychology of Apollo moon scientists.* New York: Elsevier, 1974.

POLANYI, M. *Personal knowledge.* Chicago: University of Chicago Press, 1958.

POLANYI, M., & Prosch, H. *Meaning.* Chicago: University of Chicago Press, 1975.

REIN, M., & Peattie, L. Knowledge for policy. *Social Service Review*, 1981, **55**(4), 525-543.

SANDAY, P. The ethnographic paradigm(s). *Administrative Science Quarterly*, 1979, **24**, 527-538.

SHAVELSON, R.J., & Stern, P. Research on teachers' pedagogical thoughts, judgments, decisions, and behavior. *Review of Educational Research*, 1981, **51**(4), 455-498.

SIEDENTOP, D. Teaching research: The interventionist view. *Journal of Teaching in Physical Education*, 1982, **1**(3), 46-50.

SIMON, H. Information processing models of cognition. *Annual Review of Psychology*, 1979, **30**, 363-396.

SUSMAN, G., & Evered, R. An assessment of the scientific merits of action research. *Administrative Science Quarterly*, 1978, **23**, 582-603.

YIN, R. The case study as a serious research strategy. *Knowledge: Creation, Diffusion, and Utilization*, 1981, **3**(1), 97-114.

ZUMWALT, K. Research on teaching: Policy implications for teacher education. In A. Lieberman & M. McLaughlin (Eds.), *Policy making in education.* Chicago: National Society for the Study of Education, 1982.

They Came Together

To begin . . . they came together
a meeting of minds
an exchange of ideas
imparted knowledge developed objective goals
to direct future plans
outwardly,
   they described,
   contemplating and
   determining the answers.

Magically . . . some touched
a reunion of hearts
a confirmation of ties
silent and expressed feelings
sculptured treasured moments
to be cherished forever
quietly,
   some searched,
   valuing and
   living the questions.

In time . . . we separated
most became enriched,
but for those who shared their spirit
the ensuing distances will always be ever-so small.

Andrea Cervak
Purdue University